D1582567

James Lees-Milne

The Life

MICHAEL BLOCH

JOHN MURRAY

First published in Great Britain in 2009 by John Murray (Publishers)
An Hachette UK Company

2

© Michael Bloch 2009

The right of Michael Bloch to be identified as the Author of the Work has been asserted by him in accordance with the Copyright, Designs and Patents Act 1988.

A CIP catalogue record for this title is available from the British Library

ISBN 978-0-7195-6034-7

Typeset in Bembo by Servis Filmsetting Ltd, Stockport, Cheshire

Printed and bound by Clays Ltd, St Ives plc

John Murray policy is to use papers that are natural, renewable and recyclable products and made from wood grown in sustainable forests. The logging and manufacturing processes are expected to conform to the environmental regulations of the country of origin.

John Murray (Publishers)
338 Euston Road
London NW1 3BH

www.johnmurray.co.uk

To Charles Orwin

Contents

Illustrations

Credits: the author (1, 14, 15, 22, 27, 30, 34); Beinecke Rare Book and Manuscript Library, Yale University (2, 3, 13, 17, 18, 19, 20, 21, 23, 24, 26); Nicholas Robinson (4, 6, 7, 10, 25, 29, 31, 32, 35); Lord Rosse (5); National Portrait Gallery, London (8, 28); Getty Images (9); Mrs Simon Frazer (11, 12); Estate of Robert Byron (16); Derry Moore (33).

Preface

J AMES LEES-MILNE, KNOWN to his friends as Jim, was born in 1908 and died in 1997. His life straddled the twentieth century, and saw enormous change. He retained vivid memories of an Edwardian childhood; he lived long enough to witness the advent of New Labour. He had two careers, either of which might be said to have earned him a footnote to the history of his times. From 1936 to 1950 (minus two years of war service) he worked for the National Trust in its efforts to acquire and conserve country houses. His title was a humble one: he was, as he reminded the owners he visited to discuss the possible donation of their properties, merely the secretary to a committee (which in turn made recommendations to another committee which made the decisions). But it was often largely thanks to his talents that owners were persuaded to offer their houses and the Trust to accept them; but for his tenacity and persuasive charm, such architectural treasures as Attingham, Charlecote, Knole, Petworth and Stourhead (to name but a few) might not have been 'saved for the nation'. In 1951 he retired from full-time work for the National Trust (he continued to serve it part time) to concentrate on his second career, as a writer: in the course of half a century he published some thirty books, all praised by the critics, including history and biography, autobiography and fiction (the last two categories slightly overlapping). His early works, on architectural history, were among the first of their kind for the general reader. He has been described as one of the best English prose writers of his generation. (Curiously, he longed above all for recognition as a poet, but he possessed little talent in that direction and never succeeded in having a single line of verse published.) Though he did not make much money from his writing, and few of his books remain in print, he is an interesting case of that now almost extinct breed, the independent man of letters: he had sufficient private means (for some years provided by a rich wife) not to have to worry overmuch about making a living from his pen. His friends included many noted literary contemporaries such as John Betjeman, Osbert Lancaster, Anthony Powell, Sacheverell Sitwell, Rosamond Lehmann and the Mitford sisters.

Jim, who possessed both a highly romantic nature and a strong sex drive, was bisexual. In the course of his life he fell in love with numerous men and women, with many of whom he had affairs. In his forties he married Alvilde Chaplin, an attractive and accomplished woman of his own age who was also drawn to her own sex. Their marriage somewhat resembled that of Harold Nicolson and Vita Sackville-West – and indeed, the two couples were associated in that Jim had an affair with Harold in the 1930s, Alvilde with Vita in the 1950s. As with the Harold–Vita marriage, that of Jim and Alvilde underwent a crisis, but was helped to survive by their discovery of a house they both adored, their 'Sissinghurst' – Alderley Grange in the Cotswolds, where they lived from 1961 to 1974. Whereas Jim regarded Harold as his literary mentor, Alvilde shared Vita's passion for gardening and created several famous gardens, one of them at Alderley.

However, if Jim is remembered today it is not so much for the country houses he rescued, the books he wrote, his literary friendships, his colourful love life or his unusual marriage, as for the diary he kept for some thirty-five years, which has been described as 'one of the treasures of contemporary English literature' and compared to that of Samuel Pepys. Apart from providing a wealth of fascinating detail about his daily doings and thoughts, it is remarkable for its candour, its contrasts, its sharp observation and its capture of the spirit of the times. Just as he pursued two careers, so he kept two diaries, the first from 1942 to 1949 (when he did his main work for the National Trust), the second from 1971 until shortly before his death in 1997 (when he wrote most of his books). The gap of more than twenty years in his regular diary-keeping (largely explained by his reluctance to record the details of an often turbulent marriage) presents a problem for his biographer, only slightly mitigated by the fact that both diaries contain much reminiscence, casting light on various aspects of Jim's life before 1942 and from 1950 to 1970. Another problem is that, having edited his 1940s diary in four volumes published between 1975 and 1985, Jim destroyed the original manuscripts; he did so (as he frankly tells us) partly because he felt embarrassed by some of the passages he had excised, partly because the record was largely in the form of shorthand notes which had to some extent required 'writing up'. However, several longhand pages from 1947 survived his destructive efforts and are now among Jim's papers in the Beinecke Library at Yale; as these were published exactly as written, apart from a few minor stylistic corrections and the removal of an embarrassing reference to his mother, I think one can conclude that the early diaries as Jim edited them are essentially authentic. As well as delighting an ever-growing audience, both the early and the later diaries have become recognised as important contributions to English social history: despite the recent publication by John Murray of a three-volume abridgement, most of the original twelve volumes remain in print.

The diaries highlight various unusual facets of Jim's life and personality. He was a 'slow developer' who began dim and unrecognised and ended up brilliant and fêted, a tortoise who overtook many hares (and painted wonderfully sardonic portraits of the hares as he passed them). He indulged in a self-deprecating modesty, usually making himself out to be less clever than he was, and often portraying himself as a hopeless duffer who managed to muddle through; consequently he tended to be under-estimated by his contemporaries. He was a man of contradictions, by turns timorous and brave, snobbish and egalitarian, solitary and gregarious, despairing and optimistic. He was driven by a demon (alternately manifesting itself as love, creative impulse and a passion for preserving beautiful things) which enabled him to overcome a melancholic nature and recurrent ill health. He had a gift for friendship: in his seventies he was still in touch with dozens of people he had befriended at different times, including not a few recent friends who were young enough to be his grandchildren.

As described in this book, I met Jim in 1979 when I was twenty-five and he seventy, and we became close friends for a decade. I did not however see much of him in his last years, and it came as a slight surprise, on his death in 1997, to find that he had bequeathed his literary estate to me along with the unedited remnant of his diaries. As he had edited the series up to 1978, and there was a demand for the next instalment, I found myself in the unusual position of having to prepare for publication a journal in which I often featured, sometimes in a way that was more disconcerting than flattering. It seemed appropriate to complement this task with the writing of a biography which might put into context the diaries Jim had kept during the last twenty years of a long and eventful life. He himself had undertaken the biography of Harold Nicolson, whom he had also met aged twenty-five and who had become his great mentor and father figure, as Jim had become mine.

It turned out to be a longer and less straightforward project than I had anticipated. Jim proved a complex and elusive subject; he showed different sides of himself to different people, and no one (least of all myself) had known the whole man. His imaginative life occasionally spilled over into fantasy, adding both to his interest and the difficulty of writing about him. Both his diaries, and the correspondence among his papers at Yale, provided rich sources of material, yet presented a picture which seemed curiously incomplete, like a jigsaw with most of the pieces missing. His surviving friends were usually generous in sharing memories and letters with me; but as I began my research more than ninety years after his birth, few of his contemporaries were available for interview – thus I just 'missed' the last of the schoolfriends who could have given me a first-hand account of his Eton career.

Just as Jim, in writing about Harold, felt handicapped by his limited knowledge of politics and diplomacy, so I was conscious of my ignorance about architecture and its conservation. Nor was it easy to acquire a deep understanding of Jim's work for the National Trust. There is little about it in his papers at Yale. As for the Trust itself, that great conservation body has not been remarkable for conserving its own archives, which were split up a few years ago and distributed among various repositories and regional offices, many of them going astray. I am grateful to the Trust's archivist Iain Shaw who, burdened with the task of locating and attempting to reassemble his scattered treasures, asked me to specify the material I most wanted to see; he did eventually show me an interesting selection of papers relating to Jim's first years as Country Houses Secretary. Jim's former colleagues at the Trust were kind and helpful (I am particularly indebted to Tony Mitchell); but I sometimes found myself coming up against a wall of circumspection. The National Trust has changed enormously in recent years, and now tends to regard Jim and the Trust he knew as 'elitist'; the sympathies of the 'old guard' are generally with Jim, but they are often unwilling to criticise the new regime too openly. A lingering reluctance also exists to discuss rivalries and resentments of fifty years ago. I have done my best to describe Jim's outlook and achievements as an architectural conservationist, but I recognise that there is another book to be written on the subject.

It was my good fortune to inherit, along with Jim's literary estate, a marvellous literary agent, Bruce Hunter, and a marvellous publisher, John Murray. In 2002, soon after commissioning this biography, Murray's changed hands when John Murray VII sold his family firm to Hodder Headline. I was sorry to part with my editor Grant McIntyre, but lucky to find myself under the wing of the new managing director Roland Philipps, whose grandmother Rosamond Lehmann and stepfather John Julius Norwich were both friends of Jim, and of the ever-patient Caroline Westmore, a splendid survivor of the old firm. I was lucky too in that the member of Jim's family with whom I dealt, his great-nephew and executor Nick Robinson, was himself a publisher (currently Chairman of Constable & Robinson), with an understanding of the problems involved in biography-writing; I am grateful to him for many kindnesses, as I also am to his brothers and co-executors Henry and Richard, and to Jim's nephew Simon Lees-Milne and niece Dale Sutton.

For permission to quote copyright material (as well as for other help) I must thank Bamber Gascoigne (Midi Gascoigne's letters), the late Diana Mosley (her letters), the late Nigel Nicolson (letters of Harold Nicolson and Vita Sackville-West) and Mattei Radev (Eardley Knollys's letters). I am also grateful to the following (many of whom are alas now dead): Guy Acloque; Sir Hardy Amies; Emily Aziz; Jo Batterham; the Duke and Duchess of Beaufort; Freda, Lady Berkeley; Julian Berkeley; Lesley Blanch; David Bonner; Desmond Briggs; Isabel Briggs (Isabel Colegate); Mark Brockbank; John Byrne; Rosemary, Viscountess Chaplin; Giles Clotworthy; Norman Coates; John Cornforth; George Crawshay; Father Ronald Creighton-Jobe; Angela Culme-Seymour; Robin Darwall-Smith; Juliana Deliyannis; Deborah, Duchess of Devonshire; Patric Dickinson; Francis and Libby Dineley; Ian Dixon; Sir Douglas Dodds-Parker; the Earl of Drogheda (Derry Moore); Christopher, Viscount Esher; Lionel, Viscount Esher; Sue Fox; Simon and Harriet Frazer; Jonathan Gathorne-Hardy; the Revd Thomas Gibson; Vincent Giroud; Fiona Goetz; Francis St John ('Bobby') Gore; John Harris; Wilhelmine ('Billa'), Lady Harrod; Lady Selina Hastings; Penny Hatfield; Lady Dorothy ('Coote') Heber-Percy; Richard Herner; Lady Anne Hill; Derek Hill; Bevis Hillier; Dame Jennifer Jenkins; Lord Kennet; John Kenworthy-Browne; James Knox; Jonathan Kooperstein; Deirdre Levi; Jeremy Lewis; Prince Rupert zu Loewenstein; Elizabeth, Countess of Longford; Robbie Macdonald; Harry McDowell; Professor R. B. McDowell; Peter Mandler; Philip Mansel; Colin Merton; James Methuen-Campbell; Hugh Montgomery-Massingberd; Rosalind, Lady Morrison; Charlotte Mosley; Dr Alexander Moulton; Rory O'Donnell; Frances Partridge; Burnet Pavitt; Lady Violet Powell; Stuart Preston; Theo Richmond; David Robinson; John Martin Robinson; Liz Robinson; Kenneth Rose; the Earl and Countess of Rosse; Christopher Rowell; Michael Russell; Jeremy and June Ryan-Bell; John Saumarez Smith; Tony Scotland; Richard Shone; Edith Stokes; Humphrey Stone; Michael Strassen; Sir Wilfred Thesiger; Patrick Trevor-Roper; 'Dosia' Verney; Christopher Wall; David Watkin; Moray Watson; Wynyard Wilkinson; Christopher and Mai Winn; Louisa Young. I am sorry if I have left anyone out.

While writing *Harold Nicolson*, Jim was haunted by a sense that his subject was looking over his shoulder; consequently he strove to produce exactly the biography for which Harold would have wished. I am not sure that I have approached this book in the same spirit – but should Jim be reading it, I hope he treats it with the tolerant amusement with which he indulged my follies during his lifetime.

Michael Bloch
mab@jamesleesmilne.com
January 2009

I

The Dreaming Boy
1908–26

———•———

IN 1970, AGED sixty-one, James Lees-Milne published an autobiographical work entitled *Another Self*, dealing with his life up to
1942 – the year he began his diary. It opens with the immortal line: 'My
world was the only real world.' By this he means to say that, as a child,
he led a thrilling fantasy life in which he was his own master, in contrast
to the dull, subservient life of the nursery at Wickhamford Manor,
Worcestershire, his childhood home. But perhaps he is trying to tell us
something else also – that the account which follows, while broadly true
in its outline, contains more than a touch of fantasy in its detail; that the
extraordinary (and hilarious) stories which he is going to relate owe not
a little to his imagination. *Another Self* has been hailed as 'a comic masterpiece', and remains in print after almost forty years. But literature's
gain is history's loss. For Jim kept few personal records relating to the
years covered in the book; and by the time of his death, there were few
survivors who remembered him from those years. His biographer is
therefore obliged to use *Another Self* as a starting point – though even the
rather fragmentary independent evidence which exists suggests that its
accuracy often leaves something to be desired.

In *Another Self* Jim says little about his ancestry, but conveys the
impression that he hailed from an old county family and that Wickhamford
was their native seat. This was not quite the case. His father, George
Lees-Milne, derived his fortune mainly from a cotton mill in Lancashire;
and he had bought Wickhamford, and moved from Lancashire to
Worcestershire, only two years before Jim's birth. George did, however,
pride himself on belonging to a line of small squires going back three
centuries: Lancashire is said to be a county in which it has always been
possible to be both 'of the gentry' and 'in trade'.

The Lees family came from a village of that name near Oldham, where
they had owned an estate called Clarksfield since the reign of James I.
They were a rough lot, whose motto, Jim once suggested, ought to have
been 'Sport and Booze'. The discovery of coal on their land boosted their

fortunes but did not civilise them: Jim's great-grandfather, Joseph Lees, was one of three barely literate brothers who were known, after their respective obsessions, as Nimrod, Ramrod and Fishing Rod. They were connected by marriage to two slightly grander local landowning families, the Cromptons of Crompton Hall (who could trace their holdings back to the thirteenth century) and the Milnes of Park House. Such families had traditionally run small wool-spinning mills on their land; with the arrival of steam, produced with the aid of local coal, they were well placed to set up large mechanised mills producing cotton thread. The famous mill of A. & A. Crompton in Oldham was founded in 1830 by Jim's widowed great-great-grandmother Alice Milne and her brother Abel Crompton with £2,000 lent to them by their father. Alice's daughter Sarah Milne married Joseph Lees of Clarksfield; and their son, Jim's grandfather James Henry Lees, born in 1847, came to inherit the principal fortunes of both the Milne and Crompton families, including a controlling interest in the mill and extensive properties in the Oldham area.

Grandfather James was an energetic personality, and the first of his family to go to Eton. In 1890, as required by the will of his uncle Henry Milne, he changed his surname to Lees-Milne, acquiring new arms with the Milne motto *Prudenter qui Sedulo* – he acts wisely who acts diligently. This was appropriate; for whereas most of his male relations were lazy and pleasure-loving, the first James Lees-Milne dedicated himself to the family business, turning it into a great concern with offshoots as far afield as the Balkans, and floating it on the stock market in 1898 for the impressive sum of £280,000. He became a pillar of the Conservative Party in Oldham, responsible for Winston Churchill's adoption there as a parliamentary candidate in 1899;* he is said to have refused a baronetcy (which would have descended to Jim), fearing it would burden him with having to make public speeches. In 1904 he purchased the extensive Ribbesford estate near Bewdley in Worcestershire, with a rambling house of Elizabethan origin and excellent hunting, where he was able to lead the life of a rich country gentleman far from the scene of his business activity.

In 1877 James married Mary Emma Nesbitt, daughter of a London hide broker of Scottish Border origins, whose brother married James's

---

*Unsuccessful at a by-election in 1899; successful (following his Boer War exploits) at the general election of 1900. Churchill stayed with the Lees-Milnes at Crompton Hall during both campaigns.

sister. They had two sons, Jim's uncle Alec Milne Lees-Milne and father George Crompton Lees-Milne – so named because Alec was due to inherit the former Milne properties, George those of the Cromptons. As boys, they were considered clever and gifted: Alec was fascinated by science, following the early experiments in wireless telegraphy, while George was interested in furniture and architecture, being influenced by the Arts and Crafts movement and becoming an accomplished carpenter and mason. But from the moment they attained their majorities, and started to come into their substantial inheritances, they thought of little but pleasure in the form of good living, sport, gambling and philandering. In George's case, this rake's progress was interrupted in 1904 by his marriage, aged twenty-four, to a girl four years his junior – Helen Bailey.

The Baileys were a family of rather more 'recent' origin than the Leeses, but had become far richer and grander. Their fortunes began with Jim's great-grandfather Sir Joseph Bailey, son of a Yorkshire farmer, who is said to have walked all the way to South Wales at the age of twelve to get a job with his uncle Richard Crawshay, owner of the Cyfarthfa Ironworks at Merthyr Tydfil. Joseph was eventually appointed manager of the ironworks, which during the Napoleonic Wars became the biggest in the world, and was left a third-share in the business when his uncle died in 1810. He sold his share to his cousins, started his own ironworks at Nantyglo, and later financed the construction of Welsh railways. He became one of the richest men in Britain, hated by the Welsh people for his heartless capitalism and willingness to call out the militia to break up strikes. He purchased a huge tract of Breconshire, with his seat at Glanusk Park, and sat for some years as MP for that county, being created a baronet in 1852. His senior grandson, who succeeded him to the baronetcy, sat for much of his life as MP for Hereford before being raised to the peerage in 1899 as Baron Glanusk.

Jim's grandfather, Henry Bailey, was Sir Joseph's fifth and youngest son, who devoted his life to hunting and shooting on his estate at Coates near Cirencester. In 1881, as a widower of fifty-nine, he married Jim's grandmother, aged thirty-two; she was Christina Thomson, daughter of a well-known Glasgow mercantile family. Almost alone among Jim's ancestors, the Thomsons were interested in the arts. Christina's grandfather Robert Thomson designed Camphill, his fine Palladian house in Renfrewshire; his friends included Sir Walter Scott and Sir Henry Raeburn, the latter of whom painted several portraits of him. Why Christina, coming from this cultured background, should have married the dull and philistine Henry Bailey, who was old enough to be her father, is a mystery. Their correspondence shows that she spent much of their married life apart from him, visiting friends and relations. She bore him three children – Jim's uncle Robert, mother Helen and aunt Doreen. In the seventh year of their marriage, Henry died; and Christina did not long survive him. Their orphaned children went to live with their rich relations in Wales and Scotland. Robert attended Eton and Magdalen, where he was popular both with his mentors and contemporaries; the sisters, both pretty and high-spirited, were educated by governesses, and sent to finishing schools in Paris and Heidelberg.

A Heidelberg schoolfriend of Helen was Frida Lees, a cousin of George Lees-Milne; and it was at the house of Frida's parents in the Derbyshire Peak District in April 1904 that Helen met George, who was due to ride his horse at the local races. They were attracted to each other; and when George came close to breaking his neck during his race, love blossomed. Their families were delighted at the match: there was a commercial link, for the Thomsons had introduced cotton manufacture to Scotland. They were married at St George's, Hanover Square on 20 October, and went to live at Crompton Hall near Oldham, a monstrous Victorian renovation of a house erected by the Cromptons in 1442, where their first child, a daughter named Audrey, was born in 1905. George's romantic attentions were not, however, concentrated exclusively on his wife. In June 1907 a baby boy was born to Katherine Nuttall, the Crompton Hall coachman's daughter. John Nuttall, as he was known, was subsequently raised in Australia, where he became a banker. It was only after his death in 1990 that Jim learnt of this man who had been his half-brother, possessing some resemblance to himself.

Such escapades may have made it desirable for George and Helen to live at some distance from Oldham, which in any case would have had limited attractions for the handsome young couple. In 1906 George was motoring in Worcestershire's Vale of Evesham, some thirty miles from his parents' new seat at Ribbesford, when he came across a half-timbered manor house of mediaeval origin, situated in a beautiful garden with a lake; attached to it was an ancient church containing fine memorials. With his love of 'olden tyme' architecture, he was immediately attracted to the place, and enquired about it. Wickhamford was its name, and the owner wanted to sell. George is said to have produced a cheque book on the spot, and negotiated the purchase of the property (which included six hundred acres and numerous cottages) for £2,300. It was there, at the end of 1907, that Helen conceived her second child.

Before the new arrival, there was a departure in the family. In March 1908 the elder James Lees-Milne suddenly died at Ribbesford of meningitis, aged sixty. So stricken was his widow that she could not bring herself to attend the funeral, during which she prevailed upon her pregnant daughter-in-law to stay at home with her and recite the burial service. Their father's premature death meant that George and Alec became rich men in their twenties (though the fortunes of the family business, deprived of its presiding genius, went steadily downhill from that moment on). The baby, born at Wickhamford on 6 August, was a boy; he was christened George James Henry after his father and two grandfathers, though in adult life he only ever used the middle of his three christian names and was generally known as Jim.*

Jim's mother kept a diary during the first twelve years of her married life; and although its entries are mostly brief and colourless, they nevertheless convey a picture of the life that she and her husband were leading at the time of Jim's birth and during his earliest years. They belonged to the class, far more numerous a century ago than now, which did virtually no work, lived in comfort with the aid of servants, and devoted itself to pleasure. 'Work' for George Lees-Milne meant a monthly journey to Oldham to attend a board meeting at the mill. At Wickhamford (which was not a large house) they never employed fewer than a dozen indoor and outdoor staff. However, although they had plenty of money, and lived well, they were not in the least 'smart' or cosmopolitan, and led unsophisticated, provincial lives. Their only foreign travel was an annual Easter fortnight in Monte Carlo. (On the way there and back they stopped in Paris, visiting the Moulin Rouge on the outward journey and the Folies Bergères on the return.) They did not own a house in London, or 'do the Season' – though they spent about one week out of six in the capital, where they stayed at Brown's Hotel and saw the latest musical comedies. The tailors and dressmakers they used were not in London but in nearby Birmingham. Apart from the aforementioned expeditions, an annual seaside holiday with their children in the early summer, and an annual trip to Scotland from August to October when they stayed with Helen's relations, they were rarely away from home.

Their great passion was sport, and their lives revolved around the local hunt, the North Cotswold. They aspired to attend every meeting during

---

*In her diary during the days following his birth, Helen calls him 'Augustus' or 'Gussie' – a fate he was doubtless glad to have been spared.

the season (these being the only occasions when Helen's diary becomes almost lyrical), and all their friends in the county were fellow members of the hunt. When hunting had to be cancelled owing to bad weather, they gave squash parties: George built a squash court for this purpose in the same half-timbered style as the manor. In the spring, they turned their attention to polo and racing. George was an accomplished polo player, winning trophies at Cheltenham and Hurlingham, until obliged to give up after losing an eye in 1912 as a result of a hunting accident. They never missed the National Hunt Races at Cheltenham, or the Grand National at Aintree. In June and July they gave and attended tennis parties. In Scotland during the late summer and early autumn they devoted themselves to shooting and fishing. Apart from these sporting activities, they had two main pastimes. One was motoring (still a glamorous novelty only a decade after Daimler had produced Britain's first petrol-driven automobiles). They kept a number of expensive motor cars, and the most valued member of their household was the chauffeur Haines, who was engaged by George at Wickhamford in 1906 and remained there in Helen's service until her death in 1962. (Haines's job was to look after the cars, and drive Helen; George, never happier than behind a wheel, drove himself.) Every motor journey, even to visit neighbours, was an event to be recorded by Helen in her diary. They were also addicted to gambling, and spent many of their evenings playing poker and roulette; their principal companions in these activities were Jack Muir, scion of a rich Scottish family Helen had known in childhood, and his wife Heather, who lived at Kiftsgate Court in Gloucestershire, and who joined forces with the Lees-Milnes for their annual jaunt to Monte Carlo.

Socially, they counted as prosperous minor gentry, with entries in *Burke's Landed Gentry* and *Kelly's Handbook*. The fact that they were new arrivals in the county, and that their money came from 'trade', does not seem to have impeded their acceptance among the local squirearchy. (As they lived off industrial profits, one might describe them as 'upper middle-class'; but in their vocabulary 'middle-class' was a term of opprobrium, implying suburban values, and Jim preferred to describe his background as 'lower upper-class' – both families had, after all, owned land for generations, and had their roots in the soil.) Like virtually everyone they knew, they supported the Conservative Party, and regarded Lloyd George, with his land taxes and assault on the House of Lords, as the devil. As the squire of Wickhamford and his lady, they performed local duties: George was elected to the Rural District Council; Helen concerned herself with the general well-being of the villagers. Much that they had to do clearly bored them – as when Helen presided at the Badsey Flower Show, or George sat on the board of the local workhouse. They had little contact with the magnates of the county – Earl Beauchamp at Madresfield, Viscount Cobham at Hagley, Lord Sandys at Ombersley. Socially, the grandest people with whom they mixed (both prominent members of the hunt) were Jock Campbell,* a Scottish baronet of ancient lineage who played polo with George and became one of Jim's godfathers, and Bolton Eyres-Monsell (later Viscount Monsell) of Dumbleton Hall, a naval officer who had married a local heiress and was elected as the local Conservative MP in 1910, eventually becoming First Lord of the Admiralty.

They were both country-bred people with a love and understanding of nature. George was passionate about horses; Helen adored her dogs, and also had a great affinity with birds, which she would allow to fly into the house, nest in cupboards and even sit in her hair. On the other hand, they were totally uninterested in the arts. The only music they liked was popular songs; the only theatre, light comedies. Their paintings were mostly sporting scenes and family portraits. George positively despised literature, and would have no books on display in the house except for The Badminton Library of Sports and Pastimes. Helen, however, was a voracious reader of popular novels (including some works of literary distinction): at the back of her annual diary she lists the books (generally about sixty) read during the year – the latest productions of Arnold Bennett, Marie Belloc Lowndes, R. H. Benson, Philip Gibbs, Ian Hay, Baroness Orczy, Henry de Vere Stacpoole, Edgar Wallace, Hugh Walpole and H. G. Wells. (One might ask when she found time for all this reading; the answer seems to be in the mornings, which she often, according to her diary, spent in bed.) As well as being unmoved by art, the Lees-Milnes had no great feeling for religion, towards which (as Jim writes in Another Self) his father's attitude was 'perfunctory' and his mother's 'indifferent'. Helen rarely considered churchgoing worth mentioning in her diary – though she and George did attend Wickhamford church (which was situated in their own garden) every Sunday, as

> everyone in the village automatically assembled once a week, and offered up praise and thanksgiving as much to the prevailing social system as to the Almighty . . . So my parents did not regard spending one hour a week glorifying the status quo as too great a sacrifice of their leisure moments.

* Sir John Home-Purves-Hume-Campbell, 8th Bt (1879–1960).

The patron of the living was Christ Church, Oxford, and the vicar, from 1903 to 1946, was a distinguished scholar of that college, the Reverend (later Canon) W. C. Allsebrook. Jim later recalled that his parents treated this good and learned man 'abominably' and 'would hide when he called uninvited at the manor, because he, who knew nothing of hunting and shooting, bored them'. In *Another Self*, Jim relates that something of a feud developed between the squire and the vicar: Allsebrook disapproved of George Lees-Milne's racing and gambling and introduced dark hints about the diabolical nature of such habits into his sermons, while George used his squirearchical position to retaliate in various ways.

In *Another Self* Jim, possibly influenced by Nancy Mitford's novels in which she fictionalised her parents to comic effect, depicts George and Helen as a pair of ludicrous eccentrics. If they were not quite as highly coloured as he portrayed them, they nevertheless made a curiously contrasting couple. He, notwithstanding his predilection for gambling and philandering, was conventional in outlook; she was unconventional. Despite not working for a living, he believed in filling every spare moment with useful activity, such as improving his property or making furniture; she was indolent by nature, and quite happy doing nothing. He was obsessively punctual and constantly making plans; she was whimsical and impulsive and barely capable of planning anything. She had a sense of humour; he had none. He was basically shy, but steady; she was uninhibited, with a streak of mental instability (which ran in the Bailey family, and which Jim always feared might lurk in himself).

One thing they shared was a love of Wickhamford Manor, their recently acquired but agreeably ancient property. It dated back to the thirteenth century, having originally been a monastic dependency of Evesham Abbey: the lake, fed by a rivulet known as Badsey Brook, had been the monks' fishpond, and still contained carp descended from those with which it had been stocked in pre-Tudor times. After the Dissolution of the Monasteries, it had become the property of the Sandys family from the 1590s to the 1850s. The black-and-white exterior looked romantic and impressive; inside, it was a jumble of mostly smallish rooms connected by narrow passages and staircases, the atmosphere being rather gloomy as the small leaded windows did not admit much light. Of greater architectural interest was the small adjacent church (described by Jim in his *Shell Guide* to the county as 'one of Worcestershire's best'): it featured a three-decker pulpit, Georgian box pews, and the seventeenth-century Sandys memorials. The surrounding countryside was rather flat, largely devoted to apple orchards and market gardens, their produce sold at the local market town of Evesham – though the scenic Cotswolds with their buildings of golden stone began just a few miles away at Broadway.

Jim had a typical Edwardian nursery upbringing at Wickhamford with his sister Audrey, who was three years his senior, and his brother Richard (known as Dick), two years his junior. They were looked after by a nursery maid, a 'blooming girl' from the village called Maggie; a succession of nannies (Helen does not seem to have had the knack of keeping staff); and a series of governesses who gave them rudimentary instruction, one a French *mademoiselle*. They had two sets of playmates: the children of the village with whom they mixed freely, learning their broad Worcestershire dialect as a kind of second language; and the Ashwin children at neighbouring Bretforton Manor, where the Ashwins had reigned as squires since the sixteenth century. However, Jim's closest companion in infancy was his father's white bull terrier, Tyke, 'a great blustering extrovert dog' with whom he established a relationship of deep understanding (despite Tyke's tendency to betray him when he tried to hide behind the sofa to avoid being sent to bed). On birthdays, the Lees-Milne children exchanged tea parties, featuring conjurers and magic lantern shows, with the children of their parents' friends from the hunt.

George and Helen, like most of their class, did not concern themselves much with the upbringing of their children, who were trained to be 'seen and not heard' and were often only seen when they descended to the drawing room at tea time for their daily 'inspection'. However, almost as soon as he became aware of the world around him, Jim adored his mother and was in awe of his father. Recalling his infant emotions in *Another Self*, he wrote of his mother: 'In my eyes she was beautiful, attractive, romantic and amusing. Her sense of the ludicrous and her utter indifference to the proprieties never failed to stimulate me.' And of his father: 'I longed to be admired by him. Instead I was . . . ignored by him because I never showed a vestige of bravery on any possible occasion.' He would grow up to have a close attachment to his mother and a frankly hostile relationship with his father: as he candidly admits, he was 'a cissy child', who until adolescence 'desperately wished I were a girl and felt desperately ashamed of my wish'.

To worship the mother and fear the father is not uncommon in little boys; but in two related respects, Jim was an unusual child. First, he was addicted to fantasy to an extraordinary degree. In the famous opening lines of *Another Self*, he draws a contrast between the 'real' world of his imagination and the 'unreal' world of everyday life.

I do not deny that a few of my notable fancies were sparked off by momentous contacts with the unreal, outside world . . . A riveting story or a glamorous present might . . . set the magic working. On the other hand the pattern of events in my world was often outrageously disturbed by trivial demands made by the unreal world, such as to eat tapioca pudding, to wash one's teeth, or to go to bed when one felt disinclined. With time one learnt how to condition these extraneous demands, and prevent them from totally dislocating the even flow of the true inner existence . . .

On the whole how very satisfactory the real existence was. Instead of being the victim of circumstance I was its creator. I could make it take any turn that I liked . . .

Some of Jim's fantasies related to stirring deeds he would have liked to perform to impress his father. 'I would dream of stopping a runaway railway engine by throwing myself across the track, of flashing past the winning post on Derby Day, of taking curtain after curtain call at the Stratford-on-Avon pantomime, or of advising the King over an intimate cup of tea at Buckingham Palace how to deal with the obstreperous suffragettes.' Others were genealogical in nature: he was 'consistent in my longing to become Rouge Dragon Pursuivant and spend my days in comfortable surroundings manufacturing for myself a totally fictitious but noble ancestry deriving from some Knight of the Round Table'. This 'persistent day-dreaming' was disruptive to family life and made Jim 'a serious worry' to his parents. 'Just as some children cannot co-ordinate their thoughts in words, but are otherwise normal, I could not concentrate on what I was supposed to be doing . . . My mother, hoping that I would "grow out of it", made excuses for me. My father was quite certain I was mad, and used to explain why to anyone who was interested enough to listen . . .'

George Lees-Milne's 'explanation' of his son's *distrait* behaviour focused on the second unusual streak which characterised the infant Jim – a passionate interest in religion. This was perplexing to his parents who, as noted, went to church as a matter of custom but without any particular enthusiasm or belief. However, from the moment when, as a baby, Jim was carried into church by Maggie and deposited on the floor of the manor pew, where he was 'allowed to make castles out of hassocks and prayer books', he felt that this was where he belonged. He came to love the ritual, the odour of sanctity, the sound of the harmonium, the antics of old Mrs Hartwell who combined the roles of sexton and bell-ringer. Before he was six, he believed 'wholeheartedly' in a fierce God who was all-powerful but amoral: this instilled in him a fatalism, an acceptance of all that befell him (even his father's disagreeable commands) as divinely ordained. As soon as he learned to read, his favourite book was a collection of Bible stories for children. Fantasising as ever, Jim identified himself with the heroes of the stories – Joseph, the Infant Samuel, Daniel in the Lion's Den, the Angel guarding the trio in the Fiery Furnace. According to *Another Self*, this led to some bizarre incidents.

> I followed the example of [Joseph as] Pharaoh's steward who put money and a silver cup into his brethren's sacks of corn, by surreptitiously open-ing the packed luggage of departing guests while they were at breakfast downstairs on Monday mornings, and throwing handfuls of coins – my mother always left money lying about – on top of their folded night-clothes. I even managed to jam into a full Gladstone bag the prized Hunter Cup won by my father at Cheltenham Races. Not until the owner of the luggage reached home and unpacked was this precious, but dented, object revealed. His embarrassment must have been acute, and how he managed to explain it away in his bread-and-butter letter I never learned.

The fact that his father had lost an eye on the hunting field caused Jim to identify particularly with Tobias, who, guided by the Archangel Raphael, cures his father's blindness with the entrails of a fish. In the first chapter of *Another Self*, Jim relates how, one Sunday in the village church, he attempted to smear the glass eye of his outraged parent with the mal-odorous gall of a rotting carp illicitly caught in the manor lake. It is a delightful story – though, as with others in the book, it is difficult to believe that it can have unfolded in quite the surreal fashion described. It nevertheless serves as a dramatic illustration of Jim's early absorption in both fantasy and religion – and although, as he grew up and faced life's realities, he would to some extent bring these tendencies under control, romanticism and devoutness were to remain key elements of his person-ality for the rest of his life.

Two events added variety to the life of Jim and his siblings by taking them away from home. In the early summer they had their annual seaside holiday, usually at Aberdovey in North Wales with its fine sandy beach and views of Cardigan Bay and Snowdon. And whenever their parents were absent from Wickhamford, they went to stay with their widowed grandmother at Ribbesford in the north of the county. They all looked forward to these visits; for while their parents were stern with them, they were spoilt by their doting grandmother; and Ribbesford, with its huge rambling house, army of devoted servants, and romantic wooded grounds by the River Severn, was a child's delight. ('Wribbenhall', the setting for Jim's first published novel *Heretics in Love* [1973], is based on Ribbesford, once spelt 'Wribbesford'.) Grannie Lees-Milne, as Jim later liked to recall, was a colourful relic of the Victorian age.

> When we went shopping in Bewdley, a mile away, or Kidderminster, about five miles, my grandmother would not get out of the car. Connolly [the chauffeur] would fetch the shopkeeper who would come to the pavement, washing his hands in invisible soap, and deferentially ask what Madam wanted. Madam would say, 'A toothbrush and some soap, Mr Perkins, please.' After a few minutes Mr Perkins would bring these objects wrapped in white paper and sealed with sealing wax. My grandmother would delve into her capacious bag and produce a gold half-sovereign. We children, if we had been good, would be allowed to keep the change. I aged 4 or 5 imagined that all shops had to give one change as a sort of present, and I remember bursting into tears of rage one day when, the exact sum having been tendered, there was no change.

Other red-letter days for the children were the visits of their uncles and aunts. Jim especially admired his Uncle Robert, his mother's elder brother and the apple of her eye: he worked as a clerk in the House of Commons and was both a saintly man (who devoted his spare time to boys' clubs) and tremendous fun. Their sister Doreen, known to all as 'Deenie', was beautiful and vivacious and also great fun. George's elder brother Alec was rather a shy man who suffered from poor health and was not much fun, but always brought them nice presents. At the time of Jim's birth, all three were unmarried; but during 1912, two of them entered into somewhat eccentric unions. In July Deenie married Bill Cunninghame, a heavy-drinking Ayrshire laird some years older than herself who, it transpired, had dissipated his family fortune in a long and futile attempt to claim the Earldom of Glencairn. The children travelled up to Scotland with their parents to attend the wedding, and spent some weeks there (during which Jim celebrated his fourth birthday) meeting their relations and being introduced to a country they would all come to love. And in October the mild Alec married Dorothy Edwards-Heathcote, daughter of a sporting baronet, a strident and rather masculine woman (along the lines of Bertie Wooster's booming but benevolent Aunt Dahlia) who shared his passion for shooting. (As neither marriage produced children, and Robert remained a bachelor, Jim had no first cousins.)

In August 1914, the month of his sixth birthday, the world into which Jim had been born effectively came to an end with the outbreak of the First World War. In *Another Self* he gives us to understand that his parents were leading such isolated lives at Wickhamford that they first learned of the crisis on the fifth of August, the day *after* Britain entered the conflict. 'Good God, we've declared war on Germany!' his astonished father exclaims at the breakfast table, as he drops his newspaper onto his toast and marmalade. However, his mother's diary reveals that for some days the family (in the intervals of attending tennis parties) had in fact been following the news closely and anxiously.

> *31 July*: Felt too miserable to do anything with this war hanging over us. *1 August*: Wettish day. Played tennis at Liffords. *2 August*: Horrid day of suspense. Motts [came] for tennis. *3 August*: Awful day of uncertainty. Terrified England wd back out & leave France to fight it out alone . . . Played tennis at Thomases. *4 August*: Britain declared war on Germany. At last. We breathe again. All troops are mobilized. Everyone you know seems to be off . . . Met all the Evesham territorials marching through the village, off to Swindon tomorrow . . . *5 August*: Lots of rumours about ships sunk etc. Kitchener made Secretary for War. *6 August*: Jim's birthday. He seems the only cheery looking being to be seen. Children to tea [by way of a birthday party].

Although they had led hedonistic lives and were unused to work, George and Helen were both fiercely patriotic and determined to 'do their bit'. Much to his regret, George was rejected by the army owing to his missing eye; but he turned over his land to intensive agriculture, and did a series of rather dreary war jobs, such as purchasing hay for the army's horses, which took him away from home. Meanwhile Helen remained at Wickhamford and threw herself into various forms of voluntary work – 'nursing the wounded, cherishing Belgian refugees, licking envelopes, distributing comforters, hoeing the soil' – though she was so 'pampered and flighty' that she usually brought more trouble than benefit to these worthy enterprises. Jim's parents were thus separated for much of the war; and being still handsome and libidinous in their thirties, they abandoned themselves to extra-marital flings. Most of these affairs were transient; but by the end of the war, Helen had formed a serious attachment with George's former polo-playing friend Jock Campbell, now a hero of the Dardanelles. (Jim, his godson, later described him as 'the decadent aristocrat *par excellence*'.) There was even talk of George and Helen divorcing so that Jock (whose wife had left him over the affair) could marry her – though the Lees-Milne marriage survived, albeit in an atmosphere of constant bickering and infidelity.

In his eighties Jim published a novel, *The Fool of Love*, which opens in a Midlands country house in 1917 and draws on childhood memories of wartime life at Wickhamford. It is a world of privations – disgusting *ersatz* food, unheated rooms, the reduction of an Edwardian household to three ancient servants. All are weary of war; and Rupert, the novel's boy-hero, is also colossally bored by it. Rupert is fifteen, six years older than Jim would have been, and an only child whose father is fighting at the front; but his mother – a scatterbrained but still beautiful woman who yearns for romantic adventure – seems at least partly inspired by Helen. The garden is dedicated to vegetable-growing in aid of the war effort and kept going by German prisoners of war. However, during the war Jim and his siblings spent only occasional weeks at Wickhamford; as their mother felt unable to cope with them owing to her work and reduced domestic staff, they were packed off, with their nursery maid and governess, to their grandmother at Ribbesford. Life remained comfortable there, for a home farm produced enough food for their table, and Grannie Lees-Milne was surrounded by faithful retainers who were as old as herself. As always, she doted on her grandchildren, which made a pleasant change for them after the mixture of scolding and indifference they were used to receiving from their parents. They adored roaming around the great rambling house and the vast wooded estate, and afterwards looked back on their wartime residence there, insulated from the horrors taking place in the world outside, as the happiest part of their childhood.

At some point in the middle of the war, this idyll came to an end for Jim when he was sent away to school. The facts are confused by the colourful but clearly to some extent fictional account given by Jim in *Another Self*, which runs as follows. In the spring of 1917, shortly before his ninth birthday, his mother suddenly decides to send him to a school called Upland House, which was once a private house lived in by friends of hers. On 4 June – he is specific about the date – they make the journey there from Wickhamford. Whereas Helen Lees-Milne is 'dressed to kill', Jim looks a sorry spectacle, wearing clothes which are too big for him, and shoes which are too tight; he is in a state of some nervousness, it being the first time he has either left Worcestershire or travelled by train. Their journey – in an old banger to Evesham station, by train to Paddington, across London by taxi to catch another train at Euston, finally from Hemel Hempstead station to the school in an antiquated horse-drawn cab – is depicted as a hilarious series of mishaps, culminating in the collapse of the cab's floorboards as they enter the forecourt of Upland House under the gaze of the entire school, obliging them to run for their lives to keep pace with the horse until it comes to a halt. It then transpires that they are not expected, Jim's mother in her dottiness having failed to appreciate that a boy has to be 'entered' for a school before turning up. Jim is nevertheless accepted by Upland House and remains there for four years until he goes to Eton, the boys who witnessed the humiliating circumstances of his arrival never allowing him to forget it.

The principal preparatory school in the vicinity of Hemel Hempstead, Hertfordshire is Lockers Park. It was never a private house, having been built as a school by its founder in the 1870s. Both Jim and his brother Dick were indeed sent there to be 'prepared' for Eton: but the school records show that they arrived there together just after the war, in January 1919. Before that, they must have gone to another school – but Jim's papers provide little clue as to where it was or what it was like. Possibly his original journey there, under chaotic wartime conditions, bore some relation to the uproarious tale recounted in *Another Self*. It is not the case that he had never been outside Worcestershire before going there: there had been the pre-war holidays in Wales and Scotland. But it may be that Jim had his first glimpse of London on the way there, as recalled in *Another Self*.

It seemed incredibly large and incredibly ancient. I do not suppose that the squares and crescents on our way to Euston station contained more than a dozen buildings of later date than the Regency. There was hardly any traffic and our taxi kept to the crown of the cambered, cobbled streets. I can hear to this day the soothing purr of the metal studs in the tyres as we sped along. It was however interrupted by the driver ceaselessly pressing a fat, rubber horn like a ball-cock attached to a brass serpent, which undulated over the right mudguard. The noise emitted was disappointing – the thin chirrup of an insolent sparrow. My other strong memory is of a deliciously sweet smell of petrol fumes, mingled with that of horse droppings and antirrhinums.

Jim also errs in saying that his first experience of school occurred in June 1917; for his mother already refers to him as a schoolboy in a letter written to her brother Robert, then serving with the British Army in Egypt, in February of that year. The letter itself cannot now be found, but Jim described it in his diary seventy years later (possibly before destroying it). The diary entry – dated 15 February 1987 – is worth quoting as one of the few surviving records of his childhood.

Have been reading through letters to Uncle Robert from Mama and Aunt Doreen during the last year of his life, 1917 . . . Interesting to read what my mother wrote about Dick and myself. That we adored returning to school (which we hated). That I was fearfully proud of my school (which

I wasn't). That she was vexed by my colour-blindness because I wanted to be a sailor (which I didn't, loathing it when, some years later, I was made to stay with Victor Campbell [Jock's brother] on his destroyer). In one letter to Robert, Doreen wrote that both our parents jumped on us and my father snubbed us so often that we were cowed. She was worried about it.

In Mama's letter of 11 February 1917 . . . she writes: 'I . . . took Jim to The Mall to watch the [royal] procession from Buckingham Palace to open Parliament. The whole route was lined with special constables, such cheery good sorts who let Jim stand with them so he had an uninterrupted view. When the King passed, Jim stepped out and yelled Hurray and waved his bowler so violently that the King saw and saluted him. It was *too* nice and Jim the proudest kipper in the world. It was such an excitement for a country bumpkin seeing all the colonial troops & Jellicoe & Fisher & French, Connaught & all the celebs . . . We then waddled up to Buck[ingham] Palace and stood & gazed wondering which was the King's bedroom window! We then went to Fortnums & armed ourselves with a huge cake and chocs for school and sent you your parcel. It was a memorable day in Jim's life . . .'

Another memorable though tragic day for Jim occurred in December 1917 when he heard that his uncle had died of wounds in a military hospital in Cairo following an engagement with the Turks near Acre. This was an irreparable loss, for Robert was kind, generous, profoundly Christian, good-humoured, scholarly, clever and wise – everything his own father was not. (He also differed from his brother-in-law in showing little interest in women during his thirty-five years, while remaining attached to his closest Eton schoolfriend, William Leveson-Gower, another bachelor who fell in the war: they are commemorated together in a tablet in the school chapel.) 'If only my Uncle Robert had lived', wrote Jim in 1990, 'he would surely have guided my feet into the way he saw most fitting for me, have encouraged my desire to learn, have smoothed my relations with my father, have inculcated courage in me and turned me into a more worthwhile character.' For the rest of his life, Jim revered his uncle's memory. Every August, he remembered his birthday; and he sought to follow in his footsteps by entering Magdalen College, Oxford and applying (unsuccessfully) to be a clerk in the House of Commons.

In November 1918 the war ended, Helen celebrating the Armistice in London in the company not of her husband but of Jock Campbell. Superficially, the old life resumed at Wickhamford, centred on hunting in winter, racing in summer. Money was still quite plentiful, and a full household staff was re-engaged. George enlarged the manor, personally designing and supervising the building of an extension indistinguishable from the main structure, and re-created the garden which had been given over to agriculture in aid of the war effort. However, whereas before 1914 George and Helen had led a fairly conventional existence there, after 1918 they conducted largely separate lives: one or other of them was frequently away for weeks on end, usually in the company of some paramour, and when they were together, they quarrelled incessantly. It was an unhappy home background for Jim as he progressed from childhood to adolescence, and he came to dread spending holidays at Wickhamford and to look forward to returning to school.

From January 1919 to July 1921 that school was Lockers Park. Like all such establishments, it offered a spartan regime and laid emphasis on games and the study of the classics; but the boys seem to have been quite well looked after, many of them leaving with happy memories. Its motto was *bene agere ac laetare* – work hard and enjoy yourself. The great dread among the boys was not of harsh discipline or bullying but of epidemics: throughout this period, they lived in terror of the killer influenza then sweeping the globe; though they were spared this, many (including Jim) were regularly laid low by whooping cough and other ailments. It was at Lockers Park that Jim discovered the joys of friendship. He shared a dormitory with four other boys of his own age, all of whom became lifelong friends – Tom Mitford, only son of Lord Redesdale, a charmer with a love of literature and music; Basil [Earl of] Ava (later 4th Marquess of Dufferin), a clever boy who effortlessly excelled at all school subjects; Peter Coats, heir to a Scottish cotton fortune, and a family connection of Jim's through the Thomsons; and Billy Whitaker, heir to a marsala wine fortune and a handsome house in Hampshire.* Jim became especially close to Tom and Basil, with whom he was involved in editing school magazines. Both were good-looking boys, and Jim too was developing from a weedy child into a tall and handsome adolescent, with pretty features and abundant curly brown hair. He had also ceased to suffer from the desire to be a girl (which, looking back, he thought might have been tied up with the war and his fear that, if it went on long enough, it might claim him).

In September 1921, aged thirteen, Jim progressed to Eton, following in the footsteps of his father, grandfather and Uncle Robert: Tom Mitford

---

* Other Lockers Park contemporaries included two future patrons of the arts and letters, Edward James and Peter Watson, and the future traitor Guy Burgess.

and Basil Ava entered at the same time. At Eton, one's housemaster often has a formative effect on one's development; and in this respect, Jim was unfortunate. He was sent to the House of Archibald McNeile, whose wife Mary had been a friend of Jim's mother at her finishing school in Heidelberg. Mary was a sweet woman, but McNeile himself was a cold, unsympathetic figure who insisted on a strict observance of the rules and was regarded by his boys as a remote autocrat. He was also an intolerant prude: on one occasion Jim spent his pocket money on

> a lovely nineteenth-century illustrated book of coloured prints of naked savages, ladies with full breasts and red scarves round their heads, gentlemen with spears. McNeile found it in my room, took it away and burnt it, informing my father of my unhealthy tastes.

Jim regarded him with loathing, remembering him half a century later as 'that sarcastic brute'.

Jim's five years at Eton may be briefly summarised. He was not an especially bright boy, but by no means stupid either. In December 1925 he passed his School Certificate with credit in English, Latin, French, German and Scripture Knowledge. During his last year (1925–6) he was in 'the First Hundred' (that is, the hundred senior boys who have done best in examinations, the academic cream of the school), though near the bottom of the list. When it came to games (which he hated) and other compulsory pursuits, he usually did just well enough not to disgrace himself (he was a 'wet bob', a rower); and despite his bad relations with McNeile, he managed on the whole to stay out of trouble. However, he was thoroughly 'dim' in the sense that he did not excel or stand out in any respect and, so far as one can judge, had no desire to. He won no prizes or positions of authority, and sought none. He played little part in the life of his House. He was lethargic, and generally did the minimum to get by. He did not crave the admiration of his peers: to those boys to whom he did not give his friendship, he was stand-offish. Nor does he seem to have formed any friendships with masters, or regarded any of them as an inspiring mentor.

In view of this studied dimness and detachment from the school ethos, it is curious that, in his third year at Eton, Jim became a favourite of his House Captain, Julian Hall, a handsome hero who was a member of the privileged Eton Society or 'Pop'. (He later became a minor literary figure, and succeeded to a baronetcy.) A decade later, in 1933, Hall published a school novel entitled *The Senior Commoner*, in which the hero, Harold Weir, is obviously autobiographical, and one of the lesser characters, Jim

Marsh Downe, is equally obviously based on Jim Lees-Milne (even to the fact that his mother is an old schoolfriend of the housemaster's wife, Mrs McIsaacs). Weir takes a liking to Marsh Downe, 'the only younger boy with whom he had any relationship'. Marsh Downe is 'tall for his age, with clear skin and light hair', and rather foppish, tucking a silk handkerchief into the sleeve of his coat. In his room, 'the books and pictures were arranged with care. It was an attractive room, and Harold preferred it to his own. Marsh Downe had no lists or coloured ribbons [sporting trophies] to hang on the walls.' Marsh Downe has no aptitude for physical pursuits: in the cadets, he is shouted at for marching out of step, and for flourishing his idiosyncratic handkerchief. He wears spectacles. He writes poetry, hoping to contribute a poem to a new school literary magazine. He speaks 'in a quiet voice which occasionally had a querulous note', and his general outlook is plaintive. As he tells a young classics master who shows interest in him:

> I think Ayrton [Eton] is very beautiful. But I can't really imagine why I'm here . . . I can't help it if most of the work doesn't interest me. If I was more intelligent, no doubt I should be 'up' to [taught by] more interesting people . . . It would be different if I had more brains, but I know I'm not at all clever. The things I like doing aren't of any use. I like reading . . . I love beautiful things . . . I'm not at all original. I can only admire what other people have done.

Asked what he does at home during the holidays, he replies, 'I spend my time avoiding quarrels.' Asked what he plans to do after school, he says he would like to travel, but doesn't have the money; he would like to go to Oxford, but doubts that he will have the opportunity.*

For a 1930s novel, *The Senior Commoner* is daringly homosexual: part of the plot concerns a sinister young actor who visits 'Ayrton' with a view to seducing boys there (based on an actual episode in which the American actress Tallulah Bankhead attempted to lure Eton boys to a nearby hotel until warned off by the police). Hall was himself homosexual in adult life, and one might ask to what extent his interest in Jim was sexual. In the novel, Harold Weir has a 'crush' not on Marsh Downe but on a still younger boy called Murray Gawthorne – feelings which he confides to

---

* This would seem to be an authentic account of the fifteen-year-old Jim at Eton – indeed the only one we have, as none of his schoolfriends remained alive when this biography was undertaken, both Rupert Hart-Davis and Alan Pryce-Jones having recently died. The portrait is acknowledged as being true to life in Jim's diary for 16 June 1973, and in letters from Hall among Jim's papers at Yale.

Marsh Downe, who himself fancies Gawthorne, a house contemporary of his younger brother. This brother is presumably based on Dick Lees-Milne, who entered McNeile's two years after Jim; and Gawthorne is probably based on Dick's contemporary Desmond Parsons (himself the younger brother of Michael [6th Earl of] Rosse, a senior boy in McNeile's and a contemporary of Hall): the blond and languorous Desmond was one of the most beautiful boys at the school and had numerous admirers, not least Jim himself.

If Julian Hall enjoyed physical intimacy with Jim, he was not the first to do so. In his diary for 3 June 1991 Jim noted the announcement in *The Times* of the death of one Lieutenant-Colonel Berkeley Villiers,

> who was the first boy to seduce me at McNeile's. I remember the incident extremely well, I aged fifteen at most. In the middle of the performance Michael Rosse, then his great friend, came into Berkeley's room and like the perfect gentleman he was fetched something he had left on the mantelpiece without turning his head in our direction. Michael never referred to the incident in later life, nor did B.V. whom from time to time I ran across. A prissy, affected fellow . . . The smell of his Roger & Gallet Carnation Soap never fails to remind me. Thrilling, alarming, wicked-seeming and delicious it was.

Having tasted forbidden fruit, Jim never looked back: for the rest of his schooldays, the pursuit of erotic adventures with other boys was constantly on his mind. Such activities had to be conducted with deftness and discretion, for exposure meant instant disgrace and expulsion: indeed, the elements of secrecy and danger added to the thrill. Visiting Eton in 1942 and attending Evensong in the Chapel, Jim nostalgically watched the outwardly well-behaved boys 'flashing across the nave confidential smiles that mean so much, ogling and making assignations without a word being spoken. Oh the squalid thoughts and the romance of it all at the time, I remember!' No doubt the scene brought to mind his friend Tom Mitford, and how

> on Sunday eves before Chapel at five, when the toll of the bell betokened that all boys must be in their pews, he and I would, standing on the last landing of the entrance steps, out of sight of the masters in the ante-chapel and all the boys inside, passionately embrace, lips to lips, body pressed to body, each feeling the opposite fibre of the other.

Visiting Eton in the 1980s and following the Thames upstream, Jim recalled two spots where he had engaged in trysts – an islet in the river called Queen's Eyot, and a railway viaduct known as 'Arches': the former recalled Desmond Parsons, the latter a boy named Tulloch (another future lieutenant-colonel). 'No subsequent escapades', he wistfully agreed with John Betjeman, 'have eclipsed those schoolday ones.'

Whilst healthily lustful for his age, Jim was at the same time an intensely romantic boy. As he hated his father, saw little of his mother, had little in common with his siblings and had no real friends at home, the love of schoolfriends assumed great emotional importance for him. His two great loves at Eton were Tom Mitford and Desmond Parsons. Tom he had known since Lockers Park and loved almost as a brother; Desmond was two years his junior, but a soulful, solitary and sensitive boy with whom he established a deep bond. Both were aristocratic, beautiful and artistically gifted: Jim's romantic love was enhanced by the discreet affairs he was conducting with them. They would both die young, and Jim would be haunted by them for the rest of his life. They often appeared to him in his dreams; and he was forever trying to recapture the bliss which their friendship had brought him in adolescence (to the point that he later fell in love with sisters who reminded him of them, Diana Mitford and Bridget Parsons).

Most of Jim's other Eton friendships were with boys who shared his love of literature; for although he did not excel at schoolwork, he was (taking after his mother in this respect) a compulsive reader. As he writes in *Another Self*,

> I read prodigiously, if indiscriminately, spending most of my spare time in the School Library devouring my way through the Victorian novelists and romantic poets . . . It may not have got me prizes because I was an undisciplined, unacademic child. But it did win me a number of devoted friends with similar interests, friends with whom I spent blissful summer afternoons and evenings, idly floating on the river and discussing the merits of Thackeray and Meredith, Shelley and Swinburne.

Two such friends were Rupert Hart-Davis, later eminent as a publisher, writer, editor and bibliophile, and Alan Pryce-Jones, a future editor of the *Times Literary Supplement* and literary socialite on both sides of the Atlantic. Pryce-Jones introduced Jim to a secret club which met (with the connivance of a friendly proprietress) in a back room at the Cockpit, a popular tea-shop in Eton High Street, where the members could read forbidden books, listen to a forbidden gramophone and drink forbidden cocktails. Jim also admired a set of 'enchanting, unserious, raffish boys, whose parents were for the most part cosmopolitan and rich. I was intoxicated by their glamour, but never really accepted as one of them.'

These included two clever younger sons of peers, David Herbert and Hamish St Clair-Erskine, as well as a future artist, Roland Pym, and a future actor, the gorgeous Teddy Underdown. In *Another Self*, Jim amusingly relates that he was once tricked into accompanying two of these boys in a Rolls-Royce to a roadhouse at Bray, where he was unwillingly made to participate in an elaborate prank in which they all dressed up as women and 'offered' themselves to men (including masters from the school) at a *thé dansant*, Jim proving ludicrously inept at the imposture and narrowly avoiding exposure in front of his geometry master. Apparently an episode along these lines did occur – though the 'victim' was not Jim but Alan Pryce-Jones, who was not amused, forty-five years later, to discover that Jim had appropriated his story.

It is evident that at Eton, as during his early childhood at Wickhamford, Jim lived largely in a world of his own. The school world – the world of lessons, games, rules, discipline, sense of community, exhortations to virtue – was one to which he paid attention only in so far as he was obliged to, in order to avoid trouble and have a quiet life. To him, the 'real world' was the world of loving friends, sexual adventures, art, literature and daydreams. He felt detached from Eton, observing it from the outside. He rarely wore the school tie, or attended reunions; until late in life, when his friend Martin Charteris became Provost, he never returned there except to visit the children of friends. Of course, it was something of an advantage to have gone there, as he was aware; when he worked for the National Trust, many of the leading figures on its governing committees were men he had known at Eton, as were several country house owners whom he visited with a view to discussing the possible donation of their properties, such as the Earl of Buckinghamshire of Great Hampden ('whom I knew at Eton as Hobart') and John Leicester-Warren of Tabley House.

It is also evident that at school Jim (as often happens) developed tastes and values which were remote from those of his upbringing. His parents were provincial in outlook, lowbrow in their tastes, passionate about sport, and positively suspicious of art and learning. Jim's schoolfriends were mostly aristocratic, hailing from a sophisticated, cosmopolitan world of which he longed to become part; he hated sport (especially when it involved killing animals); he had intellectual pretensions; his outlook on life was that of a languid aesthete. This did not particularly worry his mother, but it led to serious trouble with his father, with whom his relations steadily deteriorated throughout his adolescence. George Lees-Milne became increasingly 'bewildered and distressed' to find that 'he had hatched in his nest, instead of a falcon, a young cuckoo', and McNeile's disapproving reports did little to calm his irritation. In *Another Self*, Jim speculates that his father's dislike of him may have been subconsciously rooted in the fact that he so much resembled his mother.

> It was certainly true physically. It was pretty true psychically. I inherited her vagueness (what my father called 'moronic behaviour'), her love of animals, sunsets and general prettiness ('damn nonsense'), and her unfortunate incapacity for hard work and what is termed getting on with life ('utter lack of moral fibre') . . . Indeed . . . we looked more like twins than son and mother.

As George was on bad terms with his wife, but still in love with her, it enraged him to see her and Jim 'loafing around the garden arm in arm, exchanging confidences and giggling in a highly annoying manner . . . At any rate my father, sensing that there was something contrary to nature in our resemblance and our intimacy, loathed me biologically.' Had Jim been more of a sportsman and blessed with greater practical sense, George might have overcome his antipathy; as it was, the son was developing into everything the father despised.

> If my presence was pain and grief to him, my shortcomings were an unspeakable affront . . . and he never failed to deplore them loudly in private and in front of others. The consequence was . . . [that they] became more and more pronounced as the years went by and my fear of him gave way to indifference . . . Art . . . was anathema to him. The very word had on him the effect of a red rag upon a bull. He turned puce in the face and fumed at the mere mention of it; and his deadliest, most offensive adjective was 'artistic'. It denoted decadence, disloyalty to the Crown and unnatural vice. To be called artistic by him with a biting sneer used to make me shake like an aspen leaf . . . His contempt for intellectuals was profound . . . Consequently I could only read in the holidays by stealth. I spent hours at night with a torch under the bedclothes so that he should not see a light through the cracks of the door and catch me in the act. And no matter how carefully I hid my books before returning to school, he always nosed them out, like a detective on the scent of cannabis, and threw them into the stoke-hole furnace . . . I tremble to think what he might have done if he realised that I frequently took Oscar Wilde to bed with me . . .

As Jim grew estranged from his father, he drew closer to his mother, sympathising with her in the endless marital quarrels. However, this was of limited consolation to him; for as often as not she was away when he came home for the holidays, lured by the siren calls of romance. During the summer she generally sailed to Newfoundland to spend a couple of months with her lover Jock Campbell who had emigrated there. Once, when she was at Wickhamford, she asked Jim to accompany her to nearby Broadway Hill; only when they got there did Jim learn that she had gone there to meet her latest lover, an aviator, with whom she promptly flew off into the blue yonder, leaving Jim to return home alone to explain her sudden departure to his enraged father.* Among Jim's happier memories were of the new years of 1925 and 1926, when Helen joined Jock in Switzerland for skiing holidays, taking her three children with her. They were accompanied by her sister 'Deenie', whom the children adored, and who (her unsatisfactory husband having died of influenza after the war) was conveniently having an affair with Jock's naval officer brother Victor. This was probably Jim's first experience of 'abroad', and judging by the smiling photographs in his album, he enjoyed himself greatly.

Jim was neither disposed nor encouraged to invite friends to stay during school holidays, so that his only regular companions at Wickhamford were his brother and sister. Although the three got on well, they developed in very different directions. Dick did not share Jim's 'artistic' inclinations, and resembled their father both in appearance and in his interest in machinery: visitors to the manor garden would find Jim 'sitting with a pile of books under the mulberry tree while brother Dick messed about with his motor-bike'. Audrey, who had been affected both physically and psychologically by a series of childhood illnesses, was a sweet and simple girl who had inherited little of her mother's beauty but shared her vagueness and love of nature. Most days the Lees-Milne siblings visited the Ashwin children, 'the only friends we had', at neighbouring Bretforton Manor. When Harry Ashwin, last of the line, died in 1983, Jim nostalgically recalled their visits to this old squirearchical family and the ultimate fate of its members:

> We . . . rode over on our ponies, or drove in the trap, or bicycled, motor-scooted, motor-cycled or motored. In summer played tennis on the lawn before scrumptious teas, in winter hide-and-seek upstairs in the gloomy passages and bedrooms. My favourite was Clare, tall and plain with a dry sense of humour; she died in 1945 of consumption brought on by war-work. Harry always deadly dull, a lump. Mrs Ashwin a dignified, wistful, beautiful, humorous lady of the old school; Mr Ashwin, like a Cavalier in breeches and gaiters, spent all his days in a separate office building on the edge of the shrubbery and stalked into the dining room for meals,

---

*At least, in the diaries he is an aviator, Captain Butler in his Gipsy Moth (2 June 1946, 22 January 1980); in *Another Self*, he becomes a balloonist.

graciously acknowledging the presence of us children. Their enormous limousine was all windows like a greenhouse, driven by Robbins, the Plymouth Brethren chauffeur who considered it wicked to go to the pantomime. I shall never forget the unique smell of the hall, musty linseed oil on black panelling mixed with Mansion polish. The empty drawing room where for long hours Thetis thumped on the piano and resented our interruptions. There was Bobbie, the good-looking, flagrantly pansy brother, whose friends were rotters; he died when he fell out of the back of a car in Piccadilly on to his head. Lamented by his adoring mother, whose first passion was her son Jim: he died of appendicitis at school in 1907, and might have continued the line had he lived . . .

Jim also saw something of Graham Eyres-Monsell and his sister Joan at Dumbleton Hall, children of the Lees-Milnes' hunting friend who was now Conservative Chief Whip. He had a soft spot for Joan (later Mrs Patrick Leigh Fermor), but found Graham terrifying. 'At children's tennis tournaments he used to bash his racquet over my head so that I looked like a clown peering through a broken drum, and once at Wickhamford he let out my father's pet parrot so that it flew away, and drove the car out of the motor-house into a ditch.' Both Harry Ashwin and Graham Monsell were at Eton with Jim.

Happily for Jim, his holidays were largely spent not at home but visiting relations, especially in Scotland. His Uncle Alec and Aunt Dorothy often had him to stay on their 70,000-acre Knock estate on the Isle of Mull, which Jim later considered the most starkly beautiful place he had known. 'Bare moorland, windswept, cloudswept, rainswept, but how I loved it, the deer on those heights, the view of the outer islands, the scowling peaks, the treacherous waters.' They were an odd couple, his uncle shy and vague, his aunt a great blunderbuss of a woman who smoked a pipe and clearly had lesbian tendencies. Although, like Jim's parents, they lived for sport and had few aesthetic interests, they were always the soul of benevolence towards him. Scotland was also the home of his Thomson relations, who lived mostly in Ayrshire. His mother's first cousin Neale Thomson, 'Cousin Nealie', was a connoisseur and collector of pictures, furniture and *objets d'art*, and encouraged Jim's developing interest in beautiful artefacts. (Both Alec and Nealie were childless and intended Jim to be their heir, though Jim had to wait until the 1960s for these two inheritances, by which time little remained of Uncle Alec's once considerable fortune.) Jim also enjoyed visiting Cousin Nealie's widowed mother Great-Aunt Maggie and her sister Great-Aunt Netta, a delightfully eccentric pair (*née* McGrigor) who conversed in thick Scotch accents and used ear trumpets which clattered together as they talked. Netta was married to a leading Ayrshire businessman, Matthew Arthur, who had bought himself a baronetcy in 1903 and a peerage in 1918, becoming Lord Glenarthur; before meeting George Lees-Milne, Jim's mother had been in love with their son Cecil, but marriage had been forbidden by the Arthurs who did not consider Helen Bailey grand enough for their heir. Cecil now had a son, another Matthew Arthur, who was a few months younger than Jim: this handsome daredevil was the family connection of his own age to whom Jim felt closest (though there was no blood relationship, and Matthew did not share Jim's 'artistic' tastes); they were together at Lockers Park and Magdalen (between which Matthew went to Winchester), and Matthew would marry Jim's sister Audrey.

There were also holidays in Wales. Only once did Jim visit his mother's noble cousins the Glanusks at their neo-Tudor castle (by the fashionable Victorian pastiche architect Luger) in Breconshire. But he quite often stayed with his elderly half-uncle and godfather Crawshay Puleston at Emral Park, a romantic moated house in Flintshire. Crawshay was the son of Jim's maternal grandfather by his first wife, daughter of a Puleston baronet; by 1900 the Pulestons had died out in the male line, and Crawshay inherited Emral and changed his name from Bailey to Puleston. Jim was fascinated by the romance of an old line coming to an end, and later wrote a narrative poem about the fate of the Pulestons:

> Emral, there are no days for laughter.
> The moat is choked like the hollow of my left hand
> With a telltale crisscross of disaster . . .

Like Uncle Alec, Uncle Crawshay was childless and intended Jim to inherit his estate; but on his death his widow removed herself to the South of France where she succeeded in running through what was left of the money, so that in the end Jim received only the Puleston family portraits. Jim watched the demolition of Emral in 1936 and was 'much moved by the horror of it'; Glanusk Park suffered a similar fate after the war.

The only schoolfriend with whom Jim stayed was Tom Mitford, whose family lived at Asthall Manor, a lovely Jacobean house in Oxfordshire. There he got to know Tom's pretty, clever and teasing sisters Nancy, Pam ('Woman'), Diana, Unity ('Bobo'), Jessica ('Decca') and Deborah ('Debo'). Debo, born in 1920, was a baby at the time of Jim's first visit, and her earliest memory is of his lobbing a cricket ball into her pram. Jim's favourite was always Diana, the most beautiful as well as the brightest of the sisters, and the closest to Tom in age, looks and intimacy. Jim envied Tom his home life; for the Redesdales, despite their eccentricity, seemed a faithful and devoted couple at this time; and although Lord Redesdale (like Jim's father) was a philistine obsessed with field sports and given to splenetic outbursts, he nevertheless doted on his children and allowed them to behave much as they pleased, so that Asthall, unlike Wickhamford, abounded with books and the sound of music. Jim spent hours reading poetry with the sisters – in her memoirs, Diana recalled that 'he made us read Byron, Shelley, Keats and Coleridge', and that they fantasised about going to live in Greece 'where we would scorn material things and live on a handful of grapes by the sea'. The Mitfords had four cousins, the Bailey brothers (whose colonel father was married to Lady Redesdale's sister), the eldest of whom, Dick, was at Eton with Tom and Jim. Every September the Baileys invited the older Mitford children to spend a week at Maugersbury Manor, their Tudor house in Gloucestershire; and Jim, along with another of Tom's Eton friends, Ralph Jarvis, was eventually included in this 'Bailey week'. Although the Bailey boys were rather 'hearty' for Jim's taste, and the week largely consisted of tennis and cricket matches in which he participated with limited enthusiasm, he always looked forward to this annual event which reunited him with Tom and Diana.

Jim had cause to remember his last school holidays at Easter 1926, during which he had his first heterosexual experience. Among his mostly 'staid' relations was a glamorous young woman whom in *Another Self* he calls 'Janie'. (She was in fact 'Joanie', daughter of Major Siward Surtees of Redworth, a North Country landowner who had married a Thomson cousin of Helen.) In 1925, while in the throes of a divorce, she had spent Christmas at Wickhamford. As Jim writes:

> She was certainly seductive, wore very chic clothes, and was drenched in expensive Parisian scents . . . Every morning she remained in bed, leafing through French novelettes and combing her Pekingese's silky ears. In the afternoons she rolled her moon eyes at any man who happened to be about, not excluding the Vicar. She spoke in a special baby language of her own and referred to herself in the third person . . .
>
> Her effect on me was electric. In my wildest dreams I had not conjured up a being more intoxicating. The very smell of her drove me into ecstasies of excitement . . .

Jim sent her love poetry, with the result that, during the winter, she sometimes drove down to Eton on Sunday afternoons to take him out to tea – though invariably accompanied, to Jim's frustration, by some handsome escort. However, one day during the Easter holidays, while Helen was abroad, George announced that Janie would be spending the night with them on her way to Wales, his manner creating a horrified suspicion in Jim's mind that he meant to seduce her. According to the hilarious story related in *Another Self*, Jim foils this intention by surprising the guilty couple in the guest bedroom disguised as Goddard the parlour maid, come (at an unusually early hour) to deliver Janie's morning tea and run her bath. Caught in the (as yet unconsummated) act, George Lees-Milne flees, whereupon Jim tears off his maid's uniform and jumps into bed with Janie for an hour of rapturous lovemaking.

While it would be surprising if some details of this story were not fictitious, it appears that Jim did have sexual intercourse with his cousin, who was evidently fairly free with her favours. However, there was a sequel which he does not relate in *Another Self*. Some weeks after the incident, Joanie was found to be pregnant. The child was stillborn, and there can be no certainty that it was Jim's; but he was to be haunted for the rest of his life by the thought that he might have been responsible for a human soul which had been conceived in sin, and perished before birth. It conditioned his attitude towards parenthood: he felt that he had forfeited all further right to father a child. In a paradoxical way, it may also have influenced his later enthusiasm for birth control. Joanie had a tragic subsequent history: she drowned herself at Monte Carlo on the eve of the Second World War, in her fortieth year, when again pregnant with a child which was not her then husband's.

2

Further Education
1926–31

JIM LEFT ETON in July 1926, a month before his eighteenth birthday.
As indicated in Julian Hall's novel, he had little idea of what to
do in life. In the vaguest way, he wished to devote himself to literature;
but although he had read widely, he had yet to demonstrate any creative
abilities. His father lived on a private income; but this was not an option
for Jim – the family fortunes had declined considerably during the past
two decades (not least through George's addiction to racing and
gambling), and continued to do so. Moreover, George Lees-Milne, who
believed that the General Strike of May 1926 presaged revolution, was
firmly of the view that Jim ought to 'stand on his own two feet', and
refused either to make over any capital to him or give him the smallest
allowance. Nor did he (who had wasted two profligate years at Trinity
College, Cambridge in the 1890s) propose to pay for Jim to go to university. It had been settled that the down-to-earth Dick Lees-Milne would
go into the family cotton business in Lancashire with a view to eventually
running it. It was up to Jim to decide what career he wanted for himself,
and prepare himself for it. However, Jim's relations with his father were
now so antagonistic that the more George pressed him to make decisions,
the more he was disinclined to do so. 'Instead I spent hours reading out
of sight at the far end of the garden [at Wickhamford] where the water
from the great pond flowed into Badsey Brook', he writes in *Another Self*.
'I shall always associate with my wretchedness those deep, resonant and
labial notes of the pond water interminably tumbling down the wide
drain, close to the bench on which I sat, endeavouring to immerse the
future in the poetry and fiction of the past.'

Jim says that his father gave him until 1 October to make up his mind.
When that day arrived, and Jim had still reached no decisions about his
future, George took matters into his own hands. He told Jim to put on
his only decent suit and pack a bag, and drove him to London. In fact
(Jim surmised), George had no idea what to do with him, but hoped for
some inspiration. Sure enough, while they were lunching at George's

club, the Cavalry in Piccadilly, a friend of his, Colonel Percy Battye, suggested they try an employment agency called Useful Women in Dover Street. This was meant as a joke but George gratefully followed it up, with the result that, by the end of the day, after various comic adventures, Jim found himself alone in London, his father having paid in advance for him to spend twelve months at Miss Blakeney's Stenography School for Young Ladies in Manresa Road, Chelsea and lodge at half-board with a Mrs Roxburgh in Onslow Gardens, Kensington.

It is quite possible that on 1 October events occurred not dissimilar to those described in *Another Self*. However, the year was not 1926 but 1927. Jim simply misses out a year, obfuscating the fact that, after he left school, his father gave him not three but fifteen months to work out his future. What did Jim do during that missing year? There are few records from which to reconstruct it; but it is clear that he spent much of it abroad. During the autumn of 1926 he made a sea journey with his mother to Algiers and Genoa (during which he took his mind off seasickness by reading Byron's *Don Juan*), and went on to have a holiday with her in Provence; at Easter 1927 he visited Florence, Venice and Milan, marvelling at their artistic treasures. Nor was his education neglected: for the first half of 1927 he was enrolled as a student at the University of Grenoble. This was a university for foreigners, aimed at improving their knowledge of French; most of the students were women, so that Jim had the unusual experience, for one whose entire schooling had taken place in an all-male environment, of starting 1927 at an educational establishment where he was among the few men and ending it at another where he was the only one.

The secretarial course he took from October 1927 – not for twelve months, as stated in *Another Self*, but for six – was designed to prepare him for a business career. It would not in fact have been difficult for Jim to make a good start in business, for his parents had many friends and relations (such as the Muirs of Glasgow) who belonged to established mercantile dynasties and were happy to help him – though most of the jobs proposed through these connections were in India and other outposts of empire, and he showed no enthusiasm for any of them. Meanwhile he lived in poverty. Although his landlady Mrs Roxburgh, a woman of modest origins who spent her spare time reading and fantasising about the aristocracy, was kindly and maternal, his father allowed him only ten shillings a week pocket money (supplemented by occasional pound notes from his mother) with which to meet all the incidental expenses in his life (including his daily lunch, not included in his board terms). He could not even afford to travel by public transport, so that he went everywhere on foot – which had the advantage of instilling in him a good knowledge of the capital's geography and architecture.

The memoirs of Jim's contemporary Alan Pryce-Jones show that during the 1920s it was possible for an impecunious Old Etonian of nineteen to have a marvellous time in London, especially if he was good-looking – the rich (who included one's former schoolfellows) were giving endless lavish parties to which it was easy to get invited and at which one could meet fascinating people, including the leading literary lights of the day; but Jim had virtually no social life during those six months, which he later remembered as the most solitary and miserable of his life. In *Another Self* he explains that he was unwilling to accept hospitality he could not return; but the main cause of his reclusiveness was probably that, hating his current existence and seeing little future for himself, he simply felt depressed and unsociable. The only friend he saw was Rupert Hart-Davis, who after an unhappy year at Oxford had returned to London to train for the stage, and often invited Jim to spend the evening with him at his father's house in Knightsbridge. For Jim, brought up in a house without books, this was an enchanted world. As he writes in *Another Self*,

> His large living room . . . was the most civilised room I had ever entered. The walls were lined from floor to ceiling with books that had been read, the spines of their immaculate jackets flickering in the golden light of a deep coal fire. The air of wellbeing and culture was something beyond my wildest dreams of attainment. He was purposeful, busy and contented. Yet he spared time to discuss poetry and lend me books. His enthusiasms made it impossible for me to be self-pitying in his company.

When not in Rupert's consoling company, Jim spent his evenings wandering the streets alone, bemoaning his lot. Fifty years later, in a poignant diary entry, he recalled his feelings of that time:

> Last night in London I re-experienced a sensation of my youth. I was alone . . . I had tried in vain to get hold of a number of old friends . . . Before dinner I went for a walk around Westminster, looking at street buildings. Wandered into the Abbey cloisters just as the lights were turned on, in the twilight. Not a soul. There I was smitten with the loneliness of my youth when, friendless and poor, I used to walk the streets and think the passers-by so much happier than I, all so purposeful, so fulfilled, so content. Last night, I did not actually experience this unhappiness again, but I recaptured its flavour of sadness, nostalgia and utter hopelessness.

What did Jim think about as he drifted through the streets? In *Another Self*, he tells us that the subject most on his mind was romantic love (not sex, he hastens to add – though it is possible that, during his solitary perambulations, he found opportunities to gratify his sexual desires). By this time, the two great passions of his adolescence had effectively become lost to him. Tom Mitford had gone to study music in Vienna, where he soon developed heterosexual interests; Desmond Parsons had become a most unsuitable cadet at Sandhurst, eventually dropping out to devote himself to foreign travel. Jim longed to feel for others something of what he had felt for them. In *Another Self* he gives only one instance of actually falling in love during those lonely six months in London. One February evening, armed with one of his mother's pound notes which had arrived that morning, he went to hear *Don Giovanni* at Covent Garden where, standing in 'the gods', he found himself next to a young man 'of seraphic beauty' with 'a Renaissance profile like one of those candlelight portraits in chiaroscuro by Bronzino'. This was 'Theo', who forty years later he still considered to be 'the most sympathetic person I have met in a longish life'. They were immediately attracted to each other, chatted in the intervals, and afterwards consumed sausages and lager together at the Café Royal. They talked of music and art and 'laid bare our souls'. They swore to meet again, swapped tokens of affection, and exchanged names and addresses. However, in the course of valedictory embraces they somehow managed to re-exchange their slips of paper, so that, after a blissful walk home musing on his new love, Jim discovered to his horror that the name and address in his pocket were his own. Theo – Jim did not even know what that name was a contraction of, let alone his surname – was lost to him for ever.

It is a poignant tale – but is it true? When *Another Self* appeared, Jim's friend Geoffrey Houghton Brown told others that it was suspiciously similar to an early experience of his own which he had related to Jim. For that matter, Jim himself relates a similar story a quarter of a century later, on 10 April 1953, when he becomes infatuated with a man on a train who gives him his telephone number, which turns out to be the wrong number. All one can say is that, although in the course of a long life Jim had numerous 'flings' with both men and women as well as more than a few affairs of the heart, there was also a side to him which was forever in search of the unattainable, and which seems, perhaps subconsciously, to have welcomed the idea of finding love only to lose it. The story of 'Theo' may be regarded as a symbol of this recurrent theme in his life, of the many affairs contemplated but never consummated, of the romance of 'what might have been'.

In fact, during his London sojourn of 1927–8, and indeed for a year beforehand, Jim *was* in the grip of a hopeless love – the object of his passion being Diana Mitford. She is hardly mentioned in *Another Self* – perhaps understandably, since at the time of its publication she was devotedly married to Sir Oswald Mosley, former leader of the British Union of Fascists, and had become one of the controversial women of the age. It has been seen that, visiting Asthall as a schoolboy, Jim had come to admire Diana, with her beauty and love of poetry and closeness to Tom; during the summer of 1926, he transferred to the sister the love he had felt for the brother. She was two years his junior, having just turned sixteen, though unusually intelligent for her age; she was not displeased by Jim's interest in her, though she did not discourage two other suitors whom Jim had known at Eton, Bill Astor (heir to Viscount Astor and his fortune) and her cousin Randolph Churchill (only son of Winston and Clementine).*

In *Another Self* Jim describes a visit to Tom at Asthall that summer, during which he blots his copybook on the first night at dinner by suggesting that, with the war long over, the British 'ought to make friends with the Germans'. The war veteran Lord Redesdale takes exception to this remark, rises from the table, and leaves the room, fuming. At this the six sisters look at each other and chant in unison the lines of the wartime recruitment song:

> *We don't want to lose you*
> *But we think you ought to go.*

Crestfallen, Jim prepares to return to Wickhamford, but finds that it is raining heavily and that his motor-scooter will not start. He therefore creeps back into the house, only to run into his intimidating host. However, Lord Redesdale, in reality a kindly man whose bark is worse than his bite, now treats him with great friendliness, so that Jim does not leave but stays on for a week. A letter exists to Tom from his sister Nancy describing this incident; but it shows that it took place not in the summer of 1926 but in February 1928 (by which time the family had moved from Asthall Manor to Swinbrook House), and that Tom was evidently not present. And when *Another Self* appeared, the five surviving sisters delighted in pointing out that Jim had got several other details wrong. They did not insouciantly chant the words of the song – on the contrary,

---

*Lord Redesdale and Mrs Churchill were officially first cousins, but generally believed to be half-siblings as Lord Redesdale's father had been having an affair with his sister-in-law at the relevant time.

they were appalled, and speechless. As for the sequel (as they all recalled it), Jim prepared to leave, thought better of it in view of the rain, stayed the night, and only saw Lord Redesdale again in the morning, when he was indeed friendly – though in view of what had occurred, Jim cut his visit short after all.

However, Jim did visit Asthall in the summer of 1926, and his love for Diana appears to date from that visit. During the next two years it was his fate to worship her from afar, since they were able to meet only on rare occasions. They did, however, maintain a regular correspondence; Jim kept most of her letters, and she some of his. The surviving exchange begins in September 1926 with Diana thanking him for a copy of *Ariel*, André Maurois' biography of Shelley (in the original French), and expressing views which are unusually sophisticated for one of her age and upbringing, as well as indicating that she and Jim were already on confidential terms.

> I have enjoyed reading *Ariel* more than I can say – thank you so much . . . It is of course very depressing when all Shelley's lovely children die – but somehow they couldn't have lived. There will never be another Shelley. I wish I had been alive then to marry him. He was more beautiful physically and mentally than an angel.
>
> You know I think his lovely free ideas about love are just what ought to be. Why on EARTH should two souls (I wish there was a better word, I think SPIRIT is better) why on earth should two spirits who are in love a bit have to marry – and renounce all other men & women? It is SUPREMELY foolish. And yet even to speak of free love is almost a sin. But I suppose it would – if universally the custom – lead to endless misery & poverty among women. Having been deserted by their capricious lovers they would have perhaps to maintain large families on nothing for years.

Early in 1927 both Diana and Jim went to France to study French, she in Paris under the aegis of the artist Helleu and his wife, friends of Lady Redesdale, he in Grenoble. On 26 February she wrote to him from Paris that she was having 'the most superb time, which I can tell you about as you are so far from England's green and pleasant land, where scandal travels fast'. What she had to report cannot have come as a consolation to him. She misses Bill Astor 'terribly'; she basks in the admiration of Helleu, who draws endless pictures of her and 'whose compliments never become boring because they are always unexpected'; and she 'flirts outrageously' with her young French admirer, Charlie (Comte Charles de Breuil).

I do it because French flirting interests me, and because it makes me think of Bill. Round the Bois de Boulogne in a taxi alone with Charlie after dark – you can guess. Don't feel angry with me – I know that it isn't lovely to be so sensual, but it is exciting and wonderful. Charles is a count, of course. He is fairly rich and extraordinarily handsome but very vain.

Jim replied from Grenoble in an undated letter – which is worth quoting at some length, as it appears to be his first significant surviving letter to any correspondent. It is rather precious in both style and content, less witty and fluent than hers, written in an artistic hand, but poorly punctuated. He calls her 'Mona' after the Mona Lisa.

Mia carissima Mona,
. . . Your letter dropped here today like the 'gentle dew from heaven'. I cannot express my delight but imagine it as being intense . . .

I hope Charlie realizes how lucky he is . . . I agree with you, flirting is extremely good for one, even when one is plighted . . . The beautiful princess in the fairy story who, while her lover is away at the war fighting dragons (or rather catching butterflies), shuts herself up in a palace tower & refuses to see any man, invariably dies a sour old woman, and probably a jilted spinster . . . I admire you for your eternal fidelity to Bill . . .

How I wd adore to have a picture of you by M. Helleu. You must feel like Emma, Lady Hamilton sitting to Romney. I daresay you are vain, and indeed you have cause to be, and in fact I know you are vain. Have'nt [sic] you even a snapshot of yourself, your Parisian self of course, that you could send me, as I would love to see for myself, whether you have still got that Raphael face . . .

It seems as if it was in another world that I last saw you at Asthall in the summer, but I suppose it is only a few months. Do you think we shall ever all meet again? Sometimes I think I shall throw myself off the Belledonne mountains here, & be the object of beautiful Elegies and Monodies . . .

Grenoble itself is an exceptionally ugly town with nothing to recommend itself, except the Musée where there are some lovely pictures for a small provincial town, the University, which is a joke, and the Pâtisseries, which ought to be world famous . . . The mountains round are superb as the town is at the end of a long valley . . . I live outside the town in a pension, tiny, hideous, but otherwise clean & comfortable. I belong to the University, where I go every morning & occasionally the afternoon. The lectures are occasionally quite interesting, & one learns a surprising amount of French. The University is amusing, because it is for *les étudiants étrangers seulement*, & is full of every nationality in Europe.

I am having private lessons from an Italian girl, who though not pretty is very charming, & it is rather a joy learning that most beautiful lucid language from an actual Italienne.

Most of the people are repulsively ugly here, but one or two are extremely pretty. There is one Italienne I know who is quite the most fascinating little person I have ever met. She is very tiny & chic rather like my sister Audrey, but much prettier and *très spirituelle* – I am afraid I have to lapse into French occasionally, it is much easier.

At Easter I am going to Florence, Venice & Milan, & will tell you all about it after. I am naturally simply dying to go now, but am reading up & accumulating knowledge of the pictures at Florence before I go.

I forgot to tell you that in the summer I am going to climb to the top of Mt Blanc: I think the view wd be superb, & it is quite dangerous & exciting.

There is a Grecian girl here, extremely beautiful & very like Nancy [Diana's eldest sister, then twenty-two].

Will you promise to write me another of those letters one day. I am so sorry for you going home to England so soon: cant [*sic*] you come down & see me before you return?

With ever so much love

Ever yours

Jim

Diana replied on 19 March with the news that she was about to lose one of her devoted admirers.

Thank you a million times for your lovely letter. You have got an interesting & intelligent handwriting.

I am ridiculously unhappy . . . It is because Monsieur Helleu is terribly ill, and he is perhaps going to die . . . Nobody I have loved has ever died, except sometimes an adorable animal. And now a man whom I have almost worshipped, and who has worshipped me for 3 months, is going to die . . . *How* can I bear it?

You ask me if I have changed. I have grown a little older, and more intense in my passions of love, sorrow and worship of beauty. To look at I am the same. Pray for me, to your gods whatever they are. I am very unhappy.

Would you like one of Helleu's pictures of me? Answer me soon, I leave in ten days . . . I sometimes feel that I love you too much, but you *are* my spiritual brother.

Jim replied by return.

My darlingest Mona . . . It seems so fatuous to make the usual & ordinary remark, that perhaps he will get better. I hope to goodness he does. I now understand why one gets harder & colder as one grows older, and why one loves all the noble and beautiful impressions of youth. It is because one suffers sorrow and witnesses it increasingly that one becomes insensible to beautiful impressions & things . . . I always try my hardest not to let myself become callous, because I am so dreadfully afraid of losing a particle of my extreme sensibility to beauty.

I love your letters, because they are well written and you do not contain your emotions like the majority of people who write to me. Letters are usually such cold glacial things.

I would simply adore to have a photograph of one of M. Helleu's portraits of you, and beg of you to send me one. You cant [sic] imagine what a joy it is to me the thought of having your face with me. I am glad you have not changed . . . I am, I think, the same, if no uglier. In thinking over your last remark, I am convinced one can never love a friend too much, though, I will confess it now, I always think of you as something even higher than a friend.

'Your letter came the day he died,' Diana replied on 25 March. 'It was wonderfully comforting.' She enclosed one of Helleu's silverpoint etchings of her. 'Well, goodbye, my dear Jim. Write to me from lovely Italy. When shall we meet again?'

Diana returned to England; and her next letters report the alarming news that her mother, having discovered and read her diary, has found out about her 'flirtation' with Charlie. In her disgrace, she has looked in vain to her siblings for moral support.

I am so furious: Nancy says I am a bundle of sex with no soul, and Tom thinks the same . . . How *could* Tom – no really he is a brute and too too selfish. I will never be anything but *cold* towards him until he owns himself wrong. Soul is so essential. Don't mention any of this to him will you. I had to tell you, there is no one else I could confide in. Oh *damn* Tom. I really hate him. He is *far* more sensual than I God knows.

Certainly Jim (as Diana was presumably aware) would have known better than anyone about Tom's sensual propensities.

It was now almost a year since Jim had set eyes on Diana; but they finally met again during the summer of 1927. After this meeting, Jim wrote her a (somewhat cryptic) love poem, accompanied by a short note.

> Know then that one alone can give me breath
> To mutter charms so delicate, so true,
> That my poor soul torment unto the death
> The fragile heart that quivers at the view.
> My feeble head is raised to hang the wreath
> Of poesy; thus much your sight can do.
> Beauty's last balm more hurtful is than that
> Which kills with ugly shaft the jaded cat.

37

I enclose this piece of doggerel only because I wrote it in my sleep thinking of you the night I got home after seeing you. If you don't understand
it I'll explain it one day. Perhaps you will not agree with me that a cat is
a beautiful and tormented creature.

   I hope you don't think I wasn't thrilled at seeing you on Sunday; indeed
I think I was almost stunned at first.

Possibly this was the first time Jim had so openly declared his passion
for her; and although Diana kept the poem, her response was cool
and discouraging.

I think you will write lovely poetry. Read Alice Meynell's short essay on
false impressionism, called *The Point of Honour.*★ This is *not* meant to be
rude, but the best friends are those who offer advice . . . I think you are
very kind to admire me, but have you seen the beauties Georgie Curzon,
her mother, Lettice Lygon, Mary Thynne, & all the rest? I compare very
badly with them. I have got dark skin and light hair & eyes which is an
unattractive paradox.

They met again at 'Bailey week' in September 1927; and while this seems
to have been a fairly enjoyable reunion, Jim complained to her that she
was becoming too free with her favours, provoking another put-down.
'Now listen, I don't want anyone to fall in love with me . . . I am certainly
not a vamp and I don't think I am much of a flirt. Of course I used to be
when I was younger [she was then seventeen] because inordinate flattery
and adoration turned my head, but really I am not now. So don't be
worried over me.'

   While he must have been tormented, as he began his lonely six
months in London, by Diana Mitford's failure to respond to his love, Jim
had meanwhile engaged the affections of her cousin Diana Churchill†
whom he had met at the Baileys'. In January 1928 'Diana C.' invited him
to spend a weekend at Chartwell, her family home in Kent, Tom and
Diana Mitford also being asked. While he leapt at the chance to see his
'darlingest Mona' again, it must also have been a painful experience, as
they were on the home territory of his rival Randolph, then a boy of
seraphic beauty whose company and admiration 'Diana M.' clearly
enjoyed. Fifty years later, Jim recalled some other memories of the

---

★Alice's theme is: 'How many painters are painting the truth of their own impressions?'
†Diana Churchill, eldest child of Winston and Clementine, had a melancholic streak
which made her a worry to her parents. After two unhappy marriages, the second of
them to Jim's Eton contemporary Duncan Sandys, she committed suicide.

weekend for inclusion in the official biography of Winston Churchill, Chancellor of the Exchequer in Baldwin's government at the time of his visit.

> I was terrified of W.C., who would come in to dinner late, eat his soup aggressively, growl in expostulation at Randolph's cheek, then melt so as to be gallant with the girls and tolerant of the boys. One night we remained at the dinner table till midnight while W.C. gave us a demonstration of how the Battle of Jutland was fought, with decanters and wine glasses in place of ships, while puffing cigar smoke to represent gun smoke. He was like an enthusiastic schoolboy on that occasion. The rest of the visit he was in waders in the lake or building a wall, or pacing backwards and forwards in his upstairs room dictating a book to his secretaries. Thump, thump on the floorboards overhead.

After the Chartwell visit, Jim received an amorous letter from Diana Churchill; but his attention remained fixed on the other Diana. 'May I treat you as a very cherished sister to whom I can say everything?' he wrote to her. 'Why are you so amazingly *sympathique* as well as charming?' They met again at Swinbrook in February (when the incident occurred which Jim wrongly places in 1926). But Diana had moved on: she was now going to balls in London, and meeting fascinating people; her mind was already fixed on an early marriage that would rescue her from the family home which bored and restricted her, and clearly the impecunious and melancholic Jim, now training to be a secretary, was not the sort of husband she had in mind. They saw each other briefly at the Eton and Harrow cricket match in June – but after that Jim effectively passed out of Diana's life for the next twenty-five years, though she remained for a while the unattainable object of his desire. Indeed, he never forgot his feelings for her. Meeting her in 1945 for the first time in years, he recalled that 'she was the most divine adolescent I ever beheld . . . more immaculate, more perfect, more celestial than Botticelli's seaborne Venus'. And in 1972, reminded of her by a Swedish soprano singing Wagner at Covent Garden, he found that 'all my inhibited love for Diana when I was nineteen and she seventeen surged within me'.

By the spring of 1928 Jim had completed his secretarial course in Chelsea. It was perhaps the most useful part of his education, for he retained his typewriting and shorthand skills for the rest of his life, and they were to prove invaluable to him as private secretary to a statesman, secretary to a committee, a diarist recording his daily observations and finally as a professional author. But more than ever he recoiled from the business career for which it had been intended as a preparation. Instead, his heart was now set on going up to Oxford. It may seem curious that he should have been seized with a belated desire to attend the university, for the friend he had seen most of in recent months, Rupert Hart-Davis, had abandoned his undergraduate career at Balliol after only a year, considering it a complete waste of time, while another friend from Eton, Alan Pryce-Jones, had just been sent down in disgrace from Magdalen at the end of his second term, a fate he accepted without regret as he plunged into the social and literary life of London. However, as indicated in Julian Hall's novel, Jim had long dreamed of going to Oxford; and three years at university would save him from the imminent fate of working in a commercial office and give him a breathing space in which to work out his future.

In *Another Self*, Jim writes that he confided his ambition to his mother at Wickhamford while his father (who had always spoken scornfully of a university education) was absent. Helen agreed that going to university was 'the necessary culmination of every gentleman's education', and felt that Jim must go to Magdalen, where her beloved brother Robert Bailey had been a popular undergraduate during the first years of the century, distinguishing himself both as a sportsman and a scholar. (Magdalen, with its fine riverside situation on the outskirts of the historic city, is traditionally regarded as the most beautiful of the Oxford colleges, second only to Christ Church in social reputation and to Balliol in intellectual distinction.) She resolved to act quickly, before her husband returned: if by then Jim had secured a place at the college, George would probably accept the *fait accompli*. She also calculated that they could rely on two allies: Jim's former Eton housemaster Archie McNeile, who had never approved of Jim but remained under the influence of his wife, Helen's old schoolfriend; and the legendary Sir Herbert Warren, President of Magdalen since 1885, who had been an admirer of Robert. (Jim was fortunate, for Warren was on the verge of retirement; his successor George Gordon, a dour and meritocratic Scot, is unlikely to have indulged an ill-qualified late candidate.)

The next humorous passage in *Another Self* describes Jim's first visit to Sir Herbert at Magdalen. Jim had been warned that he was a crashing snob and indeed, throughout the interview the old President dropped allusions to the Prince of Wales and other eminent undergraduates to whom he had been *in loco parentis*.

With what I thought was unnecessary carelessness, he allowed a large gold pen to slip from his fingers. In attempting to pick it up he dropped it on a woolly rug. 'Dear me!' he said, as I dived to retrieve it. 'Her Majesty's present which she gave me when His Royal Highness left the College.' Reverently I placed it on his pen tray, which was an over-ornate miniature of the Taj Mahal. I gave the vulgar object a quick look of disparagement. 'I see', he remarked, 'that you admire the Viceroy's little token.' 'Oh rather,' I answered promptly.

Jim allegedly entered into the spirit by casually referring to a fictitious titled relation (though he could have dispensed with such subterfuge by mentioning his Bailey cousin Lord Glanusk, or his Scottish connection Lord Glenarthur whose son and heir Matthew was already a Magdalen undergraduate). At all events, Jim made a good impression on Warren, who was susceptible to good-looking and pleasant-mannered young men, and who readily sympathised with Jim's view that it had been a mistake for him to prepare for a business career. In *Another Self* Jim claims that, at the end of this interview, Warren promised him – 'for your Uncle Robert's sake' – a place at Magdalen conditional on his passing the university entrance examination in October, confirming this in a letter which was triumphantly presented to Jim's father on his return to Wickhamford. In fact, Jim had applied far too late for normal admission in the coming academic year, and it took Warren some weeks to 'fix' his place, probably one of the last things he did before retiring from the Presidency in July after a reign of forty-three years.

The file relating to Jim's admission survives in the Magdalen archives, and gives an intriguing glimpse into how such matters were arranged. McNeile wrote to Warren on 28 April to say (no doubt insincerely) that 'his character during his time at my House at Eton was exemplary . . . and he was most charming and attractive'. Warren replied on 1 May: 'Mr Lees-Milne's uncle, Mr Robert Bailey, was one of the most delightful Etonians we have ever had here . . . I had a great regard and, I may say, affection for him. I therefore, when his nephew turned up rather unexpectedly, felt desirous of giving him the best advice I could.' Warren first advised Jim to try for a place at Worcester College, which he knew to have several vacant places, and wrote a letter of recommendation to its head; but Jim responded that he wished if at all possible to go to Magdalen. On 31 May he again saw Warren, this time accompanied by his mother, who afterwards wrote to the President: 'More than ever now I long for Jim to get to Magdalen and I would be so grateful if you could pull all your influential strings to work it. It was Robert's greatest wish that Jim should go there.' Warren duly obliged; Jim was offered his conditional place and exempted from part of the entrance examination, though still required to sit a paper in Latin. He was already 'cramming' for this with H. B. Allen, an eccentric clergyman in the Cotswolds, who wrote to Warren that Jim seemed practically to have forgotten the language. Warren recommended that Jim leave Allen to finish his cramming with a former Magdalen tutor, one Kemshead in Lyme Regis. Warren wrote to Kemshead: 'I have reason to think he is a particularly good fellow.' In a letter designed to be placed before the admissions board, Kemshead replied agreeing that Jim 'possesses various qualities which deserve praise . . . and seems an especially desirable candidate', adding that his examination performance might not reflect his true abilities. In the event, Jim managed to get through the exam on 4 October. Warren wrote to him saying he was 'delighted you have got in all right and I congratulate you warmly . . . Now you mustn't let us down . . .'

In *Another Self* Jim writes that 'although my father was committed to paying for my board and education, he gave me no allowance. For pocket money I was dependent on my mother's generosity and whim.' This is not quite true. George (as he reminded Jim in 1935) agreed to allow him £300 a year while at the university – generally considered to be enough to get a man through Oxford* – on the understanding that he would then be on his own and could expect no more from family sources. This certainly meant Jim was on a fairly tight budget, unable to keep up with rich friends or indulge to any great extent in such things as meals in good restaurants or visits to smart tailors. But he is surely exaggerating when he claims that his 'extreme poverty . . . ruled out most forms of social intercourse' at Oxford.

Traditionally, many young men progressing from school to Oxford look forward to three years of enjoyment and pay scant attention to their studies, hoping to do enough to get by. This does not seem to have been the case with Jim. He went up to the university with the intention of working hard and doing well. He took Warren's exhortation to heart,

---

*When, in Evelyn Waugh's *Brideshead Revisited*, Charles Ryder goes up to Oxford in 1922, his father is advised that he should have an allowance of 'three hundred a year . . . that's what most men have'. However, Mr Ryder decides to give Charles £550, recalling that 'nowhere else in the world and at no other time do a few hundred pounds . . . make so much difference to one's importance and popularity'. In *Another Self*, Jim remarks that 'the difference between having no private means and £200 a year of one's own was far greater than that between having £200 and £2,000.'

and wished to show the college authorities that their indulgence in admitting him had not been misplaced. He hoped to emulate his Uncle Robert, who had gained a first in 'Mods'. He also needed academic qualifications to launch himself on a career: unlike his more favoured contemporaries (or his father at Cambridge in the 1890s), he could not afford to go down without taking a degree. And last but not least, he was aware that his education left much to be desired, and hoped to use his time at university to try to put this right.

His academic career, however, was undistinguished; and whatever his initial intentions, he cannot be said to have devoted himself to his studies. He had originally planned to read English Literature but was finally admitted to the Modern History School, having been advised by Warren that this would give him a better chance of entering the civil service on going down, as he hoped to do. There were two outstanding history tutors at Magdalen at this time, both colourful characters – the Reverend J. M. Thompson, a disaffected theologian who had become an expert on the French Revolution, and the young Scottish mediaevalist Bruce McFarlane. McFarlane in particular might have been expected to appeal to Jim (who was only five years his junior) on account of his passion for architecture: he loved visiting historic houses and churches, often taking his students with him on his expeditions.* However, these great teachers seem to have made little impression on Jim; for when, visiting Magdalen in later life, he was asked who had taught him, he hadn't a clue. Nor did he recall being tutored by two fellows in other disciplines who went on to become household names – C. S. Lewis (later famous as a novelist) and John Wolfenden (who later chaired the Committee which recommended the decriminalisation of homosexuality). At the end of three years, Jim scraped a third-class degree. In *Another Self* he asserts that he had been eager to learn, but felt let down by tutors who were only interested in undergraduates who were either intellectually or socially distinguished: as Jim was neither, he received 'no help, no encouragement' and was left to 'sink or swim', being one of the 'hungry sheep' who 'looked up and were not fed'. This is certainly unfair to McFarlane, an unsnobbish man who lived for his teaching and devoted himself to his students, most of whom revered him. The truth probably was that Jim suffered from the lack of academic discipline at Oxford: apart from having to submit a

---

* He was also (according to his close friend A. L. Rowse) a homosexual with a reputation for 'pouncing' on his pupils – possibly one reason Jim did not warm to him as a mentor.

weekly essay and attend a few lectures, undergraduates were free to do as much or as little work as they chose; and Jim did not, at this stage, possess the motivation necessary to dedicate himself to his subject.

Jim did not participate in any of the non-academic fields in which it is possible to get noticed at Oxford. He did not play games, or make speeches at the Union; he played no part in student politics or journalism or dramatics. Socially, too, he made little mark. He seems to have spent most of his time inside his own college; but this was less out of fraternity than from financial insecurity. Magdalen men had to pay for four dinners a week in the college hall whether they ate them or not; and Jim's resources were such that he could rarely afford to eat in restaurants such as the George and the Mitre frequented by richer undergraduates. His attachment to his college may also have owed something to the fact that, in his first year, probably through Warren's influence, he was allotted an unusually fine set of rooms for a dubious late entrant, on the ground floor of the fifteenth-century Cloisters: the main room (now part of the college bursary) had a large bow window looking out over Holywell Mill Stream to Addison's Walk and the water meadows beyond, an idyllic view which remains unchanged to this day.* It perhaps says something about Jim that his best college friend was the occupant of the neighbouring set, Peter Acton, a grandson of the Whig historian and a man as diffident and reclusive as Jim himself. There was a large contingent of Etonians at Magdalen, but they were mostly 'hearties' of whom Jim steered well clear. On the whole, his college friends (to none of whom he afterwards remained close) were fellow history students of middle-class background who went on to make solid careers, such as the artist Peter Greenham, future head of the Royal Academy Schools, and Oliver van Oss, future headmaster of Charterhouse. Though they had few interests in common, he also saw much of Matthew Arthur (who, though his junior in age, was a year ahead of him at the college, and who in April 1931, while Jim was still at Oxford, married his sister Audrey). Jim's first term at Magdalen coincided with the last of John Betjeman, who had been rusticated six months earlier for 'failing in divinity' but allowed to return to sit for a pass degree; rather surprisingly, given Jim's passion for poetry and the fact that Betjeman was the leading undergraduate versifier, as well as famous for his former editorship of the student journal *The Cherwell*, they did not meet at this time.

Jim's chief soulmate at Oxford was Johnnie Churchill, Winston Churchill's nephew, an aspiring artist and composer whom he had

---

* He spent the remaining two years in nearby college lodgings at 63 High Street.

befriended some months before coming up to the university when they were cramming together with the Reverend H. B. Allen: he was now at Pembroke but a frequent visitor to Jim's rooms at Magdalen, where he executed a classical mural. Unlike Jim, Johnnie was glamorous, well-connected, and high-spirited to the point of mental instability, with a taste for practical jokes; but he required a steady 'foil', and Jim fitted the role. One might compare their friendship to that between Sebastian Flyte and Charles Ryder in *Brideshead Revisited*: Johnnie, the grandson of an earl and the great-nephew of a duke, opened doors to an enchanted patrician world (their cramming in the Cotswolds had been punctuated by ducal lunches at Blenheim); and though, like Jim, he had little money, he was an accomplished sponger, in whose company Jim enjoyed a taste of good living (thus Johnnie introduced Jim to the lavish weekend parties given by his Harrow friend Harry d'Avigdor-Goldsmid, a hearty and handsome sportsman from a rich Jewish banking family, at Somerhill in Kent). The relationship also echoed that between Bertie Wooster and 'Bingo' Little in the stories of P. G. Wodehouse, in that Johnnie, like Bingo, was constantly falling in love with some girl and wishing to discuss his latest *amour* with a sympathetic friend. The greatest of Johnnie's passions during these years was for Penelope Chetwode (future wife of John Betjeman), whom he met in March 1930 ('I'm drunk with love', he wrote to Jim), and whose conventional parents were so appalled at the prospect of him as a son-in-law that by the end of the year they had whisked her off to India, where her father was Commander-in-Chief: shortly before her enforced departure, Jim took part in some form of mock pagan wedding ceremony which she and Johnnie played out in the woods of Wytham Abbey near Oxford, the seat of Johnnie's maternal grandfather, Lord Abingdon. During university vacations, Jim stayed with Johnnie's family in Norfolk (where he taught his little sister Clarissa to write sonnets); and they travelled abroad together, visiting Rome in January 1930 during the public celebrations of the marriage of the Italian Crown Prince to a Belgian princess – probably Jim's first visit to the Eternal City which would loom so large in his life.

If Jim had hoped to be reunited at Oxford with his closest friends from Eton, he was to be disappointed. Tom Mitford and Desmond Parsons chose not to go to university; Rupert Hart-Davis and Alan Pryce-Jones had already finished their brief Oxford careers before Jim got there. The schoolfriends he saw most of at Oxford were Hamish Erskine at New College and Basil Ava at Balliol. By the time Jim arrived, both had become famous figures on the university scene, Hamish as a clever and outrageous aesthete, Basil as one who combined intellectual brilliance with a great name. Hamish, as Jim recalled at the time of his death in 1973,

> had the most enchanting looks – mischievous, twinkling eyes, slanting eyebrows . . . The toast of the university, he was tossed from one rich limousine to another . . . He was everything I, then a simpleton, would have liked to be and now despise, namely a shallowly sophisticated, lithe of mind, smart society figure. For long I distantly loved him and was attracted by him . . .

Nancy Mitford, Tom's eldest sister and the future novelist, was hopelessly in love with Hamish at this time, and Jim, knowing them both, found himself roped in to their lunches as a support for the one and a protection for the other. Basil had become a protégé of the brilliant but raffish Conservative statesman F. E. Smith, Earl of Birkenhead, who in the month Jim went up to Oxford resigned from Baldwin's cabinet to spend his two remaining years mostly at Charlton, his country house near Banbury. Basil often visited Charlton and sometimes asked Jim, his friend since Lockers Park, to accompany him; there Jim met other remembered Etonians who were now politically ambitious undergraduates, including Birkenhead's son Freddie (then Viscount Furneaux) and Randolph Churchill. Jim's abiding memory of these occasions was of the prodigious quantities of alcohol consumed by Birkenhead and his guests. Birkenhead (who though still in his mid fifties was already afflicted by the cirrhosis of the liver which would soon kill him) attributed his legendary clever-ness and wit to heavy drinking, and encouraged the young men who visited him to follow his example. As a result, both Basil Ava and Randolph Churchill became alcoholics while still in their early twenties, and wasted their undoubted talents. For that matter, the lives of Matthew Arthur, Freddie Birkenhead, Johnnie Churchill and Hamish Erskine were all ultimately blighted by 'the demon drink'. Meanwhile Jim, who was painfully aware that he failed to scintillate whether drunk or sober, remained (apart from the occasional binge) a moderate drinker.

Another figure who haunted Charlton was Maurice Bowra, the clever and flamboyant but notoriously snobbish and overbearing don who was then Dean of Wadham (the college which had produced Birkenhead) and was to become its Warden from 1938 until his death in 1971. He ran a famous Oxford *salon*, and Jim attended his *soirées* and sat at his feet. It would be too much to say that Bowra only had time for the well-born – he was a mentor of John Betjeman, who was both middle-class and academically undistinguished – but he clearly had little time for Jim. It may have been his dismissive treatment by Bowra, who contributed so much to the Oxford careers of others, that Jim had in mind when he later wrote contemptuously of dons who only bothered with the aristocratic or the brilliant. At Bowra's, however, Jim had the opportunity to meet undergraduates who were later to distinguish themselves in the literary world, including the golden-haired poet Stephen Spender, whom Jim disliked for his left-wing views, and the protuberant-faced caricaturist Osbert Lancaster, with whom he struck up a warm rapport (and who was probably the only lasting friend he made at Oxford). It was also probably at Bowra's that Jim got to know a number of fascinating men of the preceding ('Brideshead') Oxford generation with whom, during the 1930s, he was to establish closer ties than with any of his own university contemporaries, notably Robert Byron, John Betjeman and Harold Acton (the last of whom he had already encountered as an older boy at McNeile's).

And what of Jim's romantic life, so vibrant at Eton? He had barely arrived at Magdalen when, in November 1928, he received a cruel blow with the news that his adored Diana Mitford, still only eighteen, had become engaged to Bryan Guinness, the clever and handsome son of a rich Conservative politician.* 'I *know* you will like him because he is too angelic & not rough & loathes shooting, & loves travelling & all the things I love,' Diana wrote to him. 'When we are married and live in London you must often come & see us.' Jim sent Diana a wedding present of books, but far from accepting her invitation he saw virtually nothing of her for the next twenty-five years. Her sudden disappearance from his romantic sights, in order to marry a man who abundantly possessed the wealth, sophistication and intellectual distinction which he so lacked himself, undoubtedly filled him with feelings of worthlessness, and blighted the start of his Oxford career. Jim did make one good female friend at Oxford, the delightful and clever undergraduate Elizabeth Harman, but the friendship seems to have been without overt sexual attraction, Elizabeth already being unofficially engaged to the eccentric aristocratic don Frank Pakenham (later 7th Earl of Longford). She found Jim charming, and particularly enjoyed his amusing observations about other people, but considered him hopelessly indolent and clearly homosexual: it caused her some amazement when he later became a man of laborious days, and eventually married.

---

*It must have been particularly galling to Jim that the news was first broken in *The Cherwell*, of which Guinness was a former editor.

It is easy to exaggerate the extent to which homosexual behaviour was prevalent at Oxford between the wars: the 'aesthetes' who flaunted such behaviour, immortalised by Evelyn Waugh in the character of Anthony Blanche, amounted to a small number of highly visible undergraduates. Nevertheless, it is true to say that many men continued to enjoy the romantic and sensual experiences to which they had been introduced at school, and that they did so in an atmosphere which was, by the standards of the day, unusually relaxed and tolerant. Although much of Jim's Oxford circle – Johnnie Churchill, Harry d'Avigdor-Goldsmid, Basil Ava, Osbert Lancaster – was resolutely heterosexual, there is no doubt that his own love life was mostly centred on other men. Through his friendship with Hamish, he had contact with the aesthetes and attended parties which sometimes developed into orgies of a fairly harmless kind. And outside that world he seems to have enjoyed casual romps with sympathetic fellow undergraduates, many of whom went on to have conventional married lives. When the Conservative politician Alan Lennox-Boyd was killed in a road accident in 1983, Jim nonchalantly recorded in his diary that 'with him I slept more than once, as indeed with his brother George,* but they were not romantic occasions'. Apart from his affair with Desmond Parsons, intermittently resumed whenever Desmond visited Oxford, the diaries allude to only one romantic attach-ment from this period – with the actor John Gielgud, who was four years Jim's senior but already something of a celebrity as a leading man at the Old Vic and a star of silent films. They were connected through both John's aunt Violet Gielgud, an 'affected but kindly' lady whom Jim had befriended on Swiss holidays, and Rupert Hart-Davis, who married Peggy Ashcroft, a young actress Gielgud admired, in 1929. Though London-based, Gielgud was at home in Oxford, where he had started his professional career as a member of the Playhouse Company in 1924. His affair with Jim took place early in 1931, when Gielgud was starring in a variety of mainly Shakespearean roles at the Old Vic. 'For six weeks I was infatuated with him,' Jim recalled fifty years later. 'Then it passed like a cloud.' The affair was partly conducted (certainly at Gielgud's expense) at the Spread Eagle at Thame, a famous hostelry frequented by rich undergraduates whose proprietor John Fothergill, an eccentric survivor of Oscar Wilde's 1890s circle, produced excellent continental cuisine.

---

* Alan and George were a few years older than Jim – but their younger brothers Francis and Donald (the first of whom was a gorgeous and much-courted 'aesthete') were his contemporaries and friends at Oxford, through whom he came to know the family.

If Jim had cut a dim figure at Eton, at Oxford he was even dimmer. None of his friends who later published memoirs of their time there – such as Osbert Lancaster and Elizabeth Longford – considered him worth mentioning. Elizabeth's sister-in-law Violet Powell recalled that, at Oxford parties, he would often retire to read a book in the corner of the room. In *Fourteen Friends*, published the year before his death, Jim describes himself at Oxford as 'particularly green, very provincial, almost retarded mentally'. No doubt he was somewhat immature, in terms of both intellect and personality – as he wrote on his fortieth birthday, 'All my life I have been a slow developer.' But one should not take his words too literally. Sir Herbert Warren, with his long experience, considered he had the makings of a man of the world; and all who got to know him seem to have regarded him as a pleasant companion. To some extent the dimness may have been cultivated: as at Eton, his attitude was that of a detached observer. And although he failed to distinguish himself academically, he strove to improve himself in other ways. He explored the vibrant religious life of the university city, experiencing the various forms of worship on offer and embarking on a spiritual quest which would lead him to embrace Roman Catholicism two years after going down; together with Johnnie Churchill and Osbert Lancaster he attended Albert Rutherston's drawing classes at the Ruskin School; and if he failed to read enough history, he continued to devour poetry and fiction,* and 'fostered secret and intensely passionate ambitions to write'.

Jim always maintained that Oxford's greatest influence upon him was in stimulating his passion for architecture. He had already developed a mild interest in the subject as a schoolboy, fostered by visits to friends and relations who lived in interesting old houses, and by cycling tours of the Worcestershire countryside. Indeed, his father was fascinated by architecture, though he liked what Jim scornfully referred to as 'ye olde', notably black-and-white manor houses such as Wickhamford, and hated the classical – to the extent that he pulled down Georgian cottages on his estate to rebuild them in 'Tudor' style. In this he was typical of his generation; for during the second half of the nineteenth century, thanks to the Victorian obsession with the Middle Ages and the influence of Ruskin and Morris, classical domestic architecture was generally derided as cold, monotonous, pompous and foreign. During the 1920s, however,

---

* Jim's taste in literature – as in painting, architecture and music – was highly traditional, and he was bewildered by the avant-garde. At Oxford, his favourite contemporary poets were the 'Georgians' and Vita Sackville-West – though he tried his best with T. S. Eliot, and admired Proust.

Georgian houses (in so far as they had not been spoiled by Victorian 'improvements') were returning to fashion, a trend both illustrated and encouraged by Christopher Hussey's profiles of country seats in *Country Life*. Jim may well have read these; at all events, by the time he left Eton, no doubt partly in reaction against the preferences of his resented parent, he had acquired a taste for the Georgian and learnt to despise houses such as Little Moreton Hall in Cheshire, a picturesque half-timbered manor which the family always stopped to admire on the way to Scotland and which George Lees-Milne regarded as 'the most beautiful house in the British Isles' (and which, paradoxically, Jim would be instrumental in 'saving for the nation' during the late 1930s).

However, it was only when he went up to Oxford that this casual interest in architecture, taken almost for granted, developed into something of an obsession. 'I do not suppose any adolescent susceptible to man-made beauty can spend a large part of three years at Oxford without being profoundly moved by those grey stones,' he writes in *Another Self*. '[T]he university city is unsurpassed in the variety of distinguished buildings. I learnt at Oxford how of all the arts architecture is the only one which cannot be ignored by the philistine or the indifferent . . . I also realised the terrible fragility of architecture. It is vulnerable to every insult, whether from mutilation or indirect neglect, ignorant improvement, or environmental change.' Jim was also impressed by the splendours of Rome which he observed with Johnnie Churchill in 1930, and by a number of interesting houses near Oxford which he visited as an undergraduate – such as Sezincote, a Regency fantasia in the Cotswolds (beloved of John Betjeman, who later immortalised it in verse). He was also moved by a book published the year he arrived at Oxford, *England and the Octopus* by the Welsh architect Clough Williams-Ellis, which warned that the insidious expansion of suburbia threatened to destroy the countryside and its architectural heritage.

In *Another Self*, Jim describes one particularly traumatic experience which 'brought home' to him how 'passionately' he 'cared for architecture', and filled him with a desire to devote himself to preserving it. The scene was a dinner party at Rousham, a romantic house near Oxford on the river Cherwell, built in Jacobean times but redecorated around 1740 by William Kent who also redesigned the surrounding landscape. It was owned (as it still is today) by the Cottrell-Dormer family which had originally built it, but had been let to 'a capricious alcoholic . . . rich, clever and slightly mad'. This tenant (unnamed by Jim) was Maurice Hastings, who did in fact have some feeling for architecture: his family owned *The Architectural Review*, on the staff of which he found a job around this time for his friend John Betjeman. On this occasion, however, after a good dinner enjoyed by all, he

> became noisy and rowdy. On leaving the dining room he got hold of a riding crop, and cracked it against the portraits. With the thong he flaked off chunks of paint. When satisfied with working off some effects of his brandy on the Knellers and Reynoldses, he fetched a rifle from the gun-room. He went to the terrace and proceeded to fire at the private parts of the statues . . .
>
> The other guests were vastly entertained. They cheered and egged on our beastly host . . . At least I can truthfully say I did not cheer, but . . . felt numb with dismay and misery. I felt sick as many people would feel sick if they watched from a train window an adult torturing a child . . . Those Rococo rooms at Rousham, with their delicate furniture and por-traits of bewigged and beribboned ancestors, were living children to me. They and the man-fashioned landscape outside were the England that mattered. I suddenly saw them as infinitely fragile and precious. They meant to me . . . far more than human lives . . .

Jim writes in *Another Self* that 'the experience was a turning point in my life', and that it caused him to make a vow 'that I would devote my energies and abilities, such as they were, to preserving the country houses of England'. In his later book of memoirs *People & Places* he repeats the story, explaining that he 'never got over this flagrant exhibition of iconoclasm' which 'aroused in me some deep atavistic compassion for ancient architecture so vulnerable and transient, and some paternal instinct to protect and safeguard all tangible works of art'.

There is, however, some doubt as to whether Jim was there at all. The episode became fairly notorious at Oxford at the time, and one man who was unquestionably present – the young Christ Church economics don Roy Harrod – was fairly sure, when he read *Another Self* forty years later, that Jim had not been a member of the party. Credence is given to this possibility by the two descriptions of visits to Rousham in Jim's diaries – on 14 May 1948, and (on his last birthday a few months before his death) on 6 August 1997. One might have expected him to make some allusion to the fact that the life-altering event had taken place there; but on neither occasion does he make any mention of it. Moreover, he writes of his 1948 visit as though it were the first time he had set eyes on the place; and his description of it is not flattering. The house he finds 'dis-appointing, for it was added to and spoiled in the last century'; the quality of the furniture so lyrically described in *Another Self* is 'not outstanding'.

If Jim was not present at the egregious dinner party, he would almost certainly have heard about it; and having heard about it, it is likely, given his propensities, that he would have relived the experience, imagining how he would have reacted had he been there. Should this have been the case, there is no reason why the experience should not have been a turning point in his life, as he says – though, as with so much else in his life and recollections, it would have been a fantasy experience rather than one he had actually lived through in the physical world.

3

Patrons and Patronesses
1931–5

TOWARDS THE END of his time at Oxford, Jim was affected by a series of family developments. The world economic recession resulting from the Wall Street Crash led to a severe downturn in the cotton trade, and his parents, who had already been living beyond their means for some years, suddenly felt much poorer – to the extent that during the 1930s they let Wickhamford Manor most summers and moved to Hody's Place, a large estate cottage built by George Lees-Milne in 'ye olde' style. Hitherto, George had refused to give Jim much financial assistance on the grounds that he needed to be taught self-reliance; now, he could plead hard times. Meanwhile George's brother, Jim's Uncle Alec, died of cancer in February 1931, aged fifty-two. He had made Jim his heir; but he too had been affected by the crash, and had had to sell the great Knock estate on Mull during the last months of his life and move with Aunt Dorothy to a more modest property in Argyll. Jim inherited some shares in the family business; but as they rarely paid a dividend during the 1930s, this was of little immediate help to him. He was in line to come in to the remainder of his uncle's fortune on the death of Aunt Dorothy (of whom he was very fond) – though she lived on in rude health until 1965, sustained by the companionship of a young Scotswoman.

In April 1931, at Wickhamford, Jim's sister Audrey married Matthew Arthur, the family connection (whose great-aunt had married Jim's great-uncle) who had been Jim's contemporary at Lockers Park and Magdalen. It was in the nature of an arranged marriage, promoted by Audrey's mother Helen and Matthew's father Cecil, who had themselves been in love thirty years earlier. It seemed an excellent match for Audrey, for Matthew was the heir to a peerage and the Arthurs were thought to be one of the richest families in Scotland. But a shock was in store. After the announcement of the engagement it transpired that Matthew's grandfather, the first Lord Glenarthur, who had died in 1928, had used the funds of the public company of which he had been chairman to finance his lavish way of life and the political donations required to secure his peerage. As a result, just before Audrey's wedding her father-in-law Cecil Glenarthur was declared bankrupt. It was an inauspicious start to a marriage which proved far from happy, for the brisk Matthew and the vague Audrey proved to be unsuited to each other, and separated after a few years (having had a daughter, Prudence, whose three sons, the Robinson brothers, were to be the solace of Jim's later years).

There were also changes in the private lives of George and Helen. Since 1918 their marriage had been under strain owing to the distraction of outside love affairs. In particular, Helen remained close to Jock Campbell, whom she visited annually in Newfoundland, while George had a long-standing relationship with another Helen – Helen Rodocanachi, the beautiful offspring (born 1898) of an Anglo-Greek shipping dynasty who lived with her sister at a house a few miles from Wickhamford where George also kept his horses. However, just after Jim had returned home for the summer vacation of 1930 there arrived almost simultaneously a telegram from Jock to Helen Lees-Milne in which he threatened to shoot himself if she did not leave her husband and cross the Atlantic to live with him, and a letter from Miss Rodocanachi to George announcing her engagement to a Mr Pilkington. Jim later recalled that 'they both took to their beds in floods of tears and I had to ferry between them with messages, the most ghastly holiday I've ever had'. Shared adversity, however, had the effect of bringing them closer together, and their marriage, despite mounting financial difficulties, was happier during the 1930s than during the 1920s – though Helen remained flirtatious until the end of her life, and never lacked admirers.

When Jim came down from Oxford with his third-class degree in the summer of 1931, shortly before his twenty-third birthday, he was in much the same position as when he had left Eton five years earlier – with few prospects and little idea of what to do. If anything, his situation was rather worse, as he seems to have made few useful contacts at Oxford, while during his time there the economic climate had dramatically deteriorated. There was no longer talk, as there had been in 1927, of his pursuing a business career (little though this had appealed to him). In September he sat and failed entrance examinations for both the diplomatic service and the home civil service. Hoping to follow in the footsteps of his revered Uncle Robert, he also applied for a clerkship in the House of Commons, only to be told there were no vacancies. In the depths of the recession, jobs of any description were hard to come by, and Jim began to despair of ever getting one.

At this juncture a welcome distraction presented itself. Jim's recently widowed Aunt Dorothy's sister Maud was the adoring mother of Sir Oswald Mosley, a charismatic politician in his thirties who had resigned from the Labour Government in 1930 in impatience at its handling of the economic crisis, and tried to 'break the mould' of British politics by founding the so-called New Party. To start with this was a respectable grouping, which attracted some talent: its misfortune was that it advocated Keynesian solutions, and the National Government, the coalition established under Ramsay MacDonald (with encouragement from King George V) in August 1931 to deal with the crisis, put forward a similar economic programme. The new government called a general election for 27 October: six months earlier the New Party had had hopes of sweeping to power; now it faced a struggle to hang on to its few seats (all belonging to former Labour MPs). Jim was invited by 'Aunt Maud' to help with her son's campaign in Stoke-on-Trent, and eagerly accepted. His job involved 'going from house to house in the back streets . . . begging for votes from impoverished and bemused citizens, usually wives in soap suds up to their elbows with babies clutching their pitiable skirts'. Mosley had not yet embraced fascism at this time; nor had he yet met his future wife, Jim's former heart-throb Diana Mitford. (Mosley was then married to Cynthia Curzon and Diana to Bryan Guinness, though both marriages were under strain.) Nevertheless, observing Mosley both in public and in private, Jim felt uneasy. As he wrote in *Another Self*:

> It became clear that he was a man of overweening egotism . . . He brooked no argument, would accept no advice. He was overbearing and over-confident . . . His eyes flashed fire, dilated and contracted like a mesmerist's. His voice rose and fell in hypnotic cadences. He was madly in love with his own words. It could be a terrible day, I fancied, when they ran away with him and took the wrong turning. The posturing, the grimacing, the switching on and off of those gleaming teeth, and the overall swash-buckling so purposeful and calculated, were more likely to appeal to Mayfair flappers than to sway indigent workers in the Potteries.

Sure enough, Mosley failed to win his seat, as did all the party's other candidates; and within a year, consumed with impatience and ambition, he had dissolved the New Party in order to found the British Union of Fascists. The main significance of Jim's brief foray into the world of electioneering is that he encountered two other New Party candidates who came to support Mosley at Stoke. One, Christopher ('Kit') Hobhouse, was a handsome, brilliant, ambitious and sexually ambiguous youth of just twenty-one whom Jim had already met at Oxford and would soon come to know better. The other was the ex-diplomatist and man of letters Harold Nicolson, then forty-five, who edited the party's newspaper: Nicolson was to become one of the great figures in Jim's life, though they were not to see much more of each other for another two years.

To reflect on his future, Jim spent the last weeks of 1931 at Haselbech Hall, Northamptonshire as the guest of Constance Ismay, the rich and sentimental American widow of a director of the White Star shipping line, whose daughter Del had been a fellow student of Jim's in Grenoble. 'Aunt Con' was one of several older women who, during the 1930s, took a fancy to this romantic, vulnerable and boyishly handsome youth and sought to help him. (A series of photographs taken at Haselbech – among the few known to have survived from this period – show Jim with matinée-idol looks, abundant wavy hair and a fine figure.) However, Jim could not accept her hospitality indefinitely, and in January 1932 he resolved to find a job, however humble. Reckoning that his undistinguished Oxford degree would be a less useful qualification than his diploma from the typing school, he entered his name on the books of a London secretarial agency.

The first potential employer to whom he was directed was George, 1st Baron Lloyd, a distinguished orientalist, statesman and proconsul, then fifty-two, who had served during the 1920s as Governor of Bombay and High Commissioner in Egypt: since being sacked from the latter post by the Labour Government in 1929, he had been active in business and Conservative politics (though he was opposed to the party leader Baldwin who had recently returned to office in the National Government). In *Another Self*, Jim recalled his first encounter with this formidable figure.

> On my arrival at the large Georgian house in Portman Square . . . a footman in a striped waistcoat and with a disdainful nose signalled me into the one empty chair out of six, telling me to wait my turn. On the five other chairs were perched in a row against the wall five strikingly plain and pinched ladies, who were also applicants (I afterwards learned that the agency had expressly selected them for their looks owing to Lord Lloyd's terror of being vamped) . . . At last the footman returned and ushered us one by one into his lordship's library.
>
> I was the last to be interviewed. As the footman closed the door softly behind me I saw a dapper figure with his back bent over a large writing-table by the window, fumbling through papers. I waited respectfully at a distance, examining the dark, immaculately groomed hair which was thinning. Without turning round the figure growled: 'Well now, Miss – er, I'm afraid I'm already satisfied.' There was a pause. Was I meant to withdraw? Instead I said sadly, 'What a pity, sir.' The figure swivelled round rapidly in its chair, and barked: 'Who on earth are you? What are

you doing here?' I apologised for my presence, and my sex. I then
explained that I too was an applicant. Lord Lloyd's demeanour changed
instantly from the proconsular to the natural. He smiled very engagingly
and became almost boyish. He fired off a hundred direct questions
without waiting for an answer to any of them . . .

The upshot of the interview was that he engaged me, not I fancy without some misgiving, and almost as a joke . . . There was an embarrassing
encounter in the hall with the lady typist whom Lord Lloyd had engaged
before he saw me. She, poor thing, was indignant to be told by the snooty
footman that she was not wanted after all. I have been haunted ever since
by her hurt expression.

At first sight, Jim's new employer had much in common with the other
mustachioed politician he had recently served, Sir Oswald Mosley. Both
came from backgrounds which were rich and aristocratic; both were
handsome narcissists, with a passion for keeping fit; both tried to get their
way through a mixture of charm and bullying; both were visionary
personalities who aspired to become Britain's dictator. Both believed in
the superiority of the British race and the destiny of the British Empire.
Both were anti-Semites (Lloyd perhaps more so than Mosley, whose New
Party had been backed by Jewish business but who later used the Jews as
a scapegoat). But there the resemblance ended. Whereas Mosley was a
populist whose belief in 'the common man' led him to embrace first
socialism and then fascism, Lloyd was an élitist who believed in the
unique fitness of Britain's traditional governing class to rule. Whereas
Mosley was a man of action who made stirring speeches and was
impatient with paperwork, Lloyd, who did not enjoy speaking in public,
was a born administrator who spent most of his life at his desk. Whereas
Mosley admired the Nazis, Lloyd, like his friend Winston Churchill,
perceived them as a sinister movement which represented a mortal threat
to Britain and her interests. Whereas Mosley was a self-worshipping
atheist, Lloyd was a devout Anglo-Catholic, troubled by religious doubt.
And whereas Mosley was a compulsively seducing heterosexual,
Lloyd – though married to a devoted wife, with a son they both adored –
was a repressed homosexual: as a proconsul in Bombay and Cairo he had
surrounded himself with handsome secretaries and equerries, who
sometimes had to be sent away when he was unable to master his feelings
for them. It is not difficult to read between the lines of Jim's account of
how he got the job, and deduce that it owed something to romantic
interest. (It goes without saying that Lloyd's relationships with young
men were entirely platonic, all physical desire being sublimated: after his

death, his First World War associate Compton Mackenzie wrote a novel, *Thin Ice*, speculating on what might have happened if a man like Lloyd had let himself go.)

From the first, Lloyd treated Jim as a protégé rather than an employee: he recognised that his new secretary, while possessing various attractions and potentialities, was immature and untrained in many respects, and he sought to further his education and make something of him. Jim had cause to be grateful to Lloyd: when he entered his service in January 1932, he still had the outlook as well as the appearance of a schoolboy; he gained much in wisdom and experience during three years in the job. Above all, Lloyd taught Jim, who had hitherto been one of nature's idlers, to work hard. He recognised that Jim, like himself, was a rather melancholic character, and that it is dangerous for such people to have time on their hands. There was certainly much to be done, for Lloyd, though deprived of public office, was a busy man at the time: he was leading the opposition to the Government's plans to grant provincial self-government to India (culminating in the Government of India Act of 1935); he was writing a two-volume work on modern Egypt (published as *Egypt since Cromer* in 1933); and he sat on the boards of several important firms. Jim had to keep Lloyd's diary, take from dictation his enormous daily correspondence, type up the drafts of his numerous speeches and newspaper articles, act as his amanuensis in the writing of his book, and see to it that everything was meticulously filed and indexed (for Lloyd had a fetish for archives). Even when business or politics took Lloyd away for long periods, he ensured that Jim was kept busy in his absence, dealing with his correspondence, sending him press summaries, compiling card-indexes. (In December 1932, Jim even refused an invitation from his beloved Desmond Parsons to spend Christmas at Birr Castle, his family seat in Ireland, explaining that, although Lord Lloyd was away in South Africa, 'cables constantly come through necessitating immediate action'.)

Though such unaccustomed industry must at first have been rather a shock for Jim, he nevertheless strained every fibre to please his master: he held him in awe and admiration, and was determined to hang on to his job. To start with, he was no more than an ordinary secretary, 'private' matters being dealt with by Colin Forbes Adam, a man of independent means who had been Lloyd's private secretary in Bombay and had married his wife's cousin; but he soon won Lloyd's confidence and established himself as a trusted aide. Indeed, before long Lloyd was treating him almost as one of his family, sending him entertaining letters about his travels, and paying for him to have an annual summer holiday on his own before joining himself and Lady Lloyd at a rented villa on the Mediterranean. (Thus in the summer of 1932 Jim visited Portugal; in 1933 he went to Majorca before joining the Lloyds at Spezia; in 1934 he toured Corsica before joining the Lloyds at Lerici.) It is not uncommon for those who are favoured by their boss to arouse resentment in the boss's family; and it is a measure of Jim's success that he was also liked by Lloyd's wife Blanche and son David. David, four years younger than Jim and a Cambridge undergraduate, was a handsome only child who was spoiled by his parents and in consequence became somewhat wild; Jim later recalled that he was 'in perpetual trouble for small peccadilloes' and would 'come into my room at Portman Square and sit on my writing table, begging me to get him out of some scrape, such as having driven his father's car into a ditch when he should have been attending a lecture'.

Indeed, there may have been moments when Jim wished Lloyd were a little less fond of him; for after a gruelling day's work at Portman Square he would sometimes be asked to spend the evening with his employer – evenings which consisted of Jim listening while Lloyd talked for hours on end. ('So precious and confidential were the talks I had with him far into the night that I cannot trust myself to refer to them here,' Jim writes in *Another Self*.) Clearly, this nervous, overworked man craved the proximity and admiration of a personable and sympathetic youth; and for three years, Jim willingly fulfilled the role. The letter Jim received when he left Lloyd's service in 1935 suggests their relations were closer than are usual between a statesman and his secretary. 'You have been very good to me these last 3 years: very patient & forbearing with all my tiresome ways . . . I think you know how much I value both your cooperation and companionship. I feel terribly bereft without you . . . Please don't forget me quite & come & see us just whenever you can, the more often the better. Bless you.'

Many men look back on their youth and recognise that some mentor – such as a parent or other relation, a schoomaster or don – played a crucial role in their early development. So far as one can judge, no such inspirational figure had existed in Jim's life up to the time he left Oxford (though he believed that his Uncle Robert would have fulfilled the role had he lived). George Lloyd seems to have been the first man of an older generation to take an intense, affectionate interest in him, who both accepted him for what he was and tried to change him for the better. However, it was not long before another such mentor came along, in the form of Harold Nicolson, whom Jim had first met at Stoke in October

1931. Nicolson was a hereditary diplomat who would probably have reached the heights of his profession had he not resigned from it in 1929 at the age of forty-three. He took this decision for a variety of reasons: as a political liberal, he did not entirely share the Foreign Office view of British power; he wished to devote his energies to literature, having already had some success as a writer of elegant biographies; and he wished to see more of his wife, Vita Sackville-West, herself a distinguished writer and poet, who refused to accompany him to foreign posts. As all the world now knows (but was then known only to their intimates), their marriage was unusual in that, while devoted to each other, they were both basically homosexual, and they allowed each other complete freedom to pursue their respective sexual interests (though they rarely discussed their affairs). In 1930 they had gone to live at Sissinghurst Castle in Kent, where they worked to restore the ancient buildings and create a paradisal garden. Henceforth they led a semi-detached existence: they spent weekends together at Sissinghurst, often with their two teenage sons, while during the week they lived apart, she at Sissinghurst and he in London, where they wrote their respective works and engaged in their respective love affairs. These affairs were somewhat different in character in that Vita, a romantic by nature, was generally in love with one woman at a time, whereas Harold, who took a pragmatic view of sex, was generally interested, at any given moment, in a variety of young male partners. During the early 1930s Harold, after parting ways with Mosley over fascism, was engaged in writing a trilogy of semi-autobiographical works dealing with diplomatic events he had witnessed,[*] while also making a reputation as a journalist and broadcaster.

At Oxford Jim had become an admirer of Vita's poetry; and he was therefore fascinated to meet Harold at Stoke, if rather shy of doing so – over dinner at the Midland Hotel he was tongue-tied, while the dashing Hobhouse, the main focus of Harold's attention, sparkled with brilliant conversation. And it was through 'Kit', with whom Harold fell in love and Jim became friendly,[†] that they next met: one weekend in August 1932, when Hobhouse was staying with Jim and two other friends at a country inn in Kent, he took them over to Sissinghurst to meet the

---

[*] A life of his father Lord Carnock (head of the Foreign Office, 1910–16), an account of the Paris Peace Conference of 1919, and a study of the foreign secretaryship of Lord Curzon (1919–24).

[†] During the 1970s Jim told his friend Billa Harrod, whose son had married Hobhouse's daughter, that he couldn't remember whether he had been to bed with Hobhouse or not.

Nicolsons and see the garden. A year after that, Jim enjoyed his first *tête-à-tête* with Harold, who wrote to him in August 1933 asking him to dine at the Café Royal. This letter, the first of many from Harold which Jim kept (the replies do not survive), begins 'Dear Lees-Milne'; the next one, inviting him to dine at the Travellers Club together with Hobhouse, begins 'Dear Jim'. During the autumn a certain intimacy developed; for in December 1933 Harold wrote to him: 'God! How I wished you could have come to Paris with me! I had not dared to suggest it – and yet it would have been amusing for you to be there – amusing for me, that is.' A few weeks later Harold had his wish, Jim accompanying him to Paris in February 1934. 'He was a superlative guide,' Jim later recalled nostalgically. 'The night of our arrival we dined at La Perouse and went the rounds of Montmartre and Montparnasse.' The next day they visited Versailles, where Harold showed Jim the *Galérie des Glaces* where he had witnessed the signing of the Treaty in 1919; later they called on James Joyce, a thrill for Jim who longed to meet famous writers. To Vita, Harold wrote disingenuously:

> I found that Jim Lees-Milne was going over to Paris on the Friday, so I decided to go with him, as it was more or less on my way . . .* Jim is such a charming person. He has a passion for poetry and knows masses about it. I like my friends to be well-read and well-bred. Jim is such an aristocrat in mind and culture. You would like him enormously.

To Jim, he wrote thanking him

> for having been so charming to me. I do appreciate it deeply, Jim. I like people, such as Virginia and you, who make life seem fuller. I really do detest unhappy people who make life seem emptier. Bless you, dear Jim.

'Virginia' was Virginia Woolf, the great love of Vita's life. It seems fairly clear that Harold enjoyed carnal relations with Jim during their Paris weekend. Jim was then twenty-five, Harold forty-seven. Harold had developed a code for writing intimate letters which sought to reveal much to those he was addressing while giving away little to any stranger who might happen to read them. His next letter to Jim contains a passage which seems designed to help Jim overcome any regrets he may have had about what had occurred between them:

---

* Harold was going out to join Vita, then staying at Portofino in Italy with Harold's sister with whom she was having an affair. It is clear from Harold's letters to Jim that the former had invited the latter to Paris and paid all the trip's expenses: his implication to Vita that Jim was going there anyway may have been a protective measure in case the letter fell into the wrong hands.

It is possible to be affectionate and tender and decent – and to extract something more than pleasure (to my mind a veritable increase of higher experience) from contacts which would by most people be regarded as grossly material. I do think that promiscuity, brutality or undiluted lechery have a bad effect upon the mind and character, but I also believe that wise concubinage has a good effect. Or in other words, I find the most facile excuses for my peculiar temptations, and leap upon the highest of moral horses the moment I am faced with temptations by which I am not myself seduced. But at least I refuse to regard as evil experiences which I am perfectly convinced have done me moral good.

In 1976 Harold's son Nigel, inviting Jim to write his father's biography, asked if they had had an affair. Jim carefully replied: 'Yes, but he did not fall in love with me for longer than three months.' This was a disingenuous reply, for two reasons. First, although Harold may only have been infatuated with Jim for a few months of 1933–4, he retained great affection for him thereafter, remaining a 'guide, philosopher and friend' to him for the next thirty years. And their sexual association also continued far beyond those initial months, possibly even up to Jim's marriage in 1951. Jim in effect joined a coterie of bright young literary men (several of whom he already knew, such as Kit Hobhouse, Robert Byron and Alan Pryce-Jones) who revelled in Harold's company and hospitality and looked to him as a father-figure, an intellectual guru, a protector who might use his influence and connections on their behalf, and (to a limited extent, for Harold was never rich) a source of material support. In return, Harold (who in the words of his grandson Adam Nicolson had 'an almost unassuageable appetite for clever and beautiful young men') looked to his protégés to 'oblige' him in his rather perfunctory sexual desires, which most of them (including Jim) were quite happy to do in view of the many delights and advantages they derived from his mentorship.

Jim also saw much of two friends of Harold who, though some years older than himself, were to play a significant role in his life. Raymond Mortimer, a brilliant and much-feared literary critic, had been Harold's great love in the 1920s and remained his great confidant. While finding him somewhat intimidating (for he was as dismissive of Jim's literary ambitions as he was later to be of his published works), Jim admired him for his cleverness. Eddy Sackville-West was Vita's first cousin, Eddy's father having succeeded Vita's in 1928 as Lord Sackville and life tenant of the Knole estate. Vita and Harold regarded him with an affection which was qualified, in Vita's case by resentment that Eddy and not she was due to inherit Knole, in Harold's by embarrassment that Eddy was an obvious, 'mincing' homosexual. A gifted dilettante in the fields of both music and letters, Eddy (who suffered from haemophilia) was both a martyr to ill-health and a self-obsessed neurotic. Jim's friendship with him antedated that with Harold, for in 1932 he accepted the first of many invitations to spend the weekend with Eddy in his private apartments at Knole. Eddy was given to crushes on handsome men, and it seems likely that he was infatuated with Jim for a time. He was a most difficult friend, and the fact that he and Jim were generally on amicable terms for the rest of Eddy's life suggests that they had a true fondness for one another. (A few years later, their friendship would play a key role in Jim's efforts to secure Knole for the National Trust.)

Towards the end of 1934 Jim, who had previously lived in a succession of Mayfair 'bedsits', became Harold's lodger in his first-floor flat at 4, King's Bench Walk. (He later described himself as a 'paying guest', but it is likely that the payment took a non-pecuniary form.) These were barristers' residential chambers of the Inner Temple, registered in the name of Harold's eldest brother Freddy, Lord Carnock, a member of the Bar who no longer practised. It was a wonderful place to live, in a fine 1670s terrace set in beautiful walled precincts on the western edge of the City, bustling by day, silent by night. The set consisted of an oak-panelled sitting room which Harold used as his study, two bedrooms, and a small kitchen and bathroom: Jim occupied the second bedroom on the understanding that he would sleep elsewhere in the event of it being required by Vita on her rare visits to London; he also had the run of the sitting room during Harold's frequent absences, and shared the services of Harold's manservant. (The previous lodger had been 'Kit' Hobhouse, then a practising barrister at the Temple, who continued to visit almost daily: there was now a note of rivalry in his relations with Jim as they competed for Harold's affections.) As well as giving him regular access to Harold's companionship and advice, Jim's residence at 'KBW' had another result. For Harold kept a fascinating (if discreet) diary, full of subtlety, humour and sharp observation. 'I remember him typing his diary at the end of the day, and early in the mornings,' Jim wrote in his own diary in 1971, soon after Harold's had been published and acclaimed. 'He . . . never wavered, never hesitated, and went straight through like cutting butter.' Though Jim was not to begin a regular journal of his own for another seven years, it was undoubtedly Harold's example which inspired him to think of expressing himself in this form.

In their different ways, George Lloyd and Harold Nicolson both influenced Jim's outlook on life. To what extent did they also influence his political and social views? They knew each other quite well, being united by their common interest in oriental civilisations and their common friendship with Alan ('Tommy') Lascelles, a courtier (and another married homosexual) who had been at Balliol with Harold and who was Blanche Lloyd's brother. Their politics were however quite different: Lloyd led the right wing of the Conservative Party in the House of Lords and was a fierce opponent of the National Government, whereas Nicolson was one of nature's liberals, elected MP for West Leicester in November 1935 as a candidate of the small National Labour Party, the party of the National Government's founder, Ramsay MacDonald.* Jim's diaries show him to have been thoroughly reactionary in some respects, surprisingly egalitarian in others, and this may be partly due to the competing influence of his two mentors. Certainly his ardent anti-Communism owed something to the fact that Lloyd was well informed about the horrors of Stalin's Russia. One thing neither mentor succeeded in instilling in him was a respect for politicians: it appalled him that two such civilised and essentially honourable men should lend their names to so many causes in which they did not really believe. Socially, both Lloyd and Nicolson, notwithstanding the political liberalism of the latter, looked down on 'the lower orders' and disliked Jews, and seem to have influenced Jim in these directions. Certainly Jim's affected disdain for 'the masses' was well-established by 1933, when he wrote to Desmond Parsons:

> Today I understand there is to be a hostile demonstration at Marble Arch of the semi-starved. I shall appreciate watching mounted police charge with flourishing batons a ragged crowd and trampling underfoot screaming women & children, while I from a safe & comfortable distance on my Park Lane balcony gloat over the carnage.

And his letters sometimes contain anti-Semitic remarks which sound rather shocking today (though they would have been considered fairly unremarkable at the time):

> Paul [Hyslop, the architect boyfriend of Raymond Mortimer] and I went to a Russian film, which I could hardly sit through it was so boring. Everyone else said it was the funniest that had appeared since the war . . . Either my sense of humour is quite distorted or I am prejudiced against a cinema full of Socialist Jews praising Stalin and the OGPU to the skies.

---

*Harold owed his nomination to pure nepotism: the chairman of the party (of which Harold had scarcely heard before being invited to represent it) was Vita's cousin, Earl de la Warr.

They make me so angry that I become more Lord Lloydish than you
would give me credit for. After the cinema we stood about being trampled
on by enormous plethoric Jewesses, pushed hither and thither by young
Fabians and jostled in the ribs by Yiddish noses till I could scream . . .

Jim had a mind of his own, however; for the greatest step he took in
the realm of personal ideology during the 1930s owed nothing to either
Lloyd or Nicolson. On 26 March 1934, at Westminster Cathedral, he was
received by Father Paul Napier-Hemy into the Roman Catholic Church.
His baptismal certificate (for converts are required to be baptised as
Catholics, renouncing any previous baptism) records two surprising facts.
The names he chose for himself were James Mary Francis: although it is
fairly common on the Continent for male Catholics to be given names
which include that of the Virgin, it is unusual in England. And the
ceremony was officially witnessed by George Cattaui, scion of a well-
known Cairo Jewish dynasty which advised the Egyptian monarchy.
Cattaui was then First Secretary at the Egyptian Legation in London, a
post from which he would depart later that year following a (presumably
homosexual) scandal.* He later wrote rather precious works on contemporary English and French literature, and became a Catholic priest in
Switzerland. It is not certain how Jim met him: Cattaui would probably
have known both George Lloyd (through his Egyptian background) and
Harold Nicolson (through his literary interests), and counted Alan Pryce-
Jones and Christopher Hobhouse among his friends.

Jim had been contemplating his conversion for some years. In 1927,
while he was still a teenager, Diana Mitford had written to him:

> Think twice before becoming a Catholic. It is a fatally attractive religion
> in that it appeals to the aesthetic sense. I quite agree that the human soul
> demands a religion, but why not the English Church? You say it is dead-
> alive; but the Anglo-Catholics are a section of it, and are very devout and
> near to God.

She did however admit that

> of all the sects into which the Christian religion is divided the Roman
> Catholic appears to be the only one which offers real relief to a soul in tor-
> ment. Also that on going into its churches one feels very forcibly the presence
> of the Divinity and a sense of rest and an atmosphere of forgiveness.

*Jim's papers contain a mildly compromising love letter from Cattaui in French, written
in 1933 on the Legation stationery, as well as a letter to Jim from the eminent Jesuit
Martin D'Arcy, dated 3 October 1934, regretting that he could not 'intercede' for Cattaui
but hoping he would 'clear his name'.

It is unfortunate that we do not have Jim's letter which inspired this reply, or indeed anything he wrote about his religious beliefs before beginning his diary in 1942. However, in *Another Self* – written in the late 1960s when he was effectively in the process of reverting from Roman Catholicism to Anglicanism – he explains his reasons for having embraced the older faith. These were essentially four – psychological, aesthetic, cultural and political. Psychologically, he 'had need of a discipline from outside, a discipline with which unaided I was incapable of providing myself'. The Roman Church, with its intricate body of rules and beliefs and its insistence on unquestioning obedience, provided that discipline. Aesthetically, he was attracted by the sumptuous rituals of the Church and the antique beauties of its Latin liturgy. 'I loved the Gothic sanctity, the Renaissance paganism, the Baroque opulence of the Catholic ritual and ceremonial. The smell of vellum missals, candle wax, chrism and incense was the breath of life to me.' Culturally, he was fascinated by the 'historical continuity' of the Papacy, its 'unbroken descent from St Peter down to Pius XI', and its associations with classical architecture. And politically, he saw the Church as 'the last and impregnable bulwark against Communism in Western Europe' at a time when Marxism was seducing so many of his contemporaries.

For some years after his conversion, Jim was devout in his practice of his new religion, regularly attending Mass and going to confession. However, various factors cause one to wonder how deep and sincere was his belief. From the first he disliked priests, a species he regarded as 'proprietary, gluttonous, boozy and dirty'. (This may have owed something to the fact that Father Napier-Hemy who 'received' him was the worse for drink during the ceremony.) There appears to have been a snobbish element in his conversion. He was attracted by the fact that, in England, Catholicism had been sustained during the centuries of per-secution by the covert efforts of a few 'old' families. In Ireland, where it was the religion of the masses, it held little appeal for him: 'Irish Catholicism is like a vice, crushing the congregation like nuts.' And when, in the 1960s, the Second Vatican Council put an end to the universal Latin Mass, along with much traditional practice and ceremonial, Jim became disillusioned and rapidly drifted back to the Church of England. Nor did he prove to be one for unquestioning obedience: the papal encyclical *Humanae Vitae* of 1968 was the final straw for him, as he considered it madness to affirm the proscription of birth control at a time of rampant overpopulation. From all this, one may deduce that it was the brilliance of the Church's spectacle and the romance of its associations which drew him, rather than its teachings. As he admitted to his diary, while at prayer he had to concentrate on the beauty of his surroundings rather than the meaning of words in order to believe. 'What I need [to feel religious] is a twilight atmosphere relieved by myriads of twinkling candles from crystal chandeliers, a plethora of gold, jewels, rich raiment, silver vessels, clouds of incense, and the tinkling and tolling of innumerable bells.'

There seem to have been two further motives behind Jim's conversion, not mentioned in *Another Self*. Between the wars, Roman Catholicism exercised a strong influence on the English literary scene, on account of its association with two strains in recent literary history – the aesthetic movement (which reached its apogee in the 1890s but still resonated in the 1930s); and the intellectual reaction to secular materialism, involving such brilliant converts as G. K. Chesterton and Ronald Knox. Jim, with his aesthetic leanings and traditionalist views, was affected by both these strains, and seems to have regarded becoming a Catholic as part of his preparation for a literary career. Several of his literary friends also converted, including Alan Pryce-Jones, Hamish Erskine, Eddy Sackville-West and (from Judaism) George Cattaui. (Interestingly, the English literary converts of this period who were to become most famous, Graham Greene and Evelyn Waugh, Jim could not abide, regarding them in their different ways as odious drunks with offensive views.) It is significant that, at the time of his conversion, Jim was attempting to write a study of another convert, the Jesuit poet Gerard Manley Hopkins (1844–89).* He was given access to papers by Hopkins' great-nephew, and discussed his religious views with the eminent Jesuits Martin D'Arcy and Cyril Martindale. By 1935 he had produced a manuscript – but he did not think it much good; those to whom he showed it seem to have agreed with him; and no trace of this work, apparently his first attempt to write prose for publication, has survived. (Cattaui published a work on Hopkins in 1947 – though whether Jim inspired Cattaui's interest in Hopkins, or vice versa, is not known.)

The other motive (as Jim later confessed) was a desire to shock his father, with whom his relations continued to be strained. Although George Lees-Milne remained uninterested in religion, and no longer even bothered with regular Sunday attendance at Wickhamford church,

*Hopkins' work was unknown to the public until 1918, when a selection was published by his friend Robert Bridges, then Poet Laureate (and great-uncle of J.L.-M's future wife Alvilde Bridges).

he was indeed scandalised at what he called Jim's 'apostasy', which he equated with treason against the Crown. He told his wife that in future they must expect Jim to sit down whenever the National Anthem was played, and put his hat on. For almost a year, Jim was unwelcome at Wickhamford. Instead he went to stay with a piously Catholic, American-born widow living nearby, 'Mamie' de Navarro of Court Farm, Broadway, who had been a famous actress (Mary Anderson) in her youth and had until recently entertained such figures as Elgar and Barrie. Jim was grateful for her hospitality and moral support, while aware that she was somewhat fanatical in her religious beliefs and that 'one misplaced word . . . would have broken the sweet spell and brought instant exclusion'. His mother went over to see him at Court Farm, while his father (as Jim had intended) regarded it as adding insult to injury that he should infest the locality as the guest of a Papist household.

Mamie was just one of several Catholic matrons who took Jim under their maternal wing: others included Mrs Astley Cooper, an eccentric millionairess who was a patroness of artists, writers and musicians both in London and at Hambleton Hall, Rutland; Lady Constance Milnes-Gaskell, a lady-in-waiting to Queen Mary and a friend of the Lloyds; the novelist Marie Belloc Lowndes, sister of the great Catholic writer Hilaire Belloc; and Mary Herbert, the formidable châtelaine of Pixton Park, Somerset (and cousin of Desmond Parsons' stepfather, Viscount de Vesci). To Jim, Mrs Cooper was 'Aunt Eva' and Lady Constance, 'Aunt Puss'. Just as Lloyd and Nicolson became substitute fathers to him, so he seems to have had a whole string of substitute mothers. Not all of them were Catholics. We have already noted Mrs Ismay, 'Aunt Con', a Protestant widow who offered him a haven whenever he required one at her pile in Northamptonshire. Nor were they all widows. Jean Hamilton was married to the eminent soldier General Sir Ian Hamilton, whose career owed much to her social talents. Both Sir Ian's family and that of Lady Hamilton, the Muirs, were distant family connections of Jim through the Thomsons, and Lady Hamilton's much younger brother Jack Muir and his wife Heather were Jim's parents' best friends. 'Great-Aunt Jean', as Jim called her, who had no children of her own, doted on him and constantly included him in her famous luncheon parties at 1, Hyde Park Gardens, Bayswater, a household which was a charming survival of the Edwardian age and which Jim came almost to regard as his family home in London.

One remarkable older woman who took a fancy to Jim had a relationship with him which bordered on the erotic. This was Kathleen Kennet, a feisty female and talented sculptor who had married first Captain Robert Scott, who perished in the Antarctic in 1912, then Sir Edward Hilton Young, a one-armed war hero who served as Minister of Health in the National Government, becoming Lord Kennet. Kathleen's quirk was a penchant for gay men; the loves of her life included Charles Shannon (who lived with his fellow artist Charles Ricketts in a famous Edwardian relationship) and Lawrence of Arabia. During the 1930s, her husband preoccupied by politics, Kathleen took up with a series of sexually ambiguous young men; and Jim, whom she met when she executed a bust of Lord Lloyd, was promptly added to her collection. Jim was enchanted by her intelligence, her directness, her zest for life and her disregard for convention: she was a woman with whom one could discuss virtually anything. (He was however made uneasy by her almost incestuous adulation of her son Peter Scott.) Kathleen regularly asked Jim to dance with her at the Savoy, and twice during the 1930s invited him on skating holidays to Villars, Switzerland: she seems to have derived a *frisson* from clinging to the body of a personable youth as they glided together on the dance floor or the ice.

Jim continued to see much of friends of his own age. He kept up with old pals from school and university: from Eton, Alan Pryce-Jones, Hamish Erskine and Tom Mitford (the last having returned from Austria to read for the English Bar); from Oxford, Johnnie Churchill, Osbert Lancaster and Harry d'Avigdor-Goldsmid. He also got to know a set of formidably talented men of a slightly earlier Oxford generation – the aesthetes Harold Acton and Brian Howard; the journalist Patrick Balfour (later 3rd Baron Kinross); the poet John Betjeman, then working as a journalist; the film producer John Sutro; and three writers who had already established reputations – the travel-writer and Byzantinist Robert Byron, the critic and essayist Cyril Connolly, and the literary historian Peter Quennell. Jim had probably met them all at Oxford, which they often revisited to see friends and mentors such as Bowra. There were other connections: Acton had been an older boy at McNeile's; Byron was in love with Jim's old flame Desmond Parsons; Betjeman married (1933) Johnnie Churchill's old flame Penelope Chetwode. Jim was a small star in their firmament; but they all liked him, and he looked up to them (for they all seemed so much more brilliant than himself) with admiration and envy. The principal venue for his meetings with them was the Café Royal in Regent Street, a huge *art déco* restaurant which had been a haunt of writers and artists since the 1890s. As he wrote shortly before his death:

Today a young person of modest means . . . cannot realise what a boon the Café Royal was to the impecunious aspirant to hobnobbery with the literary and artistic élite. There night after night the poor young person, if he had not been invited out to dinner beforehand, might in the upstairs gallery assuage hunger and thirst with a sandwich and a glass of lager in the company of his elders, betters and sometimes worsers. Even if he had previously dined at the rich man's table he might still end the night in the Café Royal . . . [and] wander around until he recognised or was hailed by a friend, at whose elbow might be sitting daedal and fuddled Augustus John, spry and jolly Compton Mackenzie, or tousled, loquacious Jack Squire . . . During these nightly vigils I may have remained inordinately mum, even anonymous, but I watched, listened and observed. The tragedy is that I remember so little.

At least three of these friends of the 'Brideshead' generation – Acton, Balfour and Byron – 'fancied' Jim. Indeed, many of the men with whom he came into contact seem to have found him sexually desirable; and while this period witnessed no serious affairs of the heart that he later cared to recall, there seems to have been much discreet romping, often after heavy drinking. For example, when David 'Boofy' Gore, 8th Earl of Arran, died in 1983, Jim, who had known him at Eton and Oxford, recalled: 'He once made advances to me when I lived in Norfolk Street off Park Lane [1932–4], and we had wined and dined, and jumped into bed. It was not a success, and neither of us referred to the incident again.' (This is of interest as Lord Arran is known to history as the supposedly heterosexual peer who introduced the parliamentary bill which decriminalised homosexuality in 1967.) Given the circles in which Jim moved, and his appealing looks, 'incidents' of this sort, successful or otherwise, must have occurred frequently. Jim sometimes attended 'debs' dances' during 'the Season'; and half a century later he told the author that the young men present, feeling sexually frustrated after dancing with the carefully chaperoned 'debs', and rather drunk, would quite often go home to bed with each other.

Jim's friends at this time also included two exotic young aristocrats with homosexual tastes, both a few years older than himself, Prince George Chavchavadze and Sir Paul Latham. Chavchavadze, son of a Russian dynasty descended from the kings of Georgia which had fled to England after the Revolution, was a concert pianist whose success owed more to panache than technical ability (though his playing 'transported' the susceptible Jim); Latham, like Jim a product of Eton and Magdalen, had been elected Conservative MP for Scarborough in 1931 at the age of twenty-six, in which year he also inherited from his industrialist father a baronetcy, a fortune, and the lavishly restored Herstmonceux Castle, Sussex. Both were favourites of Kathleen Kennet; Latham was also a friend of Eddy Sackville-West, with whom he had been conducting a sado-masochistic affair since the mid 1920s. As they were both extremely handsome, and believed in taking their pleasure where they found it, it is unlikely that Jim's friendship with them was purely platonic. (Both made brilliant marriages during the 1930s – Latham to a daughter of Lord Drogheda, Chavchavadze to the Philadelphia heiress Elizabeth de Breteuil – though in neither case does this seem to have affected their compulsive desire to make love to any desirable young men they could get their hands on.)

The female contemporary to whom Jim felt closest was 'Midi' O'Neill, a friend of Nancy Mitford whom he had met visiting Rome with Johnnie Churchill in January 1930. Midi had the bluest blood – one of her grand-fathers, Lord O'Neill, headed Ireland's most ancient family, while the other was the Marquess of Crewe, elder statesman and friend of King George V. In several respects, however, her background resembled Jim's. Her mother was a vain woman who neglected her children; after her father's death in the First World War, she found herself under the tutelage of an unsympathetic stepfather; only her grandmother loved her. She felt an outsider in the world into which she had been born. She was left to make her own way in life with little money, and worked as a secretary. She and Jim became confidants, pouring out their hearts to each other. A letter she wrote to him in 1932 shows that they considered living together – though Midi asked with cautious perceptiveness: 'Do we only appreciate each other in absence?' It is unlikely that they were ever lovers; rather (being three years his senior) she seems to have played the role of an older sister in his life, full of sensible advice. A letter she wrote to him in February 1933 gives some insight into Jim's social outlook at the time:

> Darling J . . . What you do not say or probably even realise with regard to your going about with people is that (1) you do not suffer fools or bores gladly, (2) though you have the means of a bank clerk you have the mentality of a cultured aristocrat; therefore you would like to go about on your own terms, but cannot afford this, so you are constantly refusing invitations. After years of going about on a pittance I have come to the conclusion that with no money you must go about with those who like you, who may or may not be those that you like. Had I £2,000 a year there are a vast number of people I should hope to see whom I cannot meet now

on my own terms and therefore live without. There are others who are always asking me out and, as I cannot sit alone for ever, I go. Some of these I should not see had I money of my own. You, on the other hand, will not meet people you don't like, or have not much in common with. This is right in principle but abortive in practice. I go so far as to say that had I money and a house of my own I should go out hardly ever . . .

In 1934, seeking security, Midi married a well-born but dull stockbroker, 'Derick' Gascoigne, giving her the 'money and house of her own' which enabled her to see and entertain whom she wished: she continued to see much of Jim, and remained his closest female friend. A year later, however, Jim met another woman, this time three years his junior, who both took over from Midi as his leading *confidante* and provided him with his first serious romantic interest of the decade.

4

Anne

1935–6

———•———

SINCE LEAVING UNIVERSITY, Jim had continued to see much of his soulmate Johnnie Churchill, who now made a precarious living painting murals. Though he had gone bald like his Uncle Winston, he had otherwise changed little since Oxford, being still a high-spirited and romantic adolescent at heart. From 1932 to 1934 he rented a cottage near Marlborough in Wiltshire where Jim often joined him for weekends. It was near to two country houses where they were welcome, Savernake Lodge and Biddesden Manor. Savernake was owned by the parents of Robert Byron, who lived there himself when not on his travels. Biddesden was the home of Bryan and Diana Guinness. The prospect of visiting Biddesden may have been daunting for Jim, who had seen virtually nothing of Diana in the four years since her marriage – though they probably never met there, as around the time Jim started visiting the locality she left her husband and house to live with the new man in her life, Sir Oswald Mosley. Jim did however enjoy seeing Diana's elder sister Pamela, who managed the home farm at Biddesden and lived on the estate: in June 1933 he wrote to Desmond Parsons of a jolly weekend staying with 'Pam' during which they joined Bryan and his house party – consisting of Desmond's brother Michael Rosse and his future wife Anne Armstrong-Jones, the Russian mosaicist Boris Anrep, and 'a dreadful man called Professor Joad' (the popular philosopher) – to ride across the Downs to Savernake to have tea with Robert.

In 1934 Johnnie married Angela Culme-Seymour, with whom he had been romantically involved since the end of his affair with Penelope Chetwode, now married to John Betjeman. Jim always considered Angela to be one of the most beguiling women he had known. As he wrote in *Fourteen Friends*:

> She had camellia-like skin of the softness of satin, and large glowing eyes of a dreamy quality, which smiled even when the lips were solemn. Often the only overt movement of her face came from long bewitching lashes, which, while intoxicating the beholder, gave her an air of complete

73

innocence. Indeed it was difficult to tell how innocent she was or whether, like a small child, she was amoral . . . Commonplace codes of conduct simply did not apply to her . . . She was indifferent to money, luxury, jewellery and the high life . . . She was like a ravishing cat with sheathed claws, a cat which happily settles on whatever cushion presents itself . . .

In March 1935 Angela gave birth to a girl, Cornelia Sarah (known as Sally). The Churchills had recently given up their cottage in Wiltshire and taken another near Oxford, Larkspur Cottage on Cumnor Hill, where Jim stayed with them at Easter 1935 to meet the new baby, whose godfather he had been asked to be. Also staying was Angela's cousin and close friend Lady Anne Gathorne-Hardy, sister of the 4th Earl of Cranbrook. Though not a beauty like Angela, and rather shy, Anne was quite a pretty girl, with an open, eager nature. Although she suffered from the usual lack of education of women of her generation, she had a quick and clever mind, and could be extremely funny. The Gathorne-Hardys − ennobled in the 1870s, after Anne's great-grandfather had served in Disraeli's cabinet − were a rather intellectual and unconventional family with a characteristic rapid, affected speaking style. Anne was the youngest of five children, having four older brothers whom she adored − Jock (the Earl), Eddie, Bob and Anthony. Eddie and Bob were experts in the rare book world, but best known to their contemporaries for their flagrant and rackety homosexuality. (Miles Malpractice, the outrageous 'queer' in Evelyn Waugh's *Vile Bodies*, is mostly based on Eddie.) The other two brothers (according to the son of one of them, the writer Jonathan Gathorne-Hardy) were not entirely heterosexual either. Their father had died soon after Anne was born, and Anne lived with her mother, the Dowager Countess, at Snape Priory near Aldeburgh in Suffolk, a rambling Victorian house not far from Jock's estate at Glemham. Though herself the daughter of an earl, Dorothy Cranbrook was a woman of advanced views: as well as considering homosexuality to be perfectly normal, she was an ardent socialist. Her daughter took after her in both respects, and also (under the influence of her brother Eddie) became a confirmed atheist. Anne was twenty-three at the time Jim met her, and had led a sheltered life, mostly spent in rural Suffolk or cloistered villas in the South of France. She was totally innocent of sex, and longed to meet a man − preferably one who reminded her of her beloved brothers − who would rescue her from this narrow environment.

Jim and Anne seem to have fallen in love at first sight. Eight years later he wrote some words about her in his diary which probably echo his first feelings for her: 'She is truly one of the world's worth-while women, so intelligent, male-minded and deliciously humorous. She is "a dark mare" and worth a million more than the glittering women, such as Nancy [Mitford].' Literature was a shared interest, for they were both passionate readers who spent their spare moments immersed in books. Johnnie and Angela encouraged the romance between their respective best friends which appeared to be blossoming under their roof, and by the time the weekend was over, the couple considered themselves to be engaged. The following weekend Jim went to stay with Anne at Snape. This was a success: they enjoyed romantic walks in the atmospheric Suffolk countryside, and Jim was delighted by Anne's mother – indeed, he seems to have been enchanted by the idea of marrying into a family which was as bohemian as it was aristocratic. All that seemed to stand in the way of marriage was money. At the moment, the couple had £500 a year between them – Jim £300 from Lord Lloyd, Anne £200 of her own. Jim took the view, which Anne (who cared little for material things) reluctantly accepted, that they could not marry on less than £1,000 (representing about £50,000 in early twenty-first century values).

Of course it was rash of Jim to commit himself to Anne, even conditionally, after only a few days' acquaintance, for he as yet knew very little about her. It seems strange, for example, that barely a year after embracing the Catholic faith he should have pledged himself to a woman who was not just non-Catholic, but did not believe in God. Nor can he have been comfortable with her left-wing views. (In her diary, Jean Hamilton expressed dismay that he had become 'engaged to a communist'.) As he had doubtless yet to discover, she was untidy and disorganised by nature, whereas he was fastidious in his personal habits. And such was her shyness that she was apt to be tongue-tied in the company of his friends. (Once, after a party at which he had introduced her to such alarming people as Nancy Mitford and Randolph Churchill, he complained that she had 'behaved like a housemaid'.) But that spring he was in love with her, and he promised to marry her as soon as he could increase his income. This he hoped to achieve in two ways: by securing an allowance from his family; and by leaving the agreeable but dead-end service of Lord Lloyd to embark on a career which 'offered what are called prospects'.

To Jim's dismay, his family refused to help him. At first he put this down to his father's usual selfish bloody-mindedness. However, visiting Wickhamford in September, he was shocked to discover that George Lees-Milne had in fact dissipated the family fortune. As he wrote to Anne: 'The long and short of it is that my father has been the damndest fool in the UK and lost whatever money he did have outside the cotton mill, and the mill itself has not paid its preference shares for years. So there is now no money. What has made it so difficult for us all is that my father has kept the situation so dark that none of us have known how broke we are. I am so terribly sorry that I didn't know quite how bad things were when I first met you or I should not have let ourselves fall in love [*sic*] in view of the situation.' George was only able to meet his expenses with assistance from his mother, now eighty-three. This led Jim to hope that his grandmother, who remained fond of him and fairly rich, might provide him with the desired allowance; and she was about to do so when she died early in 1936, leaving her entire estate to her surviving son, who meant to keep it all for himself. Jim was unfortunate in the timing of his appeals to his family, for his siblings were also giving them cause for concern: his sister Audrey was undergoing a traumatic separation from her husband Matthew, necessitating expensive psychiatric treatment, while his brother Dick had fallen in love with a married woman in the process of divorcing her husband whom the Lees-Milnes considered unsuitable.

In his quest for a career Jim at first seemed to have more success. With help from both Lloyd and Nicolson, he managed to get a job on the staff of Sir Roderick Jones, Chairman of Reuters' news agency, carrying a salary of £400 and prospects of promotion in that famous organisation. Jim left Lloyd's service and took up his new post in June. However, he hated it from the first. The work, while not exacting, was extremely boring. Whereas Jim had been Lloyd's right hand, sharing in the drama of his career, he was now Sir Roderick's third private secretary, performing such tedious and trivial tasks as ordering merchandise from shops and attending to the insurance of Rolls-Royces. Sir Roderick himself was a bully who seemed to delight in humiliating his underlings. Jim loathed him, and thirty-five years later, in *Another Self*, avenged himself for the slights he had suffered by painting the unflattering portrait by which his chief will probably be known to posterity.

> . . . I would describe his appearance as that of a sparrow were it not for his waist which, instead of being loose, was tight, pinched-in by a conspicuous double-breasted waistcoat which he habitually wore like a corset. This constrictive garment gave him the shape of a magnified wasp. His face too resembled that of a wasp seen under a microscope. It was long and the bulbous nose was proboscis-like. His small eyes darted rapidly in his head in the manner of that insect . . . His mouth too was sharp and vespine. His sting was formidable and unlike the bee's could be repeated.

Sir Roderick Jones was immensely proud of the exalted position he occupied in Fleet Street and the world of power. He wished his influence to be felt by the great and humble, particularly the humble. When his Rolls-Royce drove up each morning . . . a bell rang violently in every room . . . There was a general scurry and flurry of alarm. When it drove off in the evening another bell rang more softly. There was a contrasting sigh of relief and relaxation of tension . . .

As an employer he was not likeable . . . He devised an office routine from which no deviation was permissible in any circumstance . . . For instance, every object on his desk had to be arranged each morning with meticulous exactitude . . . As third secretary I was responsible for the daily arrangement of Sir Roderick's desk. I also took down and typed out the less important letters he cared to dictate to me. If he detected that a single word had been rubbed out and retyped, the whole page, complete with four carbon copies, was sent back to be done again no matter how late in the evening it was . . .

In fact, Jim may have been unfair to Sir Roderick. It was almost routine at the time for press chiefs to behave in this egomaniac fashion; and it may have been the case (as Harold suggested to Jim) that by treating Jim roughly Jones was 'testing' him for the rough-and-tumble life of a foreign correspondent. But Jim, used to Lloyd's avuncular attentions, resented such minor humiliations as being addressed as 'Mr Milne', or being kept late in the office for reasons which struck him as frivolous. By the end of the summer he was determined to leave Reuters as soon as he could find another job. He had his sights on two – private secretary to Prince Henry, Duke of Gloucester, third son of King George V, who was due to marry in November (this suggested by Midi, with her connections at Court); and a post with the publishing house of Constable (where Jim had a personal connection, a great-aunt of his mother having married into the family). Again, he prevailed upon Lloyd and Nicolson to exert their influence; but this time their efforts were in vain – the Prince chose to start married life at Aldershot, and did not require a civilian secretary, while Constable's were unwilling to accept Jim unless he could bring some money into the firm.

Meanwhile Jim's engagement to Anne dragged on for nine months – from April 1935 to January 1936. During this time he wrote to her almost daily; and she later returned the letters she had received from him during the second half of the period, now preserved among his papers at Yale. They do not make edifying reading, for their dominant tone is of unhappiness and frustration. Jim's inability to secure the income he wanted and consequent inability (as he perceived it) to marry; his dissatisfaction with his job, and failure to find a better one; his difficult relations with his family – all combined to plunge him into a state of depression sometimes bordering on despair. 'I really don't know when I have been so unhappy and positively wretched as during these last three months', he wrote to her in September. 'I try to say to myself . . . better things are bound to come along; but still I groan every morning when the clock strikes 9.45, groan as I enter Reuters, groan as I climb the stairs and carry on groaning until I leave. When I see these lovely autumn mornings I become more miserable than ever, so much would I like to be on the moors in Scotland or wandering with you through the woods. It is unmitigated hell; I contemplate all manner of escape from it.' One striking fact which emerges is how little they saw of each other: the letters cover a period of 137 days, during which they met on only 19. This included six weekends at Snape; two weekends with his family in Worcestershire; and one weekend with the Churchills. (As Jim had to work on Saturday morning, and be back in the office on Monday, these weekends were short, from Saturday afternoon to Sunday evening.) Only once were they together in London – when Anne came up to attend a wedding. Jim discouraged her from seeking a job in London; and when he gave a party at King's Bench Walk to which he invited almost everyone he knew, he found an excuse for not asking her. It is all somewhat reminiscent of his infatuation with Diana Mitford almost a decade earlier – a fantasy relationship pursued through the medium of correspondence. She was excluded from his London life; and at Snape, their intimacy did not extend beyond holding hands during their walks, and a chaste embrace on meeting and parting.

Indeed, although the letters are full of expressions of love and affection, and he treated her as a *confidante* to whom he reported much of what was happening in his life, it is clear that he was beginning to have doubts about marriage, to the point where he hardly knew himself whether he was more depressed by the prospect of being unable to marry her, or of actually marrying her. He confided his problem to Harold Nicolson, who replied in an interesting letter, couched in his usual cryptic terms, touching upon the whole issue of marriage for homosexual men.

> The worst about sensitive and therefore sexless people such as you and me is that once we really like a person that liking is, when it comes to thoughts of marriage, checked by our sensitiveness . . . But is this really a very intelligent approach? . . . So long as Anne is quite clear that the physical side may be a trifle wobbly, you will be able to give her the spiritual (if I may use such an expression) side more than any one else . . . If you are both 'affectionate' people, which I believe you to be, the actual affection

engendered by marriage will create a link more powerful than any physical complications. Unsuccessful marriages are based on lust; successful
marriages are based on intelligence and esteem. Provided that you enter
upon such a marriage with complete honesty of purpose I feel sure that
you have a 70% chance of happiness, whereas when two people fall wildly
'in love' I should allow them, after the first eighteen months, only a 30%
chance of happiness.

I feel that if you admired Anne a little less you would love her a little
more. I have the impression that you find yourself caught in a moral
dilemma which is torturing your soul. You feel that she cares for you more
than you care for her . . . You thus feel that either you must marry her and
prove inadequate or refuse to marry her and cause unhappiness . . . I admit
that in ordinary cases the 'in love' is on the man's side and the 'love' on
the woman's. Yet these balances can easily be reversed . . . You would
make an excellent husband; you very much need a person to look after
you; were I a woman I should marry you like a shot; do not be too diffident
about it. Ask only, 'Is this the sort of person with whom I should wish to
share my life?'

As Anne wanted in any case to marry a sexually ambiguous man (and
eventually did so), 'the physical side' was unlikely to present a great problem; but Jim was coming to see (as he once told her frankly) that there
were incompatibilities of temperament between them, that what he
needed was not so much a shy and innocent girl as a strong-minded,
worldly woman. Though depressing, their lack of money was also an
escape route. More than once that autumn he suggested breaking off their
engagement with a view to resuming it later on if his circumstances
improved – 'that is, if you have not found someone else you would rather
unite your fortunes with'. But Anne always assured him that she was
prepared to wait as long as necessary. Then Johnnie and Angela announced
that they were moving to the south of Spain, where life was cheap and
there was a colony of English writers and artists; they urged Jim and Anne
to marry without delay and join them there, where they could easily
manage on Anne's £200 a year. Jim demurred but suggested that, if he
had not found a better job by the new year, she should go out there alone
on an extended visit.

Although Jim's letters to Anne are gloomy and emotionally confused,
they do give a vivid picture of his life at the age of twenty-seven. He was
still living with Harold in King's Bench Walk, and Harold was clearly the
leading personality in his life: 'How I adore Harold, the most perfect of
men.' Harold gave him advice when needed, Harold did what he could to
get him another job, Harold let him give a party in his rooms and mostly

paid for it too. (In a mild and teasing way, Jim seems to have bullied and taken advantage of Harold, who had a masochistic streak and enjoyed being treated in this fashion by his young favourites.) When Harold was adopted as a parliamentary candidate at Leicester in October, and elected there in November by eighty-seven votes, Jim was not pleased, as it meant they would be seeing less of each other. Despite Jim's lack of interest in politics, he hastened to report to Anne inside details of the political crisis arising from Mussolini's invasion of Abyssinia which he had gleaned from both Harold and Lord Lloyd. Jim continued to see his former employer, who wrote imploring him to visit. When Jim told Lloyd of his money problems, Lloyd offered to pay him to reorganise his archives, which had got out of hand since Jim's departure; and Jim made regular nocturnal visits to Portman Square, where he carried out this task in a leisurely fashion while drinking his lordship's whisky and smoking his cigars. All the old ladies in Jim's life flit through the letters; he sought to give each the impression that she was the only one, and had to juggle dinner invitations with care. The friends he saw most of were Midi Gascoigne, whom he accompanied to the theatre on the evenings she did not spend with her dull husband, and (until they left for Spain in November) Johnnie and Angela Churchill, who threw bohemian parties at their flat in Paddington. Other friends he mentions more than once include Tom Mitford, Nancy Mitford and her husband Peter Rodd, the Peter Quennells, the Cyril Connollys, the Osbert Lancasters, Christopher Hobhouse, Hamish Erskine, Harry d'Avigdor-Goldsmid, John Sutro, Joan Eyres-Monsell, Raymond Mortimer, Paul Hyslop and Eddy Sackville-West. Anne knew few of these people; but she would have been interested to read about them, for Jim was already mastering the art of evoking a personality in a few vivid words or phrases, as the following extracts show.

> I had such an enjoyable evening with Hamish last night. We were really boyish together – or rather shamefully girlish . . . Between us we consumed three-quarters of a bottle of whisky and staggered out into Fleet Street to find a cab. The driver took us to the most expensive restaurant in Greek Street, the Gourmet, where we ate enormously and drank *vin rosé*. That was great fun until I had to pay the bill, Hamish producing one pathetic bent half-crown rather mingily. We then returned to KBW where we gossiped over everyone we had either of us known since we came out together in was it '26, '27 or '28. Then we branched to smut . . . Oh! how one loves one's old friends and even when one sees so little of them as I do Hamish it is absolute heaven meeting them again and spending a smutty evening together . . .

Tonight I am dining with Eddy West in Soho. Sometimes Eddy depresses me frightfully, especially if he asks if one thinks he is going off, and if one notices those bags under his eyes getting baggier as the years go by . . . At other times when he is not thinking about himself he is, besides being extremely intelligent, charming and informative, of great sensibility and understanding . . .

Dinner with old Mrs Cooper last night was extraordinary. She is the most remarkable old woman. What she does not know about one's inmost thoughts is not worth knowing. She sums up people within two minutes, and knows all about them before they have appeared in the room. It is uncanny. She is malicious, outspoken, hated and feared by all and sundry, yet extremely intelligent. Her granddaughter is being married and she does not want the mother, her daughter-in-law, at the wedding. So she, Mrs Cooper, has sent the invitations out for Saturday, but has arranged that the wedding shall take place on the Thursday, and is sending telegrams to everyone except the mother to say it is that afternoon. The mother will have bought the wedding clothes and prepared for the event only to read in Friday's morning papers that it has already taken place. It seems to me a cruel thing to do . . .

I dined with John Sutro at the Garrick off caviare and woodcock, claret and brandy. For a long time we chatted of days gone by and then set to . . . Being a friend and an extraordinarily nice person, sensitive, untough, intelligent, humorous, a Jew, he was quite frank in saying that I was worse equipped for a business career than any person in the British Isles he could think of, with the possible exception of Desmond Parsons . . .

The Connollys are marvellous people to know . . . They are quite rich, about £1,200 p.a. I should think, and they like to spend it all on food, drink, travel and their friends. They are both extremely intelligent; he is brilliant, untidy, dirty and ugly. They give lots of dinners at which 8 or 10 sit down to the most gorgeous meals . . . They never go to cinemas or plays after, instead one sits round the fire and drinks . . . Above all they know and invite all the people one likes best in England* . . .

Although Jim, in writing to Anne (or indeed to anyone else), never mentions any homosexual liaisons, such escapades (which would have thrilled rather than shocked her) are hinted at. It would have been surprising had he not ended up in bed with Hamish at the end of their 'smutty

---

*The guests on the night in question included the Peter Rodds, the Peter Quennells, John Sutro, the (Catholic) writer Christopher Sykes and his sister Angela, Countess of Antrim, Joan Eyres-Monsell, Lady Dorothy ('Coote') Lygon, and the publisher Kenneth Rae.

evening'. A few days before Christmas he spent a similarly drunken night with his 'mad but splendidly invigorating friend' George Lennox-Boyd, during which they 'behaved very badly'. On 25 September he met 'an extraordinary little man' called 'Hayward [*sic*] Hill', a relation of Anne's sister-in-law, whom he found 'very good and distinguished looking, well-dressed and almost pansyish . . . Harold likes him a lot.' Heywood Hill would go on to found the bookshop of that name in 1936, and marry Anne in 1938; years later, Jim confessed to her that he had been 'rather in love' with him at the time.

Jim's correspondence with Anne* is also of interest as they wrote to each other about the books they were reading. They were both fans of Trollope (though Jim was not impressed by his portrayal of 'country aristocrats'), and Jim read six of Trollope's novels that autumn, as well as his *Autobiography* and a biography of him by Michael Sadleir (Chairman of Constable's where he hoped to get a job). He also read Boswell's *Life of Johnson*, Aubrey's *Brief Lives* ('intoxicatingly entertaining and bawdy'), Meredith's *The Egoist*, Mrs Radcliffe's *Udolpho*, Virginia Woolf's *Jacob's Room* and *The Voyage Out* (which he admired while regretting that her characters were so 'middle-class'), and two novels by Ronald Firbank (dismissed as 'drivel'). At the end of the year he read two new books by friends – Peter Quennell on Byron, and George Cattaui on Proust. As for his own writing, he showed Anne his manuscript on Hopkins, and also mentioned his desire to produce a work on Portuguese architecture. On 5 December he wrote to her: 'I am gradually coming to think that my role in life may be that of a novelist. I should never rank with Proust, Henry James or Thomas Hardy, but rather with [her brother] Robert Gathorne-Hardy, Anthony Powell and other of our good but lighter novelists.'

In *Another Self* Jim makes no mention of Anne (a fact which rather annoyed her when the book appeared). He merely writes:

> I was extremely unhappy at Reuters. It was, with the exception of the War, the most down of all my down periods. It was made worse by an emotional entanglement (I wanted to get married) and the realisation that I was being a failure in a job from which the right sort of man would have profited.

---

* Anne's side of the correspondence, which he returned to her, is not worth quoting from here: as well as being somewhat artless, it now only survives (among her papers at the Lilly Library, Indiana) in a bizarre form, as she cut out what she regarded as the most interesting passages and pasted them undated on to sheets of blank paper, throwing away the rest.

He goes on to tell the following story. One Friday evening Jim failed to perform one of his useless duties, that of informing Sir Roderick that his Rolls-Royce was waiting at the door to take him to Sussex for the week-end. It was unnecessary for him to do so, for the car was never late; but Sir Roderick 'worked himself into a towering rage' over the incident and, as he left, ominously asked to see Jim on Monday morning. The following afternoon Jim went to stay at Cumberland Lodge in Windsor Great Park at the invitation of Lord FitzAlan, 'an extremely patrician and saintly old man' and a leading Catholic layman. The other guests were Lord and Lady Salisbury, General Sir Francis and Lady Isobel Gathorne-Hardy (Anne's uncle and aunt), Sir Edward Marsh, Mrs Belloc Lowndes, and the Prime Minister and his wife, Mr and Mrs Stanley Baldwin. Jim already knew Mrs Lowndes, and during the weekend he attracted the attention of 'Eddie' Marsh, a literary civil servant who developed platonic crushes on young writers. He also had a connection with the Baldwins, who had been neighbours of his grandparents in Worcestershire. Early on Sunday morning a footman woke Jim with the message that the Prime Minister, before leaving, hoped Jim would take a stroll with him in the grounds. Jim quickly dressed and joined Baldwin for the stroll, during which they talked of Worcestershire. Jim then confided to the Premier that he had got on the wrong side of the Chairman of Reuters (whom Baldwin knew well), and feared he was about to be sacked. According to Jim, Baldwin offered the following avuncular advice:

> What you must do is this. Get your notice in first. Immediately, without delay. Tomorrow morning. This will take the wind out of his sails. Having done so you must not repine. Friends will come to your rescue. Do not have silly scruples about accepting help and money which you cannot repay. At your age you are bound to get a job you like eventually, doubtless sooner than you expect. Remember that lean times never last for ever.

The next morning Jim confronted his boss. 'Well, Mr Milne,' said Sir Roderick, glowering, 'there is something I have to say to you.' Jim broke in: 'There is something I have to say to you first, Sir Roderick. I know I was to blame for not telling you on Friday what of course you knew already . . . I forgot. I'm sorry. But I am not sorry to tell you how much, how exceedingly much I have disliked working for you. I wish to give you notice. I am leaving now.' Flabbergasted, Jones asked Jim who had advised him to do this foolish thing. 'The Prime Minister, Sir Roderick,' replied Jim triumphantly. 'And if you don't believe me, you can ask him.'

Both the Cumberland Lodge weekend and the confrontation with his employer are mentioned by Jim in his contemporary letters to Anne. The weekend took place on 5–6 October 1935. Though it was not the first time Jim had stayed there, he looked forward to meeting the Prime Minister and was 'afraid that the [Abyssinian] situation will keep Mr Baldwin from turning up at Cumberland Lodge, that he will have to go to Geneva or something'. Unfortunately, so excited was he by what transpired during the weekend that he telephoned his report of it to Anne rather than writing her a letter. He did, however, send her a detailed account of his interview with Sir Roderick – which took place two months later, on Monday 3 December.

Sir R. said, 'Will you sit down?' And then I knew what was coming, what I wanted to avoid at all costs but thought might not come till after Xmas perhaps. He began, 'You have now been with us about six months, and I want to know candidly how you find yourself and whether you think this life is one you are well equipped for and would make a success at.' What could I say? I was absolutely calm . . . and I just said, 'Well, Sir Roderick, when I first came here we agreed that after six months we would review the situation, and I had every intention of coming to you about it, but had decided to wait until after Xmas. As you ask me now I must say that I do not at all think this is my cup of tea, etc., etc.' Then he said (he was quite charming throughout the whole audience), 'No, I have been quite aware of that and I am determined to be quite frank with you. I cannot keep an eye over all my staff, but those who deserve special attention owing to their general ability, intelligence, etc., I do. And I think I must say that you would never make a success at Reuters. I don't, my dear fellow, mean to cast the slightest shadow over your merits, etc., but you are not suited to us. I feel that temperamentally and physically you are quite unfitted, a square peg in a round hole. I think it is my duty to tell you this, because I know you are wasting your time here and with your abilities and peculiar intelligence you should be making headway elsewhere. I shall be very sorry to lose you, for I like you a lot, but I make it a rule never to let my personal feelings interfere with the good of the Company. I am only sorry that this is so. I have had to say the same thing after a period of probation to several others, so you are not the only one.' Then he said, 'You may stay on where you are for some time yet. I do not wish to hustle you away. You must just tell me when you are ready to go and I shall release you.'

'I feel very small, a failure and a hopeless ass', Jim admitted to Anne. 'I am so angry that I did not get the first word in with Roderick. Instead of which he summoned me.' Clearly Jim fantasised about an alternative scenario in which he did have the first word, and put his boss in his place; and it was this fantasy which found its way into *Another Self*. In fact, the truth was even more humiliating. Having no other job to go to, Jim saw out his month's notice at Reuters, and on the actual day of his departure, Saturday 4 January 1936, he had to endure yet more kindly words from his boss. 'He was extremely agreeable, said he was sure he was wise in speaking frankly, that if I stayed in Reuters I should never get to the top of the tree, whereas he thought I undoubtedly would in any profession I liked . . . Begged me to write and tell him the moment I was fixed with a new job and hoped I would come and dine with him and his wife . . . We parted on good terms.'

Feeling at the end of his tether, Jim decided to leave London indefinitely. He gave up his lodgings at King's Bench Walk (though Harold assured him that he would not give them to anyone else, and he could return there whenever he liked). He had nowhere to go that he might call home. Wickhamford Manor was let, and his parents were the last people he wanted to see anyway. Anne suggested he retreat to Snape; but though Jim had quite enjoyed his weekends there, walking, riding and discussing literature with her, and meeting her mother, her brothers, and local literary personalities such as John Strachey and A. J. A. Symons, he wanted to be apart from her to reflect on the future. Fortunately, two convenient invitations came his way. One was to join Mary Herbert's New Year's hunting party at Pixton Park, Somerset, a house soon to be immortalised by Evelyn Waugh as Boot Magna Hall in *Scoop*. The other was from Mrs Ismay, urging him to visit Haselbech Hall 'whenever I like for as long as I like with as much luggage as I like, adding that she hopes I may not get a new job for six months so that she doesn't have to lose me . . . How kind women are to one . . . Men are inclined to shun others in misfortune, whereas women are so sympathetic and nice.'

Jim arrived at Pixton on Monday 6 January 1936 for a two-week stay. 'What a wonderful thing is a country house full of congenial people,' he wrote to Anne. 'One meets at meals, has intelligent conversation, then disperses either to study or to take exercise. I could stay here for ever, only I have not yet quite established my position and am not altogether absolutely at ease.' The Herbert family – consisting of Mary, widow of the swashbuckler Aubrey Herbert, her three daughters, and her young son Auberon – were

> more u.c. [upper-class] than it is possible to conceive.* Their whole life is so
> 18th century with Pixton and Bruton St and their villa in Italy, and the life

---

* Mary was a daughter of the 4th Viscount de Vesci, her late husband the younger son of the 4th Earl of Carnarvon.

they lead, a mixture of sport and culture. They never waste a moment of the day except in talking. Yesterday, on returning from hunting at 4.30, Mrs H. suddenly started giving a singing lesson to the village in the drawing-room; after dinner she did accounts with the estate agent. They do things like getting all of us to read Father D'Arcy's book on St Thomas Aquinas out loud, having a debate after on the Thomist philosophy. She is very sweet, Mary H., and extremely intelligent but I am rather alarmed by her.

Jim was obliged to hunt in muddy conditions, which (though he normally abhorred such pursuits) he seems rather to have enjoyed: the wooded, hilly country was beautiful, and the exercise dispelled his depression. He was thrilled that his fellow guests included Hilaire Belloc, doyen of Catholic writers. 'I have as you know always looked upon him with the utmost veneration. He is certainly brilliant and witty. But his views are so reactionary as to shock me to the quick . . . Looks like an old English squire but is really more French in his habits and culture. I have been doing some work for him, taking down in shorthand a synopsis and typing it out on a prewar Corona.' The Herberts were ardent Catholics, with whom Jim felt spiritually at home: they had turned their old laundry into a chapel where they held Masses surrounded by geysers and mangles (a scene Jim was to reproduce in his novel *Heretics in Love*). 'One day,' he told Anne, 'I shall at great length explain to you that Catholicism is not all my eye or make-believe.'

Anne was due to sail for Spain to visit Johnnie and Angela on 25 January, and had arranged to meet Jim to say goodbye as he passed through London on his way from Pixton to Haselbech. However, on Sunday 12 January, after a week at Pixton, Jim, in the midst of a letter saying how much he was enjoying life there, suddenly dropped the following bombshell:

I think of you still a good deal of the day but I do believe now that I am away from London and my old life that I could if I had to do without you . . . This is a very bald gauche statement I know . . . But I do think that altered circumstances make such fundamental changes in one's life more easy to bear, and I cannot help thinking that we are both being extremely foolish going on in this way month after month . . . If we are to part would this not be the best moment, just before you go to Spain and while I am loose like this? I don't want you to have any idiotic feelings of chivalry about sticking to your man at all costs while he is on the rocks. I shall be all right. I also wonder whether it might not be better that we should not meet in London when I go through to Haselbech. It is meetings that revive old wounds (silly sentimental word) and old hopes . . . I cannot honestly believe we shall do ourselves any good lingering in this way and

nourishing hopeless ideas . . . Our families would never understand and
be tiresome, but that is always the way . . . I am almost inclined to be angry
with you now because I feel sure that you will agree with me whatever I
decide and so I shall consider myself responsible for the ultimate action.

This cannot have come as a total surprise to Anne, as he had been suggesting to her for months that it might be best to call off their engagement
until his circumstances improved, and indeed that they might not really
be suited to each other. However, the manner of his declaration can only
have distressed her. It was couched in peremptory terms; it made no
mention of any future resumption of their relationship; it was inserted
into an account of the joy he felt at Pixton, as if to draw a contrast with
the misery of their engagement. He did not wish to see her to say goodbye; and he ended with a curious reproach. Although Jim had certainly
by now concluded, probably correctly, that the engagement had been a
mistake, and was probably also correct in thinking that, if it was to be
broken off, the sooner this happened the better, it seems cruel of him to
have delivered the blow in these terms.

There was, however, another factor, probably unsuspected by Anne at
the time. Of Mary Herbert's three daughters, the eldest, Bridget, had
recently married, while the youngest, Laura, was a mere girl of eighteen
(who would marry Evelyn Waugh the following year). The middle
daughter, Gabriel, was a young woman for whom Jim had a considerable
fondness, and whom he had met several times in London during the
autumn. In fact, it was at Gabriel's suggestion that Jim had been invited
to Pixton. Just before he arrived she sustained a hunting accident which
put her on crutches, and he spent much of his stay comforting her. It
seems that, amid the heady sense of freedom which he felt after leaving
Reuters, and in the magical atmosphere of Pixton which so delighted
him, he fell in love with her. (When she died, Jim wrote in his diary that
'there was a time in the mid-thirties when I thought I was in love with
Gabriel, and she seemed a little in love with me'.) She was the same age
as Anne; but with her ardent Catholicism and her daredevil personality,
she was as different from Anne as could be imagined. (She would soon
be off, like Waugh's Cordelia Flyte, to drive ambulances for Franco in
the Spanish Civil War.) One may conjecture that, under the influence of
this sudden infatuation, Jim felt an almost furious desire to disengage
himself from Anne. (Jim soon realised, however, that Gabriel too would
make an unsuitable wife for him, and she eventually married one of his
fellow guests of that January, Alick Dru, described by Jim to Anne as 'an
ugly bore and the most pious and nauseous kind of Catholic'.)

Anne was an extremely sensible girl. Whatever her hurt feelings, she immediately wrote back saying that she respected his decision, having long sensed that his heart was not in their marriage, and hoped they would remain the best of friends. She then embarked for Spain, hoping to console herself with the company of Johnnie and Angela in their Moorish villa overlooking the sea at Torremolinos, intending to stay with them for at least three months. However, her holiday turned into a nightmare, thanks to two events which occurred soon after her arrival. A radical left-wing government came to power in Spain and violent incidents broke out all over the country (culminating within six months in civil war). And Angela suddenly decided that she was bored living with Johnnie, and casually went off with another admirer. Before the winter was over, Johnnie and Anne had returned to England, both feeling forlorn and bereft.

Jim had predicted that their families 'would never understand'. In fact, Anne's brothers understood all too well; but her mother, who had for nine months cherished him as her future son-in-law, was heartbroken. An expert needlewoman, she had spent the autumn embroidering linen with the initials 'A.L.-M.', and she now passed her days unpicking the letters while the tears coursed down her cheeks. Jim's parents were also dismayed, and his father lost no time telling his hunting friends about his son's caddish behaviour, making Jim's name mud in his native locality. When Jim next visited Wickhamford (to see his mother, who had not been well and was about to embark on a recuperative cruise), his father 'hardly spoke to me at all but looked stern and cross, and finally at lunch said that my hair was so long and clothes so odd that he thought I was a pansy. To which I said I was, whereupon he shut his mouth in a rigid set attitude and did not speak one word more.' As for Jim's aged grandmother, who had decided to settle £100 a year on him when married, her shock at the news seems to have contributed to a fatal stroke she suffered soon afterwards.

Jim had meanwhile made his way from Pixton to Haselbech, passing through London on 20 January while the nation was in mourning for King George V. Two more different houses could hardly be imagined: Pixton was an ancestral pile, shabby but redolent of past generations and full of fascinating people; Haselbech, the Edwardian acquisition of a rich business family, was the last word in modern comfort, but full of bores. He was however welcome to stay at Haselbech for as long as he liked. He wrote to Anne (to whom he resumed his letters) that he avoided boredom by observing a daily schedule. After breakfast, he wrote on Portuguese architecture; after lunch, he took exercise (usually in the form of riding); after tea, he wrote letters; after dinner, at which he made himself agreeable to Mrs Ismay and her dull guests, he read. He was currently reading *Tom Jones*, which he thought

> a good, facetious picture of English country life among squires in the 18th century. However attractive in the idyllic sense English squires are, what bloody philistines they have always been, narrow, hard-headed, hard-drinking, hard-hearted and dilapidated. Pretty hopeless, and when you see them legacied in individuals like my father today you feel it is time they made way for some better species of humanity.

Once a week he went up to London, seeing Harold and the Lloyds and hoping to hear some news regarding jobs. On 18 February, after a month at Haselbech, he reported that, thanks to Harold, he had just had a job interview at the National Trust.

> I dare say you know they are the people who buy up open spaces, beauty spots etc. and get left legacies etc. Well, they are now starting a scheme for preserving country houses, hoping to get Government support. They want someone to run that side. It would necessitate going all over England, staying with the Devonshires at Chatsworth, and Farmer Gubbins at Ye Olde Tudor Farme House in the depths of the Wrekin, trying to induce landowners and proprietors to join the scheme. I think that if I searched the whole world there is no job I would rather have. It would suit me down to the ground and would be a job really worth doing, sympathetic and interesting, for I would be doing something of use to the world, instead of writing letters in an office about ults and proxes. The trouble is that the pay would be a bare £200 p.a. and there are at least three other applicants. I shall know by the middle of next week one way or the other.

5

The National Trust
1936–9

THE NATIONAL TRUST for Places of Historic Interest or Natural
Beauty was founded in 1895. It developed out of two older charities,
the Commons Preservation Society (CPS), founded in 1865 to oppose
the development of open spaces, and the Society for the Protection of
Ancient Buildings (SPAB), founded in 1877 to oppose the destruction or
over-restoration of historic (notably late mediaeval) architecture. Unlike
these campaigning organisations, whose aims it broadly shared, the
National Trust was a holding body, whose constitution enabled it to
acquire and preserve land and buildings 'for the nation'. Under an Act of
Parliament of 1907 it was entitled to declare any of its property 'inalienable', unable to be transferred to another owner except by a further Act
of Parliament. The prime movers behind its foundation – the CPS solicitor Sir Robert Hunter, the Lake District clergyman Canon Rawnsley,
and the housing reformer Octavia Hill – were Victorian idealists inspired
by the 'Christian Socialism' of John Ruskin and William Morris (the
latter being the SPAB's founder); but it was also supported by some landowning aristocrats, its first Presidents being the Duke of Westminster and
the Marquess of Dufferin and Ava. During its first forty years it attracted
some dedicated enthusiasts and acquired, either by donation or purchase
(with money raised through public appeals, the generosity of rich individuals, or grants from other charitable bodies), a scattering of worthy
properties; but its membership remained small and its achievements
(except in the Lake District, where it rescued large tracts of scenic landscape) relatively modest. By 1914 it had 725 members and held 63 properties covering 5,814 acres; by 1929, the year in which its membership
reached 1,000, it held some 200 properties covering 37,000 acres; during
the years 1930–5 its holdings increased to some 50,000 acres, while
its membership almost quintupled to 4,850 owing to a surge of public
interest in preserving the countryside. It had little regular income
and depended on unpaid volunteers; before Jim joined, its salaried staff
consisted of two officials and some clerical workers at its London office,

and (to look after its substantial holdings there) a representative in the Lake District.

Before the 1930s the National Trust had acquired various buildings – ranging from cottages and barns to two mediaeval castles bequeathed to it by Lord Curzon – but had shown little interest in country houses, traditionally regarded not as part of the 'national heritage' but as bastions of social privilege, owned by families (often those that had originally built them) which generally had the means to maintain them. Its sole experience of taking on a country house, the Tudor Barrington Court, Somerset in 1907, had not been encouraging: it had found itself with insufficient funds to repair the derelict property (a portent of problems to come), and had had to be rescued by a rich tenant. By the 1930s, however, the way of life associated with country houses was becoming increasingly difficult to sustain, and their very existence as a social and architectural phenomenon seemed threatened. Fifty years of agricultural depression, coupled with the inflation of prices and wages and dramatic increases in the taxation of income and estates, had subjected owners to mounting financial pressure: as Clough Williams-Ellis wrote in 1928, there were now 'more great country houses in England than rich men able and willing to inhabit them'. The First World War, which resulted in the deaths of many owners and heirs and a decrease in the pool of domestic servants, added to the problems of ownership, as did the Crash of 1929 and the policies of the Labour Government of 1929–31. Many owners gave up the struggle; others were only able to make ends meet and to continue to enjoy something of their traditional life by selling land or contents which had been associated with their houses for generations. Altogether the outlook was bleak; and *Country Life* had already warned throughout the 1920s that the glories of English domestic architecture were at risk of falling into eventual ruin unless steps were taken to protect them.

The Government was not yet inclined to accept ownership of country houses with a view to their preservation; and virtually the only organisation constitutionally equipped to do so was the National Trust. As it happened, there had been a change in the complexion of its committees in recent years: the founding zealots in the tradition of Ruskin and Morris had largely died out and been replaced by enlightened aristocrats who belonged to the country house world, such as the historian G. M. Trevelyan, whose brother owned the Wallington estate in Northumberland, and Oliver Brett, 3rd Viscount Esher, owner of Watlington Park, Oxfordshire. Its Chairman from 1932 to 1945 was Lawrence Dundas, 2nd Marquess of Zetland, a Yorkshire landowner active in Conservative politics. These men were naturally sympathetic to the idea of the National Trust concerning itself with the fate of country houses. However, it was another peer, not previously involved in the Trust's affairs, who set the ball rolling. In 1930 the Liberal politician Philip Kerr had unexpectedly inherited from a cousin the Marquessate of Lothian, along with half a dozen country houses and their estates. Dealing with this inheritance, which came with a bill for a quarter of a million pounds in death duties, presented him with considerable problems. Invited to address the Trust's annual meeting in July 1934, he declared:

> I venture to think that the country houses of Britain, with their gardens, their parks, their pictures, their furniture and their peculiar architectural charm, represent a treasure of quiet beauty which is not only specially characteristic but quite unrivalled in any other land. In Europe there are many magnificent castles and imposing palaces. But nowhere, I think, are there so many or such beautiful country manor houses and gardens, and nowhere, I think, have such houses played so profound a part in moulding the national character and life. Yet most of these are now under sentence of death, and the axe which is destroying them is taxation, and especially that form of taxation known as death duties [the top rate of which, he noted, had risen from 8 per cent in 1908 to 50 per cent in 1930].

Lothian had two recommendations to deal with this situation. First, he suggested that a list should be drawn up of the most important houses, and that the government should be pressed to grant these houses, together with their parks and collections, immunity from death duties in return for public access. (A scheme already existed to provide such immunity in the case of listed works of art.) Secondly, he expressed the view that 'if a body like the National Trust were willing to equip itself to become a landlord on an ampler scale, it would gradually draw within its ambit quite a large number of historic furnished houses'.

This speech aroused some public interest, but evoked little response from the Government: at a time of political uncertainty and economic hardship, it could not be seen to be making tax concessions in favour of the landowning class. However, in May 1935 Lord Zetland became Secretary of State for India, and was able directly to approach his cabinet colleague, the Chancellor of the Exchequer Neville Chamberlain, about the country house problem. As a result the Treasury did, early in 1936, come up with two tentative schemes which amounted to pale reflections of Lothian's proposals: both involved the National Trust, which was invited, in collaboration with government officials, to draw up a list of the houses most worthy of preservation. The first scheme proposed to relieve the listed houses, and any associated land, contents and endowments, from death duties in the event of their owners donating them to the National Trust – it being accepted that the donors and their heirs might continue living in them as tenants paying a nominal rent. For those owners unwilling to donate their properties, the second scheme proposed a form of 'affiliation' to the National Trust: in return for allowing a degree of public access, the 'affiliated' owners would have the right to establish a common maintenance fund to be administered by the Trust, which would not be subject to tax and to which the public and other charities might also contribute. Only if both schemes aroused sufficient interest to make them practicable would the Treasury agree to the necessary changes in the law.

These were meagre pickings, but the National Trust quickly put together a Country Houses Committee with a view to drawing up a list, contacting owners to see which of them might be interested in entering into arrangements, and continuing discussions with the Government about the (still nebulous) details of the two schemes. Two leading figures in the nascent movement to preserve country houses were persuaded to serve on it – Paul, 4th Baron Methuen, the artist owner of Corsham Court, Wiltshire, and Christopher Hussey, editor of *Country Life*. It was also decided to employ an extra official to assist the new committee's work. Jim heard about the vacancy from the Nicolsons. Through Harold he had got to know Vita, to whom he had confided his desire to help save country houses. Hilda Matheson, a formidable lesbian who had worked for the secret service and the BBC, learned about the job from her brother Donald MacLeod Matheson, the Trust's Secretary since 1934; she mentioned it to Vita (her former lover), who mentioned it to Harold, who mentioned it to Jim. Jim was interviewed by two members of the Trust's Executive Committee, one of whom, 'Rob' Holland-Martin of Overbury Court, Worcestershire, knew his parents, a fact which he was not sure would help him. He need not have worried: early in March 1936, at Haselbech, he learned that he had been appointed to the post of Country Houses Secretary at a salary of £300 a year.

As Jim wrote to Anne, no job could have appealed to him more; and it would be interesting to know how his appreciation of country houses had developed since he had (according to *Another Self*) become an enthusiast for their preservation at Oxford in the late 1920s. Unfortunately no diary survives from those years, and little of his correspondence apart from his letters to Anne. These do not give the impression that he was a dedicated country house visitor: during the second half of 1935, apart from visits to his own family in Worcestershire and Anne's in Suffolk, he stayed (twice in each case) in just two (hardly typical) houses – Cumberland Lodge (in 'Wyatville baronial') as the guest of the FitzAlans, and Somerhill (a Jacobean mansion converted into a luxurious Edwardian residence) as the guest of the d'Avigdor-Goldsmids. He did however admire a book published in 1935, *The English Country House* by Ralph Dutton, copies of which he gave as Christmas presents that year. Its short but elegant text, lavishly illustrated with photographs, covers the main styles of building from the Plantaganets to Queen Victoria, as well as explaining developments regarding interior features, parks and gardens, and various aspects of social history. Destined to remain the standard guide to the subject for some years, it was published by Batsford, which specialised in producing popular illustrated works on 'heritage' subjects. Jim had probably read other Batsford titles dealing with the architecture, furniture, painting and decoration of various periods; and when he himself came to write works of architectural history a decade later, it was to this publisher that he would turn.

Dutton was one of three close friends who, since the 1920s, had played a leading role both in 'the Georgian revival' and the movement to preserve country houses, the others being Christopher Hussey and Lord Gerald Wellesley, the Duke of Wellington's architect brother. (Dutton and Hussey were both heirs to houses – Hinton Ampner, Hampshire and Scotney Castle, Kent – which they would eventually donate to the National Trust, while Wellesley would inherit the dukedom and its seat at Stratfield Saye, Hampshire on the death in action of his nephew in 1943.) 'Gerry' was already known to Jim, for he was an old friend of Harold Nicolson, with whom he had served as a diplomat in Constantinople in 1914, while his wife 'Dottie' had left him to pursue an affair with Vita (and was now living with Hilda Matheson). As for Hussey, Jim was undoubtedly familiar with his profiles of country houses in *Country Life* (of which he had become editor in 1933), which had done much to inspire popular interest in the subject and had recently been collected in book form. All three of these aesthetes were to serve on National Trust committees and become friends of Jim.

Also friendly with the Dutton–Hussey–Wellesley trio and sharing their scholarly interest in country houses (though too exclusive and patrician to become involved with an organisation like the National Trust) were the brothers Osbert and Sacheverell Sitwell. Osbert contributed a foreword to Dutton's book, expressing sentiments which would have appealed to the romantic in Jim. ('How curious it is that works of art only begin to obtain a wide appreciation when they are on the verge of being destroyed . . . What country house of any size, one wonders, can hope to survive the next fifty years?') While still in his twenties Sacheverell had written *Southern Baroque Art* (1924), one of Jim's favourite books which had been his companion on holidays in Italy and the Iberian Peninsula; it contributed to his becoming a devotee of Baroque architecture, which may in turn have influenced his decision to become a Roman Catholic. Jim spent much of a visit to Portugal in the summer of 1933 studying and photographing Baroque churches and palaces; and he was writing on this subject at Haselbech when he received the National Trust's 'call' in 1936. 'Sachie' was another figure whom Jim had already encountered and who would become a friend.

Jim had two brilliant literary friends of his own generation (both in fact three years older than himself) who cared deeply about architecture – John Betjeman and Robert Byron. Some of their first writings were on architectural subjects – Byron's *The Appreciation of Architecture* (1932), Betjeman's satirical *Ghastly Good Taste* (1933). Until 1935 Betjeman was on the staff of the *Architectural Review* (for which Jim's Oxford friend Osbert Lancaster also worked as an illustrator), and in 1933 he had founded the Shell county architectural guides which he would edit for the next forty years. Byron specialised in the architecture of the Near East (the subject of his celebrated travel book *The Road to Oxiana* [1937]), but he was also angrily concerned about the destruction of good British architecture, and had in 1932–3 played a leading role in the successful campaign to prevent the demolition of Carlton House Terrace. Jim saw much of them during 1933 when, weekending in Wiltshire with Johnnie Churchill, he visited both Savernake Lodge, Byron's family home, and Biddesden, where Betjeman was a regular fixture; he was impressed by their knowledge and crusading spirit, and looked up to them as aesthetic mentors.

Jim later described himself as 'raw and ignorant' at the outset of his conservationist career; and while he had seen and read much, and was one of nature's aesthetes, his knowledge of architecture, and of the various categories of art which adorned country houses, must have been decidedly haphazard and amateurish at this time. He had much to learn. He did, however, possess an innate understanding of the traditional landed class from the lower reaches of which he sprang – a class which had long been in decline, much of its membership becoming decadent or eccentric. He was not an unconditional admirer of that class, and certainly had little sympathy with those who, like the spendthrift aristocrats of the 1920s, or indeed his own father, took an *après nous le déluge* view, and frittered away their patrimony. But he passionately believed that the most splendid and durable creation of that class, their country houses, ought as far as possible to be preserved (preferably still inhabited by the families which had built them) both as works of art in themselves and as monuments to their creators' grandeur, taste and way of life. He had seen enough of England to share Lothian's view that something unique and precious was slipping away. Thirty years later he recalled, in a preface to what would be the final edition of *Burke's Landed Gentry*:

> Until about 1930 . . . [a]t an average of two miles throughout the country there was what local people referred to as 'the big house'. It might be liter-ally a palace like Blenheim, or a small manor house like Owlpen in the Cotswolds. Quite apart from size it was noticeably different from its neighbours in that its carefully groomed elevations and sprucely mown lawns radiated a beneficent well-being denoting authority and ease. The surrounding fields, checkered with neatly laid hedges and punctuated by ancient low-spreading trees like gigantic tea cosies, still belonged to the nearest big house, the capital of its little kingdom. The resident squire – and the less grand and rich the more resident – cared for the village on his estate . . . In rural districts his guiding hand was everywhere apparent, and that parish in which for some reason there was no squire was instantly recognisable by its neglected, unkempt, unloved appearance . . . Indeed during the 1920s the physical aspect of the countryside still resembled what the squires, with the help of Capability Brown and Repton, had made it in the eighteenth century, namely one vast luxuriant park . . .

In 1936 Jim undoubtedly hoped that, through his new job, he would be able to make a contribution to saving some small part of this vanishing world of 'big houses' in their landscapes. At the least, it would give him an unrivalled opportunity to make his own personal study of that world and the families who still owned it.

Jim took up his post in time to be present at the inaugural meeting of the Country Houses Committee on 12 March 1936. This was attended by two political grandees, Zetland (who took the chair) and Lothian; two other liberal-minded peers, Esher and Methuen; 'Ronnie' Norman, the Trust's Vice-Chairman and sometime chairman of the LCC and BBC; Sir Alexander Lawrence, a retired civil servant; Major (later Sir) Michael Peto, a cultivated squire (and friend of Methuen); and the veteran Nigel

Bond who had been the Trust's Secretary in Edwardian times. All were country house owners; four of the eight were Etonians. Matheson was present to keep the minutes and deal with any serious business; his new subordinate was there to listen and learn. After Zetland had explained the background and aims of the new committee, the meeting focused on two issues: the negotiations Matheson was conducting with the Government to clarify the still imprecise 'schemes'; and the establishment of a sub-committee under Esher to draw up, in consultation with the Office of Works, a list of eligible houses.

Jim spent the next few weeks familiarising himself with life and work at the National Trust's headquarters, 7 Buckingham Palace Road, a red brick house facing Victoria Station. Although it was undistinguished without and 'cramped and stuffy' within, it was, on the whole, a happy place. Its occupants, 'united by a strong missionary zeal', felt more like priests than office workers. The Secretary Matheson, a Balliol man and a follower of the Russian mystic Ouspensky, was a man of some intellect, able to master difficult problems, but perhaps not ideal for his job: he was 'a bad delegator of business' (as Jim soon discovered when he found his reports redrafted), and 'his previous job as Secretary of the Gas Light & Coke Company had not made him an aesthete'. However, he suffered from poor health, and during his frequent absences 'a jolly atmosphere reigned' and his subordinates could do much as they pleased. Apart from Jim, these subordinates consisted, in 1936, of the Deputy Secretary Christopher Gibbs, a Wykehamist 'with the benevolence and dedication to duty of a scoutmaster', and the Lake District representative Bruce Thompson, 'a gentle giant of a Norseman'. Jim found them both congenial, and also became fond of the head of the clerical team, Miss Florence Paterson, 'a saintly nanny figure'.

Of the original members of the Country Houses Committee, two were to loom large in Jim's life over the next twenty-five years – Oliver Esher and Paul Methuen. Esher, who took over the Committee's chairmanship from Zetland that summer (being already chairman of the Finance and General Purposes Committee which held the Trust's purse strings), became Jim's boss and his third great mentor during the 1930s after Lloyd and Nicolson. He was the son of Reginald, 2nd Viscount, the Edwardian *éminence grise* (whose biography Jim was to write fifty years later); and although he had been out of sympathy with his father, he had inherited all his charm and guile. (While 'Regy' – as Jim would be fascinated to discover – had led a secret homosexual life, Oliver had no such inclinations, differing from Lloyd and Nicolson in that respect.)

Having married an American heiress he had no need to earn a living and devoted himself to various charities connected with the arts and amenities – he was also Chairman of the SPAB and the Old Vic. Jim later remembered him as

> a shrewd, genial, irreverent and witty man – in fact the funniest I have met . . . To be in his company was a delight; to witness his handling of committees was an education. With infinite merriment he always got what he wanted, and what he wanted was invariably right . . . He was the most loyal boss and friend who supported me through thick and thin in whatever argument or tiff I might be engaged in with what he termed the 'mangel-wurzels' of this world.

Methuen (an artist first and foremost) was by contrast a somewhat melancholy and abstracted character, but dedicated himself to the preservation of country houses in general and Corsham in particular, and came to have much respect for Jim, who shared his single-minded fervour. He invited Jim to become a trustee of the Corsham estate; and when Jim, shortly before his own death, wrote a book of essays about departed friends, it was Methuen and not Esher who featured in it.

The Sub-Committee met on 31 March with Esher in the chair, the other members being Christopher Hussey, Gerry Wellesley, W. A. Forsyth, an architect prominent in the SPAB, and Sir Charles Peers, retired Chief Inspector of Ancient Monuments at the Office of Works* (which had to approve the list). According to the minutes kept by Jim, the meeting 'drew up a list of some 230 houses' with the proviso that they would leave it to the main Committee to decide whether London houses should be included. It seems amazing that such a list could be approved at a single meeting, but *Country Life* had already published one of some six hundred houses which it (that is, Hussey) considered to be national treasures, and Jim had been busy conferring with the Sub-Committee's members in the fortnight before the meeting with a view to establishing an agreed choice. Jim later wrote that he had 'misgivings about this hastily compiled and definitive list. I only knew that England was crammed with wonderful country houses, many of which we must have overlooked, and several of which, little regarded in 1936, might be highly esteemed by the next generation.' Esher, indeed, shared this point of view – though

---

*Known from 1940 as the Ministry of Works (which was subsumed in 1971 into the Department of the Environment, the section concerned with the listing and preservation of buildings, monuments and archaeological sites being known from 1984 as English Heritage).

as officialdom required a list he was happy to produce one in the confident expectation that he would later be able to add to it any other properties he considered suitable. Although it is unlikely that Jim was yet acquainted with many of the houses on the list, he was certainly responsible for adding one item to it – Emral Park, Flintshire, the former property of his recently deceased half-uncle Crawshay Puleston: its inclusion was a mere act of piety, for there was no realistic possibility of saving the house, which had already been sold to speculators who were about to demolish it.

The main Committee met again a month later. It decided to exclude London houses – except for Holland House in its park, which could be considered a country house. Otherwise it approved Esher's list. It regretted that the talks between Matheson and the Office of Works had not yet made much progress, but resolved without further delay to submit the list to the Office and write to the owners of the listed houses with a 'memorandum' outlining the two proposed schemes and suggesting, if they were interested, a meeting with Matheson or Jim. When the Committee held its third meeting on 22 June, Matheson reported that the Office had accepted the list almost in its entirety, adding six houses and deleting three, and that the owners had been written to. He received a severe wigging from Esher, as it turned out that without further consultation he had submitted the memorandum as well as the list to the Office, where it had been rewritten by the officials: it now read awkwardly and uninspiringly, though sent out in the National Trust's name.

The owners were invited to make known their views on the two schemes either to Matheson (at Buckingham Palace Gardens) or Jim (who was available to visit them in their houses): the Committee hoped to hear from them by October, when it was due to report to the Government, which would then decide whether to introduce the necessary legislation (for the schemes were still merely proposals). It was, Jim later wrote, 'the most enjoyable summer of my existence, visiting . . . a succession of stately homes and their forbearing owners'; but his task was not easy, for both schemes possessed drawbacks which were likely to discourage all but a few. Under Scheme 1, owners who wished their properties to be preserved by the National Trust would have to donate not just their houses (preferably with their parks and historic contents) but also a substantial endowment, in land or securities, to provide for future maintenance. In other words, they would have to part with much of their income as well as their homes. And under Scheme 2, owners who wished to become 'affiliated' would have to accept a legal obligation to admit the public in return for a measure of tax relief which seemed paltry. To sweeten the pill, the memorandum suggested that a mere thirty days' opening a year should suffice; but even owners who were already opening their houses voluntarily tended to feel that, once they were required to do so, they would no longer be masters in their own domains. It is hardly surprising that, of the 225 owners who were sent the memorandum, only eighty-three bothered to reply at all; of these, ten wrote merely to register negative interest; of the remaining seventy-three, only forty-two had taken up the invitation to a personal interview by mid October.

Of these, Jim visited about a score in their country houses that summer, usually travelling (for the National Trust as yet possessed no motor car) by train to the nearest station, then on an old bicycle which accompanied him in the guard's van. No doubt it was an adventure for him to meet the often eccentric owners *in situ*; but he did not always receive a cordial welcome. At Charlecote Park, Warwickshire, he failed even to get through the front door.

> Sir Henry Fairfax-Lucy, military, dapper and arrogant, walked me quickly round the park and garden. It was a rainy day I remember. On returning to the porch, whence we had set out immediately on my arrival, Sir Henry stretched out his hand and bade me goodbye . . . Nervously I asked if I might see inside. The reply was, 'There is absolutely no need. Charlecote is known to be one of the great, the *greatest* houses of England. Good morning.' So, without disputing, I went off with my tail between my legs. On my return to the office I was told I had been a fool.

Others received him courteously but clearly had no serious interest in the schemes. At Longleat, Wiltshire,

> old Lord Bath, the most distinguished and courteous of patricians, received me in a frock coat . . . At the conclusion of a fruitless interview he rang the bell and ordered my motor-car to be brought round. He insisted on accompanying me to the front door. The steps to the drive were flanked on either side with a row of footmen in livery. In place of my uniformed chauffeur an extra footman wheeled my bicycle to the front of the steps. I shook my host's hand, descended the perron and mounted. At the end of a straight stretch of drive . . . I looked back for a last view of the glorious façade. Lord Bath, attended by a posse of open-mouthed and doubtless disdainful servitors, was in the old-world manner of true hospitality still standing at the top of the steps until his guest was out of sight.

However, such humiliations were offset by the rare but gratifying cases of owners who looked to the National Trust as a potential saviour and greeted their representative with open arms. At Attingham Park, Shropshire, Jim was warmly welcomed by the shy Lord Berwick and his handsome younger wife Edith (it being immediately clear to him that the latter made the decisions).

> They were surprisingly unreserved in explaining to me that in spite of a large estate the house was a cruel burden to them. But it had to be preserved at all costs, however onerous, and the marvellous contents kept intact. The estate was what they called 'embarrassed' . . . Nevertheless not an acre should be sold. Perhaps fortunately, they had no children and no heirs with claims on them . . . Now would and could the National Trust help them, and if so, how? I said I was sure they somehow would and could, although it was not for me to unravel the means. When I left at the end of the day, my pockets stuffed with delicious sandwiches for the return journey to London, my kind host and hostess stood above the portico steps watching me take to saddle and pedal, he fluttering a nervous smile, she a royal but affable wave. While I bicycled back to the station I was so intoxicated by Attingham and a determination to save it that I nearly missed my train.

In some cases Jim was able to benefit from prior knowledge of either the house or the family. Bishop Abraham, owner of Little Moreton Hall, Cheshire, the picturesque black-and-white manor house (semi-derelict and long uninhabited) which Jim's father so admired and Jim himself had come to detest during his boyhood, asked him to tea at his London club and begged the National Trust to take over the house, but had no money with which to endow it. Putting his own prejudices aside, Jim assured him that a way would somehow be found; and it proved possible to raise at least the funds needed for urgent repairs. At the other end of the spectrum, Knole, Kent, one of the largest inhabited houses in England, still filled with much of its original contents, presented far greater problems; for although both Lord Sackville and his heir Eddy Sackville-West longed to offload this great white elephant onto the National Trust, the endowment required was enormous and the legal difficulties (arising from the fact that it belonged to a settled estate) daunting. Although a decade would pass before the house finally came into the Trust's possession, Jim's friendship with Eddy, who often invited him to Knole, helped maintain Lord Sackville's confidence that these problems would eventually be overcome.

He also visited several houses (mostly of the smaller gentry) which did not yet feature on the 'list' but whose owners had heard about the schemes and wished to know more about them. In his early reports to the Committee on the merits of such properties, it is evident that he was just as interested in the houses' family associations as in their purely physical charms. When he visited Mrs Baker Baker at Elemore Hall, Durham, he was fascinated to learn that Byron's wife had been born there, her aunt having been the Mrs Baker of the time; it was, he reported enthusiastically, 'the finest kind of live, unmuseumy house; been in family since 1520; never once empty or even let; nearly every content of family interest . . .'

On 10 October 1936, four months after the 'listed' owners had been written to, Jim submitted a lengthy report on their reactions to the Country Houses Committee, copies being sent to the Treasury and the Office of Works. The results were not encouraging: just nine owners had expressed serious interest in Scheme 1, a mere six in Scheme 2. The trouble was that Scheme 1 only appealed to the richest of owners, who could afford to part with a substantial endowment, while Scheme 2 only appealed to the poorest, since the idea of a 'common fund' implied that rich owners would be subsidising poor ones. Virtually all owners were bitterly disappointed by the tax reliefs proposed by the government, and many of them suspected that both schemes represented a sinister attempt to nationalise private property (a view shared by Jim's father). As the Treasury had intimated that it would not agree to the necessary legislation unless *both* schemes aroused substantial interest, it looked as if Jim would soon be out of a job. However, Zetland and Lothian brought their influence to bear on the Government, as did a new member of the Country Houses Committee, Lord Brocket, a personal friend of Chamberlain (who was shortly to succeed Baldwin as Prime Minister). During 1937, therefore, Scheme 2 was quietly dropped while legal provisions were introduced, in the Finance Act and a new National Trust Act, to give effect to Scheme 1, which was up and running by the middle of the year.

As Jim later wrote with wry understatement, 'it cannot be claimed that the surviving Scheme started with a bang'. Before the outbreak of war in 1939, just one large house was actually transferred under it – Wightwick Manor, Staffordshire, an Arts & Crafts creation of the 1890s. Not only was this absent from the 'list', but it contravened an understanding between the Country Houses Committee and the Office of Works that no house less than a century old should be considered. However, as it was a perfect example of its type and the owner, the Liberal MP Sir Geoffrey Mander (whose grandfather had built it), offered a generous endowment, it was duly approved and accepted.* Five other owners, all childless,

---

*Two small manor houses – still occupied today by the donor families – were also accepted in 1938–9, Owletts, Kent (donated by the architect Sir Herbert Baker) and Bradley Court, Devon.

arranged to bequeath their houses in their wills – Lord Berwick of Attingham; Sir Henry Hoare of Stourhead, Wiltshire; Lord Lothian of Blickling, Norfolk; Colonel Lutley of Brockhampton, Herefordshire; and Sir George Vernon of Hanbury, Worcestershire – and these properties effectively passed to the National Trust on the testators' deaths in the 1940s. Another important property, Wallington, had been offered to the Trust even before the formation of the Country Houses Committee; but its owner, the radical socialist baronet Sir Charles Trevelyan, brother of Professor G. M. Trevelyan who chaired the Trust's Estates Committee, raised so many conditions and difficulties that his much-trumpeted gift did not take effect until 1941. Lords Sackville of Knole and Methuen of Corsham – as well as Hal Goodhart-Rendel, an architect friend of Esher who owned Hatchlands, an Adam house in Surrey – wished in principle to donate their properties but were frustrated by the fact that, as life tenants of settled estates, they lacked the legal power to do so. To make such donations possible, a second National Trust Bill was tabled shortly before the outbreak of war in 1939 – but the aristocracy closed ranks, and in the Bill's passage through the House of Lords the proposed authority of a life tenant to dispose of such property was severely restricted (so that the transfer of Knole and Hatchlands finally succeeded, but that of Corsham did not).

Despite this meagre progress, Jim was kept extremely busy during the late 1930s, dealing with the correspondence generated by the Scheme and visiting owners who expressed interest in it (as well as performing his share of other jobs which fell to be discharged by the National Trust's tiny and hard-pressed staff). His most important work was to 'nurture' those properties coveted by the Trust whose owners hoped eventually to donate them, and deal with any circumstances which threatened to frustrate this intention or cause a change of mind. In the case of Attingham, Brockhampton and Stourhead there were no heirs likely to cause trouble, and Jim got on well with the hereditary owners (whom he later poignantly depicted in *People & Places*) – though a cloud appeared over Stourhead when the RAF announced its intention of requisitioning part of the estate for an airfield, and Sir Henry Hoare not unnaturally looked to the National Trust to minimise the ensuing disruption. More complex were the cases of Lacock Abbey, Wiltshire and West Wycombe, Buckinghamshire. These were magnificent properties, consisting in each case of a house representing the best of its type (mediaeval ecclesiastical and Georgian Palladian), complete with park, village and estate. Their respective owners, Miss Matilda Talbot and Sir John Dashwood, wished to donate them to the National Trust; but there were heirs to be considered, and endowment presented problems: Miss Talbot drew her entire income from the Lacock estate, the donation of which would leave her penniless, while the West Wycombe estate (parts of which Sir John had already donated) generated insufficient funds for the maintenance of the house. Despite strenuous efforts to find a solution, these problems were still unresolved when war broke out, though Jim had by then befriended both the saintly Miss Talbot and the debonair young Dashwoods. A case which presented rather different problems was Hanbury Hall in Jim's native Worcestershire. The rakish Sir George Vernon, the last of his line, wished to leave the Hall, together with a few farms by way of endowment, to the Trust; but the bequest was subject to his estranged wife's life interest in the house after his death, and Sir George proposed to leave everything else, including the house's contents and park, to a girlfriend he had adopted as his daughter, the two women being at daggers drawn. Though difficulties would only arise on Sir George's death in 1940, their resolution would eventually require all Jim's tact and skill.

These were all traditional country houses in which it was then envisaged that representatives of the donor families, or some other tenants, would carry on living under the National Trust. Rather different were the cases of smallish houses which it was in effect proposed that the Trust should maintain as museums. Little Moreton Hall was one such property. Another was Smallhythe Place, Kent, an ensemble of farm buildings acquired by the actress Ellen Terry who lived there until her death in 1928: her daughter Edith Craig, hoping for its preservation by the Trust as a memorial to her mother, approached Jim personally in 1938 on the recommendation of her neighbour Vita Sackville-West. As both properties were in an appalling state of disrepair and there were no adequate sums available for their maintenance, they should, according to the rules, never have been taken on by the National Trust. However, Jim, who was touched (in the case of Little Moreton) by Bishop Abraham's devotion to his historic ruin, and fascinated (in the case of Smallhythe) by both the mother's lingering spirit and the daughter's jolly lesbian entourage, seems to have talked the Country Houses Committee into accepting them virtually unendowed. Both were to cause the Trust endless problems; but thanks to craftsmen (notably from the SPAB) who were willing to give their services for minimal reward, and to philanthropists rich and poor who responded when funds became urgently needed, it proved possible to restore and preserve the crumbling edifices, which are places of pilgrimage today.

Most of the above-mentioned houses eventually came into the National Trust's possession; but the majority of properties which Jim visited on the Trust's behalf were not destined for this fate. In many cases they were simply judged to be of insufficient merit; and Jim in his reports could be caustic about their shortcomings, particularly where artless 'improvements' had altered the original style. In other cases he wrote lyrically about their virtues, and evidently felt sympathy with the owners, but lack of adequate endowment proved an insuperable obstacle (though frustrated donors could still safeguard their properties to some extent by granting restrictive covenants empowering the Trust to prevent future development). A rather surprising case was that of Herstmonceux Castle, Sussex, a moated mediaeval ruin which had been rebuilt as an Edwardian residence in the early twentieth century. Its acceptance in principle by the Country Houses Committee in 1938 was no doubt largely due to the circumstance that (like Wightwick) it was offered with a munificent endowment, but may also have owed something to the fact that the owner, the rich and reprobate Sir Paul Latham, was a friend (and some-time lover) of Jim. (Changed personal circumstances later led Sir Paul – who went to prison in 1941 after attempting to seduce his batman – to withdraw his offer.) In the case of Holland House, Kensington, Jim had no doubt of its architectural and historical importance ('very little altered since the great Lady Holland's time, and filled with Byronic associations . . . there is no single room that is not full of art treasures'), and the owner, Lord Ilchester, was eager for it to become the inalienable property of the National Trust in order to frustrate the London County Council's threat to build roads through his splendid park; but while the problems of transference were being worked out, the house was all but demolished in the Blitz.

Jim's visits to country houses with a view to assessing their architec-ture, contents, geographical settings and historical associations led to a steady development of his relevant knowledge and skills. As he wrote during the Second World War after inspecting some furniture offered to the Trust, 'I rely upon instinct sharpened by years of experience, rather than upon imbibed knowledge from books'. Of interest is a bound note-book, now in the National Trust's archives, which he began in 1938 and entitled 'Architectural Notes'. He divided it into sections dealing with external features, internal features, decorative work and artistic contents, and jotted down a wide range of information he picked up – concerning the characteristics of various styles, the practitioners of various arts, and the country houses which best exemplified various developments. Today, information of this sort is readily available in works of reference; but such works hardly existed in Jim's day, obliging him to put together a hand-book of his own. Much of its content is practical rather than historical – he explains, for example, the techniques used for repair, giving the names and addresses of current craftsmen. (He had recently learnt much about the repair of old buildings by observing the work done by the experts of the SPAB on Little Moreton Hall.)

At the same time he was perfecting what he later described as 'the manner which used to endear me to owners'. In all his contacts with them he was courteous, deferential, tactful and attentive. He never showed off his knowledge, or corrected them when they displayed ignorance about their houses and possessions. He affected to share their enthusiasms, whatever these might be, and tried to conceal any strong likes or dislikes which he felt for either their property or themselves. In explaining the scheme and its advantages he was always careful to represent himself as a mere servant of the National Trust, unable to influence decisions (though his committee was in fact usually ready to accept his advice). This policy of discreet dissimulation proved salutary in embarrassing situations.

> It would happen that an enthusiastic owner, fired by the prospect of the National Trust preserving for all time his ancestral seat and thus immortal-ising himself and his forbears, invited the Country Houses Secretary to pay him a visit in remotest Wales or even Cumberland. The Country Houses Secretary must stay a night, sometimes two, in order to allow adequate time to take in the architectural beauties of the house, the historic contents and the spectacular park and surroundings . . . Then it might happen that before dismounting from whatever vehicle had borne me 400 miles from Buckingham Palace Gardens one glance told me – the flat terrain, the immoderately restored façade or the lamentable Edwardian excrescences – that Colonel So-and-So's seat was totally unacceptable. Nevertheless I was still faced with forty-eight hours' examination of every nook and cranny, maybe a contained revulsion, and certainly the obliga-tion to gush appreciatively. I had to answer a thousand questions relating to the anticipated acceptance of a property of no merit whatever. If directly asked whether or not Tantivity Towers was worthy I would reply that, charming though I found it, I dared not predict what might be the opinion of my committee. Even in favourable circumstances I tried to be non-committal, though not always with success. My enthusiasm would get the better of me.

In his dealings with owners Jim had two advantages. As the scion of a minor landed family, raised in a country house and educated at Eton, he was able to identify with them in various ways and win their trust. And since coming down from Oxford he had become adept at touching the hearts of susceptible men and women of an older generation, his youth and good looks being assets in this regard. When confronted with blimpish owners, he had to rely on tact and deference rather than charm; but he often had remarkable success with their wives, and in some cases (such as the Berwicks of Attingham, or the Throckmortons of Coughton Court, Warwickshire) he found himself entering into conspiratorial relationships with sympathetic châtelaines in order to achieve results not necessarily favoured by their husbands or sons who were the owners in name. Such was Lady Berwick's fondness for him that she asked him to 'squire' her to balls in London – though even in such cases Jim guarded himself against taking liberties or becoming over-familiar.

In travelling around the country visiting owners who expressed interest in the National Trust's scheme, Jim availed himself of any opportunities which came his way to visit other houses which appeared to be of note. Soon after taking up his job in 1936 he began a remarkable compilation which would occupy him intermittently for the rest of his life. Gleaning his basic data from county histories, he sought to list every country house worthy of the appellation in England and Wales, together with such details as the name of the current owner, the chronology of the buildings, the distinguishing architectural features, the location of descriptions and illustrations (published and unpublished), and the dates of his own visits (if any). In small, neat writing he drew up his lists alphabetically, county by county, on long sheets of paper which he would later bind into 'red books'. He aimed to visit as many of the houses as possible to obtain information to include in the survey (though long before his death the vast majority had either been demolished or ceased to be used as single residences). Though never completed or published, this undertaking constitutes his principal written legacy from the 1930s, before he began his diary and started to write architectural history, and testifies to his desire to produce a comprehensive record of the doomed world a fragment of which he was trying to save.

Between 1936 and 1939, such was Jim's absorption in domestic architecture and its preservation that almost all the friends, old and new, with whom he associated were people who shared these interests. He became close to those two brilliant pundits he had known since Oxford, John Betjeman and Robert Byron. Jim thought Betjeman 'sweeter and funnier than anyone on earth'; they shared a puckish sense of humour, and during architectural strolls in their lunch breaks would stop at the deserted Geological Museum and 'insert into the dusty glass cases old chestnuts and pebbles which we labelled with long names in Latin'. Betjeman influenced Jim's architectural taste, teaching him not to despise the then unfashionable Victorian Gothic. Jim's reliance on his knowledge and judgement is evident from a letter he wrote to him in April 1936, soon after Esher's sub-committee had produced its 'list'. Jim begs 'dear old John' to comment on this document, having himself 'already found about 50 to 60 houses not on [it] that in my estimation certainly should be'. He thanks him for providing information on the neo-Gothic Toddington, Gloucestershire, agrees that Sezincote 'is a most important house indeed', and asks whether Sheffield Place, 'the house Gibbon used to stay in', remains standing. He looks forward to spending Easter with the Betjemans in Berkshire and to riding on the downs with Penelope (his friend since the days of her courtship by Johnnie Churchill).

Meanwhile Jim and Robert were drawn together by their common love not just of architecture but of Jim's Eton flame Desmond Parsons. During the early 1930s Robert had become infatuated with the beguiling Desmond, who enjoyed his friendship while treating him coolly and refusing to go to bed with him. In 1933 Desmond went to live in Peking with his friend Harold Acton; and in November 1935 Robert, who had been travelling in Central Asia, joined him there. He was shocked to discover that Desmond had been taken ill and diagnosed with the incurable Hodgkin's Disease (as Jim was also dismayed to learn when he stayed with Desmond's step-cousin Mary Herbert in January 1936). Back in England, Desmond received treatment which gave him some respite; and during the autumn of 1936 he rented a house in Northamptonshire from Sachie Sitwell where his greatest pleasure, on the days he felt well, was to go on motoring tours to see country houses, Jim and Robert joining him on these expeditions when they could. Early in 1937, however, his condition worsened, and he retreated to a sanatorium in Switzerland where he died in July at the age of twenty-six. On hearing the news Jim and Robert drowned their sorrows together at the Savile Club, later accompanying each other to the funeral at Birr Castle in Ireland, the Parsons family seat. An embarrassment for Jim was that Robert promptly transferred to him the passion he had felt for Desmond. Though they had for some years had a teasing relationship, Jim was initially no more interested than Desmond had been in having a serious affair with Robert, who was of porcine appearance. On their return from Ireland, Jim's rejection of Robert's advances led to a tiff. However, this was soon made up, and later that summer they went on holiday together, staying as guests of Nancy Mitford at the villa of her father-in-law Lord Rennell at Posilipo near Naples. Jim admired Robert for his forceful personality and uncompromising principles, and during the following months he seems to have relented and they embarked on an affair.

Ever since his successful campaign to rescue Carlton House Terrace, Robert had been a vociferous crusader for the preservation of Georgian London; and in the spring of 1937, with the aesthete Lord Derwent and the writer Douglas Goldring, he founded the Georgian Group to advance this purpose. Jim, a Georgian enthusiast since his adolescence, was involved from the outset, and it may have been at his suggestion that the Group started life under the aegis of the SPAB, of which Esher was Chairman. However, the cosmopolitan 'Georgians' did not get on with the insular mediaevalists of the SPAB, and in the autumn the Group relaunched itself as an independent entity, with its own office in Cork Street. Jim was offered the joint honorary secretaryship with Goldring, but had to refuse, as he was 'kept very busy [at the National Trust] from 9.30 to 5.30 every day of the week, when not about the country'. He did however serve on the committee and devote much of his spare time to the Group's work, notably its successful campaign in 1938 to save from demolition a pair of exquisite Palladian houses in Old Palace Yard, Westminster. Fellow committee members included two old friends, Betjeman and Osbert Lancaster, two members of the National Trust's Country Houses Committee, Hussey and Wellesley, and Desmond's elder brother, Michael, 6th Earl of Rosse. Rosse, an Eton schoolfriend of Robert whom Jim had also known as an older boy at McNeile's, was an altogether more serious and purposeful character than Desmond, following whose death (which renewed his contact with both Robert and Jim) he dedicated himself to the Group. Jim came to respect and admire this civilised and public-spirited aristocrat and was drawn into his social orbit, getting to know his wife Anne, whose sense of style befitted a sister of the theatrical designer Oliver Messel, and his unmarried sister Bridget, for whom Jim conceived romantic feelings on account of her resemblance to Desmond. He also established a lasting friendship with Wilhelmine ('Billa') Cresswell, the daughter of a Norfolk squire who was employed as the Group's organiser from September 1937 until her marriage the following year to the Oxford economics don Roy Harrod; Jim loved her for her breezy forthrightness (a quality which had also endeared her to Betjeman, who had briefly been engaged to her before his marriage to Penelope).

On starting work with the National Trust in March 1936 Jim returned to live with Harold Nicolson at King's Bench Walk, staying there until early 1937 (when he moved into rooms of his own in Gloucester Place, Marylebone). Jim remained close to Harold while deploring his absorption in politics, an interest he could not share. ('Harold is completely caught up in the Mother of Parliaments, and has no mind of his own left', he wrote to Desmond in November 1936. 'He lives on intrigues, scares, rumours, and what Victor Cazalet may say to him about Ramsay, and whether it will get to the ears of Tom Mosley, and then what will Mrs Simpson say, etc.') In August 1936 a new young man burst into Harold's life in the form of James ('Jamesey') Pope-Hennessy, then at Balliol with Harold's son Nigel. Jamesey was the younger son of Richard Pope-Hennessy, a retired general and something of a dullard, and his wife Dame Una, a formidable literary bluestocking who brought up her two boys to have wide intellectual and artistic interests. As well as being extremely quick and clever he was a gorgeous creature, with a lithe figure, birdlike movements and exotically handsome features. (He was part Malay, his grandfather, a colonial governor, having married a lady of mixed blood.) He was a born charmer and quickly seduced Harold, who would remain infatuated with him for the rest of his life. (When Nigel, who was in love with Jamesey, discovered that he was his father's lover, he received a shock which seems to have affected him emotionally for the rest of *his* life.) Jim also capitulated to the advances of this enchanting twenty-year-old, and they began an intermittent affair which would last for a decade. There was much to draw them together: Jamesey loved architecture and was already planning a book on the subject (to appear in 1939 as *London Fabric*); and Jim was fascinated by Jamesey's piously Catholic family – by mid 1937 he had got to know Dame Una, who was helping him plan a country houses exhibition in aid of the National Trust.* Some of their early correspondence has survived: while this is written in the cryptic style which Harold enjoined on his protégés, one may deduce from it that Jim became somewhat exasperated by Jamesey, whose constant attentions were interfering with his work, but that Jamesey wooed him back by writing him delightful letters, whereupon Jim wrote assuring 'dear, dear Jamesey' that 'my feelings are ever the same' and 'you will always be welcome any time you like to come along'.

---

*A further link was that Jamesey's closest female friend, the precocious teenager Clarissa Churchill (future wife of Anthony Eden), was the younger sister of Jim's old soulmate Johnnie.

On the afternoon of 1 March 1938, a date which would remain etched on his memory, Jim visited a house which had been offered to the National Trust in Queen Anne's Gate, Westminster, where he was to meet one Richard Stewart-Jones, a committee member of the SPAB (some venerable greybeard, Jim supposed) with whom he was to inspect and evaluate the premises. There being no sign of the SPAB man, Jim let himself in, locked the front door behind him and explored on his own, reaching the conclusion that the building was of little interest. He was about to leave when he 'heard from upstairs a sinister tinkle of broken glass, followed by a screech of wrenched woodwork, followed by an oath'. He braced himself for an encounter with a burglar, when there nonchalantly trotted down the staircase a scruffy but ravishing youth who resembled the poet Shelley. He looked eighteen (he had in fact just turned twenty-four); the movements of his slender body were 'nimble as quick-silver'; a cigarette dangled from his lower lip in working-class style, though he was clearly a gentleman. He introduced himself as 'Rick' with the words, 'Why the hell did you lock the front door and oblige me to scale the drainpipe and force my way through a bedroom window?' Still marvelling at the apparition, Jim riposted, 'Why the hell couldn't you have rung the bell or banged the knocker like any self-respecting person?' Following these bizarre preliminaries, they re-explored the house together, Stewart-Jones pointing out various fine architectural and decorative details which Jim in his ignorance and haste had overlooked. They went on to spend the evening (and probably the night) together. 'Our friendship did not slowly develop,' Jim later wrote. 'It exploded like a rocket, instantly, there and then . . . Our mutual sympathies induced a sort of *coup de foudre.*'

Richard Stewart-Jones – with whom Jim, a few months short of his thirtieth birthday, had fallen madly (and requitedly) in love – was six years his junior, having been born just before the First World War, in which he lost his father, a shipping agent. The father-figure of his child-hood was A. R. Powys, a distinguished writer and craftsman who was Secretary of the SPAB and through whom he acquired his love of old buildings. Rick did not enjoy his schooldays at Pangbourne Nautical College, though he developed resourcefulness and quirky charm. He went into the Merchant Navy but left it at the age of twenty after coming into an inheritance from his paternal grandmother. By investing this wisely, he might have enjoyed a pleasant, bohemian existence – but he had other plans. As a boy living in Carlyle Square, Chelsea he had become fascinated by nearby Lindsey House, a palatial residence, originally erected in the 1670s and largely rebuilt in the 1750s, which during the 1770s had been split into seven separate houses, known as 95 to 101 Cheyne Walk; Rick's ambition was to buy them all up and restore the edifice to its former unity and glory. By the time he met Jim he had managed to acquire 95 to 97 (as well as 94); after 1945 he would get 99 to 101.* The grandest of these addresses was 96, formerly the house of the artist James McNeill Whistler, which included the ballroom of the 1750s house: its last owner had been Bryan Guinness, who was so intrigued by Rick and his 'project' that he agreed to part with it on easy terms. Stewart-Jones spent all his money buying these properties, so that for the moment there was no question of 'restoring' them and he had to find ways of making them pay. He let the ballroom for parties and dances, and installed the Royal Historical Society as a tenant; he put his mother and sisters into the best remaining rooms, and turned the rest of the ensemble into a huge lodging-house in which he invited young friends and relations to stay for modest rent. He had a natural grasp not just of the architecture and decoration of buildings but of the practical arts of keeping them in decent repair and running them with a minimum of funds. He impressed all he met with his charm, energy, kindness and eccentricity, and by the age of twenty-four had been elected to Chelsea Borough Council as well as to the SPAB Committee.

Jim confided details of his new love to Jamesey Pope-Hennessy, who wrote him two long letters on the subject in April 1938. These are so cryptic that it is not easy to divine their meaning; but it seems that Rick, while returning Jim's feelings, suffered from 'Protestant guilt' over the affair, and also wished to be assured that he was Jim's sole romantic interest, whereas Jim, apart from sleeping with Jamesey, was still involved with Robert, as well as with a woman called Ursula. (This was probably Ursula Brocklebank, a general's daughter with whom he had had 'a flirtation' before – and apparently after – she was married off by her mother in 1934 to the eccentric John Strutt, later 5th Baron Rayleigh.) At all events, Jim soon left his current lodgings† and moved in with Rick in Cheyne Walk, taking the room next to Rick's. He quickly succumbed to the magic of this stretch of pre-war Chelsea, later nostalgically recalled by one of his fellow lodgers in the following terms:

---

* Owing to financial problems, Rick subsequently sold most of these properties (suitably covenanted) and by the time of his death in 1957 only owned 99–100, which he bequeathed to the National Trust.
† He had recently moved from Gloucester Place, Marylebone to Upper Grosvenor Street, Mayfair.

n's birthplace, Wickhamford Manor, Worcestershire: the church he loved as a child is on
e right

ith his parents and siblings on Aberdovey beach, June 1914: Jim, aged five, stands between
s sister Audrey, eight, and brother Dick, three

Jim with Tyke, his closest childhood friend

At Eton

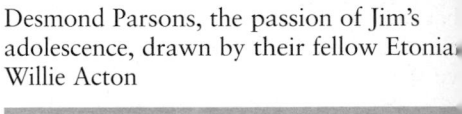

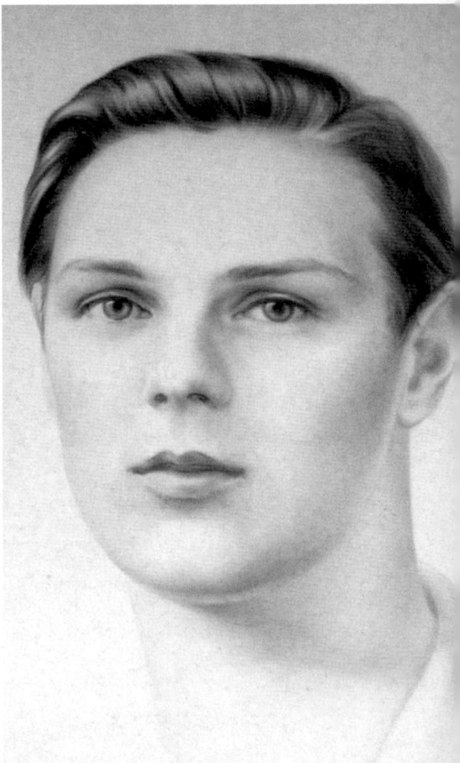

Desmond Parsons, the passion of Jim's adolescence, drawn by their fellow Etonian Willie Acton

ight: Jim with his mother in
rovence in 1927 – 'We looked more
ke twins than son and mother'

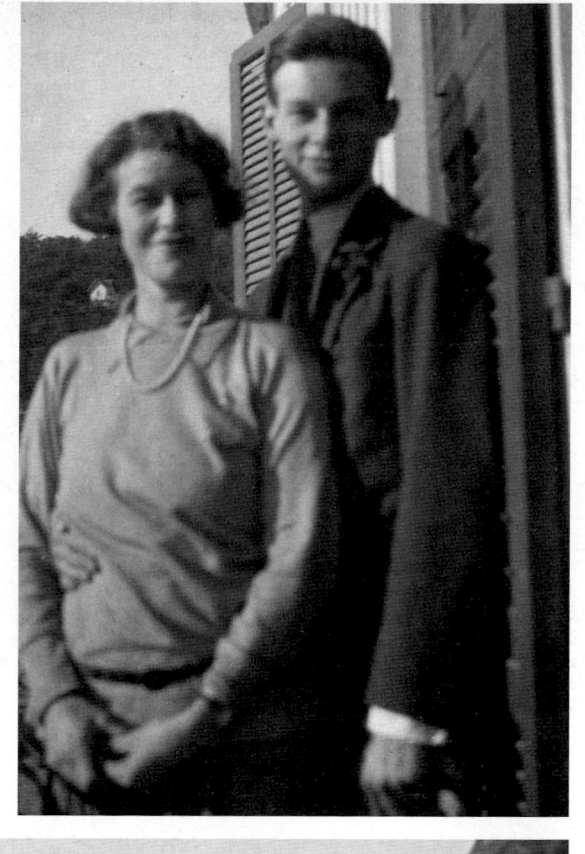

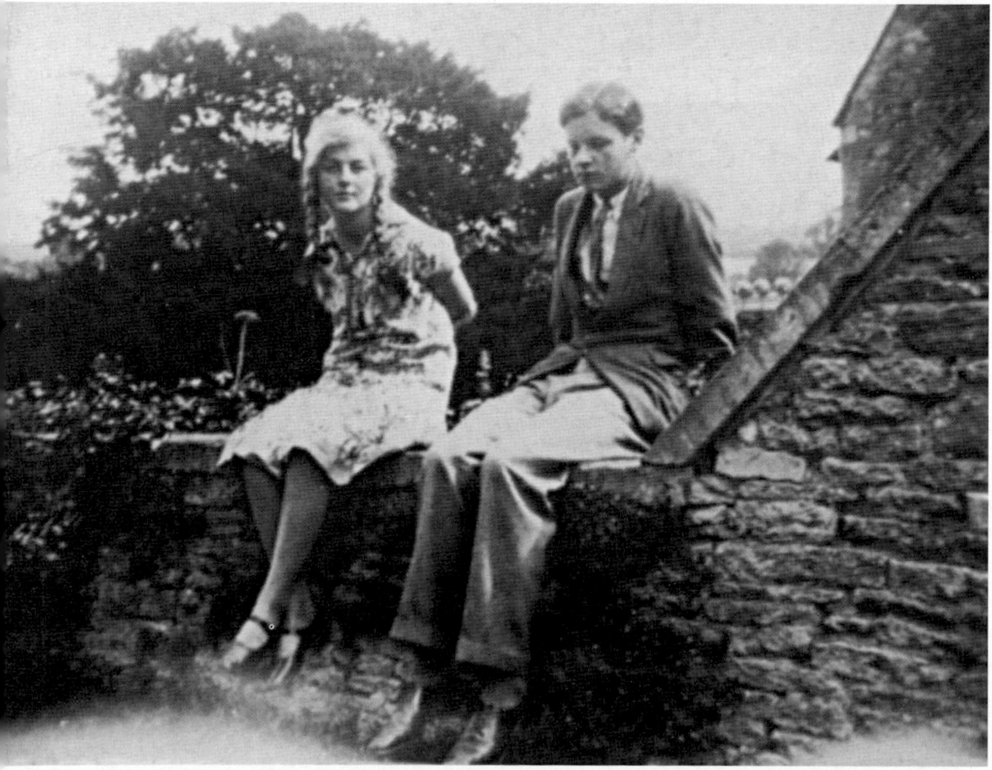

elow: Jim with Diana Mitford,
hat radiantly lovely Botticelli
enus . . . whom I, her elder by
vo years, worshipped'

In his twenties, Jim was helped by two father figures who harboured romantic feelings for him: the statesman Lord Lloyd (*left*), whom he served as private secretary, and the writer Harold Nicolson (*right*), who helped him get a job with the National Trust

Kathleen Kennet, a mother figure with whom Jim had 'a relationship which bordered on the erotic', holidaying in Switzerland with Jim and her son Wayland (later 2nd Lord Kennet)

Right: Riding with Penelope Betjeman

Below: At Easter 1935, staying near Oxford with his old friend Johnnie Churchill and his wife Angela (*right*), Jim met Angela's cousin Anne Gathorne-Hardy (*left*), to whom he became engaged for eight months

Above: Jim at his desk
the National Trust

Left and below: The h
and park at Stourhead,
offered to the Trust by
Henry Hoare during Ji
first months as Country
Houses Secretary

Clockwise: Three of Jim's lovers before and during the Second World War: Robert Byron; James Pope-Hennessy; Stuart Preston

Jim and Rick Stewart-Jones on a tour of Irish country houses in 1938

Holidaying in Italy

It is not that the summers were always fine, but rather that the winters were smokey. There was for much of the year a mist on the riverside recorded in the pictures of Whistler and Steer. The Embankment carried very little traffic . . . On the river there was much more and varied activity. Facing its wide bend Lindsey House and the surrounding Georgian terraces stood out like ocean liners dominating the cottages around them, while the great chimneys of Lots Road power station belched smoke across Chelsea Reach.

Jim soon felt at home in his new abode: he was accepted as one of the family by Rick's mother and sisters and old nanny who acted as house-keeper, all of whom he adored, and befriended several of the thirty-odd lodgers, including Fred Oppé, a young man who worked in advertising, and the pretty teenager John Russell, later a famous art critic. Although the lodging-house was a bohemian establishment which included several couples 'living in sin', Jim and Rick still had to take care to preserve the appearance of being friends rather than lovers. The need for discretion is the theme of the only extant pre-war letter from Jim to Rick, dated 11 March 1938, just ten days after their first meeting. It shows that feelings were as strong on the part of Rick (who had evidently been upset that they would not be meeting that day) as on Jim's.

> I just want to say this: that I hope you don't suppose my inclinations urge me against putting off all and every engagement, especially weekends, in order to be with you. On the contrary, it is some kind of outside prudence or rather discretion that dictates to me – warns me to carry on as I should normally be doing. I somehow feel this is right (as I am sure you do) if as I am determined this thing is to continue happily. I just thought this morning however after I had told you rather abruptly on the telephone that I saw no chance of seeing you today that I would like to give you my explanation. It is probably so cryptically put that you will not understand at all.

The rest of the letter deals with architectural matters: Jim describes the latest progress of the Georgian Group's campaign to save Abingdon Street, Westminster, and mentions the efforts on which he had embarked to persuade Chelsea residents to grant restrictive covenants over their properties to prevent future development (though he had not had much success that morning with 'Mr Caesar Cohen of 28, Cheyne Row'* whose 'attitude is what you would expect').

---

* 24 Cheyne Row, a shrine to Thomas Carlyle who had lived there for most of his life, had been donated to the National Trust in 1936.

Jim and Rick effectively lived together as lovers until the outbreak of war, remaining intimate for some time thereafter. Their shared interest in architecture created a powerful bond; and Rick influenced Jim as a conservationist, teaching him never to lose heart in the struggle to preserve what he loved. But the course of their love did not always run smooth: once the early raptures had passed, temperamental differences led to problems in the relationship. Jim was fastidious in his habits and tactful in his dealings with his fellow men, whereas Rick dressed like a tramp, chain-smoked, and didn't care a damn what anyone thought of him. Rick's political outlook was that of a radical, and he mocked what he saw as Jim's reactionary views, pernickety manners and admiration for the aristocracy. Rick was also notoriously unpunctual, and on more than one occasion chucked an engagement with Jim to attend to some soul in distress (for he took a pastoral view of his duties as a borough councillor). In 1975, eighteen years after Rick's untimely death, Jim recalled in his diary: 'My opinion of Rick is that he was something of a saint, but maddening . . . I know now what I knew at the time but refused to admit to myself, that he was not my 'sort' . . . For he was a Roundhead, and I am a Cavalier.' Elsewhere, he wrote of him: 'He was one of the chief loves of my life [and] I suffered more on his account than anyone else's, almost.' At some point in late 1938 or early 1939, Robert Byron, who was renting a charming Georgian house in Swan Walk nearby where he lived comfortably with a manservant, persuaded Jim to leave the relative squalor of Cheyne Walk – 'that refined brothel', as he called it – and move in with him. But Robert, with his neurotic personality and constant demands, was not an easy friend to live with; and within a few weeks, Jim had returned to Rick.

Robert was not the only person who was in love with Jim while Jim was in love with Rick. Jim enjoyed the platonic attentions of an older admirer, Ted Lister, a retired diplomat with antiquarian interests who had restored Westwood Manor, Wiltshire, a ravishing early Tudor house where he lived with his Bulgarian servant Christo (formerly a footman at the Bulgarian Legation in Paris). Lister – a somewhat old-maidish character whose hobbies included needlework and playing the harp – begged Jim to visit him at Westwood whenever he wished and with whatever friends he wished, and often declared his intention of leaving him his house and fortune. Another admirer from this period was Geoffrey Houghton Brown, a fellow Catholic convert and a clever businessman who bought derelict houses and made them habitable while stripping them of any fittings suitable for separate sale. Jim respected his

knowledge and taste; and Geoffrey, like Lister, showed much generosity
to the impecunious Jim, eventually providing him for many years with
agreeable London accommodation at a modest rent.

During these years Jim saw much of two beloved women friends who
were aware of his homosexuality, Midi Gascoigne and Billa Cresswell
(later Harrod); but otherwise women do not seem to have played a great
part in his romantic life. His 'flirtation' with the married Ursula Strutt
was unlikely to lead anywhere; and although he was mildly infatuated
with Bridget Parsons, she did not encourage his interest at this time.
However, at one moment he found his heart-strings tugged by two
women he had loved in the past, Diana Guinness and Anne Gathorne-
Hardy. On 11 December 1936 he visited Wootton Lodge, a romantic
Jacobean house in Staffordshire whose owner, Captain Unwin, VC, was
thinking of offering it to the National Trust, and which was currently let
to Diana, who lived there with Sir Oswald Mosley. Doubtless to Jim's
relief, Mosley was not present (and Jim was probably unaware that Diana
had married him in Berlin a few weeks earlier, a fact the couple wished
to keep secret). Jim had hardly seen Diana for nine years (and would see
no more of her for another nine); but what promised to be a sticky meeting was turned into an emotional reunion by the fact that Edward VIII,
whom they both adulated, had just abdicated: they listened together to
the ex-King's farewell broadcast with tears running down their cheeks.
(Jim was a 'King's man' for the rather odd reason that, as a Catholic, he
believed in 'Divine Right'; when, two nights earlier, Harold Nicolson
had told him the King would have to go, he had replied testily,
'Goodnight, regicide.') A few weeks later Jim proposed again to Anne,
barely a year after he had broken off their engagement: she had shown
kindly concern for him when, in January 1937, he had been confined to
hospital with a fever. However, she informed him that she 'couldn't be in
love with him again' and that she now loved Heywood Hill, at whose
bookshop in Curzon Street she had been working since the previous
summer, and whom she would marry in February 1938. (A year before
his death, Jim wrote to Anne begging forgiveness for his 'caddish behaviour' at the time, adding: 'Of course, the sequel turned out wonderfully
for you in marrying Heywood who in every way seemed to suit you
ideally. How attractive he was when you married, I remember having
fancied him a lot then.')

Jim did not lose sight of his ambition to become a writer; but he now
had little leisure in which to contemplate literary work. At Haselbech,
just before joining the National Trust, he had started his book on

Portuguese architecture and completed the chapter on the Manoeline Period (1495–1521): this appeared as an article (illustrated with his own photographs) in the *Architectural Review* for October 1937, probably his first published work. He captures the flavour of the unique style of architecture which flourished during those years, reflecting Portugal's brief flurry of maritime glory and exhibiting an exotic mixture of Gothic, Moorish and Asiatic elements; his knowledge and enthusiasm are impressive, but his turgid style and opinionated remarks testify to inexperience. (He writes that while in Britain 'a religious Protestantism was disastrously affected', in Portugal 'a concomitant strengthening of the Catholic faith was most miraculously attained'.) A year later Jim published two further articles, on Spanish Baroque and Palladio's Vicenza, the product of holidays during which he had studied and photographed these architectural styles. In July 1939 the *Review* carried an article by him on the buildings owned by the National Trust: although these as yet included few country houses worthy of the name, he declared that 'what the Trust has actually achieved in the preservation of historic buildings is but a fraction of the work it has in mind and confidently hopes to achieve'. During the late 1930s Jim also wrote a series of 'autobiographical sketches' which survive in manuscript, describing episodes of his childhood and schooldays: this was his first attempt at a literary form he would later employ in *Another Self* (though the humour and surrealism of *Another Self* are lacking in the earlier effort). He showed these essays to a new mother-figure in his life, Doreen Colston-Baynes, a successful writer of popular history under the name of Dormer Creston, who told him that he had great potential as a creative writer but so far 'lacked technique'.

In 1937 Jim was elected to Brooks's Club, his proposer being Tom Mitford and his seconder, Eddy Sackville-West. He was to remain a member for sixty years; but looking back in old age on his pre-war experiences there, his memories were not altogether rosy: the atmosphere was stuffy; it was not easy to get to know other members; the old constantly put the young in their place; the committee, reflecting the prejudices of Jim's father's generation, seemed rather ashamed that they were inhabiting a fine Georgian building, and certainly had little idea how to care for or embellish it. The annual subscription of fifteen guineas was a sacrifice for him, and he was grateful whenever prosperous fellow-members, technically breaking club rules, treated him to meals. Nevertheless, Jim loved the club's antiquity, its Whig traditions, and the fact that most of the members could be described as gentlemen, almost half of them peers or the sons of peers. As a bachelor living in modest rooms, he enjoyed using the club's facilities, especially at weekends. Best of all he loved the library with its tradition of absolute silence. As he wrote in 1944:

> I am always happy in this stuffy, dingy Victorian library, in which the silence is accentuated by the relentless ticking of the old, stuffy clock. I love the old stuffy books on the stuffy brown shelves, books which nobody reads except Eddie Marsh, and he falls fast asleep over them. The very atmosphere is calculated to send one asleep, but into the gentlest, most happy, nostalgic dreams of nineteenth-century stability, self-satisfaction and promise of an eternity of heavenly stuffiness, world without end. How much I adore this library, and club, nobody knows.

As war-clouds gathered, Jim took on various odd jobs on behalf of the National Trust. The Country Houses Committee decided to propose a 'supplementary list' of about one hundred houses to the 'approved list' of 1936; and Jim was deputed to discuss this with George Chettle, the 'whimsical' Chief Inspector at the Office of Works, who seemed to treat the whole matter as a tremendous joke. He was also deputed to organise exchange visits between the National Trust and the *Demeures Historiques* of France and Belgium. These were mutual self-help associations of chât-eau owners which sought to obtain tax concessions from their respective governments; they had long been cultivated by Paul Methuen, who hoped that something similar might be established in England (though the British Government's 'Scheme 2' of 1936, which had proposed the setting up of an analogous association of English owners under the National Trust, had aroused minimal interest). In July 1938 a party from the two *Demeures* visited England as guests of the Trust and, basing themselves in Bath, spent ten days touring country houses and being entertained by their owners. Jim, who spent months planning the tour, had nightmare visions of the foreign visitors following their custom of formal presentations and elaborate speech-making on meeting the English owners: fortunately he managed to prevent such jarring occur-rences, and the visit was a success. In July 1939 he conducted a return visit to Belgium, the party including several of his own friends such as the Methuens, the Rosses, Kathleen Kennet, 'Puss' Milnes-Gaskell and Paul Latham, and the itinerary including a formal reception by King Leopold III. This too was a success (though the King rather disappointed the visitors by his banality), and Jim was asked to look into the possibility of a similar visit to Portugal in July 1940 (by which time English country house owners were no longer going anywhere except on active service, and the Belgian châteaux where Jim and his friends had been entertained were receiving a different species of visitor).

The summer of 1939 also saw the last of Jim's pre-war love affairs — with a handsome young American friend of Harold Nicolson visiting London, Stuart Preston. The rich and erudite Stuart hailed from New York's 'Irish aristocracy' but was himself a passionate Anglophile; armed with dazzling looks, charming manners and a seductive baritone voice, he arrived in England hoping to take both Society and the literary world by storm. Meeting him at Harold's, Jim found his social ambitions slightly absurd, but was also envious of his success — within a few weeks Stuart had succeeded in meeting and delighting many of the great and good and penetrating some splendid houses which Jim had yet to see. But Jim too was conquered by him — though their brief affair may have meant more to Stuart than to Jim. Back in America on the eve of the European war, Stuart wrote to him:

> Whatever may happen, I have known and still know one perfect thing . . . Oh the folly of not stopping over another week in August when I could so easily have . . . How many things there were to say and thrash over . . . I should like to talk over everything in the world with you . . . Your medal is beside me . . . Dear Jim, it cheers and saddens me to think of you.

6

Soldier Blue

1939–41

———•———

J IM GREETED THE outbreak of war in September 1939 with gloom
and despair. Three and a half years after he had joined the staff of
the National Trust, its Country Houses Scheme at last seemed to be
gathering momentum, with half a dozen splendid properties effectively
promised under it and another half-dozen looking fairly hopeful. And
now the machinery ground to a halt. Apart from matters in progress, it
was decided to suspend the work of the Country Houses Committee, and
dispense with Jim's job: his last act of service was to help Matheson move
the office from Buckingham Palace Gardens (situated next to a military
target) to two Lutyens pavilions in Runnymede, Surrey. (These turned
out to be cramped and unsuitable, and within days it had moved again,
to a house coveted by the Trust – West Wycombe.) What depressed Jim
even more than the abrupt termination of his work was an awareness that,
thanks to the war, the general outlook for England's country houses was
bleaker than ever. They were at risk not just from enemy bombardment
(which was to destroy one house the Trust hoped to acquire and damage
several others*), but also from the fact that, on the outbreak of hostilities,
most owners of large residences ceased to live in more than a corner of
them, being obliged to hand over the rest to institutional tenants (of
whom units of the armed forces were generally the worst) who were
unlikely to pay much attention to their care and preservation. At the same
time, confiscatory wartime taxation threatened to complete the financial
destruction of the landowning class. Jim foresaw the ruination of the
work to which he had hoped to dedicate his life.

A pacifist by nature, he also had doubts about the morality of Britain's
declaration of war on Germany. However, two close friends whose
judgement he respected, Harold Nicolson and Robert Byron, persuaded

---

* This is not to mention the vast devastation which the war was to cause to Britain's urban
architecture, the historic buildings destroyed including several Trust properties such as
the Bath Assembly Rooms.

him that the use of force to restrain Hitler, who threatened the peace of all Europe, was a lesser evil than supine inaction. Both these mentors hoped that the war might lead to a new era of international cooperation; and Robert founded a 'Federal Union Club' in London to promote the concept of a future world government, which Jim duly joined. (It became something of a joke, as its leading lights were mostly upper-class aesthetes such as the Rosses, the Antrims, Sir Michael Duff and John Sutro, and its principal activity during 'the Phoney War' was holding cocktail parties.) One factor which made it easier for Jim to reconcile himself to the conflict was the Nazi–Soviet Pact which had preceded the invasion of Poland: as far as Jim was concerned, if Hitler was not the devil incarnate, he was certainly now in league with him.

Another worry for Jim was that Rick Stewart-Jones, with whom he was still living at Cheyne Walk, suffered a nervous breakdown, caused by guilt over the fact that he had been responsible, as a Chelsea borough-councillor, for the corporation failing to build any air-raid shelters: convinced that war would not come, he had used the funds earmarked for the shelters to buy housing for the poor and elderly. Jim did what he could to console his lover, who soon recovered sufficiently to enlist as a gunner in an anti-aircraft battery in Dorset. Meanwhile, Jim – who at thirty-one was not liable for immediate call-up – joined the Red Cross and was posted to a Civil Defence detachment at West Brompton. A photograph of his detachment shows eighteen women of various ages in nurses' uniform, two elderly gentlemen in suits, and a solitary young man – Jim. When not training as an ambulance-driver and stretcher-bearer he had little to do, as until April 1940 no British forces were engaged on land and no German war planes appeared over England.

Jim had some experience of organising exhibitions for charity, having set up a 'country houses exhibition' in aid of the National Trust in 1937. During the first months of the war he helped mount an exhibition in Richmond of divers works of art depicting or connected with that borough for the benefit of the local Red Cross. This gave him the idea of organising a similar Chelsea exhibition in the main rooms of the house in Cheyne Walk (which he was helping Rick's sister Dione manage in Rick's absence): it was to be in aid of the Finns, whose gallant resistance to the Russian invasion of their country in the last weeks of 1939 had caught the imagination of Londoners. Through 'Puss' Milnes-Gaskell, his friend at Court, he arranged for Princess Helena Victoria, a granddaughter of Queen Victoria, to be the exhibition's patron and for some Chelsea scenes from the Royal picture collections to be lent. Augustus

John and other Chelsea artists lent samples of their work. The exhibition occupied Jim from February to April 1940. It proved rather an Alice-in-Wonderland exercise, for while it was being put together the Finns surrendered, and by the time it was opened by the Princess on 16 April the war had begun in earnest, British forces having become engaged in bitter fighting in Norway. Queen Mary came to see it when in London from her wartime retreat at Badminton, Jim finding her 'rather splendid and awful'. It raised £237 for 'Finnish Relief', £30 of which was repaid to Michael Rosse who had advanced that sum for the exhibition's expenses.

At February's meeting of the exhibition's organising committee, Rosse had urged Jim to join him in the Irish Guards: the regiment had many Roman Catholics among its officers, and Rosse was confident of being able to get him in through his personal connections. At the time Jim demurred, as he still hoped, when the time came, to go out to the scene of battle as an ambulance-driver. However, in mid May, with the German invasion of France under way and Britain in a state of national emergency, it was announced that all able-bodied men between the ages of eighteen and thirty-six who were not in reserved occupations or regis-tered as conscientious objectors would be required to serve in the armed forces, service with the Red Cross no longer being an option for this age group. A few days earlier Churchill had become Prime Minister and Jim's two great mentors had taken office in his coalition government, Lord Lloyd as Secretary of State for the Colonies and Harold Nicolson as Parliamentary Secretary at the Ministry of Information. Jim appealed to them both to use their influence to have him exempted from military service, as he had just completed his Red Cross training and felt he would be of far more use as a humanitarian auxiliary than as a soldier. Had it been possible to obtain an exemption for him, Harold would in fact have liked to engage Jim as his private secretary; but the rules were now strict and he was told he would have to join the Army. Michael Rosse was still working on his behalf, and at the end of May he applied for a commission in the Irish Guards and was immediately gazetted a temporary ensign.

As Jim awaited his call-up, Rick returned to Cheyne Walk, having been granted sick-leave following an attack of appendicitis: he arrived back in London on the final day of the now somewhat irrelevant 'Chelsea Exhibition for Finland'. While the world crashed in ruins, with the defeat of France and the evacuation of the British Expeditionary Force from Dunkirk, Jim and Rick seem to have enjoyed something of a second honeymoon. In 1951, the year they both married, they returned each other's letters; and Jim kept those he had written to Rick from June 1940 onwards, for as he wrote in one of them, 'I do think our comments on military life from 2 essential civilians may be of interest in future years'. They also reveal other aspects of Jim's life at that dramatic time, not least his love for Rick which he proclaims with unusual frankness, addressing him affectionately as 'Rockling', 'Rocko' or 'Rock' (while signing himself 'Jabs'). The first surviving letter is written from Brooks's on 18 June, just after Rick had returned to his unit in Dorset and just before Jim was due to leave London to join the Irish Guards Training Battalion at Lingfield, Surrey.

> Dearest Rocko, imagine my disappointment yesterday when I got back [from Wickhamford] to find that you had gone. I felt very sad and had some tea with Nanny who told me about the latest disaster – the French capitulation . . . My aunt has given me 21 guineas to pay my club subscription (hence my being here today for lunch) and will pay for my uniform . . . My father is really angry at my going into the Guards and kept quoting you as an example of pluck, guts, etc. for going into the ranks; in other words a subtle rebuke of me for being extravagant – not that it will cost him personally one penny . . . Although I am terribly sad without you and miserable to think how seldom we may now see each other, I am at least happy at the recollection of these three weeks we had, almost the best ever. I could not exist without you and it is almost disturbing to realise that my feelings are absolutely unchanged since March 1st 1938 . . .

> *Lingfield, 27 June.* My dearest Rockling . . . How I wish we had gone into this together for there are several lots of brothers and friends here who have come in together and are allowed to share rooms . . . The little I have so far seen of the men makes me hate the Army and its appalling social distinctions . . . Here the men seem to be treated like helots, and tho' the officers are certainly efficient and according to their aristocratic 18th century standards strictly just and impartial, to hear the men being treated like slaves and abused by bloody NCOs makes me sick . . . Then the honeyed way in which the NCOs have to address officers is such unnatural, maudlin nonsense. Just because we are officers, however incompetent – and I shall never be competent I know, for I simply cannot order people about and curse them for a slip . . . The other thing I intensely dislike is bayonet drill and lectures on firing guns of whatever kind. I cannot disassociate from my mind the fact that this cold-blooded instruction is for the purpose of shooting men's brains out and sticking knives into them . . . Apart from this I am really quite happy. There is a great deal to do and so much healthy drilling and out of door work that one becomes very tired physically . . . So far I have made no friend . . .

Lingfield, 1 July . . . I am not a social success [with fellow officers]. I don't know what to say to them and most of them are much younger and very huntin' and shootin', the rest just rather m.c. [middle-class] and boring . . . A ghastly experience happened last night. Certain officers of my Company had to go out with a section on Road Block duty between 10 and 12 p.m. I as a new officer was to have gone with a senior officer just to see how it was done. When I arrived on parade I was told to my dismay that my senior officer would not be coming, and I was to order the section to right about, march, form fours and entrain in the track. I endeavoured to learn it by heart from the officer commanding the section before me, but when my turn came I could not remember it all and suddenly became stuck and tongue-tied. To my undying humiliation I then had to ask the Corporal, whom I was supposed to be drilling with his men, what the next order of command should be. When we arrived at our post I just told him to carry on himself, while I tried to regain my lost dignity by silently walking up and down & occasionally throwing out a terse comment to remind them of my presence. Most humiliating and this sort of thing does take years out of one's life . . .

Lingfield, 15 July. Divinest R, I loved yesterday and it was well worth the effort. Even seeing you for that short time has set me up. I just have to see you from time to time. I wish though you were more contented and in better health . . .

Lingfield, 22 July . . . I felt so unlike [*sic*] being back after the weekend [at Wickhamford] that after tea I borrowed a bicycle, put on battledress, and biked 20 miles with map in hand, eastwards. I went down luscious country lanes into the Eden Valley and then made for Chiddingstone, a small hamlet the N.T. bought a year ago. Typically N.T. it is bijou, olde and the timbered cottages claim to have been built of oak from the Armada. But the surroundings are lovely . . . It is a constant strain remembering one is in uniform. Even on my old bicycle this evening I could not quite escape from it, for while clambering over gravestones in Chiddingstone churchyard my gasmask bumped against me to remind me that I was an officer and must not forget all its beastly implications . . . Never a day passes that I do not think of you . . .

Cheyne Walk, 30 July . . . On Sunday I dined alone with Lloyd in his flat. He is in the Cabinet and so sees a lot of Winston, who he says is in very good form, happy and confident. Randolph whom I met in my club yesterday said the same. Lloyd too was confident. He thinks the invasion will not come off but that fighting will ultimately develop in the East . . . Yesterday as I was up here I went to the National Trust Annual Meeting – a pathetic affair in the Society of Arts building. Very few people and that awful old Zetland delivering a pedantic and dead boring speech. The Trust is practically dormant now . . .

West Wycombe Park, 4 August . . . I came here for the weekend. It is rather refreshing to stay in a country house again with a comparative degree of comfort still: certainly good food (sucking pig for dinner wh I had never before tasted), a butler, early morning tea and one's bath turned on. There is only Helen [Dashwood] here . . . very companionable and an invigorating personality. Johnny Dashwood, now at the F.O. again and looking after Greenland and Iceland, came down for dinner last night and made my visit an excuse for copious whisky and port to wh I was not averse. He is a dear, nice, simple creature, and curiously good and religious-minded under a rather cloddish, rustic, back-slapping exterior . . . The N.T. here★ behave in an odd manner . . . Not one of them even considers West Wycombe an unusual, far less a beautiful house. Helen knows this and resents their boorish ignorance. Now W.W. is a beautiful place, each time I come here I am more sure about that. It is very lovely here now and this morning I walked round the park and lake amongst the swans, classical temples and Greek statuary, reading and ruminating, while a faint autumnal mist hovered around. I wrote James [Pope-Hennessy] a long letter disabusing him of his theories about my guardsmanship. I am still alas only too pacifist for words and in no way can I put my heart and soul into this utterly hateful Army life. How I long and pray for the end of it, to get back to my old interests, for you to be happy and safe meanwhile, and indeed happy and contented afterwards . . .

Lingfield, 16 August. Dearest Rock, it looks as though a new phase of the war has begun with all these tremendous air battles. I must confess in a sense that I welcome it, for anything seems preferable to a stagnant war. It is rather terrible however to think that places like Wickhamford and Leckers [Leckhampton, the Stewart-Jones country house in Berkshire] stand just as great a chance of bombardment as you and me. I went up to London to dine with the Rosses but found on arrival that they had not returned from Ireland. Instead I had a drink with Harold [Nicolson]. He said that the previous day when we shot down 78 planes the real number was 120 but the M. of I. did not dare announce the full figures for fear the public would not believe them . . . Last night was rather fun, for Midi and I arranged to meet at Croydon for dinner, as a place where both our buses converged. After half an hour there was a terrific explosion and the Aerodrome was bombed. We all went to look at it. There was a mass of flames and smoke and

---

★ It is not clear whether Jim is referring to the Trust's staff – then consisting of Matheson and such volunteers as were assisting him at the time – or the members of the Country Houses Committee.

considerable damage. I have been working out my finances & find I shall have practically nothing left to live on. I have given up drinks and am going to try & give up smoking too . . . It sounds as though they [the German bombers] are over London, I do hope not . . .

On 1 September, after ten weeks at Lingfield, Jim was posted to Dover, a town in the forefront of the raging Battle of Britain – it was being simultaneously bombed from the air and shelled from the French coast and seemed the obvious first target for the German invasion which was expected at any moment. What possessed his superiors to send Jim, who had not distinguished himself in training and was quite unprepared for any form of action, into this inferno one can but guess, as apparently no other officers from his batch went there at the time. In *Another Self* he gives a dramatic account (largely drawn from his letters to Rick) of the month and a half he spent there, and lightens this with a marvellous comic story – of how, drilling his men on the Western Heights, he managed, by giving some incorrect words of command, to march them over the cliffs, where they survived by 'clinging on to tufts of sea thistle and ledges of rock'. This episode (of which there is no mention in his letters) is unlikely to have taken place as Jim described it, for just after he arrived at Dover all outdoor drilling ceased in view of the double bombardment and imminently expected invasion: it seems to derive partly from a story heard from Michael Rosse, who had served at Dover earlier that summer, partly from his own humiliating experience at Lingfield described in his letter to Rick of 1 July quoted above.

Those apocalyptic weeks at Dover were both traumatic and exhilarating for Jim, who had hitherto led a fairly comfortable life and witnessed nothing in the way of serious violence. The worst aspect was the claustrophobia, for his company was largely confined to its underground fortress and only rarely was he able to get even a few hours' leave to inspect the bomb damage to the town and visit Tom Mitford who was serving with his own regiment nearby. A great blessing, on the other hand, was that, whereas at Lingfield Jim had met no officer with whom he felt much affinity, he now 'hit it off' with his company commander Simon Combe, as well as with his two fellow platoon commanders, one of whom, Patrick O'Donovan, became a firm friend. (On Patrick's death in 1981, Jim recalled: 'Ten years younger than I, he was gay, amusing, amused, very bright and clever, always with a smile and a giggle. A pious Catholic, yet ready to laugh at his religion. He really was adorable, and as queer as a coot in those days.') Jim's letters to Rick again give a vivid picture of this episode in his military career.

Grand Shaft Barracks, Dover, 2 Sept . . . My first reaction was acute depression at being confined to a small town with absolutely no chance of getting away . . . I am for some unknown reason the only one of my lot of officers to be sent here. Everyone else is comparatively seasoned. I have only just completed a very elementary course & have had no dealings with the men at all. Now I have a platoon of my own! . . . The first few weeks will I foresee have some terrifying moments of making a fool of myself. I must also say it is rather thrilling here too and will I think be an excellent way of being broken in to warfare, for it is undoubtedly the front line at present . . . There are raids the entire day long . . . AA fire never ceases and one watches huge formations of German bombers flying over the town and the shells bursting all around them . . . A number of our men have been killed by machine-gunning . . . It is rather curious just awaiting invasion, for we work on the assumption that it is coming any day. This afternoon I was taken round my platoon area, shown my weapon trenches and the likely places where I should have to repel the invader . . . These barracks were constructed to repel the Napoleonic invasion and are centered on the other side of the town to the castle, just above the harbour. They are surrounded by a vast walled moat with intricate thick walled tunnels and passages in the bowels of the earth which afford splendid defensive positions today. It was all made by French prisoners of war in the early 19th century and is rather impressive. Dover will either make me or break me. I am trying to take it as I wd were I to be thrust into a monastery: reconcile myself to strict obedience and hard work with no communication with the world as I know it . . .

Dover, 10 Sept. Dearest Rock, during the last few days all kinds of dramatic things have happened . . . We have suspended all training and live on an imminent emergency system; we sleep at our posts and in fact are absolutely prepared for the worst at any moment now. The extraordinary thing is that I find it rather invigorating and hardly experience any fear, but a feeling of relief that at last things may be beginning to happen . . . But the long and short of it is that I fear any moment now I may be cut off from you for ever . . . Will you make a pact that if either of us shd become a prisoner of war the other will do his utmost to get in contact? Last night we were shelled for 6 hours – a curiously thrilling experience; I watched the flashes of the guns from the French coast quite clearly: then after 60 to 75 seconds the crash came this side . . . You wd be fascinated by our underground life. The fortress my Company lives in most clearly resembles the Alcazar. Today we spent assiduously converting it into a tolerable dwelling, clearing away debris, opening up original fireplaces and making our sleeping facilities, etc. as attractive as possible . . . Dearest Rockling, when shall I next see you? . . . I feel I might fight like a tiger if only it were with you . . .

Dover, 21 Sept. Dearest old Rocky, I was so delighted when your lovely long letter arrived and kept it all day unopened for the full enjoyment of it at leisure . . . We are still keyed up for the invasion . . . This morning for instance an order came through – 'Invasion at Dover expected at 1330 hrs. All men to be standing to at 1300 hrs, etc.' It was cancelled less than 10 minutes after issue . . . Thank goodness so far we four officers seem to have hit it off . . . the truth is that the 100% male is outside our orbit . . . There are certain unforgettable pictures of Dover which I shall always remember with aesthetic satisfaction. One is our Sunday morning Mass in a bastion which is a natural cathedral like a catacomb in which early Christians must have worshipped. With the oil lamps burning, the men all round in the gallery, their rifles and bayonets slung on the bare walls, the simplicity of the architectural construction and the hardiness, unaffectedness and sever-ity of it I find most moving . . . As for me, perhaps I have become a shade less frightened by and strange to the Army. At times in flashes I see the satisfaction that cd be got from leadership of men. But I am awfully bad still, constantly indecisive, frightened of my position and without self-confidence. Some of the men I do like a lot but I doubt if I shall ever be able to learn leadership. One thing I can say without false modesty is that since I have been at Dover I have not been a 'gloom' or felt cross with anyone. I am fairly resigned to my lot for the first time since the war . . . Poor London, the destruction must be pretty bad. Simon Combe, a brewer, heard yesterday that 112 Watney Combe pubs in London had been hit. Chelsea Hospital hit. What is one to think? . . . Dearest R., remember in your blackest moments that your continued existence in no matter what moods or conditions is quite essential to your devoted J.

Dover, 1st Oct 1940. I have been here a month now and am heartily sick of it . . . The invasion scare seems to have died down a bit. The shelling however persists and at times is rather disagreeable. But the confinement and the discomfort is getting us all down . . . One alarming thing is that we get absolutely no training here. I am sad that Patrick O'Donovan is going off in a week's time to the 2nd Battalion. He is the only person I have yet met in the Army to whom I can talk rationally. Dover is getting very mutilated. London sounds so ghastly. The Ormond Street Hospital was hit so I suppose the SPAB may be injured. I think I told you that for the last 3 weeks I have been sleeping in the dungeons with the men. I hear them talking and singing amongst themselves as though I was not there, and it makes me wonder how on earth you can endure their society for a year . . . Many of them I like quite a lot but I realise that many are out to get away with doing as little as they can – I don't blame them – and with tacitly making a fool of anyone in authority over them. I suspect they think I am rather soft and gullible. In fact I am as bad a soldier as ever in all respects and every single officer young and old is more self-confident and efficient than me . . . The war will obviously not end for years and is generally going against us I feel. If we finally win after a great length of time I suppose we will again muck up our chances as before . . . Dearest, dearest R., I am so devoted to you. The war will end one day . . .

On Thursday 17 October Jim's company was finally relieved after seven weeks at Dover and returned to Lingfield to await reposting. The following day he went to London for his first leave in two months. He was shocked at the transformation of the capital during that time. 'The damage inflicted is appalling. Lovely St James's, Piccadilly is a wreck. So is St Anne's, Soho. Carlton House Terrace has 2 or 3 houses in ruins. St James's Sq, Grosvenor Sq and the north (one of the old sides) of Berkeley Sq gone. Holland House quite destroyed. Howard de Walden's house, Belgrave Sq, hit. In fact there is no single square or street that has not some tragedy of this kind. As though the late Bishop of London & the LCC* had not already done enough destruction.' After collecting his new uniform and visiting the shaken residents at Cheyne Walk, he went to spend the weekend at Wickhamford – a frustrating journey as the trains were hours late in both directions. When he returned to Paddington on Sunday night an air raid was in progress; there being no taxis, he put on his steel helmet and started to walk with his bag to a club where he had arranged to meet a fellow officer who was driving back to Lingfield. Crossing Hyde Park Square, he heard 'the familiar whine of a falling bomb', and crouched for safety under the portico of the nearest house. The blast threw him some ten yards across the street, where he picked himself up in a daze beside the railings of the square gardens. It was a narrow escape: the house received a direct hit and was more or less demolished, little more than the portico remaining intact.

Somehow he managed to keep his appointment and return to Lingfield, but within a few hours of arriving there he began to experience fainting fits and blackouts and was confined to the barracks infirmary. 'I feel so utterly humiliated being reduced to bed here over a trivial cause,' he wrote to Rick. At the beginning of November he was given a week's sick-leave and returned to Wickhamford where, to his delight, he was joined by Rick. But illness and inactivity had induced depression, and he was filled with gloom about the war. Passing again through London, he

---

*The London Diocese and London County Council were among the *bêtes noires* of the Georgian Group: Robert Byron had denounced the Bishop, who had shown himself indifferent to the fate of much fine Georgian architecture near Westminster Abbey, as 'a mitred serpent'.

saw Robert [Byron], who was fairly cheerful, and dined with Harold
[Nicolson], also quietly optimistic. How can they be? How can there be a
clear-cut victory for us and how can people of intelligence envisage any
cheerful outcome? Harold was as charming and fatherly as ever – I do care
for him – but his views are far from mine. We walked in the moonlight
through devastated Bloomsbury streets back to his Ministry of Information
where he lives now. I remarked, 'Poor London, I am fond of her now'.
Harold replied, 'I am proud of her scars' in such a 1914 manner of gleeful
patriotism that I was horrified. I returned to Cheyne by tube & saw the
people lying in heaps along the platform and even sprawled upon the
staircase up to the topmost step. It is a terrible sight but they were all most
cheerful and wonderful. But can this spirit survive the winter?

Jim rejoined his company, now posted to Northwood in Middlesex,
and resumed his duties, but suffered from 'woolliness of mind and
incapacity to take things in or concentrate'. The district was being
severely bombed, and whereas at Dover he had been 'more or less indifferent' to the noise and danger, he was now made anxious by it, especially
after a bomb destroyed a house only fifty yards from the one he was
billeted in, killing the inhabitants. His blackouts soon returned, now
accompanied by painful spasms in his left leg. By the end of November
he was again on leave in London, staying at Cheyne Walk while awaiting
instructions from an army medical board. He saw various friends –
Hamish Erskine, Midi Gascoigne, Anne Rosse, Gabriel Herbert – but
continued to feel anxious and depressed. 'Really, there are so few
incidents of my past life that on reflection do not strike me as abjectly
shaming that I feel almost too ashamed to appear in the streets for fear
that people I know will suddenly jeer at me for some folly committed in
their presence in 1930 . . . Was there ever such an unfulfilled life as mine?'
He also suffered from amnesia, being 'unable to remember what I was
doing yesterday, what a familiar face's name is, what the last book I
finished was about'. On the evening of 29 November he was sitting
'ruminating' with Nanny at Cheyne Walk when a series of deafening
explosions took place very close to the house, smashing most of the
windows, bringing down heaps of plaster, and causing cracks in the walls
– but leaving the inhabitants uninjured and the structure intact: for the
third time in less than six weeks, Jim had a lucky escape.

He spent the next ten months in and out of five military hospitals while
the army medical authorities attempted to discover what was wrong with
him. It was a frustrating experience, for apart from his periodic 'absences',
and the trouble with his leg which at times became severe, he felt fairly

well physically, and dreaded being considered a 'funk'. Finally, at the Birmingham hospital where he spent June and July 1941, he was diagnosed as suffering from Jacksonian Epilepsy and advised to 'go rather easy for a year or so . . . They told me that had I not been messed about by Army doctors during the past year it would not have got such a hold as it seems to have now.' The condition, which was controllable by drugs (which he continued to take for the rest of his life), was also one from which his mother suffered, and Jim's main fear (which proved unfounded) was not so much of the physical effects of the illness as of the possibility that he might be destined for the 'vagueness of mind' into which she had descended. His prevailing gloom was not improved by the war news: from his hospital bed he was appalled to hear Churchill's broadcast welcoming the Soviet Union as Britain's ally.

He spent most of his time in hospital reading: during his seven weeks in Birmingham he claimed to have read twenty-four books, including such weighty tomes as George Eliot's *The Mill on the Floss* and Meredith's *Diana of the Crossways*. He also wrote an autobiographical novel entitled *Dust and Ashes*, no trace of which survives: it was his second experiment with this form, after his 'autobiographical sketches' of 1937–8. (The third attempt, almost thirty years later, would produce *Another Self*.) He showed the manuscript to Eddy Sackville-West, who replied that 'I should be untrue to you if I told you that I thought *Dust and Ashes* a good or even a presentable book'. He did however admit that 'the characters are acutely observed' and 'you feel it all intensely and seem to have the power of making your reader feel with you'. Jim's mother, on the other hand, thought it quite brilliant, and was flattered by the portrayal of herself. Her main criticism was that the characters were too obviously based on their originals, which risked causing offence to those (such as the vicar's wife) who were unflatteringly portrayed. She also objected that 'anyone reading the book might jump to the conclusion that you came of a very old established family'. (The same might be said of *Another Self*, whose readers are given little clue to the fact that the author's family was 'in trade' and had settled in the county just before his birth.)

In April 1941, after being discharged from his third hospital, Jim was distressed to learn from Harold Nicolson that Robert Byron had lost his life at the end of February when the merchant ship taking him to Cairo, where he had been appointed correspondent of the *Sunday Times*, had been torpedoed by a German submarine. This was not the first war casualty among Jim's friends: Midi Gascoigne's brother Brian O'Neill had been killed in Norway in the spring of 1940, Christopher Hobhouse a few months later in a bombing raid on Portsmouth (where he was serving in circumstances similar to those of Jim at Dover). Robert's death filled Jim with particular regret as their last meeting, just a few days before his sailing, had ended in a row. Jim had gone to say goodbye to him at the Great Western Hotel where he was staying, but Robert was in a bad mood and made various provocative remarks, notably to disparage Lord Lloyd who had just died, aged sixty-one, of a sudden illness brought on by overwork. Jim was in a state of frayed nerves, and in no mood either to argue with Robert or put up with his inevitable sexual pass. He stormed out of the room, followed into the hotel lift by Robert who proceeded to strike him in the face in front of a terrified American lady. 'I shall never see you again, Robert,' Jim declared furiously, as he picked up his cap. 'This is the end.' This had proved literally to be the case, and Jim mourned a friend whom he had loved for all his peculiarities. Soon after hearing this news he dined in London with an Eton contemporary, the dapper Peter Montgomery. That night saw the worst bombing raid of the war, during the first part of which Jim and his dinner companion lay half-clad in their uniforms on a bed in the Piccadilly Hotel: Jim's description of the episode (which saw his fourth narrow escape from death in six months) in *Another Self* ranks as one of the great descriptions in literature of the London Blitz.

During the first half of 1941 Jim grieved not only for a beloved patron, George Lloyd, and a beloved patroness, Jean Hamilton, but also for a woman he had never met – Virginia Woolf, who drowned herself in the River Ouse in March. He knew about her great love affair with Vita and had heard much about her from Harold, and venerated her as a writer. ('Oh how I wish I had seen her, even had a glance on a railway platform,' he wrote half a century later to Harold's son Nigel. 'She has been perhaps the greatest inspiration of my dull life.') While in hospital during the following months, he read (or re-read) most of her books. After his discharge from Birmingham he spent August 1941 convalescing at Wickhamford; and for four weeks, beginning on his thirty-third birth-day on 6 August, he kept a detailed journal, running to some 50,000 words, which is obviously influenced by his literary heroine – though he was leading a totally uneventful existence at the time, he minutely observes the small incidents of everyday life, with frequent disgressions into the past or his 'stream of consciousness'. As a literary experiment, it does not quite succeed: the long descriptions of trivial encounters and the mental processes they unleash are prolix and precious. But it is not without interest. It provides a vivid snapshot of life in a remote

English country district two years into the war. (What surprises is how comparatively little the conflict had yet changed his parents' way of life. They continue to live in the Manor, assisted by a maid-of-all-work, a gardener and the invaluable Haines; as a major in the Home Guard, his father continues to rule the local roost; food is still fairly plentiful, except for such commodities as eggs and sugar; the routine of exchanging visits with neighbours carries on much as before.) It contains some interesting set-pieces, including a visit to relations in Lancashire and the crash-landing of a Spitfire on the Wickhamford estate. It also reveals various things about Jim at that point in his life. He seems to be getting on quite well with both his parents (and they with each other) for the first time since his childhood. Physically he seems quite fit, except for intermittent trouble with his bad leg: he works in the garden, and goes for bicycle rides. On the other hand, he seems quite fragile psychologically, given to frequent bouts of what he calls 'angst'. Whenever he visits a building – be it a country house, an inn, or Worcester Cathedral – he analyses its architecture and associations; and he dissects the personality of everyone he meets, known or unknown, like a novelist. It was a useful preparatory exercise for the regular diary-keeping he would begin five months later (though whereas he would then be leading a hectic life, writing succinctly about fascinating encounters, he was now leading a life of idleness, writing interminably about trivia).

Jim left Wickhamford in September for his fifth and final hospital at Lichfield; as a result of tests carried out there, he was declared unfit for active service and formally discharged from the army at the end of October. Though it was a relief to give up a vocation to which he was manifestly ill-suited, he felt an abiding sense of humiliation that his military career had been so brief and inglorious and that he had been given so little opportunity to share the hardships of former regimental comrades. He had meanwhile seen something of former National Trust colleagues, on social visits to West Wycombe to stay with the Dashwoods and at the first wartime meeting of the Country Houses Committee in March 1941 which he had been invited to attend. Matheson told him that they were desperately short-staffed and would be happy to take him back if his services became available. On 6 October he saw Esher, who explained that the Trust had recently received several new properties and a host of offers under the country houses scheme, and that he was urgently needed back at his old job. Jim did not immediately seize this opportunity, feeling that he ought first to seek some official war-work: he applied for a position with the British Council in Lisbon (a possibility which may have been suggested to him by Lloyd, the Council's Chairman, before his death). However, he was rejected for this on health grounds, and on 30 October he wrote to Esher from Pixton where he was staying that he could 'quite conscientiously return to the Trust as soon as you are prepared to receive me'. (It is possible that Esher, that arch-operator, played a part in contriving both his discharge from the army and his rejection by the British Council.)

Thus it was that, in November 1941, aged thirty-three, Jim resumed his work as Country Houses Secretary after an interval of two years and two months. It was an unusual form of civilian employment in wartime, and one which Jim felt worth recording for posterity: on 1 January 1942 he began the diary which he would keep regularly for the next eight years.

7

'The Man Who Saved England'

1941–5

THE NATIONAL TRUST was still based at West Wycombe, to which (together with a maternity hospital and the Wallace Collection) it had been evacuated in 1939; and it was mostly there that Jim was to live and work for the next fourteen months. The first entry of his published diary begins[*]:

> West Wycombe Park is a singularly beautiful eighteenth-century house with one shortcoming. Its principal living-rooms face due north. The south front is overshadowed by a long, double colonnade which induces a total eclipse of the sun from January to December. Consequently we are very cold in winter, for the radiators work fitfully these days.

He was no stranger to the house, which he had visited before the war in connection with Sir John Dashwood's offer of it to the Trust. Though negotiations had foundered owing to lack of endowment, the Dashwoods had taken a liking to Jim and often had him to stay. Indeed, despite its institutional tenants and the shortage (less drastic than in many large houses) of servants, food and fuel, West Wycombe still had something of the atmosphere of a pre-war house party; and Jim joined a trio of 'paying guests', friends of the Dashwoods and himself, who were determined to entertain each other and have a jolly time. These were Nancy Mitford, who was convalescing after a miscarriage; her cousin Clementine Beit, whose husband, the millionaire MP and art collector Sir Alfred, was stationed nearby with the RAF; and Eddy Sackville-West. After dinner, huddled around the fire in the Tapestry Room, they would make humorous conversation while engaging in such pursuits as knitting in aid of the war effort. (Clementine once described the article Jim was attempting to knit as 'the true sock' which would unravel on St Milne's Day.)

[*] In fact, the original entry for 1 January 1942 begins with a characteristic moan about getting old; but Jim, on the advice of Rosamond Lehmann, cut this out before publication in 1975. (Diary, 1 January 1972; Rosamond Lehmann to J.L.-M., 16 February 1974, in Chatto & Windus archives, Reading University.)

At weekends they would be visited by friends from London such as the hostess Sibyl Colefax and the photographer Cecil Beaton, both of whom Jim met there during the first weeks of 1942. Presiding over the household was the imperious figure of Helen ('Hellbags') Dashwood, who deserved respect for her heroic determination to keep up pre-war standards, but was regarded warily by her guests owing to her haughtiness and inquisitiveness. (Nancy would later caricature her as Lady Montdore, the hostess from hell, in *Love in a Cold Climate*, in which Eddy also features as the intellectual hypochondriac Uncle Davey.) It was a blow to Jim when all three lodgers left in the spring of 1942, Clementine to move into her own house, Eddy to work at the BBC, Nancy to take up a job (found for her by Jim) at Heywood Hill's bookshop; though their departures enabled him to move to the warmest bedroom in the house, he had little rapport with their successors, mostly Foreign Office colleagues of Sir John.

West Wycombe was only half an hour from London; and Jim seems, during 1942, to have spent as much time in London as in Buckinghamshire. His work constantly took him to the capital, which was also the centre of his social life. If he wished to stay overnight, he could usually return to his old bed at either King's Bench Walk or Cheyne Walk. Then, in January 1943, London having been relatively free from bombing for eighteen months, the National Trust left West Wycombe and returned to its old headquarters in Buckingham Palace Gardens, obliging Jim to look for new lodgings. Owing to the general exodus from the capital it was still quite easy to find inexpensive accommodation to rent, provided one was not too choosy about its condition; and Rick drew Jim's attention to the fact that 104 Cheyne Walk, an early nineteenth-century house next to his own property, was on the market. Though no architectural gem, it was well-proportioned, and owing to its triangular position on the corner of Milmans Street it offered two different views over the river. Jim snapped it up, inviting the Trust's chief clerk Miss Paterson to become his lodger, and spending what small savings he had on hiring builders to make it habitable. This left him with no money with which to furnish it (the owner having removed everything movable); but friends came to the rescue by lending odd items. Ten days after moving in, he recorded:

> My house is settling down. The room with three large and long windows on the front faces the river and the big barge moored alongside. A fourth window at the west end faces Lots Road power station and the bend in the river opposite Battersea and the next bridge upstream . . . My glazed curtains have white sheaves of flowers on a cherry ground, and are torn

and shabby. The floor is parquet. In one corner beside an Adam hob-grate is the Empire bureau with fall flap on which I write this diary. Other pieces are my unsightly bed with hideous servants' pink cover; an upright winged armchair in crimson damask; a silk covered sofa of a different crimson; a mahogany half-circular fronted commode; an anthracite stove always burning in the other fireplace; Persian rugs; a large painted tin tray of Margate, *circa* 1850 over one chimneypiece. The room is thoroughly unpretentious and on the whole pretty.

The windows were still so grimy that he could hardly see out of them; but once they had been cleaned, the views were a constant delight. 'I have been sitting for an hour on my window seat looking at the cheerful river, with the evening sunlight dancing upon the wavelets, and at the gay motor boats, painted black and yellow, dashing down the river and growling busily . . .' Jim was to live at '104 Cheyne' for two and a half years: it was one of the war's consolations that it briefly allowed him, who spent most of his life living in other people's houses, to have a home of his own.

At West Wycombe the National Trust office had occupied Sir John's study, with the archives and secretarial staff in the Brown Drawing Room next door. For a year, after the call-up of Christopher Gibbs, Matheson had been the sole official in the office, until in the spring of 1941 he had acquired an assistant in the form of Eardley Knollys. Eardley was a pre-war art dealer whose friends included such contemporary artists as Duncan Grant and Graham Sutherland; as the son of a land agent, he had some knowledge of estate management. Jim was already slightly acquainted with him, as he was a friend of Eddy Sackville-West and Harold Nicolson (having been at Oxford with the former and admired by the latter). Eardley was to become one of the greatest friends of Jim's life; but the relationship developed slowly and they did not become close until after the war. Indeed, one of the first of the many expeditions which they made together on the Trust's behalf, to the archaeological site at Avebury, Wiltshire in April 1942, resulted in a sharp disagreement, as Eardley felt that the Trust's first duty was to preserve the prehistoric stone circle while Jim was far more concerned by the historic village which lay within it. Although they had many friends in common, their tastes and outlook differed in many respects: Eardley, who was on the fringes of the Bloomsbury Group, held atheistic and left-wing views which Jim could not share. But Eardley was one of those rare beings in whose company Jim felt totally relaxed and uninhibited; and they had a similar sense of humour, chortling together for hours about the houses they visited and the foibles of the owners. Apart from shared laughter another bond between them was that, while they did not fancy each other in the least, they felt able to confide in each other, over almost half a century, about their respective homosexual infatuations and love affairs.

The task Jim faced was daunting. Since the outbreak of war, four large country houses had come to the National Trust – Blickling, bequeathed on the death of Lord Lothian in 1940 while he was serving as British Ambassador to Washington; Wallington, finally donated by Sir Charles Trevelyan in 1941; Packwood, a Tudor mansion in Warwickshire 'restored' by the Ash family, Birmingham industrialists; and Cliveden, Berkshire, a Palladian palace on the Thames transformed into the last word in Edwardian luxury by the American-born tycoon Viscount Astor.* (Of these, Blickling and Wallington were of outstanding architectural and historical importance; Cliveden and Packwood had been much messed about by their rich owners, but were accepted owing to their fine parks and the generous endowments offered.) This, however, was merely the tip of the iceberg. During its first years the Country Houses Scheme had been of little interest to the majority of owners, who tended to see it as a sinister and socialistic ploy to relieve them of their property. On the whole it had only tempted owners who were either left-wing in their views (such as Trevelyan), so rich that the donation of a large house and endowment hardly dented their finances (such as Astor), or childless (such as Lothian). After two years of war, however, the situation was very different. In view of the requisitioning of properties, the disappearance of servants, and the egalitarian spirit which had swept the embattled nation (reflected in confiscatory levels of taxation), few owners could envisage ever living in their houses again in anything resembling their pre-war style. Indeed, for most the prospect of maintaining and inhabiting them at all seemed all but impossible for the foreseeable future. It therefore happened that scores of owners who had spurned the approaches of the National Trust in the 1930s began to see it as the only body offering a solution which might permit the preservation of their estates and the (at least partial) continued habitation of their houses by their families. All such owners up and down the land who had written expressing belated interest in the scheme, often making outright offers of their seats, had to be visited and their properties inspected; and this was the job which confronted Jim on his return to the

---

*Also Little Clarendon, a small but exquisite house in Wiltshire, was donated in 1940; and Hanbury Hall passed to the Trust the same year on the death of Sir George Vernon, subject to his estranged wife's life interest.

office. (Eardley was responsible for the management of existing properties – though he and Jim often co-ordinated their visits and travelled together, particularly in the West Country which Eardley knew well and where many properties, both actual and prospective, were situated.)

Of course, various factors impeded the Trust's acceptance of new properties; but ways of dealing with at least two of these were found during 1941–2. Under the original Country Houses Scheme, only 'listed' properties approved by the Office (known from 1940 as the Ministry) of Works were eligible – and many of the houses now offered did not feature on the current 'list'. However, 'Works' had already agreed to add several properties to the first list of 1936, and in 1939 Jim had been discussing with them the composition of a second list. Owing to the outbreak of war, the latter was never finalised or approved; but early in 1941 the Ministry announced that henceforth it would no longer bother with lists but would consider the suitability of each property on its merits – to the relief of Jim, who had always considered the listing process absurd. A more serious problem was that of endowment. Owners might be eager to donate their houses; but, apart from the seriously rich, few amid wartime uncertainties were willing to surrender substantial wealth in the form of land or cash in order to ensure future maintenance to pre-war standards. One of the first owners Jim visited after returning to his job was Earl Spencer, who contemplated handing over his seat at Althorp, Northamptonshire but changed his mind when told what endowment would be required of him, writing to Esher that, unless the Trust changed its policy, it should not expect to receive many offers. Esher heeded such warnings, and in a memorandum dated 17 February 1942 recommended that the Trust, when offered a worthwhile property, should for the time being insist only upon 'a minimum endowment . . . to keep the roof watertight and dry rot at bay', further upkeep being the responsibility of the donor family or other tenants. To the horror of the Trust's Treasurer (but the satisfaction of Jim, who had long pressed for such a development) this was eventually agreed to by the Country Houses Committee. Appropriately, one of the first properties to be accepted under the new rules – in April 1943 – was West Wycombe; Lacock, that other gem which had previously eluded the Trust on the endowment issue, followed in 1944.

The wartime progress of the Country Houses Scheme following Jim's return may be summarised as follows. Apart from West Wycombe and Lacock, a number of fine houses were handed over outright by their living owners, notably Great Chalfield Manor, Dinton House and Holt

Court, all in Wiltshire, and Gunby Hall, Lincolnshire. Sir Richard Acland, like Sir Charles Trevelyan an aristocrat with radical socialist views, donated his Killerton and Holnicote estates on Exmoor, mainly notable for their scenery but including several substantial houses. A few 'modernised' houses which in Jim's view were 'not up to our usual standard', such as Dorneywood, Buckinghamshire and Lindisfarne Castle, Northumberland, were accepted as their tycoon owners (following Lord Astor's example) offered them with 'preposterously large' endowments. Several splendid properties which the Trust longed to accept presented problems owing to their size, which imposed huge costs of even basic maintenance and made it unlikely that they would ever again be used as private residences: these included two houses near London, Ham House, Richmond and Osterley, Middlesex, and two in the north-west, Speke Hall, Lancashire and Lyme Park, Cheshire. A precedent which suggested at least a temporary solution to these problems was established when Liverpool City Council agreed to lease Speke from the Trust in 1944; subsequently the Trust felt able to accept Lyme to let it to Stockport Council, and Ham and Osterley to let them (with government support) to the Victoria & Albert Museum. (Though Attingham had not yet become the Trust's property, Jim similarly persuaded the Berwicks to let most of the house to Shropshire County Council for use as an adult education college.) Of those houses belonging to settled estates whose life tenants wished to donate them under the National Trust Act of 1939, just one – Hatchlands – was successfully transferred during the war. The transfer of two others – Knole and Coughton Court, Warwickshire – encountered legal problems and had to await judgments of the Chancery Division in 1945–6. Polesden Lacey, Surrey, an Edwardian jewel, came to the Trust under the will of the society hostess Mrs Ronnie Greville in 1942; and Charlecote was donated by the heirs of Sir Henry Fairfax-Lucy after his death in 1944. Attingham, Brockhampton and Stourhead had already been bequeathed to the Trust before the war by owners who were still alive in 1945; and during the war several other owners, such as Wyndham Ketton-Cremer of Felbrigg Hall, Norfolk and Lady Binning of Fenton House, Hampstead, arranged for their houses to pass to the Trust on their deaths. In addition a number of modest houses which had belonged to famous figures, such as Batemans, Sussex (Rudyard Kipling) and Woolsthorpe Manor, Lincolnshire (Sir Isaac Newton), were given to the Trust during the war, while George Bernard Shaw bequeathed his cottage in Hertfordshire and Ralph Vaughan Williams donated his estate in Surrey.

Given the conditions of war and the fact that the National Trust operated with a tiny budget and staff,* this was a considerable achievement – and it was largely Jim's personal achievement. In fact, during these years he effectively ran the Country Houses Scheme by himself, exercising his own judgement as to which properties were acceptable and on what general terms: that National Trust stalwart Professor G. M. Trevelyan thought he had saved the Scheme by returning to take charge of it. Nominally he was subordinate to Matheson; but Matheson's ill-health was now chronic and Jim deputised for him during his frequent absences from the office. Nominally, too, all decisions were for the Country Houses Committee; but its wartime meetings were infrequent, and Jim generally had little trouble in getting it to agree to what he wanted. On 24 February 1942, after taking a meeting of the Committee in Matheson's absence, he wrote that 'all went fairly well. The old gentlemen are so fearfully ignorant of the intricacies of most items on the agenda that one need have little fear of them. Besides they one and all are *so* nice.' In effect, Jim was responsible only to Esher; but between the two men there seems to have existed a perfect rapport. 'Esher said he had no quarrel to make with my plans and schemes,' he wrote in March 1943; and when, two years later, he proposed an administrative reorganisation, he was 'pretty confident that Esher, who is my consistent ally, will agree'. As for Jim's policy as Country Houses Secretary, he expressed this in a nutshell when he wrote in his diary that his loyalties were 'first to the houses, second to the donors, and third to the National Trust. I put the Trust last because it is neither a work of art nor a human being but an abstract thing, a convenience.' Both from sympathy with the families and because he believed it was best for the houses, he generally set out to help the former continue to live in the latter; but where a conflict arose, it was the future of the houses which was uppermost in his mind.

Jim's influence was largely exercised behind the scenes and it is not always easy to chart it from the records, particularly as he himself was always studiously modest about his role; but a few examples may give some idea. Gunby was a house which came into the Trust's possession largely as a result of his efforts. Since being built in 1700 it had descended through the same family, whose current representative was Lady Montgomery-Massingberd, married to the Field Marshal of that name.

---

*During the years 1942–4 the permanent staff was augmented by two – when Hubert Smith was taken on as Chief Agent, and Christopher Gibbs was demobilised and returned to his old job.

It had featured on the 'list' of 1936 but the Massingberds had not responded at that time. However, in March 1943, having already been disturbed by the creation of an RAF aerodrome on neighbouring land, they were horrified to learn of a proposal to extend the runway in a manner that would necessitate the demolition of Gunby Hall and the felling of all the trees in its park. In the process of contacting anyone who might help avert this catastrophe, the Field Marshal wrote to the National Trust. In reply, Jim pointed out that the Trust could only intervene if a threat existed to one of its own properties – or prospective properties. The Field Marshal responded that, if the Trust was able to save the house, his wife would consider handing the entire estate over right away. Jim made haste to visit Gunby. He was immediately enchanted both by the plain squire's house in its romantically isolated setting and by his hosts, 'true county squirearchy' who were the soul of kindness and decency; discussions seem to have been helped by Jim's friendship with the Massingberds' nephew and next-of-kin Peter Montgomery (though they had not made him their heir as they knew him to be 'not of the marrying sort'). 'They are such dear people', Jim wrote, 'that even if the house was worthless I would walk to the ends of the earth to help them.' And help he did. He got Christopher Hussey to publish an article on the house and the peril it faced in *Country Life*; he mobilised the Ministry of Works; he approached Sir Geoffrey Mander MP, donor of Wightwick Manor and now Parliamentary Private Secretary to the Air Minister Sir Archibald Sinclair. The upshot of these efforts was that within a month the Air Ministry had given an assurance that the house would not be touched and only a few trees would be topped. The delighted Massingberds were as good as their word and immediately set about donating the house and estate. When Jim next visited, in November, the formalities were almost complete; he was 'overjoyed that the Trust has been instrumental in preventing this dear old place from being razed to the ground'.

Gunby was a rare example of a house which passed to the Trust with a minimum of delay and fuss. In most cases, years elapsed between initial approach and final transfer, either because the donation had to await the death of the owner, or because (in the case of settled estates) heirs and law courts had to be consulted, or because practical problems (usually concerning endowment) had to be resolved, or simply because owners hesitated before committing themselves to the irrevocable act. During these intervals Jim often had to exercise tact and patience to keep prospective donors happy and prevent them changing their minds. Sir Henry Hoare of Stourhead, having made the National Trust the main beneficiary of his will, expected it to sort out during his lifetime every kind of problem affecting the estate it was to inherit on his death. When not in correspondence with the Air Ministry trying to limit their incursions onto the estate, Jim was writing to the Ministry of Labour begging them to release those the Hoares wished to employ as domestic servants. At one point, Sir Henry suddenly insisted that the Trust undertake to maintain his pedigree cattle herd, and Jim had to introduce this item at successive meetings of the Country Houses Committee until they granted assurances sufficiently firm to satisfy Sir Henry. Thanks to these efforts, Hoare remained steadfast in his intention to bequeath Stourhead along with an endowment of £100,000. Jim appeared to have less success with another eccentric Sir Henry, the 'arrogant and peevish' Sir Henry Fairfax-Lucy of Charlecote (who had refused to let him see inside the house in 1936). This sadist and bully, who resembled his wife's ancestor Justice Shallow in his pedantry, delighted in making repeated offers of the property, negotiating an adequate settlement, and then at the last moment raising some new condition which scuppered the deal. Jim came to dread the arrival of his querulous letters. The process of offer and withdrawal went on for eight years, until Sir Henry died in 1944. Jim's patience paid off, however, for the following year Sir Henry's children handed over the house without conditions (though virtually without endowment – it would probably have been refused but for Professor Trevelyan's eagerness to acquire it on account of its Shakespearean associations, and Jim's liking for Sir Henry's younger son Brian and his wife Alice who were to live at Charlecote).

Jim sometimes managed to secure houses for the National Trust in the face of opposition from heirs, trustees, professional advisers, even owners. One property he was determined to save was Knole, which was of interest to him not only as the greatest 'olden tyme' mansion in England but because of its connections with Vita and Eddy. (Vita, who had been brought up there, wished she had been born a boy so as to inherit it; Eddy, who rather disliked it, wished he had been a girl so as to avoid responsibility for it.) Eddy's father Lord Sackville wished to transfer it under the Country Houses Scheme, provided this could be achieved without too much financial sacrifice to himself; but his trustees were sceptical and his agent was positively hostile. Jim overcame their opposition by securing a deal which was so generous that it could hardly be refused: the Trust would let most of the property back to the family on a 999-year lease, and much of the endowment would come not from them but from the estate of Mrs Ronnie Greville, who had made the Trust her residuary legatee.

The agreement was announced to the press in the autumn of 1943 (though contingent on a court ruling exempting endowment funds from estate duty, only forthcoming in 1946). Another property of special interest to Jim was Coughton, seat of the Catholic Throckmortons, 'a thoroughly romantic house . . . the family associations – the papistry, recusancy, Gunpowder Plot and intermarriages with other Catholic families – are thrilling'. The life tenant Sir Robert Throckmorton and his heirs were far from enthusiastic about relinquishing the house, but unable to resist the wishes of Sir Robert's formidable mother, whom Jim befriended and encouraged. 'It is entirely owing to her that Coughton is to become Trust property, in the face of seemingly insuperable obstacles raised by the entail and the hostility of the Throckmorton family.' In the case of Holt Court, Jim persuaded the mentally unstable owner, a great-grandson of William IV, to hand it over without consulting his son, the harpsichord maker Tom Goff, who was serving overseas and not pleased to learn that he had been (as he put it) 'diddled out of his inheritance'.

Jim was often responsible not only for the National Trust's acquisitions but also for its refusals: he was perfectly capable of putting a spanner in the works if he disliked a house or an owner, even in the case of a quite famous property. Knebworth House, Hertfordshire had been built by the novelist-statesman Bulwer Lytton and had for generations been a noted centre of political hospitality. While admitting that it was 'a perfect specimen of a Disraelian Gothic mansion', Jim found it 'hideous' and its owner, Lord Lytton, pompous and patronising. Despite prospects of an ample endowment, it was rejected by the Country Houses Committee. Pyrland Hall, Somerset was a borderline case architecturally; but Jim 'cordially disliked' the owner Colonel Pemberton, 'a fiendish old imbecile' who offered him 'an exiguous lunch of bread and cheese, both hard as wood, a baked potato in its skin, dry as sawdust, and watery apple pie with Bird's custard – ugh!' It too was rejected. And Jim would doubtless have engin-eered the rejection of the mediocre Dorneywood had not its crafty owner, Sir Courtauld Thomson, secured the personal support of the Prime Minister (and earned himself a peerage into the bargain) by stipulating that the National Trust should make the house available to the government as a ministerial residence. But in the case of a really splendid house he was prepared to put up with much from a difficult owner. Lord Leconfield of Petworth, Sussex, 'a pompous old ass with a blue face and fish eyes', at first treated Jim, and the very idea that the National Trust might help him, with scorn. He offered Jim no refreshment, but on seeing him out by the street door pointed to 'a tea house with an enormous notice CLOSED hanging in the window'. But Jim, who was determined to secure for the Trust the historically fascinating house with its Adam interiors, Repton park and sensational collection of pictures and sculpture, 'decided to stress upon the feudal, reactionary Lord L. that during his lifetime he will not be disturbed in any particular . . . and by transferring now he will establish the only assurance that his successors can live at Petworth'. With patience, persistence, a generous offer of arrangements and the support of Leconfield's nephew and heir Jim gradually succeeded in putting across this point of view, and within two years of his first meeting with his lordship, Petworth had been made over to the National Trust.

Sometimes a donation was largely due to an owner's personal liking for Jim. Lady Binning (*née* Salting), heiress to a nineteenth-century Australian sheep-farming fortune, owned both the exquisite seventeenth-century Fenton House, Hampstead and a priceless porcelain collection. Jim went to see her in 1944 as, having left the porcelain to the V&A, she was thinking of leaving the house to the National Trust. Jim found 'an elderly, delicate, hot-housey lady' expressing 'ridiculous' views (she was outspokenly pro-Nazi and anti-Semitic); but so bowled over was she by his charms that she not only confirmed her intention to leave the Trust her house, but changed her will to leave it her porcelain too. 'It is nice being loved so much,' wrote Jim; it was all he could do to stop her giving valuable contents of the house to him personally, though he could not resist accepting a sixteenth-century book on Roman palaces. In the course of his visits to her, her generosity to the Trust became ever more munificent: when he admired the pretty garden, she decided to make further provision for its future upkeep. Jim also touched the heart-strings of several bachelor squires, such as Ted Lister of Westwood and Wyndham ('Bunny') Ketton-Cremer of Felbrigg (though his relations with such men were always correct): Lister seems to have vacillated for years over whether to leave his house to the National Trust or to Jim, though the latter's marriage eventually settled the question for good in favour of the former.

Writing in 2007 about Jim's wartime efforts to rescue a representative selection of the nation's country houses, Sir Max Hastings described him as 'the man who saved England'. If his achievement was rather less than this, it was certainly rather more than he himself would have us believe. At the end of the war, in a rare moment of candour, he wrote:

The lengths to which I have gone, the depths which I have plumbed, the concessions which I have (once most reluctantly) granted to acquire properties for the National Trust, will not all be known by that ungrateful body. It might be shocked by the extreme zeal of its servant, if it did. Yet I like to think that the interest of the property, or building, rather than the Trust has been my objective. I have to guard against the collector's acquisitiveness.

Of course, Jim's great weapon in his campaign of conquest was charm: it would later be said that he knew how to 'wheedle' houses out of their owners. At the end of 1943 he noted that, of the many owners he had visited, there were only two with whom he had 'failed to make friends', both crotchety individuals whose cherished properties were refused by the Trust – the 'fiendish' Colonel Pemberton of Pyrland Hall, and a pathetic old lady whose house was genuinely fourteenth-century, but a squalid ruin. In another moment of candour in 1944, after he had visited two contrasting households in Gloucestershire – those of the wealthy bohemian musician Violet Woodhouse at Nether Lypiatt Manor, and the impoverished 'bluff ex-naval commander' Bruce Metcalfe at Woodchester Priory – he admitted to an ability 'to adjust myself to different sorts of people . . . from the sophisticated to the simple, the rich to the poor, the clever to the stupid . . . Which means of course that I am a chameleon . . . a mirror of other people's moods, opinions and prejudices.'

Jim was not merely a rescuer of country houses during the Second World War. He was also a social historian, whose diary is noteworthy for its accounts of his visits to their embattled owners. He had the gift of conjuring them up, with all their dignity and absurdity, in a few words. Lord Hastings is 'a sort of Edwardian stage peer with a purple visage'. Lord Lytton is 'pompous, courteous in a keep-your-distance manner, patrician and vice-regal'. Lord Brocket is 'breezy and good-natured', 'amusingly convinced of his nobility' (he was the son of a brewer), and 'fundamentally stupid'. Old Lady Throckmorton is 'delightful, plain, unfashionable, intelligent, *très grande dame*'. Lady Trevelyan 'looks as though she may have been the first woman chairman of the LCC'. Sir Henry Hoare is 'an astonishing nineteenth-century John Bull hobbling on two sticks'. Sir George Leon is 'rather an absurd, opinionated man, but public-spirited and pathetically patriotic like so many rich Jews on this side of the Channel'. Field Marshal Montgomery-Massingberd is 'a little ponderous . . . yet very gentle and kind'. Mrs McGrigor-Phillips is 'a tall, ungainly, exceedingly coy woman, and a low-brow writer under the pen name of Dorothy Una Radcliffe'. Lord Fairhaven is 'a slightly absurd, vain man, egocentric, pontifical, and too much blessed with the world's goods'. The Duke of

Argyll is 'a short old man with white hair and a smooth white face . . . very eunuchy'. Lady Clementine Waring is 'a handsome and forbidding woman' who 'looks at one with the intensity of a psychoanalyst'. The nonagenarian Sir Lyonel Tollemache is 'courteous and charming . . . very sprightly and straight' but 'hopelessly defeatist, anti-Government, anti-people and anti-world'.

Needless to say, Jim was quick to notice evidence of sexual peccadilloes. He supposes Lord Lytton 'to be what my father would call "effeminate" by the well cut but long silver hair deliberately curled round the nape of the neck'. Major Greaves of Finedon Hall, Northamptonshire 'has photographs of smiling choirboys about the house and patted little boys on the head in the village'. At Smallhythe, Edith Craig's lesbian entourage dresses in men's clothes and uses men's names. Inspecting the house of one notorious peer, Jim finds a baby-faced American GI asleep in a double bed. The donor of Lindisfarne Castle, Edward de Stein, 'puts his arm round one's waist and makes rapid, sly remarks which I think it best to leave unheeded'. At Tredegar House, Monmouthshire, the heir has discovered 'instruments of the most bloodcurdling nature' in his late lordship's bedroom cupboard; Jim remarks that by throwing them out his host 'gave the dustmen ample opportunity of circulating scandalous gossip about the family'. A set-up which particularly fascinated Jim was Faringdon House, Berkshire, where the aesthete Lord Berners lived in apparent domestic harmony with his wild young paramour Robert Heber-Percy ('the *enfant terrible*, all right'), Heber-Percy's wife Jennifer and their baby daughter Victoria. 'I thought how enviable their ménage.'

Like La Rochefoucauld, Jim believed that one must laugh lest one should cry; and the eccentricities of owners provided him with material for humour and anecdote. Lord Berwick of Attingham is a spiritualist who thinks that ghosts have invaded the vacuum cleaner, while his neighbour, the orange-haired Lady Sibyl Grant, has moved out of Pitchford Hall, which she believes to be haunted, to live in a tree house. Lord Brocket takes Jim 'after hours' to the pub of the village he owns, where he 'beams, bows, and receives the homage of a dozen demi-mondaines and flash alfs'. Mr Frank Green, a 'wicked old tyrant' who receives Jim in bed wearing a nightcap with a bobble at the end of a string which flies around as he speaks, threatens to 'haunt him until his dying day' unless he restores the furniture at The Treasurer's House, York to its precise arrangement when Green donated that property to the National Trust. Over dinner at Stourhead, Lady Hoare remarks that in 1918 they were 'reduced to eating rats', prompting her husband to correct her: 'No, no, Alda, you get your wars wrong, that was when you were in Paris during the Commune.' The Trevelyans at Wallington force Jim to play intellectual games after dinner at which they score 100 per cent and he gets nought; they assure him he will do better next time, but he 'inwardly vows there will never be a next time'. During a pre-war dinner at Polesden Lacey, Mrs Greville hands her steward a note reading 'you are drunk, leave the room immediately', whereupon he sways down the table and presents it to that most sober and humourless of politicians, Sir John Simon. Lady Leconfield of Petworth is 'certified for descending in the lift at Claridge's stark naked'; when reprimanded, the lift boy protests that 'he could not see above her knees, she was so tall'. The Duke of Devonshire disapproves of Catholics because 'they put God before their country'. The blimpish Colonel Wingfield-Digby of Sherborne Castle, Dorset, who also hates Catholics (Jim remains tactfully silent during his diatribe), 'climbs to one of the castle towers and with a rifle peppers the ice to make it crack' when locals come without permission to skate on his frozen lake.

Yet when not making fun of the owners, Jim was often overwhelmed with sympathy for them. He admired those, like the Montgomery-Massingberds and Miss Talbot of Lacock, who felt so attached to their ancestral properties that they were prepared to part with them in order to preserve them, impoverishing themselves in the process. He pitied those who felt unable to cope with the modern world. At Lyme Park, Lord Newton 'is hopeless. The world is too much for him, and no wonder. He does not know what he can do, ought to do or wants to do. He just throws up his hands in despair.' The Newtons feel 'that their day is done and life as they had known it is gone for ever. How right they are, poor people.' Lord Braybrooke is 'at his wits' end' as to what to do with the Tudor palace at Audley End which he has just unexpectedly inherited along with his title. 'Who wouldn't be?'

One wartime privation which afflicted all owners was scarcity of servants. As Jim later wrote of the Hoares of Stourhead, who regularly sought his help in their desperate search for cooks and housemaids,

> for people in their position who had been born in mid-Victorian times and owned enormous houses, lack of adequate staff was a hideous depriv-ation. The husbands hadn't a clue how to turn on and off the central heating system. The wives often couldn't boil an egg. They were too old to adapt to their adversity. They could not move into the lodge with one servitor as ancient as themselves and leave the great house either to rot

or to fall to the mercy of troops, lunatics or Borstal boys. Their plight . . .
in many cases brought their grey hairs in sorrow to premature graves.

Jim admired those who coped stoically. At Elsing Hall, Norfolk, two
sisters, last of their line, have 'one indoor servant only', but 'in spite of the
terrible *délabrement* among which they live, these ladies with their long
Plantagenet pedigree, their courtesy and ease of manner, were enchanting'. At Kedleston, Derbyshire, 'whereas Lord Curzon thought he was
pigging it with thirty indoor servants', his nephew and wife make do with
'one woman for three hours each morning'. At Little Hempston Manor,
Devon, the Dundases, cousins of the National Trust Chairman Lord
Zetland, have sacrificed their health to keep the house going with no staff
at all; Mrs Dundas has not taken a day's holiday since the war began 'but
slaved all these years single-handed'. And he pitied those who could not
cope. Lady Leicester has suffered 'a nervous breakdown brought on by
the anxiety and worry of keeping up Holkham [Hall, Norfolk] with
practically no servants'; at Ham House, where all the staff have left except
for the cook, the middle-aged son of the house has taken on the role of
butler-caretaker and been driven to the verge of suicide by his impossible
burden. Yet some owners manage to retain a staff which, though reduced,
is adequate to run their houses properly and ensure a fairly comfortable
life: these include not just the very rich, but those living on feudal estates
in remote districts where ancient traditions of service survive. At the
Duke of Argyll's castle in the Highlands, 'the moment one leaves the
room, the ashtrays have been emptied and one's things straightened';
the Massingberds at Gunby, though frugal in their habits and strict in
their observance of wartime regulations, still employ a butler, cook,
pantry boy, two housemaids and a chauffeur in 1944.

Another aspect of wartime social history on which the diary casts
fascinating light is meals. Here again, there is much disparity: on the
whole, public-spirited aristocrats make a point of sticking to the rules and
serving sparse fare, while sybaritic plutocrats continue to entertain well.
Thus luncheon with the Spencers at Althorp consists of poached eggs and
cabbage, and with the FitzAlans at Cumberland Lodge of a bowl of soup
and a potato, while Sir Edward du Barry at Ockwells Manor serves a
hearty meal of roast beef and rhubarb tart, and Lord Fairhaven at Anglesey
Abbey a dinner of soup, lobster, chicken and savoury. Many owners, on
the principle of *après nous le déluge*, drink up the best wine in their cellars,
while the Massingberds at Gunby (to Jim's annoyance) eschew alcohol for
the duration. Another subject treated is wartime taxation. Lord Astor is

happy to endow Cliveden with an astronomical £200,000, as it brings him after tax a mere £150 a year. At Ham House, the nominally rich Tollemache family 'does not receive sixpence from each pound'. Lord Bradford lets the stable block at Castle Bromwich Hall for £100 a year, of which he is allowed to keep two pounds ten shillings. On the death of his nephew in 1943, Lord Gerald Wellesley inherits along with the dukedom an income of £40,000 a year, of which he manages (thanks to certain privileges granted to his family after Waterloo) to hang on to £4,000. (This confiscatory regime was of course to the advantage of the National Trust, which as a charity paid no tax on endowment income.) Another tribulation common to most wartime country house owners, concerning which Jim was sometimes able to help, was the requisitioning of their gates for scrap. He does not lament the gates of West Wycombe, 'very indifferent ironwork, about fifty years old'; but he manages to save the late Georgian gates of Stourhead (and thus pacify Sir Henry Hoare) by getting their historic value recognised by the Ministry of Works, just as he saves the William IV railings of Brooks's by appealing to members with influence.

Jim was moved by the plight not just of the owners but of the houses themselves, which take on almost human characters in the diary. If they were not falling into ruin through absence of servants and lack of funds, they were often being wrecked by the tenants foisted on them. At Blickling, the RAF have 'out of devilry' smashed the crown-glass windows and forced the locks of the stateroooms. 'This sort of thing is inevitable,' sighs Jim − though even he is shocked to find sarcophagi forced open in the mausoleum. Chawton House, Hampshire, once the home of Jane Austen, has suffered badly from the Barnardo children evacuated there. At Kedleston, American soldiers have stolen the door handles as souvenirs; at Picton Castle, Pembrokeshire the latest troops have removed stair balusters, kicked in mahogany doors, ripped up floorboards and caused flood damage. At Lyme, 'the park is cut to pieces by thousands of lorries'. Even the Hearts of Oak Benefit Society at Herstmonceux Castle have 'caused much damage' to contents foolishly left there by Sir Paul Latham. But such houses were perhaps fortunate compared to those which could find no tenants, and consequently suffered total neglect. By the end of the war two architectural masterpieces in the Richmond area, Ham House and Syon Park, too large and too close to London to have been of interest to either the armed services or evacuated institutions, were all but falling apart.

In his preface to *Ancestral Voices* Jim says that he has 'pruned' architectural descriptions so as not to bore the general reader; but enough architecture remains (bad as well as good) to delight enthusiasts as well as to give an idea of his own taste, which had developed considerably since he started work for the National Trust. Unlike the scholars of the SPAB, he is rarely impressed by antiquity for its own sake: 'It is extraordinary how quite intelligent people think that a house's site mentioned in Domesday is a better qualification than its architecture by Wren.' His preference is still for the refinement and regularity of the classical; as he exclaims on beholding the neo-Grecian Dinton: 'How splendidly proportioned, clean-limbed and precise this great house is . . . All my cravings for proportion, propriety and solving of architectural problems are satisfied.' But the former Georgian purist is now also fascinated by Victorian 'fakery', provided it is well done. Stragglethorpe Hall, Lincolnshire, 'a misleading, fakey sort of house', is 'not unpleasing'; Somerleyton Hall, Suffolk, 'a hideous red brick edifice of 1860', is 'fascinating and more than just a Jacobean pastiche'; Charlecote, a genuine Tudor house 'drastically altered' in the 1850s to make it look even more authentically Tudor, and at the same time stuffed with bogus Elizabethan relics, is 'amazing'. (When in 1944 Jim was asked by Cyril Connolly to contribute an architectural article to *Horizon*, he chose as his subject the great nineteenth-century *pasticheurs* Decimus Burton, Anthony Salvin and George Edmund Street.) The houses he likes best of all are those where interior, exterior, landscape and outbuildings express a harmonious whole; where everything speaks of the history and taste of the owning family; and which exhibit a variety of styles which have developed naturally down the ages. At the end of the war he identifies his 'dream country house in which I would gladly be incarcerated for the rest of my life' as Compton Beauchamp, Berkshire.

> It is completely surrounded by a moat, for romance. It has a pleasant, square courtyard, for shelter. The approach is by a symmetrical forecourt with two detached flanking stable wings, retaining wall, stone piers and magnificent iron gates, for grandeur. The principal façade is classical Queen Anne of rustic simplicity, for cosiness and dignity. The other façades are mediaeval and Jacobean, for historic continuity . . . It is a small paradise in the fold of the downs, with tinkling fountains in forecourt and courtyard.

'I once firmly believed in the permanency of human relationships,' wrote Jim on 9 March 1942. 'Now I know [impermanency] to be a fact, just as every physical creation is transitory.' This reflection may have been prompted by the fact that he had spent the previous day with Rick

Stewart-Jones, with whom he was slowly falling out of love after four years. They had wandered around the devastated areas of Chelsea. 'It is the slums in which he is most interested. I am not at all.' They remained quite close for the rest of that year: in May Jim joined the family at the bedside of Rick's dying mother; and in November he helped Rick organise a concert at Cheyne Walk, featuring Benjamin Britten and Peter Pears, to raise funds to buy railings to protect the ruins of Chelsea Old Church (on whose rebuilding Rick had set his heart after the war). But when in January 1943 Rick, now an officer, unburdened himself to Jim about his hatred of army life, Jim was frankly bored. 'For the first time I have known him I made an excuse to leave, and slunk home to bed.' Jim does not seem to have missed Rick overmuch when the latter was posted to Egypt in 1943; at their last meeting, Rick complained that Jim was going to too many grand parties in London.

By then, Jamesey Pope-Hennessy seems to have taken over as Jim's closest friend: 'there is no one with whom I can be happier,' Jim wrote in July 1943. They were bound together by numerous common friend-ships and interests, and spent exhilarating nights strolling among the ruins of London discussing life and literature, sometimes pub-crawling in disreputable districts in search of adventure. (Such escapades were more in Jamesey's line than Jim's, and the fact that Jim went along with them is a sign both of his closeness to Jamesey and of the frenzied wartime atmosphere in which one lived for the moment.) Jamesey could be mad-dening, with his self-centredness and indiscretions and habit of leaving Jim to pick up the bill; but Jim found him 'so engaging that . . . I forgive him all his trespasses'. Jim also saw something of Jamesey's mother Dame Una (now a widow) and brother John (then serving in the Air Ministry), and spent Christmas with them in 1943. He admired them for their clev-erness, learning and Catholic ethos, but found them rather forbidding and exclusive as a family group: when Dame Una suggested that he 'write a book and join us', he reflected that 'even if I could write a book I would not be permitted to join them, however much I might want to'. While sleeping with Jim, Jamesey declared that he wished to become a lover of women and sought Jim's advice on the subject: Jim assured him 'it was as easy as falling off a log'. Soon afterwards, Jamesey introduced Jim to the woman by whom he hoped to be seduced – Bridget (Lady Victor) Paget, a famous beauty of the 1920s whose lovers had included Edward, Prince of Wales. Fascinating though she was, Jim found her a strange choice, now in her fifties and a confirmed alcoholic and drug–addict. But although Jamesey believed himself to be in love with both Bridget and her teenage daughter Ann, he could not bring himself to go to bed with either. After a course of psychoanalysis he finally announced in November 1944 that he was 'to sleep with his first woman' and asked Jim to pray for him: he later telephoned to say that he was 'still alive' and that the experience had been 'quite easy but not riotous'.

Jim was at first delighted when another former lover, Stuart Preston, arrived in London in the last days of 1942 with the deceptive rank in the US Army of 'Sergeant attached to Headquarters' – he in fact had an intelligence brief to move in the highest English social circles and report on their attitude towards the American ally. 'I "saw" or rather "slept" – and not alone – the New Year in,' Jim wrote. 'Could there be a happier augury for 1943?' Within a few days 'the Sergeant' (as he became known to his English friends, to his annoyance) had dined with the Duff Coopers and gone to stay at Panshanger, Hertfordshire, with Lord and Lady Desborough. When he went to Eton to visit the Desboroughs' grandson, Jim accompanied him and was included in Stuart's invitation to lunch with the Provost, Lord Quickswood. 'Lord Q. was . . . full of solicitude for Stuart . . . who seems to be treated by all society as a lion,' Jim wrote. 'But then Stuart is attentive to the old and throws off anecdotes and literary quotations like pearls before swine.' In February, Stuart contracted jaundice. 'The whole of London congregates around the Sergeant's bed,' wrote Jim. 'Instead of meeting now in Heywood Hill's shop, the intelligentsia and society congregate in public ward no. 3 of St George's Hospital.' Jim had to jostle with Lady Cunard, Harold Nicolson, Logan Pearsall Smith and Stephen Spender for the favour of a word with the invalid. After his recovery, Stuart confided to Jim that Alan Lennox-Boyd, an earl's son-in-law and a minister in the wartime government (and a former lover of Jim), had fallen in love with him. By this time Jim had become tired of hearing about Stuart's conquests, a feeling not unmixed with envy. 'His social activities arouse the worst instincts in me,' he wrote on 28 July. Dining at Brooks's on 9 October they had a row, Jim accusing Stuart of snobbishness and Stuart accusing Jim of callousness. Although they made this up, their friendship was never the same again, and Jim responded rather coolly when Stuart came to see him on 15 July 1944 to say that he was leaving the next day to join the American forces in Normandy.

It was a relief for Jim to see old friends who returned safely from the war. He was distressed to learn in July 1943 that Hamish Erskine had been captured by the Germans in North Africa, and jubilant when he returned to England at the end of the year, having escaped from a prisoner-of-war camp in Italy. They celebrated with a drunken dinner at Brooks's at which Hamish related his exploits, 'treating it all as a great joke', and ended the evening at Hamish's mews house where they went to bed together. Another returnee in 1944, back from a tour of duty in the Mediterranean, was Tom Mitford: they had a joyous reunion, notwith-standing their contrasting views on politics and the war. (Tom declared himself to be 'an unrepentant Nazi', while Jim described himself as 'an unrepentant pacifist' who 'would prefer to live in a country of tenth-rate power provided there was peace and freedom of speech'.) For a few months, they resumed something of the close friendship of their adolescence – until Tom announced that he was off to fight the Japanese in 1945, 'for he does not wish to go to Germany killing German civilians'. A different kind of survivor was John Betjeman, who returned from neutral Dublin where he had worked for British propaganda and narrowly avoided assassination by the IRA; meeting him in 1944 for the first time since 1939, Jim was delighted to find him just as ever, 'jumping up and down in his chair and snapping his fingers in laughter . . . totally unselfconscious, eccentric, untidy and green-faced'.

The war, with its intimations of mortality, led to a loosening of morals and an explosion of promiscuity; and even from his discreetly expurgated diaries it is clear that Jim (though essentially romantic in nature) was not averse to casual flings when opportunities arose. During a train journey in 1943 he mused that, although one could simultaneously be in love with more than one person, indeed with both a man and a woman, such infatuations were 'damnable and devilish' and there was much to be said for 'unadulterated jolly old lust exclusively'. While waiting to meet Sir Henry Hoare of Stourhead in the lounge of the County Hotel, Salisbury he saw 'a young RAF sergeant . . . of ineffable beauty' who 'smiled in a most beseeching manner. He took out a cigarette, offered me one, and was about to introduce himself when, damn it! – Sir Henry Hoare was announced.' But one had to be careful. He had been shocked, in August 1941, to learn of Paul Latham's arrest and disgrace after 'pouncing' on his batman. 'I would write to him if I knew where,' he wrote to Paul's former worshipper Eddy Sackville-West, 'but . . . it might be unwise in his interests as well as my own.' Still, soon after Paul's release from prison in 1943 Jim went to stay with him at Herstmonceux, Paul having intimated that Jim was one of the few old friends he wished to see.

Jim continued to see his (platonic) women friends – Midi Gascoigne (who spent most of the war living with her children in one of the estate cottages at Wickhamford); Anne Hill (who ran the Curzon Street bookshop after Heywood's call-up); Nancy Mitford (who helped Anne run the bookshop, and was a constant source of merriment at grim moments) and Billa Harrod (whom he visited in Oxford). His published wartime diaries mention only two women with whom he was involved romantically. The first is a married society lady cryptically referred to as 'Q.'. She first appears in July 1942 when Jim takes her to dine at the Mirabelle, a restaurant he can ill afford, and later reflects that what they are getting up to in a taxi 'must have happened a hundred, no a thousand, no a million times'. On 9 January 1943 he treats her to a similarly ruinous meal at Prunier's, followed by a night at Duke's Hotel, St James's. Some weeks later, after another expensive dinner (to which she contributes £1), he is overcome with loneliness on parting from her at 11.30, and reflects: 'Every day I have a letter, sometimes a postcard too. There can be no mistaking their underlying meaning – which is now, and not for ever.' On one occasion she asks him to dine with her husband, which he feels he must refuse. 'Q.' is mentioned for the last time on 12 October 1943, when he telephones her and she answers in a voice of unconcealed excitement, 'Is that you, Terry?' – whereupon Jim gently replaces the receiver. After that, the woman Jim most often takes to dinner (and presumably to bed) is Bridget Parsons – 'ravishingly beautiful with her long, arrogant neck, golden hair, fair complexion and sulky mouth' – whom he loved as she reminded him of his adored Desmond.

In the final pages of *Another Self*, Jim writes that he was 'sustained' during the war by 'perhaps the most intimate friendship of the many with which I have been blessed' – with a woman a few years older than himself whom he not only never met, but of whom he did not even know the name. They encountered each other on a crossed telephone line: he liked her 'euphonious and clever' voice and called her back, having heard her give her number to the operator. This proved to be the first of many intimate conversations. They agreed not to identify themselves to each other, which would be 'a restraint' on their 'totally unguarded talks'. They discussed the war, the books they were reading, even their private lives – Jim heard about her unhappy marriage and the recent death in action of her only son aged eighteen. He came to depend on their talks, which usually took place late at night, and spoke to her almost daily – until one day his call was greeted with the siren wail of the disconnected tone, and he learned from the operator that the address corresponding to the number had been destroyed in an air raid: he did not hear from her again, or try to find out who she was. This story recalls Jim's epistolary romances with Diana Mitford and Anne Gathorne-Hardy, and the tale of 'Theo' whom (we are told) he met once aged nineteen and remembered longingly for the rest of his life. How far it is true is difficult to say. In *Another Self*, Jim says the telephonic affair began during the first half of 1941, between two of his hospital spells, and continued for 'just over a year'. The only reference to the 'affair' in his published diaries occurs on 17 August 1943, when it is described in obsessional terms.

> Neither last night nor the night before has the voice spoken to me. In the office today I hardly dared leave the room in case the telephone should ring. Whenever it did my heart jumped. And when the voice at the other end was not the right voice I was in despair. I could hardly bear it when colleagues were using the line in case my voice was trying to get through to me. And what am I doing now? Waiting again for the telephone to ring. I must snap out of it.

Jim's correspondence with his publishers reveals that the first entries of his original diary for 1944 also referred to 'the voice' – but his editor asked him to remove these references as no one who had not read *Another Self* would understand what they meant. If (as Jim alleged to the publishers) the 'voice' of 1944 was the same as that mentioned in *Another Self*, the affair seems to have continued for not one year but almost three. Quite possibly the story in *Another Self* (like others in that book) is drawn from several episodes which Jim either experienced himself or just heard about. (Perhaps some of the 'voices' were male rather than female, which would explain the need for anonymity.)

Jim continued to visit his parents at Wickhamford, staying with them on average once a month, though owing to the shortage of servants they let the Manor in 1942 to the local 'Land Army' and moved to their main cottage, Hody's. (These visits also enabled Jim to see his beloved Midi.) During these years Jim's relations with his father improved while those with his mother deteriorated. In 1942 he was still having rows with his father, such as one sparked off by George Lees-Milne's sneering reference to the Duke of Kent, who had just been killed in an air crash, as 'a pansy'. 'Words flew, as of old, as of old. I cannot, alas, stay here more than two days without allowing myself to be provoked beyond endurance.' But at Christmas 1944 Jim could report that 'my father has been perfectly charming, and companionable. I believe that by . . . showing sympathy for his not inconsiderable difficulties . . . I may at last have broken down his suspicion and reserve.' A few weeks later he was surprised when George, unannounced, paid him a friendly visit at Cheyne Walk, where they had a cosy dinner in the kitchen and talked of family history.

Meanwhile his formerly close relationship with his mother was being undermined by exasperation at her vanity, self-centredness and mental vagueness: possibly a subconscious fear that their shared epileptic condition might cause him eventually to share her scatterbrained state contributed to the gradual process of estrangement, as did the fact that wartime strains drove her increasingly to resort to the bottle. During the war, Jim saw little of either his brother Dick, who served as a major with the RASC in North Africa and Italy, or his sister Audrey, who contracted a second marriage with Cecil ('Tony') Stevens, a charming adventurer of whom her parents disapproved.

Jim remained close to the substitute father in his life, Harold Nicolson, their closeness reinforced by the fact that Jamesey was a fellow protégé of Harold. The three of them often dined together, such occasions some-times resulting in arguments about the war, which Harold, unlike Jim and Jamesey, regarded as a noble crusade. Otherwise they talked of literature – one of the first entries in Jim's diary records a memorable dinner during which they discussed Byron's sex life. Harold seems to have settled the bill after the dinner at Boulestin's restaurant which Jim gave to celebrate his thirty-fifth birthday in August 1943,* following which Jim returned to spend the night with him at King's Bench Walk, where Harold discoursed on the possessiveness of women and 'extolled the advantages of homosexuality and relationships between men, who allowed individual independence'. Of the other men and women of an older generation who had enhanced Jim's life during the 1930s, several (George Lloyd, Eva Cooper, Jean Hamilton, Mamie de Navarro) died during the war while others (Constance Ismay, Doreen Baynes) sat out the conflict far from London. He continued to stay with Ted Lister at Westwood and Mary Herbert at Pixton, and to visit Kathleen Kennet and Mrs Belloc Lowndes at their London houses. Jim was always fascin-ated to meet distinguished literary personalities; and during the war (as well as spending a day with George Bernard Shaw to discuss the donation of his 'very ugly' cottage, Jim recording his every utterance for posterity) he befriended two famous eccentric writers living in London – the English novelist Ivy Compton-Burnett and the American essayist Logan Pearsall Smith. With her greed for food, unexpected remarks and sparring relationship with her companion Margaret Jourdain, Miss

---

*Jim's guests were Harold, Stuart, Jamesey, Emerald Cunard, Joan Moore, and the novelist Henry Yorke and his wife Dig. It is significant that Rick (who appears to have been on leave in London at the time, as Jim dined with him the following day) was not included in the party.

Compton-Burnett provided good material for Jim's diary. The venerable Logan – a bachelor admirer of young men, whom Jim met through Stuart – had become a bit of a bore, given to repeating long-winded stories; but Jim became a devoted visitor and adopted several of the new words he had coined, such as 'swimgloat'.

Between 1942 and 1945 Jim was taken up by the rival hostesses Lady (Sibyl) Colefax and Lady (Emerald) Cunard: he first met Sibyl at West Wycombe where she was visiting Eddy, Emerald at the house of Lady Crewe, a *grande dame* cultivated by Jamesey. Both were elderly widows at this time, and though they had been entertaining in London longer than anyone could remember, neither was truly English – Emerald was an American from San Francisco, while Sibyl had been born in India and reputedly had Indian blood. Their common practice was to hold perpetual luncheon and dinner parties to which they would invite a wide diversity of people who had achieved note in their respective fields to see how they would get on. Otherwise they differed much: Emerald (the more intelligent of the two) was a mischievous personality who teased her guests; Sibyl (who had shown considerable initiative, after her family had been ruined in the Wall Street Crash, by founding the interior decorating business which still bears her name) was earnest and kind. Both carried on entertaining throughout the war as if their lives depended on it, Sibyl (who required her guests to contribute financially to the cost of meals according to their means) at her house in Lord North Street, Emerald at the Dorchester. They shared a reputation (as Jim wrote on meeting Sibyl) of being 'hell-bent on collecting scalps'; but this is rather belied by the fact that they both took Jim, who was of little social consequence, to their hearts. For his part Jim, who on first meeting them felt sure he would dislike them, soon became devoted to them both. When Rick expressed disgust that Jim was attending their parties, Jim excused himself by saying that he just went 'out of curiosity'. But apart from having the opportunity at their tables to meet a great variety of interesting people – of whom some (such as the conductor Malcolm Sargent and the poet-Viceroy Lord Wavell) provided good copy for his diary while others (such as the handsome Garrett, Viscount Moore, later 11th Earl of Drogheda, and his glamorous pianist wife Joan) became friends – he found much to admire in them. Sibyl, for all her absurdity, he discovered to be a gallant woman full of interesting social knowledge, while Emerald he considered a woman 'out of the common run . . . a rare and inspired talker' whose 'nonsense can be funnier than any nonsense I have ever enjoyed'.

Among the fascinating people Jim met with Sibyl and Emerald was 'Princess Winnie' (Princesse Edmond de Polignac, *née* Winaretta Singer [1865–1943]), the sewing-machine heiress who had for half a century been a leading light of Paris society and patroness of writers, artists and composers. Jim was especially keen to meet her as she had been an intimate of Marcel Proust, a writer Jim venerated. He evidently made a favourable impression on her, for within the space of a few weeks she invited him to several dinner parties at her Park Lane flat, during which she enthralled him with her memories of the French novelist. At these *soirées* – just after the last of which, in November 1943, the Princess dropped dead of a heart attack, to Jim's distress – he met Alvilde Chaplin, a woman a year younger than himself who had been the Princess's devoted companion for the previous six years. He was impressed by her beauty, elegance and domestic skills – with servants scarce, she had cooked the delicious dinners he had eaten at the Princess's table, an unusual accomplishment for a woman of her background (she was a general's daughter). For the rest of the war Alvilde continued to give dinner parties in which Jim was often included: like most of his other close women friends, she enjoyed the society of homosexual men. But it seemed unlikely that their intimacy would develop further; for she was safely married, with a daughter, to Anthony Chaplin, a handsome composer and zoologist who was the heir to a viscountcy and serving gallantly in the RAF; and the Chaplins declared their intention of living in France after the war, where Alvilde had inherited a house from the Princess together with a slice of her considerable fortune.

Although Jim's diary is one of observation rather than introspection, one cannot keep a daily record for years without revealing much about onself; and thus we have a far clearer picture of his personality during the 1940s than during the 1930s or 1950s. He shows himself to be a man of contradictions – by turns timorous and brave, self-pitying and stoical, selfish and considerate, snobbish and egalitarian, angry and cheerful, solitary and gregarious, prejudiced and tolerant, caring and indifferent, profane and devout, pessimistic and hopeful. He possessed (as he once wrote) an essentially cyclothymic nature, forever swinging back and forth between the dark and the light. He is often close to despair; but morning follows night. Before the diary begins, he had experienced some narrow escapes from death and the tedium of lengthy sojourns in military hospitals; while the war lasted, the future remained precarious; and one senses his determination to live life to the full and extract the greatest value from every situation – a process which his diary seems designed to assist. He loved his work (agreeing with Michael Peto of the Country Houses Committee that he 'had the most enviable life'); and the delight of touring country houses, coupled with the prospect of helping preserve some fragments of a disintegrating civilisation, gave him the courage and inspiration to keep going in an otherwise mad and miserable world.

While Jim spares us tedious details, it is clear that two matters were an almost daily worry to him – his health and his finances. Having been discharged from the army on medical grounds, he was far from robust. He is laid low by frequent fevers; his bad leg gives recurrent trouble; he suffers side-effects from drugs prescribed to control his epilepsy. But he struggles stoically on – not until April 1943 does illness force him to take a day off work. Financially, he seems to have returned to civilian life with scarcely a penny to his name. He was re-engaged by the National Trust in 1941 at an annual salary of £400, increased to £500 in 1942 and £600 in 1943. (In 1944, after he had served for six months as Acting Secretary in Matheson's absence, the Committee voted him a bonus of £200; but to avoid tax he took this not in cash but in the form of surplus furniture from Polesden Lacy.) With wartime inflation these sums were scarcely enough to meet life's necessities, and his enjoyment of such additional pleasures as money could buy depended on the generosity of friends and relations. His Aunt Deenie pays his subscription at Brooks's; Harold Nicolson settles restaurant bills and offers accommodation when needed (as does Geoffrey Houghton Brown); well-wishers assist with occasional cheques. Even so, it was a constant struggle to make ends meet: in May 1944, having discovered that he was £200 overdrawn and unable to settle his household bills, he was reduced 'in desperation and shame' to seeking help from his father.

During the war Jim continued to be a believing Catholic and to derive satisfaction from visiting Catholic households such as the Herberts at Pixton, the Throckmortons at Coughton, and the FitzAlans at Cumberland Lodge. He defends Pope Pius XII against the charge of 'condoning fascism' (though he privately wonders whether His Holiness believes the English deserve to win the war). His religious observance was however becoming occasional: in April 1942, after going to confession at the FitzAlans', he recalls that he had last done so eighteen months earlier while serving at Dover. He recognises that his religion is of a mystical kind – 'the moment reason takes over, faith flies out of the door'. Nor does it have much connection with conventional morality – while taking a bath (using more than the regulation allowance of hot water), he reflects that 'the worst sins are the most enjoyable' and that 'the lusts of the flesh, instead of alienating me from God, seem to draw me closer to Him in a perverse way'. After a decade it is possible that Jim was becoming slightly bored with Catholicism, which no longer shocked his parents or gave him a thrill of exclusivity; but he agreed with Jamesey Pope-Hennessy that 'no matter how much we might kick against the pricks and no matter how disloyal we were to the Church, Catholic principles were for us the only right and true ones'.

It has been alleged that Jim's wartime diaries show him to be snobbish, reactionary and xenophobic. Certainly one does not have to look far for evidence to support such allegations (and Jim himself, in his 1974 preface to the first published volume of his wartime diaries, admits that 'the priggish young man who wrote them is . . . someone with whom, upon re-acquaintance, I am not wholeheartedly pleased'). But one can equally find evidence for the opposite in each case. Jim may be intrigued to meet the great, the famous and the aristocratic; but he always sees what is ridiculous about them, and is contemptuous of vulgar snobs (such as Sir Vere Hobart of Gatcombe House, Isle of Wight) who never stop talking about their ancestry. His political and social views may reflect nostalgia for a lost age; but he has little time for the likes of Derek Jackson with his Nazi sympathies and visceral hatred of the lower classes. Despite occasional disparaging remarks about Jews, Americans and foreigners, he is wary of the arrogant and the exclusive, and remains attached to liberal ideals of pacifism and international unity. (Amid the fraternal rejoicing of VE-Day, he reflects that 'if we could . . . once a month . . . invite the Poles, Germans, even Russians to do what we were doing now, there might never be another war'.) Significantly, he is fascinated to learn that one of his friends is an anarchist, and claims to be one himself when an intrusive guest at Sibyl Colefax's enquires about his political loyalties; for the diaries, as well as showing him to be a man of paradoxes, suggest that, while outwardly conventional, he possessed a distinctly subversive streak.

One of the themes of Jim's wartime diary is the bombing of London – both the destruction wrought by the Blitz of 1940–1 and his personal experience of air raids in 1944–5. After his return to the National Trust he spent much time inspecting bomb sites in the capital, out of both professional and personal interest. Some he found rather beautiful: the gutted remains of St John's, Smith Square 'would make a fine Piranesi ruin'; the devastated area around St Paul's Cathedral 'was like wandering around in Pompeii'; the SPAB in Great Ormond Street stood in solitary spendour surrounded by 'empty blankets of snow'. Others induced nostalgia: observing the burnt-out shell of Holland House, he recalled attending a ball there before the war – though he was opposed to rebuilding it 'as the point about it was its historical associations, which have now gone for ever'. Although London was spared heavy bombing in 1942–3, the Luftwaffe turned its attention to other historic cities in the so-called 'Baedeker raids': one of the first, in April 1942, destroyed the Bath Assembly Rooms which were owned by the National Trust. Jim was appalled to learn that the raid had been in retaliation for an RAF one on Lübeck. 'Both raids are sheer barbaric bloody-mindedness, anti-culture and anti-all that life stands for. I positively want not to survive the war when things like this can happen.' He was however grimly amused by a German announcement 'that they will make a point of bombing English country houses, those haunts of bloated plutocrats and aristocrats, especially the famous "Tudor" ones'. Among Tudor houses suffering bomb damage was Knole, where the fall-out from a landmine dislodged masonry and shattered stained-glass windows on the west front; Jim noted that 'the heraldic beasts on the gable finials turned round on their plinths and presented their backs to the outrage committed'.

The London raids resumed in earnest in February–March 1944. Jim was alarmed to hear them while at home, but fascinated to observe them from the roof of the National Trust offices when he was on fire-watching duty. 'It was beautiful but shameful to enjoy the glow of fires, the red burst of distant shells and the criss-cross of searchlights. I suppose Nero derived a similar thrill from watching Christians used as human torches.' One raid targeted St James's, where he went the next day to view the devastation.

> The [St James's] Palace front sadly knocked about, the clock awry, the windows gaping, and shrapnel marks on the walls. A twisted car in the middle of the road. Geoffrey [Houghton Brown]'s Pall Mall flat devastated, and the Lelys from Castle Howard he had just bought presumed lost. The staircase to the flat quite gone. A colonel who lived above him has entirely disappeared, only two buttons of his tunic and part of his cap have been retrieved. In King Street Willis's Rooms finally destroyed, one half having gone in the raid of [May] 1941 when I was sheltering in the Piccadilly Hotel. Poor Frank Partridge's shop devastated, Drowns, the picture restorers, where I took the two Greville primitives, gone altogether.

To Jim's relief, Brooks's remained unscathed. On the other hand, the London Library in St James's Square, of which he was a devoted member, had received a direct hit. After lunching at Brooks's, he joined a 'human chain' trying to rescue the books.

> They think about 20,000 books are lost. It is a tragic sight. Theology (which *one* can best do without) practically wiped out, and biography (which *one* can't) partially. The books lying torn and coverless, scattered under debris and in a pitiable state, enough to make one weep. The dust overwhelming. I looked like a snowman at the end. One had to select from the mess books that seemed usable again, rejecting others, chucking the good from hand to hand in a chain, in order to get them under cover. For one hour I was perched precariously on a projecting girder over an abyss, trying not to look downwards but to catch what my neighbour threw to me.

The next great excitement was the Germans' long-heralded secret weapon, the V-1 bombs or 'doodlebugs', pilotless planes whose terrifying screech eerily cut out before the explosion, which started arriving in mid June 1944, soon after the Allied landings in Normandy.* Hearing about the first batch, which had fallen short of London, Jim thought they sounded 'like an H. G. Wells story . . . almost inconceivable'. Soon familiar landmarks – Tyburn Convent, Charing Cross Bridge, the Guards Chapel filled with Sunday worshippers – were hit and destroyed. 'For sheer damnable devilry, what could be worse than this terrible instrument?' Lying in bed, he heard them getting nearer.

> Another fearful night. Nothing dropped in Chelsea that I know of, but before midnight one just across the river made a hideous clatter, and the house shook like a jelly. The guns have ceased firing now because they merely bring the rockets down to explode in the streets . . . Whereas previously I cursed the guns for the noise they made throughout the night, now without them I find I am more frightened. Instead I lie awake for hours, my ears waiting for the sound of rocket planes. Here in Cheyne Walk we have distant trams, trains, motor vehicles and river traffic which one mistakes at first for a plane.

On 26 June, at 2.30 in the morning, he was woken by 'the most terrific con-cussion' accompanied by 'a cascade of glass, plaster and broken woodwork'. He rushed down to the room where Miss Paterson was sleeping, to find her

---

*After the Allied invasion, in which several of his friends were participating, Jim was overwhelmed with guilt at his civilian status and applied to serve in France with the Red Cross. Esher wrote to him that the National Trust could hardly oppose his going *if* he should pass his medical test. Needless to say, he did not pass. (Diary 14 July 1944, 9 August 1944, 17 August 1944.)

almost buried in broken glass and masonry, but miraculously unharmed. A doodlebug had landed in the river a hundred yards away: amazingly, all the riverside buildings remained standing and no one was hurt, though Jim's house became temporarily uninhabitable. A few days later, in the midst of another raid, he went on a crawl of dockside pubs with Jamesey, witnessing scenes of wild abandon. 'Women sang into the harsh microphone, sailors stamped, and peroxide blonds and the worst characters in London danced like dervishes and swilled gallons of beer . . . [an] operatic scene.'

On 12 September 1944 he was woken by 'an explosion like an earthquake, followed by a prolonged rumble, which I at first mistook for thunder'. This was the first of the V-2 rockets. At first he made light of them. 'They are very exciting and not frightening at all, for when you hear them, you know you are all right.' By the end of the year he had changed his tune. 'The V-2 has become more alarming than the V-1, quite contrary to what I thought at first, because it gives no warning sound. One . . . jumps out of one's skin at the slightest bang or unexpected noise, like a car backfire or even a door-slam.' Most of them fell around the river, making Jim's windows rattle, and his nerves. 'No anti-aircraft device can stop them.' He mused that, if the European war continued to the end of 1945 and they kept on coming, 'I do not see how they can fail to get most of us in the end'.

'The year has opened in a melancholy way,' wrote Jim in his first diary entry for 1945. The V-2 rockets continued to strike terror – one fell a few hundred yards from his house, demolishing the east wing of Wren's Chelsea Hospital. He felt bereft as his two most intimate friends had gone overseas, Jamesey to America to serve with the British Military Mission in Washington, Tom to fight the Japanese in Burma. He did, however, form intimate friendships with several other personable bachelors around this time: these included John Fowler, a talented decorator of country houses (formerly in partnership with Sibyl Colefax); George Dix, an art-loving American naval officer; and two conscientious objectors, the artist Derek Hill and the architectural journalist Ian McCallum. (Jim was introduced to Fowler and McCallum by Geoffrey Houghton Brown, and to Dix by Stuart Preston; Derek he had met before the war with Pamela Mitford.) He also got to know two rich young bachelor aristocrats, the louche Sir John Philipps, owner of Picton Castle, Pembrokeshire (which he contemplated leaving to the National Trust), and the enigmatic John Egerton, 7th Earl of Wilton, who asked Jim to find him a country house to rent after the war (Jim tried to interest him in Audley End). A new female friend was Mrs Reginald ('Daisy') Fellowes, a sophisticated Anglo-French society figure (and a niece of 'Princess Winnie') whom he met at Emerald Cunard's. Though she was almost old enough to be his mother, and dangerously mischievous, he found her 'bewitching': he took her to see houses in which she was interested, squired her to parties, and summoned the courage to invite her to a tête-à-tête dinner, at which he felt 'mesmerised like a rabbit by a stoat'.

Another consolation was that he could at last look forward to publishing a book.* He had been asked to edit a collection of essays to mark the fiftieth anniversary of the National Trust's foundation in 1895, a task which occupied him intermittently from July 1944 to March 1945. G. M. Treveylan wrote the Introduction, in which Jim begged him to 'stress the Trust's opposition to museumisation and its wish to preserve the face of England as it was under private ownership'. Jim himself contributed a chapter on the history of the English country house, showing that the National Trust now owned examples of every period and type, from the pre-Tudor Great Chalfield to the late Victorian Wightwick, from the monastic Lacock to the Palladian West Wycombe, from great palaces like Blickling to modest squires' houses like Gunby. When the volume appeared in August 1945 as *The National Trust: A Record of Fifty Years' Achievement*, the first printing of 7,500 copies sold out in a week. The publisher was Batsford; and both the head of the firm, the lovably eccentric Harry Batsford, and his editorial director, the 'satanic' bisexual drunkard Charles Fry, took a fancy to Jim and invited him to write a book of his own. Jim chose as his subject the great Scottish neoclassical architect Robert Adam (1728–92), about whom little had been written for the general reader, and began his research with a pilgrimage to Adam's tomb in Westminster Abbey. The prospect of examining Adam buildings and interiors added new interest to his National Trust tours, and within a few months he had visited such masterpieces as Syon Park, Middlesex and Kedleston, Derbyshire. (Visits to the sites of Adam's London buildings were less rewarding, as they had generally suffered more from pre-war developers than from Hitler's bombers.) He also benefited from the advice of experts such as Professor Sir Albert Richardson of London University (already a friend from Brooks's), Rudolf Wittkower of the Warburg Institute, and John Summerson of the Soane Museum.

---

*When Jim started his diary in 1942, he seems to have been contemplating a study of Thomas Carlyle and his wife Jane; but this came to nothing, like all his previous book projects.

In April, as the European war drew to a close, dreadful news arrived from the East. On the 4th, after dining with Daisy Fellowes, he read in the evening paper that Basil, Marquess of Dufferin and Ava, his brilliant friend from Lockers Park and Eton, who had served in recent years as a minister in the government, had been killed in Burma. Jim lamented that they had seen so little of each other since Oxford ('on the rare occasions we did meet the affection was still there'), and that his short and promising life had been blighted by drink. But four days later came a worse blow, when Nancy telephoned to say that Tom Mitford had died of injuries sustained on the same battle-front. 'Beloved, handsome Tom, who should have married and had hosts of beautiful children; Tom, caviare to the general, possibly, but to me the most loyal and affectionate of friends. It is hell.' Jim wrote an appreciation of him in *The Times*, and attended a family luncheon in his memory, where he saw Tom's sister Diana for the first time since 1936, finding her as alluring as ever. (She had spent most of the war sharing the captivity of her husband Sir Oswald Mosley, and had declined Jim's offer to visit her in prison, wishing to reserve the few visits she was allowed for her children and siblings.) Tom had been Jim's first and perhaps greatest love, and within weeks Jim was experiencing the first of the Freudian dreams about him by which he would be haunted for the rest of his life. ('I rushed up to him and he threw his arms around me. I said, "Tom, they told me you were dead . . ." He laughed and said, "Yes, it was all a mistake . . ."')

In May came the news of Hitler's death and the German capitulation. Jim was unable to feel much relief – 'we have waited and suffered too long' – but left a vivid account of the VE-Day revels, which he experienced in the company of Bridget Parsons and John Sutro. Soon afterwards he was in the turmoil of a move, as the owners of 104 Cheyne Walk required him to vacate the property by the middle of June. Fortunately his admirer Geoffrey Houghton Brown came to the rescue, offering him 'the first floor and one spare room upstairs' of a terrace house he had recently bought in South Kensington, 17 Alexander Place (round the corner from the Brompton Oratory where Geoffrey was a devoted attender). The National Trust was also moving, from its rented premises in Buckingham Palace Gardens to a small but handsome house which had been donated to it, 42 Queen Anne's Gate. With both his new flat and his new office in a chaos of building works, Jim took a fortnight's holiday at one of his favourite National Trust houses, Blickling, where the formidable secretary-caretaker inherited from Lord Lothian, Miss O'Sullivan, had become a friend. Sitting in the great Jacobean library, looking out over the splendid park, he felt blissfully happy, and hoped to make a start on his Adam book. But there were pleasurable distractions. Wyndham Ketton-Cremer came over almost daily from nearby Felbrigg and took him to see other local houses of note. John Wilton turned up (the diaries hinting at some romantic involvement). And when Wilton left, Stuart Preston came to stay, having spent a year with the US Army in Europe rescuing art treasures: despite their former coolness, Jim was overjoyed to see him again, and for a few days they resumed their affair.

The general election took place on 5 July while Jim was at Blickling, but he had no thoughts of returning to London to vote.

> Polling day, but not for me . . . My dislike of Socialism is almost equalled by my dislike of what Mr Churchill stands for. What has the end of the war in Europe brought us? Perhaps the answer is that it has brought us nothing positively good, but saved us from something infinitely bad. But it has brought us something else infinitely bad, if not worse, namely Russian occupation of Eastern Europe. Moreover, this damnable occupation of Christian countries which form part of our civilisation will spread like a disease, and we, being too tired and feeble to resist, will complacently defer, in our phlegmatic way, resisting this disease until it is too late. No, politically speaking, I am miserable. Nevertheless, my joy at the ghastly fighting having stopped is great.

Three weeks later came the surprise news that Labour had won the election by a landslide, which would have profound implications both for the life of the nation and the work of the National Trust during the following years.

8

A New World
1945–9

———•———

O N 1 OCTOBER 1945, a month after the Second World War officially
ended with the surrender of Japan, Jim discontinued his diary.
As he wrote: 'Its background was the war. Its only point was the war.
And the war is now over . . . isn't it?' However, three months later,
on 1 January 1946, he resumed it, explaining that he 'missed it like
an old friend . . . If a man has no constant lover who shares his soul as
well as his body he must have a diary – a poor substitute, but better than
nothing.' He would keep it regularly for another four years, until the
end of 1949.

As well as chronicling Jim's own life during those years, it vividly
evokes life in England as a whole. And the picture it paints is grim. Many
things seemed worse after the war than during it. Food was more severely
rationed, and poorer in quality; housing was scarcer, taxation heavier. A
succession of bitterly cold winters, with fuel in short supply, caused the
entire nation to shiver. Nor was there much prospect of escape to warmer
climes: overseas travel, which during the conflict had been compulsory
for many, became largely impossible. For all its horror and destruction,
the war had been an hour of glory for Britain and her Commonwealth;
now she was bankrupt, her empire disintegrating. Having achieved
victory, she could look forward only to decline; the slog of peace (and a
seemingly precarious peace at that) was as arduous as that of war, while
lacking its excitement. Another transformation was that, whereas
the country in wartime had continued to be ruled by the traditional
establishment, headed by the grandson of a duke and guided to some
extent by an *après nous le déluge* philosophy of enjoyment, a new order had
come to power with Labour's election victory; although it offered hope
to millions, and proved in various respects to be less revolutionary than
feared, it represented the economic and cultural triumph of the masses
over the élite, and its watchword was 'austerity'.

How did Jim view this brave new world? As usual, his feelings were
mixed. As one of nature's élitists, he did not take kindly to socialism.

When he met the new (Old Etonian) Chancellor of the Exchequer Hugh Dalton at Sibyl Colefax's, his blood boiled with indignation. He was shocked when Harold Nicolson, who had lost his parliamentary seat in 1945 and hoped to resume his political career (preferably with a peerage) under the red flag, joined the Labour Party in 1947. Wandering one fine June evening around Brockhampton, which had recently come to the National Trust on the death of its last squire, he felt that the fate of this beautiful ancient estate symbolised 'the tragedy of England':

> A whole social system has broken down. What will replace it beyond government by the masses, uncultivated, rancorous, savage, philistine, the enemies of all things beautiful? How I detest democracy. More and more I believe in benevolent autocracy.

On the other hand, the earnest and egalitarian temper of the times rubbed off on him to the extent of making him contemptuous of those members of the traditional ruling class (including many of his friends and contemporaries) who remained as cynical and hedonistic as in the past. The postwar diaries are littered with references to 'worthless society people', 'pre-war good-timers', the 'staleness and futility' of those who 'are sophisticated and in the swim'. In February 1948, after attending a London cocktail party thrown by Hamish Erskine at which he sees many old friends, he writes: 'I believe my generation to be, for the most part, "unreal"; cliquey, dated, prejudiced, out of touch with the new world and preposterously exclusive – arrogant, arrogant, with few redeeming qualities of any kind. They have nothing original to impart . . . I truly don't mind if I never see these people again. They are only tolerable singly or in very small groups. In a mass they are detestable and contemptible. Am I one of them?'

Jim's begrudging acceptance of the 'new world' owed something to the fact that it was not unfriendly towards the National Trust. The idea of 'saving for the nation' landscape or buildings which had once been enjoyed by the few was one of which any socialist could approve. Both Dalton and his successor as chancellor Sir Stafford Cripps were enthusiastic members of the Trust, as was Dalton's wife Ruth who joined the Trust's executive committee in 1946. Dalton established the important new principle that land or buildings could be accepted by the Treasury in part payment of death duties and, where it seemed appropriate, handed over to the National Trust. A great worry to the Trust was that the government might seek to nationalise it, a fate which befell other 'national' institutions such as the Bank of England; but there was never much risk of this happening, and Dalton and Cripps helped ensure that socialist planning legislation barely affected the inviolability of the Trust's inalienable estate. In 1948 Cripps set up a committee under the civil servant Sir Ernest Gowers to advise on what more the government could do to help preserve historic houses: this sat during 1949 and reported in 1950, Jim being in charge of presenting the Trust's case. During this time, the great debate within the Trust was over whether to seek direct financial help from the Government to assist with the mounting cost of maintaining its properties; Jim felt it essential that it should do so, and unlike some others believed that this need not compromise the Trust's independence. ('I have very strongly urged that the Trust ought to come to terms with the Government and indeed ask for . . . government subvention, in spite of our hitherto having set our faces against the risk of state interference . . . The Trust is at a critical juncture and I seem to be playing a backstair role in guiding its affairs.') Largely as a result of his representations, Gowers recommended the establishment of a system of government maintenance grants both to the National Trust and to private owners: the Labour Government was about to implement this when it fell from power in 1951, and it was given statutory effect two years later under the Conservatives. (When it came to architectural conservation, Jim found little to choose between the two main parties; in the first postwar general election in which he is known to have voted, in 1959, he supported the Liberals, whose then leader Jo Grimond was a former Secretary of the Scottish National Trust.)

The transition from war to peace brought other changes to the National Trust. With the retirement of Zetland and Matheson, it had to find a new Chairman and a new Secretary. Jim hoped that his boss and mentor Esher would succeed Zetland as Chairman; but the position went to David Lindsay, 28th Earl of Crawford, who would hold it for twenty years. Jim was slightly in awe of this great aristocrat, who was already a towering figure in the amenities world as chairman of the National Gallery, the Royal Fine Arts Commission and the National Library of Scotland. (Crawford was unusual in that he combined a profound aesthetic sense with a reputation for being homophobic: when, in the early 1960s, there was talk of offering a National Trust job to Princess Margaret's husband Lord Snowdon, Michael Rosse's stepson, he caused alarm by informing a meeting which included Jim and several of like persuasion that he would not tolerate 'buggers' in the Trust.) However, as Crawford was busy with his other duties, and refused to come down from Scotland more than once a month, Esher, who chaired the General

Purposes Committee as well as the Historic Buildings Committee, remained in charge for everyday purposes. Matheson hoped that Jim, who had deputised for him during his wartime absences, would succeed him as Secretary, but Jim would not hear of this as it would have meant giving up his beloved country-house tours for a life of paperwork. Jim in turn hoped that Harold Nicolson would accept the job; but Harold declined owing to his hopes of returning to politics. Two new Secretaries were appointed in quick succession, neither of whom proved satisfactory. The first, George Mallaby, a former civil servant, made the mistake of trying to run the Trust like a government department; Esher and Jim realised he would have to go when he expressed the view that the government was 'just as fit to hold country houses as the National Trust' and 'bound eventually to take over the Trust's activities'. He left within a year and was succeeded by Admiral Oliver Bevir, who was warned by Crawford that the staff was 'not a bureaucratic team of experts but a dedicated group of happy-go-lucky enthusiasts who ought not to be bossed about'. However, the Admiral's problem was not bossiness but dimness: he simply did not have the mental equipment for the job. Nor was he suited to deal with aesthetes: when he accompanied Jim to Buscot, Oxfordshire to stay with its flamboyant owner Lord Faringdon who was offering it to the Trust, he was 'well out of his depth and kept trying desperately to surface like some moribund dolphin'. The secretaryship finally came to rest in 1949 with Jack Rathbone, a genial solicitor from a well-known Liverpool shipping family and a bachelor friend of Eardley Knollys, who would hold it for nineteen years; it was a comfortable appointment for Jim, who had known Rathbone at Oxford.

Meanwhile Jim's own job had been redefined. In March 1945 it was decided that the Country Houses Committee should take charge of all the Trust's historic architecture, not just the rural and domestic; it changed its name to the Historic Buildings Committee and Jim became the Historic Buildings Secretary. After the departure of Matheson, Jim was the Trust's longest-standing official (except for Christopher Gibbs, who returned towards the end of the war in the somewhat lowly capacity of Assistant Chief Agent); he also exercised an unusual degree of independence owing to his closeness to Esher and the committee, whose new members included Harold Nicolson and Michael Rosse. In 1945–6, he was responsible for a major reform. During the war it had been decided, in view of the growing size and complexity of the Trust's holdings, to discontinue the old system of appointing local firms of agents to manage its properties and instead to employ its own network of regional agents, reporting to a Chief Agent in London and responsible to the Trust's Estates Committee; Matheson set up the new system during his last years in office. However, Jim felt that these regional agents were not competent to oversee 'aesthetic' matters such as repairing historic buildings and showing them to the public; he was supported by Esher, who regarded the agents as 'only plumbers' and 'was very outspoken in his objection to [their] encroachment upon the aesthetes' work'. By the end of 1946 Esher had approved a scheme devised by Jim to appoint 'representatives' to assist him in the regions, who would be responsible to the Historic Buildings Committee and whose word would be law in all questions involving 'taste'. To begin with, only two regions had full-time, paid represen-tatives – the West Country, where the job was undertaken by Eardley, and South-East England, where Robin Fedden combined it with the post of custodian at Polesden Lacey. Elsewhere, local grandees of independent means were found to undertake the role in a part-time, honorary capacity – such as George Howard in Yorkshire, owner of Castle Howard, and Peter Fleetwood-Hesketh in Lancashire, whose family ruled the roost in the Southport area. Such men were used to giving orders to agents, and Esher made it clear that they would have precedence over them.

In theory Jim should have found his work easier in peacetime, espe-cially after the appointment of representatives. In fact he must have yearned for the wartime years, when his committee rarely met and there were few other staff and he had effectively been left to decide things on his own. Bureaucracy was rearing its head and it was far more complicated getting a property accepted in 1949 than 1944 – especially as the rules regarding endowment were toughened up as it became apparent that many of the endowments with which houses had been accepted during the war were inadequate for their long-term maintenance. Still, the period 1945–50 marked the Trust's golden age of country-house acquisition. Attingham, Brockhampton and Stourhead, nurtured by Jim since the 1930s, finally fell to the Trust on the deaths of Lord Berwick, Colonel Lutley and Sir Henry Hoare. Many cases on which he had worked during the war – Coughton, Ham, Knole, Lyme, Osterley, Petworth – came to fruition. Among the 'new' properties he succeeded in securing were Uppark, Sussex, Upton, Warwickshire and Cotehele, Cornwall. Uppark, a romantic house in the South Downs, had been lovingly cared for by its impoverished owners, Admiral Sir Herbert and Lady Meade-Fetherstonhaugh, who were only able to donate it by selling the contents for £50,000, the sum required to endow it, to a philanthropist who presented them to the Trust; Jim placed the Meade-Fetherstonhaughs in the same noble category as Miss Talbot at

Lacock and the Massingberds at Gunby – sacrificing all they had to ensure the survival of their house in the Trust's hands. By contrast the owner of Upton, Viscount Bearsted, was the son of the Jewish oil tycoon who had bought and 'improved' it (though Jim found that the Bearsteds possessed 'the unassuming manners of the well-bred'); the house was of little consequence, but its contents – furniture, china, and above all pictures – took Jim's breath away, and there was no problem with endowment. Cotehele, romantically isolated in its wooded setting on the Tamar (Jim hoped it was so out of the way that few of the public would want to visit it), was an amazing time-warp, the buildings almost unchanged from the fifteenth century and most of its contents from the seventeenth; it was the first house to be given to the National Trust by the Government, which accepted it in part payment of death duties from Lord Mount Edgcumbe who had inherited it during the war.

The Trust also received a number of properties which were of interest not for their architecture but for their historical associations. These included two prime ministerial residences, Disraeli's Hughenden and Churchill's Chartwell, which Jim thought 'deliciously hideous' but 'fascinating as the shrines of great men'. Chartwell, where Jim had stayed in 1928, was bought, endowed and presented to the Trust soon after the war by a group of rich friends of the once and future premier on the understanding that he could continue to live there undisturbed for his lifetime; visiting the new acquisition with the great man's nephew, his old friend Johnnie, Jim noticed a characteristic aroma which had not changed since his last visit – cigars and brandy. Other donations included T. E. Lawrence's cottage, Clouds Hill, and Thomas Hardy's house, Max Gate, both in Dorset. Jim thought the first 'a pathetic shoddy little place', and noted that visitors seemed to have stolen the entire contents down to the window clasps, but nevertheless felt that it gave an idea of Lawrence's asceticism. Max Gate he considered not just 'perfectly hideous and shapeless' but 'shoddily built' and likely to be 'a constant expense', and he urged the Trust to sell it (it was held alienably) in order to buy the more evocative thatched cottage which was Hardy's birthplace. He had no such doubts about the early Georgian Lamb House, Rye, where Henry James had spent his later years: so thrilled was Jim by this acquisition (which between the wars had been rented from James's estate by another novelist, E. F. Benson, who used it as the model for 'Mallards' in his 'Tilling' novels) that he committed the Trust, despite its lack of funds, to buying those of its contents which had belonged to 'the Master' and rebuilding the destroyed garden house where he had done most of his writing.

Just as impressive as the list of houses which came to the Trust during these years was the list of those whose owners longed to donate them, and which Jim and his committee would have loved to accept, but which could not be transferred for some reason. Often it was not just a matter of insufficient endowment. A particularly frustrating case was Corsham: Paul Methuen was a pioneer of the Trust's operation to rescue country houses, but despite frequent attempts before, during and after the war he never succeeded in transferring his own, as it belonged to a settled estate with numerous living heirs whose consent could not be secured as required by the National Trust Act of 1939. Similar considerations frustrated the donation of Holkham Hall, Norfolk by the 4th Earl of Leicester, Madresfield Court, Worcestershire by the 8th Earl Beauchamp, and Ragley Hall, Warwickshire by the 8th Marquess of Hertford. Sometimes bequests failed through the incompetence of lawyers, a profession Jim came to regard as 'the enemies of the human race'. A case he particularly lamented was Westwood Park in his native Worcestershire, 'a weird Jacobean house planned like a starfish, all turrets and spikes'; its owner, the 3rd and last Baron Doverdale, died in 1949 believing he had bequeathed it to the Trust, but his relatives found a loophole in his will, as a result of which both the house and park were finally sold in lots. (It should be added that, forty years on, the owners of Corsham, Holkham, Madresfield and Ragley were probably thankful that their properties had stayed out of the Trust's hands; but it was impossible, in the grim late 1940s, to foresee that things would develop so favourably, politically and economically, for the owners of large historic houses; and the example of Westwood shows that the alternative to the Trust was often extinction.)

Another concern for Jim was that, although the Labour Government received a number of covetable houses in part payment of death duties, it did not invariably hand these over to the Trust but sometimes kept them to be managed by the Ministry of Works, Audley End being a notable instance. At one point, while the Trust was preparing its case for the Gowers Committee, it was suggested that the Trust should confine itself to holding 'inhabited' houses while the Ministry was the proper body to run 'uninhabited' ones as museums – a suggestion fiercely (and successfully) resisted by Jim, 'because I foresee all families leaving these anachronistic white elephants in time – and then what will be left to us?' At this period, indeed, Jim and his committee developed considerable disdain for the Ministry, regarding its officials as bureaucratic philistines ill-equipped to show buildings to the public: as Jim remarked on observing an ugly wooden hut erected in front of one government-owned romantic ruin, 'the Ministry lacks taste and sensitivity in spite of its academic superiority'. When, in 1947, King George VI's brother-in-law, the 6th Earl of Harewood, died, Jim suggested that 'the family might approach the Treasury and ask for the house [Harewood House near Leeds], some 4,000 acres of land around it and also the chief objects of art to be taken in lieu of death duties and handed over to the Trust'. The new Earl and his mother the Princess Royal were both interested, and Jim made a fascinating visit to Harewood, being struck by its well-ordered beauty ('God, what England owes to the landed gentry for the trim appearance of their estates') and his royal hostess's love and knowledge of the house and its contents. However, the Treasury intimated that, if it accepted the property, it would *not* be inclined to pass it to the Trust; whereupon the family decided to hang on to it.

The acquisition of new properties represented only part of Jim's work for the National Trust during the postwar years. With the coming of peace the Trust's architectural estate, which had been closed to visitors throughout the war, had to be prepared for opening to the public. This involved Jim in visiting all Trust properties which were suitable for opening, appointing custodians, organising repairs and redecorations, and 'arranging the rooms'. (Later, such tasks would largely fall to the representatives; but during 1945–7 Jim mostly had to undertake them himself.) Given difficulties of finding staff, shortages of almost everything and severe financial constraints, arrangements generally had a makeshift character, and there was often near-panic as the opening day approached. At Charlecote, which (Jim later recalled) was 'about the first country house of which I supervised the showing after the war', there was no sign of either the (volunteer) guides or the guidebooks on the eve of opening; but both turned up on the day (1 June 1946), and the opening ceremony was a stirring occasion, with speeches from G. M. Trevelyan and the Shakespearean actor Barry Jackson, the former launching an appeal for (much-needed) funds with a munificent donation of £5,000. Altogether it proved possible to open eleven historic buildings during 1946, and a further nineteen during 1947; visitor numbers were at first modest owing to petrol rationing but rose rapidly, from 120,000 in 1948 to 433,000 in 1950. Although the showing of country houses to the public went back several centuries, the National Trust was a relative newcomer to it, and ever-rising visitor numbers presented problems to which solutions had to be found as they arose; it was some time before the Trust mastered the art of managing the influx, and there was never any standard method, each house adopting a regime suitable to its usage, size, layout, fragility, and the numbers it attracted.

In charge of 'showing' each property was the (usually resident) custodian, and Jim showed some imagination in filling these posts. Several of the original custodians of 'uninhabited' houses were men of considerable taste and substance who were destined to rise to senior positions in the Trust's hierarchy, such as Joshua Rowley at Packwood (later the Trust's Deputy Secretary) and Robin Fedden at Polesden Lacey (who would succeed Jim as Historic Buildings Secretary in 1951). Where there was a resident donor family, Jim naturally encouraged them to assume the custodian role, which some of them relished. At Gunby, the Massingberds were relieved that only two people turned up on the first day of opening in May 1946, as it enabled them to forget about the extra staff proposed by the Trust and show the visitors round themselves with the help of their elderly servants. At Hatchlands, visitors were guided by Goodhart-Rendel's Jeeves-like butler, who proved as much an attraction as the house itself. Elsewhere the results were not so satisfactory. At West Wycombe, Helen Dashwood insisted on being in charge of all showing arrangements (for which the Trust paid her £64 a year), but made no secret of the fact that she resented the public coming to the house at all. At Knole (which became the Trust's most visited property), problems were created by the fact that some staff were employed both by Lord Sackville as servants and by the National Trust as custodians and tended to look down on the visitors, who often complained about the manner of their reception.

Another of Jim's responsibilities in connection with opening was the publication of guidebooks. As with custodianship, a member of the donor family was often the most appropriate person to whom to entrust authorship. Jim approached Vita Sackville-West to write the guide to Knole; although she had not set foot in the house since 1928, when her father had died and her hated American aunt had become the *châtelaine*, 'every stick of furniture and every picture was accurately recorded in her prodigious memory' and her text (which serves to this day) required no correction. Similarly, Hal Goodhart-Rendel, a distinguished architectural historian, wrote the Hatchlands guide (though unable to refrain from describing those parts of the house which the public never saw). Where the family produced no such literary talent, Jim usually wrote the guide himself; he often had to do so at speed and errors inevitably crept in which were corrected in revised editions issued during the 1950s. In August 1946 Batsford commissioned Jim to produce a popular guide to all the National Trust's historic buildings. Appearing in 1948, this was a delightful little volume, handsome drawings by the illustrator Stanley Badmin complementing Jim's concise and elegant essays (organised by county in the traditional gazetteer manner) on the properties' history and architectural features. (It is now a collectors' item, and certainly more diverting to read regarding the houses it deals with than the Trust's annual *Handbook*.) It also sheds interesting light on the opening regime of the period. Great attractions like Knole, which now open seasonally from March to October, were then visitable all the year round. To view small municipal buildings, readers were instructed to apply for keys to 'Mr Frank Wooding at the cottage opposite the church' or 'the blacksmith in the High Street'. Entrance fees (not payable by Trust members) ranged from twopence for the Old Post Office at Tintagel to half a crown for Knole. Many houses were not yet open, though it was hoped they would become so 'as soon as staff is available' (Cliveden), 'as soon as it is possible to make the necessary arrangements' (Osterley), or 'at a later date' (Petworth).

Out of love, Jim devoted himself to arranging some houses far beyond the call of duty. Two examples, both in the West Country but presenting totally contrasting problems, were Montacute, Somerset and Stourhead, Wiltshire. (Both properties included magnificent parks; but it was with the houses that Jim was mainly concerned.) The acquisition of Montacute, an Elizabethan jewel, predated the Country Houses Scheme; it was bought and donated to the Trust in 1931 by the philanthropist Ernest Cook (of the travel agency dynasty) after the Phelips family which had originally built it were obliged to sell. By 1946 it was empty of both inhabitants and contents; but Jim felt strongly that it should nevertheless be shown as a 'living' house, filled with appropriate furniture, pictures and other artefacts. He therefore set about amassing a suitable collection – by way of gift or loan, as there was no money to buy anything. In March 1946 he succeeded in borrowing 'piles of dusty furniture' from the basements of the V&A; in June, visiting Lord Crawford at Haigh Hall, the nineteenth-century house near Wigan which he was having to give up, he persuaded the National Trust Chairman to lend twenty-five imposing pictures – 'several Teniers, a Ruysdael, Ostades, van der Neer, a Pintoricchio, Reynolds of Lady Eglington at the harp, Opie of Dr Johnson, Romney of the young Pitt, and so forth'. (A year later, when Crawford threatened to move the pictures to the Travellers Club, Jim 'implored him not to . . . telling him how they made Montacute what it now is', prompting Harold Nicolson to remark, 'that is precisely how he wheedles things out of old ladies'.) Jim personally placed all the items he collected; and by the time the house was officially opened in July 1946, its vast rooms no longer looked bare. He nevertheless continued his hunt for items with which to embellish it; when Brockhampton came to the Trust at the end of the year and it was decided that the 'big house' (unlike the black-and-white farmhouse) was unsuitable for showing, he transferred the best of its contents to Montacute – including a collection of antiquarian books which filled the empty shelves of the Montacute library. Stourhead, which became the property of the National Trust when Sir Henry and Lady Hoare died on the same day in March 1947, presented precisely the opposite difficulty: nothing seemed to have been thrown out for generations and it was overstuffed with treasures of every description, to the point where one could hardly move in the rooms, let alone show them to the public. Jim spent almost a year sorting out the mass of things, and sought the advice of various experts – Anthony Blunt on the pictures, Leigh Ashton on the porcelain, Graham Reynolds on the miniatures, Margaret Jourdain on the furniture, Katharine Esdaile on the sculpture, 'Bob' Gathorne-Hardy (Anne's brother) on the books. (With this exercise originated the practice of appointing 'honorary advisers' to the Trust.) He finally divided the contents into three, with a view to keeping the best of everything in the house, selling a mass of 'surplus clutter' to local dealers, and sending the remnant – too good to be got rid of, but too voluminous to remain – to other Trust houses (including Montacute) which might benefit from them. A difficulty was that Sir Henry's prickly cousin Rennie Hoare, who inherited the right to live in the house, resented and tried to resist the relocation of many items; he succeeded in enlisting his fellow Wiltshire grandee Paul Methuen as an ally, but Jim was able to rely as always on the support of Esher, who 'approved wholeheartedly' of Jim's plans when he visited Stourhead for its opening in June 1948.

Something which gave Jim particular joy during his labours at Montacute and Stourhead (and also at Cotehele, where the rooms were already well-arranged but the furniture and fabrics required much restoration) was the assistance and comradeship of Eardley Knollys, who was appointed the Trust's West Country representative in 1947 (having already kept a protective eye on the Trust's holdings in the region since 1941). Indeed, during the years 1946–8 Eardley ceased to be a mere colleague of Jim and became his most valued friend and confidant. Jim wrote that he was 'the dearest and best companion on expeditions', that it was 'more fun being with Eardley than anyone in the world', that 'there is no one . . . with whom I have shared more cherished moments of giggling, *vide* yesterday carrying the grandfather clock down the stairs at Cotehele, clankings coming from the mechanism . . . I thought I would have a stroke we laughed so much, yet could not put it down'. After they had spent three days at Stourhead, toiling from dawn till dusk, he wrote:

> We had to start from scratch . . . with the minimum of help, carrying heavy furniture and busts together, back-breaking, yet giggling work . . . It was the greatest fun, and oh how I enjoy Eardley's companionship. We think we make a splendid team, because we never spare criticism, neither taking offence; on the contrary each relishing outright condemnation of the other's efforts. I know we shall eventually succeed in making the house look splendid.

At the end of the war Eardley, together with two other friends, Eddy Sackville-West and his fellow music critic Desmond Shawe-Taylor, had gone to live in a pretty house in Dorset, Long Crichel near Wimborne, which they decorated in the 'Bloomsbury' style. Jim often stayed there on his West Country expeditions, and soon became accepted as a member of the household, one of the few people (another was Raymond Mortimer) who was welcome to stay whenever he wished. He always enjoyed his visits. 'Eardley, Desmond and Eddy lead a highly civilised existence here. Comfortable house, pretty things, good food. All the pictures are Eardley's and a fine collection of modern art too.' He appreciated the welcome he received from his hosts, 'greeting me like three big affectionate dogs'. Best of all he loved the conversation, an unrestrained mixture of gossip, jokes and intellectual chat. Jim thought Desmond (whom he had befriended towards the end of the war) 'the gayest, sweetest-tempered, most informative person in the wide world', who contrasted agreeably with the neurotic (but still lovable) Eddy. In 1947–8, while he was sorting out Stourhead with Eardley, Jim spent long periods at Long Crichel, writing that 'the inmates . . . are angelic to me and this house has become a sort of second home'.

Jim had meanwhile acquired a new London home. He lived at 17 Alexander Place for little more than a year; for in September 1946 his landlord Geoffrey Houghton Brown moved to the grander 20 Thurloe Square at the end of the same street, a Regency corner house with a garden. Jim was alotted the ground floor; two dear old sisters, Emily and Dolly Bradford, inherited from the previous owners, lived in the basement and looked after him as cook and housemaid, enabling him to throw occasional lunch and dinner parties for the first time in his life.

(Geoffrey had his own housekeeper, Miss Hall, whom he installed in the attic.) Jim had grown to love this pretty corner of South Kensington, which was conveniently round the corner from both the Brompton Oratory and the Victoria & Albert Museum, visitors to 20 Thurloe Square including priests from the one and curators from the other. Neighbours with whom he exchanged hospitality included the 'wicked and amusing' Viva King (a celebrated 'fag-hag' immortalised in the novels of Angus Wilson, who gave rise to the expression 'a friend of Mrs King' as a euphemism for homosexual) and Cecil Beaton in Pelham Place. As Geoffrey was a restless buyer and seller of houses, Jim feared they would not stay there long either; but it was to remain his principal home for the next fifteen years.

As with King's Bench Walk a decade earlier, one may assume that the rent was modest; since their meeting in 1937 Geoffrey had had a *tendresse* for Jim and shown him many kindnesses (such as taking him, when he badly needed a holiday in 1943, to stay with his friend the Duke of Argyll at Inverary Castle); when he died in 1993, Jim admitted that he had 'rather traded on his generosity'. Jim still had need of such patrons, for his finances remained precarious. His salary at the National Trust was raised to £1,000 in 1947; Batsford paid him £250 for his writing in 1946; his shares in the family cotton mill paid a dividend of £123 in 1948. Under inflationary postwar conditions this (heavily-taxed) income scarcely enabled him to lead a modest life; in July 1948 he was obliged to appeal to his father (who proved surprisingly forthcoming) for help in paying off an overdraft of £600. Yet if there was something he really wanted, he generally found ways and means – thus at the start of the postwar diaries in January 1946 we find him spending £600 on a second-hand Rolls-Royce.

Jim's diaries show that he continued to lead an active and varied social life after the war: most evenings that he was in London he either went to a party or dined with friends. He continued to be a regular attender at the gatherings of Sibyl Colefax ('my respect for her kindness and gallantry has developed into true fondness') and, until her death in July 1948, Emerald Cunard ('I admired her for her lightning perception, her wide reading, her brilliant repartee, her sense of fun, and sparkling, delicious, wonderful nonsense . . . no one will ever take her place'). Everyone in London aspired to get onto the guest list of an embassy or legation, where one might be treated to lavish meals not subject to rationing, and Jim, having got to know 'Paz' Subercaseaux, the Chilean Minister's lively wife, at Emerald's, was often to be found at the Chilean Legation; there he befriended the exotic legation attaché 'Tony' Gandarillas, a bisexual millionaire and patron of artists who attributed his perpetual youthfulness to a daily pipe of opium. Another fascinating hostess who took Jim up after the war was the American-born octogenarian Mrs Carnegie, widow of the statesman Joseph Chamberlain (1836–1914), whose daughter by her second husband was married to Michael Peto of the Historic Buildings Committee. 'Such a flavour of Edwardian London this evening conveyed to me,' he wrote after dining at her house in Lennox Gardens. 'Mrs C. is still young in spirit and quick in uptake, with perfect old-fashioned manners [and] slighly husky . . . very beguiling intonation.'

In Jim's postwar diaries it is noticeable that, with the exception of a few old chums from Oxford such as Johnnie Churchill and Harry d'Avigdor-Goldsmid, a few literary figures such as Peter Quennell and Sachie Sitwell, and a few fellow aesthetes such as Kenneth Clark and Michael Rosse, most of the male friends with whom he associated were predominantly homosexual. Some were old friends from before the war, such as Hamish Erskine, Paul Hyslop, Patrick Kinross and Paul Latham; some he had got to know during the war, such as George Dix, John Fowler, Ian McCallum and Johnnie Philipps; some he befriended on their return from the war, such as the 'cosy and sympathetic' Mark Ogilvy-Grant, who had been a prisoner in Germany, and Harold Nicolson's son Ben, who gave up his position as Deputy Surveyor of the King's Pictures (under Anthony Blunt) in 1947 to edit the *Burlington Magazine*. (Similarly, most of the women to whom he was close – Alvilde Chaplin, Daisy Fellowes, Midi Gascoigne, Anne Hill, Nancy Mitford, Bridget Parsons, Anne Rosse – were known for their liking of 'queer' male society.) That Jim had sexual affairs with some of these men (as well as with various women) is perhaps less significant than that he shared with them a sense of complicity as members of a clandestine society, and enjoyed with them a certain kind of gossip. He has a 'jolly talk' with John Fowler about 'sex problems and how to overcome them by the most practical, mechanical and cynical means'; Patrick Kinross, back from Greece, opines that 'true love can only exist between man and woman, true sex between man and man'; at an all-male dinner party at Mark Ogilvy-Grant's, Jim 'nearly choked with laughter' at the stories he hears – 'lust *is* a jest! How *would* we laugh without it?' Although this was the society in which Jim clearly felt at home, he did not regard himself as irredeemably homosexual. At Long Crichel, 'Eddy maintained that born homosexuals could never become heterosexuals, whereas I maintained, with no intent to annoy, that this was not the case. People were not necessarily born one way or the other; heterosexuals could become homosexuals, and vice versa; and there were people capable of falling in love equally deeply with men and women.'

While far from chaste ('sometimes I am in the arms of God, sometimes of Satan, as a priest once remarked when I confessed to one of the loveliest lovers I ever enjoyed'), Jim was becoming more fastidious, even prudish in carnal matters. When Harold Nicolson told him (somewhat disingenuously) that 'he scarcely requires sex these days', Jim remarked, 'I too find sex without savour or even degrading unless with someone who attracts me mightily'. (He does appear, however, to have been sufficiently attracted in this regard by two handsome but unstable young protégés of Harold who eventually committed suicide, the writer Richard Rumbold and the poet Michael Clayton-Hutton.) In his twenties Jim had been responsive to older admirers, but this was no longer much the case. He was more repelled than fascinated by Queen Victoria's youngest grandson Lord Carisbrooke, a neighbour in Kew of Mark Ogilvy-Grant. 'He reminded me of an old, spruce hen, cackling and screeching in the dust of a chicken-run – really, a typical old queen . . . He likes bringing the topic of conversation to venereal disease and unnatural vice; and he chases one into a corner and talks so close that one expects him to pounce at any moment.' Nor did he encourage the advances of the Queen's brother, Sir David Bowes-Lyon. 'His conversation very strange. Did I not think women's thighs ugly? Men's figures more aesthetic? Did I like wearing shorts? . . . I did not commit myself to any opinions.' He was becoming intolerant of 'lechers' such as the 'drunken, dissolute and destructive' Charles Fry of Batsford, 'the worst and most depraved man I know' – though perhaps Fry's fault was to combine his license with being middle-class, as Jim expressed amusement rather than disapproval at the equally rakish antics of the aristocratic Johnnie Philipps, and was upset when he drowned in his bath in November 1948, aged thirty-three.

When Jim was preparing his postwar diaries for publication in the 1980s, he wrote that he was deleting references to sexual encounters because 'lust . . . is uninteresting unless the circumstances are amusing, horrifying or titillating, my affairs having been none of these things'. What *was* interesting, he added, was love – but he was 'not in love during those years'. He continued to see something of his wartime paramours Rick Stewart-Jones, Jamesey Pope-Hennessy and Stuart Preston; but in all three cases love had died (a development possibly not unassociated with the fact that all three were on the way to becoming confirmed alcoholics). It was difficult to resume his old intimacy with Rick when the latter returned from Egypt in 1946. They continued to collaborate as conservationists; but Rick cannot have been pleased when Jim, as a fellow-member of the SPAB committee, opposed his cherished project to rebuild Chelsea Old Church on the grounds that 'there is too little of it left' and they could only reproduce 'an exact fake'. (In the event Jim was in a minority of one, and the rebuilding went slowly ahead.) Jim had an up-and-down postwar relationship with Jamesey, still affected by his charm and delighting in his gossip, but increasingly irritated by his amorality and penchant for 'rough trade'. In September 1946 they had a '*rapprochement*' following an 'estrangement', Jim writing that 'there are certainly enchanting sides to his volatile little character'. But a more typical entry expresses disapproval of Jamsey's latest boyfriend, a 'grubby house-painter', and of the fact that Jamesey 'borrows from his mother and poor friends what they cannot afford in order to make frequent trips abroad, taking friend'. Still, Jim was bound to Jamesey by their common attachment to Harold Nicolson, who remained devoted to them both (though particularly to Jamesey). Stuart kept in touch with Jim and stayed with him on postwar visits to London; Jim still found him attractive (though he had gone quite bald) and enjoyed his well-informed literary gossip, but a letter from Stuart begging forgiveness for a drunken incident suggests that this friendship was starting to become a trial.

There were in fact one woman and one man with whom Jim came close to falling in love in 1947–8. The woman was Sarah Churchill, Winston's daughter, whom Jim met with her cousin Johnnie in May 1947 and got to know in Rome in October that year, finding her far more seductive than her elder sister Diana (who had had a *tendresse* for him twenty years earlier and was now unhappily married to Jim's Eton contemporary Duncan Sandys); she was the black sheep of the family, having gone on the stage and contracted an unsuitable marriage (recently and acrimoniously ended) with the entertainer Vic Oliver. In the romantic atmosphere of Rome, Jim spent several evenings alone with her and found her entrancing.

> Her beauty is of a frail sort, her hair Botticelli gold. She is of a romantic disposition. There is something guileless about her, like Johnnie . . . She is bright, independent, bohemian yet elegant . . . She explained to me why she loved Rome. She does no sightseeing and has no understanding of architecture. She says it is the movements of the statues, the fountains, the bridges, the curves of façades of churches, the actions of the Romans in the streets, even the mudguards of the *carozze*. I really am intrigued by

her. I walked her home and was amused by the impression this blonde beauty, apparently unnoticing, makes upon the staring, lascivious Italians.

Back in London, Jim had further amorous meetings with her ('the sound of her voice again . . . made me jump to hear') – until she invited him to a dinner party to introduce her future husband Anthony Beauchamp, 'a dark gigolo with a scar': Jim spent a miserable evening sitting next to her mother Mrs Churchill whom he disliked – 'jerky and precise . . . laughs and speaks as though she feared to swallow dirt'. (Jim had not much love for the great war leader either and it is curious to imagine him as a possible son-in-law.) The man was Burnet Pavitt, a former diplomat with a distinguished war record, born the same year as Jim, who now ran the British subsidiary of the Swiss pharmaceuticals company Hoffman-La Roche; he was also a gifted amateur pianist and a friend of that former professional, Joan Moore. He and Jim met in February 1948 and found each other sympathetic: within a fortnight they were talking daily on the telephone. Jim took Burnet to visit Blickling; Burnet took Jim to visit the Moores at Parkside near Windsor (a house Jim was to get to know well over forty years), where he played duets with Joan 'with much gusto and giggling'. In April Burnet, on his fortieth birthday, invited Jim to stay alone with him at his farmhouse in Hertfordshire: he was still moving in and Jim helped him paint the rooms. Several further visits followed. Clearly they were much attracted to each other; and they might have gone on to have a serious affair, except that Burnet was fundamentally unromantic by nature. As Jim recorded on a visit to him in June:

> We discussed the cussedness of inclinations beyond one's control. Something inside may whisper futility, and caution against the inevitable backfire of passion. Affairs of the heart mean not a fig more than the grip of momentary drunkenness, rendering one rudderless and unreliable. Civilised beings must rise above the distractions of lust.

Although Jim professed to share these 'pious thoughts which tomorrow may wither beneath the sun of a new love', he may also have been discouraged by them; for Burnet, having featured frequently in the diary during the previous four months, is mentioned little thereafter. They did however remain lifelong friends.

Apart from his work for the National Trust and his social life, these years marked Jim's *début* as a professional writer. That he found time for writing when busy with so much else signifies considerable self-discipline; he managed to combine his research with his job, never missing an opportunity to consult relevant experts and visit relevant buildings. His first book, *The Age of Adam*, appeared in December 1947 to good sales and mostly enthusiastic reviews, and Batsford commissioned him to write another volume dealing with 'the dawn of English classicism', published in 1951 as *Tudor Renaissance*. (Both works will be considered in Chapter 10 along with the rest of Jim's pre-1960 literary output.) Batsford also did well with the National Trust commemorative volume edited by Jim in 1945 and his *National Trust Guide* which appeared in 1948, both of which ran into several editions. When Jim's first books came out he was almost forty, and had been hawking manuscripts to publishers for over a decade; having waited so long for his writing career to take off, he lacked self-confidence and was easily stung by criticism. But he was always grateful to fellow writers for advice and interested to hear about their working methods. The eccentric Doreen Baynes told him that 'when she got going on her writing she became an instrument, a gigantic machine or fountain pen through which outside thoughts and ideas poured, sometimes to the extent of alarming her, the *she* remaining a passive, uncontrolling feature of the process'. Sachie Sitwell, when Jim stayed with him in Northamptonshire in 1948, amazed him by saying that he had seven books coming out that year (having already published fifty), though he admitted that 'writing is a terrible effort for him and for weeks he cannot put pen to paper'; he advised Jim to set aside more time for writing, which may have encouraged him to start thinking of giving up full-time work with the National Trust to devote himself to his literary career.

While writing books and articles, not to mention reports and guides for the National Trust, Jim kept up his diary. As noted, it lacks the excitement and exuberance of the wartime diary; there are fewer laughs; his own frequently depressed mood reflects the temper of the times. Yet much of the writing is inspired; he could pack an ocean of meaning into a few words. The following entry from December 1947, with its contrasts, its note of regret and its capture of the fleeting moment, may serve as typical.

> On the way from the Ivy – the best food I have had since my return from Italy – a man accosted me and I, so Bridget [Parsons] said, was very snubbing. Indeed I did not recognise him until we had passed on. Then I suddenly remembered the sad, second-rate, hopelessly unpractical member of the A.R.P. who was in my platoon at the beginning of the war. The last person in the world I would wish to be unkind to. I left B. and tore after him. Alas, he had gone. Now for ever he will remember me as a cad, a man too proud, while with a beautiful woman, to acknowledge him. He

looked so thin, yellow and *dégringolé*, which makes my behaviour worse. Perhaps he is starving and would have welcomed five shillings. Instead B. and I continued to her flat in Mount Street where we drank whisky, were warm and happy.

Like the wartime diary, the postwar diary is largely taken up with descriptions of the houses he visits and their (often eccentric) owners. While students of these will find much of interest, his accounts of both are sometimes rather jaded: Jim had visited so many houses by this time that he was less easily moved to rapture, and the spectacle of owners struggling to survive was less poignant in peace than in war. One house which thrilled him, however, was Chatsworth, which he visited for the first time in August 1948 as the guest of Andrew Hartington, heir to the 10th Duke of Devonshire, and his wife Debo, youngest of the Mitford sisters, whom he had known since she was a baby. The Hartingtons were then living in one of the estate villages, and working to open the big house (into which they would not move for another decade) to the public the following year.

> The site of the house, the surroundings unsurpassed . . . The scale of Chatsworth is gigantic, beyond comprehension (like St Peter's, Rome) until experienced . . . The Hartingtons, eager to know their possessions, intend to spend several hours a day systematically looking through papers in the library, like schoolchildren at a holiday task . . . As a couple the Hartingtons seem perfection – both young, handsome, and inspired to accomplish great things . . . Both full of faith in themselves and their responsibilities. She has all the Mitford virtues and none of the profanity. I admire them very much.

As with many of Jim's visits to great houses, pleasure was combined with an element of business; for there was a prospect of the house being offered to the National Trust (as was indeed to happen a couple of years later, when Andrew's father died aged fifty-five, leaving him to face a night-mare of death duties); and in the library Jim discovered drawings by Inigo Jones, a subject he had in mind for a book, which the Hartingtons were happy for him to return to study at his leisure.

If the great set-piece description in Jim's wartime diary is of the bombardment of London by the 'doodlebugs' in June 1944, in his postwar diary it is of the freezing winter of 1947. It began snowing on 24 January, and by the 29th London was officially experiencing its coldest weather for fifty years. Electricity supplies were interrupted and it was scarcely worth turning gas fires on as the pressure was so low. Jim sat at home huddled in blankets, his plumbing having packed up as the pipes had frozen. 'Even the basic elements of civilisation are denied us.' On 8 February he reported 'the jolly news' that 'all fuel is to be cut off'. On 13 February he wrote:

> This week is being a veritable nightmare. On Sunday afternoon it started to thaw and the snow mostly went. On Monday it froze again very hard, so that the slush is like slippery brick. Since Monday we have had no heating in the office apart from one electric fire. And now this is turned off from 9 to 12 and again from 2 till 4 each day. Wrapped in my fur coat with three pullovers underneath, my snowboots kept on, I am still too perished to work properly. People are unanimous in blaming the Government for a hideous muddle, yet Mr Shinwell remains Minister of Fuel.* I seldom sit in the office now but walk about and dictate letters. Have twice been to the National Gallery, which is heated, to look at the Spanish Exhibition . . . A number of poor old people sit on the benches, their feet wrapped in brown paper, striving to keep warm. At an Historic Buildings Committee yesterday all sat in fur coats, moaning in misery, for no one could concentrate on the agenda. Lord Esher however was as cheerful as ever. He told a member of the Cabinet, 'You Labour people never let us have a dull moment.' Bridget [Parsons] says that if this Government goes an extreme left one will take its place, and that she is quite ready to go to the barricades and shoot. I asked, whom? Well, almost anyone, she replied. Most of the large shops are closed; those that are open have no electricity, and no light except from the odd candle. The streets are blacked out, as in war time, and millions are unemployed for industries have come to a standstill. Food is becoming very short and the situation is as critical as ever it was during the war.

Early in March he was staying at Wickhamford when a snow blizzard began which continued for days, creating drifts up to six feet deep. 'No one remembers anything like it before. There are icicles over three foot long hanging from the thatch of the cottages. I spent the morning on the roof of the pantry at the Manor shovelling the snow off.' (Jim's parents had long been struggling at Wickhamford owing to shortage of staff, and this experience finally persuaded them to sell the Manor and move into the more manageable Hody's, which they did the following July.) On 16 March began the great thaw, causing flooding all over the country; visiting Worcester, Jim saw 'water in the bedrooms of all the cottages along the river . . . there has been nothing like these floods since 1770'. At Easter

---

*With unfortunate timing, he had overseen nationalisation of the coal industry at the start of the year.

on the 30th it was 'perishing cold' again 'with relentless rain'. Not until
11 April could Jim report 'a beautiful day, dry and sunny' on which 'all
Londoners were singing or whistling with joy over escape from an
appalling winter'.

In August of the same year the diaries describe a happier episode, when
Jim accompanied Harold and Vita on a ten-day motoring tour to inspect
National Trust properties in the West Country and Midlands. (Harold
now sat on the Trust's Executive Committee as well as its Historic
Buildings Committee, while Vita was about to become a founder
member of the new Gardens Committee.) They stayed at small inns and
hotels, except for three nights at Long Crichel where Eddy was a perfect
host; they also visited friends along the way, such as David Herbert at
Wilton. Vita did the driving, and whenever she saw from the road a house
which interested her, would shoot up the drive uninvited to have a good
look; Jim was enchanted by this habit – 'she does it not as a tripper but as
an eighteenth-century aristocrat who has the right' – but Harold was
embarrassed when they inevitably encountered a red-faced colonel who
demanded to know what they were doing on his property. Jim was
intrigued by the Nicolsons' architectural taste, which resembled that of
his own parents: 'They do not really care for classical buildings, only
liking the Gothic and Elizabethan.' But their opinions were always interesting. The excursion set the seal on Jim's friendship, now fifteen years
old, with both parties to the unusual marriage, whom he loved as much
for their eccentricities as their civilised attributes. 'Harold is wonderfully
untidy, dust and ash all over his hat and clothes. Vita wears one terracotta
dress . . . yet is always distinguished and "grande dame".' Soon after their
return, Vita sent Jim in appreciation an engraved silver pencil which
became one of his most cherished possessions.

Jim had spent the war entirely in Great Britain, and as soon as it was over
he yearned to travel overseas. His first opportunity to do so came in
August 1945 when Michael Rosse invited him to accompany him on his
homecoming from the war to his Irish seat, Birr Castle. From the quay-
side at Kingstown they motored directly to Birr, a Georgian garrison
town in the centre of the island. Their arrival, late at night, was feudal.
A crowd of townsfolk clustered around the castle gates, another of servitors and tenants awaited them on the sweep of the drive. Every light was
ablaze. Anne, their two boys and the agent stood on the steps, with the
butler, housekeeper, footmen and maids ranged behind them. Michael
made a short speech, greeted with cheering and 'For he's a jolly good

fellow'. The staff then went off for 'a beano' while the Rosses and their guest sat down to a midnight supper with champagne.

Jim found Ireland agreeably old-fashioned and relatively prosperous ('this shows how English standards and conditions must have deteriorated during the war'). He loved the ubiquity of horses, the lack of motor traffic, the fact that the streets were redolent with the aroma of horse-droppings rather than petrol fumes. In a country which had largely been spared food rationing, it was a treat to enjoy lavish meals full of cream and butter. The climate was relaxing, indeed too much so. 'There is something dead about the country and the people. It is like living on a luxuriant moon. I dislike the way the inhabitants remain for hours on end standing and staring into space.' Jim treated his week at Birr as a rest-cure, and found himself falling for his hostess Anne, who played 'the proud châtelaine' with style and was full of 'efficiency, vitality, keen wit and good nature'. A nightmare return train journey to Dublin, during which he almost lost his luggage, gave him a taste of Irish chaos. Jim was fascinated by the dilapidated Georgian architecture of the Irish capital, the 1890s atmosphere of the streets, the brightly lit and fully staffed hotels, and the churches which were so full on Sunday one could hardly enter them.

He returned to Birr in the spring of 1948 when the kind Rosses invited him to stay for a fortnight in their absence at a time when he felt under the weather and wanted to get down to work on his current book (*Tudor Renaissance*). This however he found a creepy experience.

> I do not like Ireland. I do not like the country here. It is horizonless and dead. One cannot see further than one's hand. I wish I could define properly what it is I do not like about the climate, the people and the scenery. My dislike is almost intuitive, certainly temperamental and racial. I fear the native hostility under the mask of deceit. At Mass the church here is so crowded that one cannot worship . . . The Irish God is not loving. He is a tyrant. The people are tight within his grasp . . . One senses that their appalling mendacity and untrustworthiness are the consequence of their age-long abortive attempts to escape the clutch of the priests. Oh, I do hate the whole island . . .
>
> The family are treated like royalty . . . There is too a sanctity about Desmond's memory. If you mention his name there is no respectful hush, but eyes sparkle and he is referred to as if still alive. The Irish are all eyes, and nothing else. No compassion, and I doubt whether there is any love, except for the dead. Much hate for the living.

Owing to exchange controls and transport shortages it was difficult, during the first years of peace, to travel outside the British Isles; but in the

summer of 1946 Jim managed to visit two countries (both of which had
been neutral in the war) thanks to the kindness of pre-war boyfriends.
Geoffrey Lemprière, an Australian whom he had met in Corsica in the
1930s and who had since survived being a prisoner of the Japanese, turned
up in London and invited Jim to join him on a business trip to Sweden.
'He is exactly the same, like a startled kangaroo, his age only betrayed by
a fold behind the ear.' The air journey to Malmö via Copenhagen was
Jim's first flight since 'looping the loop' in the Gipsy Moth of his mother's
lover Captain Butler over Broadway Hill in 1925. 'England looks small,
compact and very beautiful from the air. Most striking features are the
fields and hedgerows, chequer-board fashion, and the number of country
houses and demesnes.' Even the modest city of Malmö struck him as a
paradise after the miseries of war-torn London. 'The shop windows are
replete with everything one could possibly want to buy. The air of well-
being and luxury at the Hotel Kremer . . . is exhilarating. The beauty of
the boys and girls. Everyone is young. The cream complexion of the men,
their blond thick hair. Women with pale blue eyes and bare arms. The
standard of good looks immensely high.' In the hotel restaurant Jim
gorged himself on the smörgåsbord, surrounded by handsome waiters in
trim uniforms. In Malmö, Göteborg and Stockholm, while Geoffrey
attended to his business, Jim savoured the (mostly eighteenth-century)
architecture and visited picture galleries. He was fascinated by the
Swedish 'Versailles' at Drottningholm, associated with the romantic
figure of King Gustav III who had been assassinated there in 1792, but
was also impressed by Swedish modern architecture, with its 'wholeness,
convenience and neatness' and 'air of gaiety and happiness'. He bought as
many clothes as he could afford to pay the customs duty on. Jim felt guilty
as Geoffrey would accept no financial contribution for his hospitality, nor
did Jim feel inclined to resume their former relationship. 'Do tarts who
fail to requite the attentions of rich business men ever harbour these guilt
feelings?' He did however attend a louche party which Geoffrey gave on
their return to London, meeting such characters as 'an ugly Greek prince
with a soldier from the Horse Guards'.

The second holiday was in Switzerland at the invitation of George
Cattaui, the disgraced Egyptian diplomat of Jewish origin who had witnessed Jim's Catholic baptism in 1934 and was now a priest in Fribourg.
Jim travelled there by train, an uncomfortable journey of a day and a half.
'Greedily I inhaled the strong, dry, torrid southern heat, which I have not
experienced for seven years.' He found George 'a terrible bore', with his
hypochondria and endless enquiries about everyone they had known in

London a dozen years earlier, and was glad to escape his company and move to a hotel at Lugano. There he relaxed in idyllic surroundings, though he found no one to talk to, suffered sunstroke (a warning that he was going bald) and found himself being 'merely disturbed' by the beautiful bodies bathing in the lake. The locality was full of pretty churches which he explored.

After this taste of Italian-speaking Switzerland Jim longed to revisit Italy itself, where he finally spent the month of October 1947 after his publishers, Batsford, had been permitted to advance him some Italian *lire* on the grounds that he needed to visit Rome and other cities to research his architectural books. He had only found time for brief visits to Rome before the war and was overjoyed to spend a fortnight there. 'I walk everywhere, intending to know every street and square inch of the city before I leave.' He began his sightseeing with the Pantheon, 'the proto-type of so much I love and endeavour to preserve'. He was received at the Palazzo Doria, one of only two Roman palaces still inhabited by the families which had built them, by Prince Filippo Doria, a cousin of Michael Rosse. 'He is rather bent from the waist like an old apple tree . . . For two hours we were shown round the piano nobile of this gigantic and gloomy palace. Pictures v. important . . . to crown all the Velasquez of Pope Innocent X . . . In one room the Pope's velvet-covered throne [the Dorias had been one of the few Roman families entitled to receive the pontiff] turned to the wall, a customary protest by the Roman nobility against the Pope's incarceration within the Vatican in 1870.' Jim was appalled by the condition of some monuments; the Baths of Caracalla, where Shelley had written *Prometheus Unbound*, was 'a dump for old war material and barbed wire', which at least meant that he had the place to himself. After sightseeing by day Jim enjoyed a full social life at night, for Garrett and Joan Moore were staying in the city and introduced him to fascinating people, including Sir D'Arcy Osborne, former British Minister to the Vatican, and two beautiful, recently divorced women, Sarah Churchill and Barbara Rothschild. (Sarah, as we have seen, provided the main romantic interest for Jim in Rome in 1947; Barbara would fulfil a similar role the following year.)

He continued to Florence, where Harold Acton entertained him at the Villa La Pietra and advised him on sightseeing. He also visited Bernard Berenson at the Villa I Tatti with an introduction from Sibyl Colefax, one of the many old ladies infatuated with the great American art histor-ian; he was 'mortally frightened' of this encounter and relieved to find that Raymond Mortimer was a fellow guest.

Then in came the great man, who is tiny, white-bearded and eighty. Looks frail and tired, and is neat. When he speaks it is to the point. No irrelevancies, no pleasantries. I felt very shy and tongue-tied. He saw at once that I had nothing to communicate to him. But I was fascinated by his talk to others. Berenson is tiresome in that he is very conscious of being the famous art-dictator and sage, surrounded by applauding disciples. This expectancy of deference does not make for ease . . . He conveyed to me the impression of a great man striving to be something which he isn't. Perhaps he wishes he were an aristocratic connoisseur, and not a self-made professional expert.*

After a few days in Florence, Jim concluded that 'one should walk at night, when the main streets are empty and quiet. The narrow, tortuous streets are mysterious by lamp- and particularly by moon-light. Then you can appreciate the vast, rugged, abstract beauty of the palaces in the sharp shadows of semi-darkness. Things not noticeable by day loom into sight – here a window pediment, there an armorial escutcheon suspended over a doorway.' Nocturnal wanderings had other attractions: he encountered a handsome young Italian sitting on an embankment wall who took him into the Boboli Gardens by a secret entrance. 'His fine classical features were illuminated [by lights from cars on the adjacent road] as in a succession of celestial visions. It was as though the whole history of Tuscany was bared to me in that strange, silent conjunction of understanding and love.' He ended his tour in Venice, staying with George Chavchavadze and his wife Elizabeth who were renting Princess Winnie's Palazzo Polignac on the Grand Canal, their other guests being Hamish Erskine and his current lover, a young cellist. From the moment when, outside the railway station, he stepped into his hosts' sumptuous jet-black gondola, festooned with coronets and black silken ropes and propelled by two liveried gondoliers ('there can be few things more romantic, more transposing from this dismal modern age'), he gave up thoughts of serious sightseeing and abandoned himself to 'the superb meals, the flow of wine and the late hours'.

Jim returned to Italy for another month-long visit in September 1948, this time travelling in the company of Desmond Shawe-Taylor. He did

*Berenson in his own diaries described Jim as 'rather stern, melancholy, youngish-oldish' and was interested to hear about his work for the National Trust – though he thought it best for country houses bereft of their traditional owners to 'fall into ruin . . . for we then enjoy their picturesqueness, and can indulge in nostalgic romances about the kind of people who once lived in them' (*Sunset and Twilight: From the Diaries of 1947–1958* [ed. Nicky Mariano, 1964], p. 43).

not experience the same careless rapture as the year before, and Rome seemed shabbier, and nervous after elections narrowly lost by the communists. It was school holidays and the city was overrun by Catholic schoolgirls. ('What we now want', said Desmond, 'is some Protestant boys.') The high point of the visit was an audience with Pope Pius XII, arranged by D'Arcy Osborne, at Castel Gandolfo, the papal summer residence outside Rome. Unfortunately when the day arrived Jim was suffering from a heavy cold. He did not think much of the building, 'a shapeless yellow thing towering over the village'. The pre-audience ritual consisted of an elaborate game of musical chairs, as he joined a seemingly endless queue of pilgrims moving slowly from room to room and chair to chair. 'It is I suppose what the immediate after-life may be . . . moving through the mansions of Purgatory towards Heaven.' Immediately ahead of him in the line were a Brazilian lady in black who compulsively munched biscuits and 'an uncouth young American from Texas' who showed Jim a pocketful of gold trinkets and asked if he thought he might offer these to the pontiff: Jim 'advised him to consult the Brazilian lady whose fourth audience with a different Pope this would be'. Jim received a jolt in the final anteroom when the Pope himself walked in – 'a tall, erect, brisk figure, all in white, wearing a white biretta' – and immediately approached the American, who 'fumbled in his trouser pocket but mercifully thought better of it'. When it came to his own turn, Jim was so overcome with emotion that he was merely aware of 'a benignity, calm and sanctity that I have certainly never before sensed in any human being'. He did however notice that the heraldic medal in a blue envelope with which he was presented at the conclusion of the two-minute interview was a cheap object, and that a cardinal hastily placed another envelope into the pontiff's 'desperately wagging fingers' for the next guest.

A few weeks earlier, on 6 August 1948, Jim had reached his fortieth birthday. He wrote in his diary:

> The shock is not too great because during the past year I have been telling people that I was forty, in anticipation. But I am rather less good-looking and very bald now. My figure is as slender as ever. Only occasionally does my stomach swell, owing to the bad bread, but it soon flattens itself. I have lately found that the skin of my jaw and chest is slacker than formerly. I am less stirred by desire than I used to be. It is the forms of falling-off that I most resent: the fact that the life-line only reaches an angle of 89.9 rather than 90 degrees. Oh dear, to say nothing of the decay of teeth, eyesight and hair. When in another twenty years I am too old to work I shall retire to a monastery and pray, for I shall presumably no longer see to read . . .

At present my mental faculties, never first-rate, are better than they have
ever been. All my life I have been a slow developer.

It was Friday, a working day, and Jim saw no cause to celebrate; but
during the weekend he got together with Rick Stewart-Jones, his great
love of a decade earlier. Jim told Rick what he did not really believe, that
he had no true friends; Rick replied that he was too fickle to deserve any.
In his diary, Jim thought of some of the many friends with whom he was
in fact blessed – 'James Pope-Hennessy, Ben Nicolson, Mark Ogilvie-
Grant, Patrick Kinross, Johnnie Churchill, Michael and Anne Rosse,
Bridget Parsons, Harold and Vita, besides A., B. and C.' And he added:
'I have however no lovers and with folded hands await some devastating
romance.'

Within six months of writing those words he would find that romance
in the form of Alvilde Chaplin who would become his wife.

9

Alvilde

1949–51

T HE FUTURE Mrs James Lees-Milne was a woman of accomplishments. Though no intellectual, she was alert and decisive, and a born
organiser: under other circumstances she might have made a brilliant
career as a business or professional woman, or the head of a school or hospital. She was an excellent hostess, socially adept and possessing perfect
taste in clothes, food and interior decoration. Her conversation had a sharp
edge which many found refreshing. She was knowledgeable about natural
history; and although her familiarity with literature and the visual arts was
sketchy, she had a sophisticated appreciation of music, having known
during her twenties many of the great composers and performers of the
day. Slim and svelte, she carried herself with poise; though her head was
perhaps too equine to be pretty, she was undoubtedly handsome in a statu-
esque way. Jim wrote that 'her beauty is proud, guarded, even shrouded . . .
Pre-Raphaelite in manner if not in substance'; the young Garrett Moore
was driven into 'ecstasies of frustrated desire' by her resemblance to the
severe-looking film star Dolores del Rio. The trouble about her was that
she tended to be aloof, impatient, dictatorial, querulous, rebarbative and
possessive. Her admirers (of whom there were many) insisted that such
tendencies arose from a mixture of shyness, vulnerability and extreme
perfectionism, and that she was a warm, generous, companionable woman
at heart; but many of those who experienced her snubs and sulks did not
bother to explore further to discover these hidden depths.

She was born on 13 August 1909 (a year to the month after Jim), the only
child of parents who were then in their late thirties. Her father, Colonel
(later Lieutenant-General Sir) Tom Bridges, was a nephew of the Poet
Laureate Robert Bridges, and himself a poet and artist, but made his name
as a dashing cavalryman in the Boer War and other colonial campaigns. At
the time of his marriage to Janet Marshall in 1907 he was serving in military
intelligence as an attaché to the British legations in Scandinavia; his wife,
who hailed from a family of rich Edinburgh distillers who had established
themselves as Scottish gentry, the Menzies of Halliburton House, Forfarshire,

was a widow with a son at Eton (later killed in action). Bridges was a notorious philanderer, as illustrated by the following account of how his daughter came to be called Alvilde. While pregnant, Janet Bridges discovered that her husband, then stationed in Oslo, was conducting an affair with a Norwegian ballerina of that name; she subsequently insisted on bestowing it on their child as a permanent reminder to him that he had been caught out in his adultery. Whether true or not, the fact that this story gained currency gives some idea of both Bridges' reputation and the personality of his wife. Bridges went on to cover himself with glory during the First World War, in which he lost a leg at Passchendaele, and may have saved the Allied cause in August 1914 when, during the retreat from Mons, he rallied demoralised elements of the British Expeditionary Force with the aid of a penny whistle and a tin drum. Winston Churchill admired him for his swashbuckling qualities, and as Colonial Secretary secured his appointment as Governor of South Australia, where he served from 1923 to 1927.

Alvilde accompanied her parents to Adelaide. Until then she had seen little of her father, absent on his military campaigns and missions, and it was her mother who had been the formative influence in her life. Lady Bridges was an impressive but imperious matron of the Lady Bracknell variety, and Alvilde took after her. As captain of Woodlands, the smart girls' school near Adelaide, she was a byword for bossiness (as some junior girls of the time still recalled in 2004). She was also an attractive girl whose mother gave her a thorough schooling in the domestic arts, and she helped her father by charming the troublesome local politicians who came to dine at Government House. She also (as she later confided to Jim) succumbed to her father's sexual advances, an experience which resulted in some trauma, making an already prickly personality more so, and giving her an ambivalent attitude towards men. The contemporaries to whom she felt closest in adolescence were Margaret Newlands, her inseparable schoolfriend at Woodlands, and her handsome cousin Angus Menzies, who turned out to be gay.

After the family's return from Australia Alvilde caused a stir as a debutante with her 'proud beauty'; her many suitors included Garrett Moore and Johnnie Churchill. In 1933, aged twenty-three, she married a family connection three years her senior, Anthony Chaplin, son and heir of Viscount Chaplin. Though it was no love-match but an arranged marriage fixed up by their mothers,* Anthony seemed to have much to

---

*Lady Bridges' brother, the whisky heir Jack Menzies, had married Lady Chaplin's first cousin, the shipping heiress Susanna Wilson (though the fortunes of both families diminished somewhat during the twentieth century).

offer as a husband: he possessed Byronic looks and charm, excellent social connections, and a wide if dilettantish knowledge of the arts and sciences, having ambitions as both a composer and a zoologist. The Chaplins had an unusual honeymoon, joining a zoological expedition to New Guinea organised by Lord Moyne (father of Bryan Guinness who had married Diana Mitford). Alvilde tried to share her husband's interests, and enjoyed their life in high society: they attended the lavish receptions and house parties of Anthony's formidable aunt Lady Londonderry, and spent their summers in Scotland as guests of Anthony's cousin the Duke of Sutherland. Unfortunately Anthony had little money of his own (as the only child of fairly rich parents, she had more), and was obliged to work in the City; but he became bored with his job and with English social life, and in 1937 moved with his wife to Paris to study composition with the famous teacher Nadia Boulanger.

While based on a certain mutual esteem, the Chaplins' marriage was not altogether happy. Alvilde found their lovemaking a trial; and although she gave birth in 1934 to a daughter, Clarissa, she later told Jim that her relations with Anthony had been so perfunctory that she found it difficult to understand how the child had been conceived. Anthony for his part turned out to be a serial seducer of young women in the mould of General Bridges. While they lived in London Alvilde tolerated his infidelities (she could hardly do otherwise in view of her reluctance to fulfil her own conjugal responsibilities); but when, in Paris, he flaunted his relationship with a young violinist, she retaliated by going to live with Princess Winnie de Polignac – whom the Chaplins had come to know as the city's great musical hostess, and who had fallen in love with Alvilde. Despite the difference in their ages (the Princess was then seventy-two, Alvilde twenty-seven) they began a lesbian affair, in which Alvilde at first took the submissive role. The sexual side of their relationship probably subsided as the Princess began to suffer from angina during 1938, but Alvilde remained her inseparable companion, being named as a leading beneficiary in the Princess's final will signed in April 1939. In a reversal of their original roles, Alvilde seems rather to have bossed the old lady in what became something of a love–hate relationship; as Nancy Mitford wrote to Gerald Berners in 1947, 'Alvilde . . . told me she suffers dreadful remorse over having been horrid to the Princess – I never thought it was quite her fault, they were thoroughly on each other's nerves.'

For forty years Princess Winnie, with her wealth (derived from her American father's sewing-machine) and her ability to recognise genius, had been Paris's leading patroness of the arts, especially music; and living with her was an education. For two years before the war Alvilde rubbed shoulders with the numerous distinguished people who flocked to the Princess's famous *salon* on the corner of the avenue Henri Martin and the rue Cortambert: these included composers such as Stravinsky and Poulenc, performers such as the pianist Cortot and the singer Chaliapin, artists such as Cocteau and Bérard, writers such as Colette and Rosamond Lehmann, cultivated French aristocrats such as Charles de Noailles and his wife Marie-Laure, and society lesbians such as Violet Trefusis and Gertrude Stein. Alvilde brought her infant daughter to live with her at the Princess's, where they were often visited by Anthony: she continued to be interested in her husband's career and had no desire to end a marriage which gave her social position and respectability. In this she may have been influenced by the Princess, who had been the best of friends with her own husband, Prince Edmond de Polignac, though they had eschewed sexual relations and led separate lives; like Winnie, Alvilde seems to have married her husband largely for his name and connections (though Edmond differed from Anthony in that he was old enough to be his wife's father, and homosexual). Indeed, there is evidence that Anthony encouraged his wife's relationship with the Princess and (for he himself was an aspiring composer in search of patronage) profited from it. When, in January 1940, Lady Londonderry criticised Alvilde for neglecting her nephew and bringing scandal on the family, Anthony wrote to her angrily: 'I'm not surprised she is hurt, for anybody less selfish and more determined to sacrifice herself to those she loves I have never met. It is thanks to Alvilde that I am able to lead a creative life of comparative sanity in a world driven mad by muddlers, whose names will be forgotten when those of superior minds, Princess Winnie's among them, remain monuments among the ruins of European culture.'

Winnie and Alvilde were in England when war broke out in September 1939, and decided to remain there for the duration. Alvilde's mother had died in 1937; her father followed in November 1939; Anthony joined the RAF as a rear gunner (telling Jim, when they met at Emerald Cunard's, that 'the camaraderie among the crew was such that it could only be described as pure love'). Alvilde trained as a hospital nurse and otherwise devoted herself to looking after the increasingly ailing Princess until her death in 1943 at the age of seventy-eight. By her pre-war will the Princess left Alvilde her jewellery, her summer house at Jouy-en-Josas near Paris, complete with contents, and a slice of the residue of her complex estate (which was otherwise divided among her numerous nephews and nieces) – though it took a year or two to come into this inheritance after the liberation of France. Meanwhile Alvilde had been left fairly well off by the deaths of her parents, though all the possessions she had inherited from them were destroyed when the warehouse storing them was bombed.

After the war Alvilde moved her main residence from London to Jouy, for life was far pleasanter in France than in England, and she was able to avoid paying crippling British taxes on her now substantial income: as a tax exile, she could only come to England for ninety days of the year. She joined a set of smart English society women in Paris, including Diana Cooper (whose husband Duff was Ambassador until 1947 and who stayed on afterwards), Nancy Mitford (who used the royalties from her novel *The Pursuit of Love* to move to the French capital and be near her great love Gaston Palweski), Daisy Fellowes and Violet Trefusis. She continued to see artistic protégés of Princess Winnie such as Poulenc and Cocteau, and through her friendship with Charles de Noailles and the Duchesse d'Harcourt she moved in the highest French social circles. Anthony joined her quite often, sometimes bringing his mistress of the moment, though Alvilde was now enjoying a complex love life of her own, mostly but not exclusively lesbian.

Alvilde's experiences with her father and husband gave her a horror of womanising 'rotters' (though she allowed herself to be seduced by another example of the species, Duff Cooper), and a consequent liking for sexually ambiguous men. Her beloved cousin Angus Menzies (whom Jim found 'a seductive creature, just slightly affected' with 'glossy black hair and a Michelangelo mouth and eyes') was homosexual, as were many of Princess Winnie's protégés, such as the English composer Lennox Berkeley. In London during and after the war she gathered around her a circle of well-bred bachelors: apart from Angus and Lennox these included Jamesey Pope-Hennessy, Eddy Sackville-West, David Herbert, Derek Hill, the eye-surgeon 'Pat' Trevor-Roper and the American-born horticulturist Rory Cameron. All these men were (or soon became) friends of Jim, who himself joined the circle after meeting Alvilde at Princess Winnie's, being invited to the (largely male) dinner parties she gave after the Princess's death. He admired her from the first for her beauty, elegance, sophistication and resourcefulness; like many of her male friends, he also got something of a thrill from her rather bossy, nannyish personality. Alvilde was not averse to having physical relationships with her bisexual admirers; she had a postwar affair with Rory

Cameron (mostly conducted in France where they were both domiciled*) and became pregnant by him (but aborted the child). On 4 May 1946, after Jim had taken her to dinner and the cinema in London, he wrote that 'I almost loved her this evening and kissed her affectionately on leaving her at her hotel' – which may signify more than it says. But after she moved to France they ceased to see much of each other until 1949: in Jim's published diaries, she is mentioned eight times in 1944, but only twice in each of the following four years.

A feature of Jim's psychology was that he tended to feel romantic about people because they reminded him of others he had known in the past. (Hence his feelings for Diana Mitford and Bridget Parsons, who recalled their brothers, his Eton loves Tom and Desmond.) The person Alvilde brought to mind was almost certainly Kathleen Kennet, another woman of diverse talent and determined personality who, after being sexually abused in her adolescence (in her case by an older cousin), came to enjoy the proximity of gay men. When she died in 1947 in her late sixties, after a battle with cancer, Jim was grief-stricken. After his last visit to her he wrote that 'this woman is dear to me because with her I need never dissemble in mind or spirit; with her there is no call for flattery and insincerity, no barriers of any kind'. (It is clear from the context that he especially means to imply that he could be open with her about his homosexuality.) He noted that no loss had affected him more apart from that of Tom; he found it curious that, for days afterwards, he was 'tormented by sex'. Possibly Alvilde was aware of this association in Jim's mind; for on 31 December 1948 she invited him to see the film *Scott of the Antarctic*, in which the young Kathleen was played by Diana Churchill (a blonde beauty unconnected with Winston Churchill's daughter of that name who twenty years earlier had declared a fondness for Jim). 'How strange to see featured in a film a woman I had known so intimately as K.,' wrote Jim. 'She played the part quite well and K. would not have objected, I fancy. No sentiment she would have been ashamed of.' Alvilde and Anthony (for they continued to keep up the appearance of their marriage) had recently rented Cecil Beaton's house in Pelham Place for a month, just round the corner from Jim's flat in Thurloe Square; and she and Jim saw much of each other in January 1949. On the 2nd the Chaplins dined

---

*At Emerald Cunard's Jim had met Rory's Australian-born mother Enid, Countess of Kenmare, known as 'Lady Killmore' as her four husbands, each grander than the last, had all died within a short time of marrying her. Soon after the war she used her accumulated wealth to buy La Fiorentina, a magnificent villa on the tip of Cap Ferrat, where she went to live with Rory, who created a fabulous garden there.

with Jim to meet the Dashwoods; on the 10th Jim dined with the Chaplins to meet Eddie Marsh; on the 16th Alvilde (without Anthony) dined with Jim to meet Eardley; on the 19th Jim dined with the Chaplins to meet the Sachie Sitwells. Anthony then faded out of the picture. On 20 January Jim took Alvilde to the theatre; the following day they dined at Sibyl Colefax's; the day after that, they went together to a memorial service for Jim's fellow 'Georgian' Peter Derwent. Alvilde invited Jim to stay with her and Anthony at Portofino in February, but Jim regretted that he could not afford to go.

Alvilde then left for the Continent; but on 13 February she telephoned Jim from Amalfi urging him to join her and Anthony in Rome. He could not resist; and two generous friends helped him out, Rick Stewart-Jones paying his fare and Paz Subercaseaux giving him enough Italian *lire* for his expenses. 'It is heavenly being in Rome again [last visited the previous September] after so short an interval,' he wrote a week later. For the first time he realised the full oddity of the Chaplins' marriage, for while Alvilde wanted to see the artistic treasures of the city with Jim, Anthony declined to accompany them, claiming to be absorbed in a study of Italian amphibia: as soon as Jim joined them at their hotel, Anthony insisted on showing him a rare toad he had discovered at Paestum and was keeping in a chamber pot. Jim took her to see the Castle of St Angelo, the Sistine Chapel, the Vatican Museum and the Villa d'Este. After three days they left by car for Florence. Alvilde was 'the perfect travelling companion', while Anthony positively refused to look at buildings or pictures on the way and would 'stop only to look at frogs in ponds'. In Florence they met Harold Acton, and Jim showed Alvilde the Ognissanti church, the Uffizi and the Duomo. When the hotel staff made Alvilde remove her pekinese from the dining room, Anthony wondered what they would say if they knew he had two toads in his pockets. After a stop at Pisa they proceeded to Portofino, where they spent a week at the *castelletto* of the Chaplins' friends the Cliffords. This was a rather disappointing experience: there was a biting wind; the terrain was too hilly to allow much walking; Jim suffered from toothache and had to visit a dentist in Rapallo. But the three of them got on well. 'Such laughter we have. They say I must come and live with them in Paris. Alvilde is incredibly generous and pays for everything.' Jim parted from them at Genoa on 5 March to return to England by train.

Back in London, Jim wrote: 'My mind a turmoil. A fire has been lit.' He and Alvilde were presumably lovers by this time, though the diaries never refer directly to the fact: this is not merely for reasons of circumspection but also because, under the divorce laws of the time, the validity of Alvilde's subsequent marriage to Jim might have been jeopardised had it been established that they had had an adulterous relationship while Alvilde was still married to Anthony. Within ten days of Jim's return Alvilde followed him to London, staying for a week on her own at the Dorchester.* They refused invitations from friends and spent their evenings *à deux*, dining and going to the theatre. 'I am in a daze,' he wrote on 19 March. 'I do not quite realise what has happened to me. This is the first time that a woman I have loved has loved me. I say "loved" which is totally different to "lusted after". I have had plenty of reciprocal lust of one sort or another. I want to be with her all the time.' Next day he continued: 'The reality of this love dawns on me slowly like a creeping paralysis. One becomes a victim to a great power which is irresistible. How selfish I have been hitherto, all the stony way to middle age.' When Alvilde returned to France, Jim promised to join her there for Easter.

Jim was now extremely busy: apart from his normal work at the National Trust, which had accumulated during his unscheduled holiday in Italy, he had to introduce the new Secretary, Jack Rathbone, to his duties, and give evidence before the Gowers Committee which had started sitting. Moreover, a new set of emotional circumstances arose which provided a contrast to those arising from his love for Alvilde. At the beginning of April his father was diagnosed with bladder cancer, and underwent an apparently successful operation in London to remove two growths. The specialist told Jim that the reprieve was merely temporary and that George could live for two years at most. However his parents, who were now devoted to each other, remained blissfully ignorant of this news and returned to Wickhamford happy in the thought that he was on the way to recovery. Feeling more than a twinge of guilt, Jim left to spend Easter at Jouy; Alvilde, 'looking radiant and beautiful', met him in Paris and drove him there. 'Her house most picturesquely set on a hill with a Turneresque view over a valley, crossed by a Louis XIV aqueduct in the background. The village hidden by misty trees below. The moon was shining in the sky, the nightingales singing like sopranos, everything as romantic as could be desired while, arm-in-arm, we walked into the garden and into the house where Anthony was playing Mozart on the piano.' Anthony's presence was no impediment to their affair. On the contrary, 'Anthony behaves wonderfully to me. We are a sort of blood

---

*The hotel was built on the site of the house of Alvilde's aunt Lady Holford with whom she had lived during the First World War.

brothers . . . He is delighted because A. is made happy. It is all A's, the house, the money, everything. Was there ever such a topsy-turvy business?' Clarissa, aged fifteen, was present too, and her father's talk with her 'about his love affairs and sex life makes my hair stand on end, but not hers, evidently'. Anthony took them all to a marsh to hear a chorus of frogs sing at night. 'He says their voices were the first animal voices to be heard on earth – an impressive thought.'

Jim and Alvilde were now passionately in love and could only think of being together, a complicated matter owing to Jim's work in London and Alvilde's inability to join him there for more than a few days at a time. Within a fortnight of his Easter visit Jim was back at Jouy, 'I having to make untruthful excuses in the office, and feeling guilty and unhappy . . . Terrible black moments of despair are mercifully redeemed by moments of unadulterated bliss. I suppose this is often the case. Neither can be described.' They visited Versailles, which they were shown by Alvilde's friend the curator; they heard Jim's old lover George Chavchavadze perform a piano concerto (badly, Alvilde thought); they went to Chantilly to have tea with the Duff Coopers, Jim finding Diana 'very offhand'. Jim noted with pride that 'A. is considered one of the best-dressed women in France, which for an Englishwoman is some compliment'. When Alvilde next came to London, Jim accompanied her to Clarissa's confirmation at her school near Cirencester. At Whitsun Jim was again at Jouy, 'a curious party à quatre' as Anthony's young mistress (and future wife) Rosemary Lyttelton was staying ('very pretty and slight . . . musical, talented, and extremely intelligent, well-read for her age, and much in love with Anthony'). They all got on well. In London a few days later Alvilde bought a ring for Jim in the Burlington Arcade, while he gave her a ring he had worn for eleven years (presumably since the start of his affair with Rick Stewart-Jones in 1938) and had had reduced in size to fit her. 'We realise this exchange is sentimental but believe it is the best troth plight available . . . Our love is now established and permanent.'

They now had to endure five weeks of separation, during which they both brooded on their predicament. How were they to make a life together without either his giving up his work for the National Trust or her giving up her French tax residence (and hence 80 per cent of her income)? A possible solution was for Jim to seek a part-time job with the Trust, which would leave him free to spend the rest of his time with her abroad, pursuing his writing career. As Anthony and Rosemary wished to live together, it seemed to make sense for Alvilde to divorce him to marry Jim. But as a Catholic, Jim could only marry her if the Church granted an annulment of the Chaplin marriage. He also felt uncomfortable about living off a rich wife. Jim consulted his friends. Jamesey was encouraging, assuring him that 'it is middle-class to have financial scruples because she has money and I have none, and ridiculous to have religious scruples about divorce'. Harold, who did not care for her (though he naturally did not say so), was non-committal, while Vita advised him to marry if he had the chance. Other women took a less friendly view. Anne Rosse asked him, 'Is it true that you are in love with that hard little thing Alvilde?' Midi Gascoigne urged him 'to bear in mind that you may be sacrificing your country, your religion, your career and your independence'. Eardley advised Jim to pursue the dictates of his heart and said 'that he would chuck Long Crichel and his perfect life there for love and give all he possessed to the loved one'. Lord Esher, when Jim told him (as they were driving to Attingham for the opening of the state apartments) that he was thinking of leaving the National Trust to live abroad and devote himself to writing, was appalled. 'He said that nobody else could do my job but me, whereas thousands of people could write books better than me. I said yes, I was sure of that, but my health was not so good and I was tired.' Esher suggested that if such was the case they should find him 'a very rich deputy' who could take the pressure off him without having to be paid.

In July Jim and Alvilde spent a week motoring in Provence, where Alvilde (a great sun-worshipper) was thinking of buying a house in the event of Jim being able to live with her. Their reunion after more than a month's separation was not as joyous as it might have been, and in fact proved to be the first unsatisfactory time they had spent together. Weeks of pondering their problems had set them both on edge. At Chalon-sur-Saône he 'made a confession [one can but guess what] which greatly disconcerted' her. He was also discovering things about her which disconcerted him. He found her 'a fussing car owner who shouts directions all the time and gets rather impatient with me. In fact she is impatient with inefficiency, hesitancy and hopelessness, which are among my many failings.' Although he thought Aix 'a ravishing little town set like a jewel in open country', he was 'a little depressed' at the thought of living in Provence, and asked if they might not live in Italy instead, to which she replied that she could never do so because of the Italians' cruelty to animals. 'It is so frequently the case that people who care so vehemently for animals do not care for humans,' Jim commented to his diary. After Jim's return to London Alvilde wrote to him admitting that she had become rather bad-tempered in view of the frustrations of their situation, but assuring him that she would not be so if married to him. Jim commented: 'I don't believe this because she was cross when we were together. I am extremely cross now too, and I fear it would be so with her after we were married, though not at first.'

The next episode in their affair was a three-week Italian holiday in September, during which they visited Lake Garda, Verona, Milan and Venice. They ran into many people they knew, some of whom, such as Kenneth Clark and Cyril Connolly, were a boon, while others, such as the Permanent Secretary to the Ministry of Works, had to be avoided. While they were there, Anthony's father died and Alvilde became Viscountess Chaplin (on which Connolly congratulated her, which she and Jim considered in poor taste). At the end of the trip, Jim wrote: 'Now my relations with A. have entered a new phase, undergone a sea change from the first fine careless rapture into something richer and possibly stranger. It is part of the inevitable process of love.' And he added (in a passage which, at her request, he expurgated before publication in 1985):

At times we had rows, mostly slight, but some of them deep. Since I do not know which of my tiresome habits rile her I cannot enumerate them. No doubt there are plenty, for she gets cross and snaps at me and grouses like a spoiled child. This conduct has a most unfortunate effect on me, makes me want to escape, turns me in on myself, makes my love grow tepid. A. instantly recovers from these bouts which leave me unhappy and disturbed. Dwelling on them I say that I do not think after all I can live with her permanently. She says I have changed and gone back on what I repeatedly wrote to her during the summer. There is some truth in this. I am very worried. I still believe I can live forever with the Alvilde I knew before we went to Aix; whereas the other Alvilde I could not live with, the Alvilde that fusses over inessentials and takes things badly. There was a night on Lake Garda when I left her in the garden in anger, and walked by myself under the moon along the shore, and sat on the shingle praying for help from the lapping waves. When I returned A. was in tears. Then I was all penitence. There were other moments when she taxed me angrily with no longer loving her. I could give no honest answer for during those moments I had temporarily ceased to love her.

Jim thus foresaw that life with her would expose him to much nagging and recrimination, and it occurred to him to end the affair at this point. But he had made commitments to her from which he could not easily extricate himself; and their next meetings, during her visits to England in October and November, though not entirely free of difficulties, were happy on the whole, and made him feel that, in this relationship as in others, the rough had to be taken with the smooth. As he wrote:

> A. and I have reached a happier and even high plane but she wants to be with me all the time. This is where I fail for I cannot be with anyone all the time . . . I console myself with the certitude that no true and enduring love affair ever runs entirely smoothly. How can two individuals, who choose to coalesce, not clash fairly frequently? The triumph of love consists, not in winning, but enduring. Marriage is a very unnatural state. But then so are logic and art unnatural. All the most worthwhile and glorious things achieved by mankind are unnatural. To be natural is to be animal. Only fly-by-night lovers expect to have no ups and downs – for six weeks at most.

Meanwhile Jim had to attend to the other domestic crisis in his life, resulting from his father's rapid decline. The seriousness of his condition could no longer be concealed – 'when he does not come to talk to me in the morning then I knows how ill he is', remarked Haines, the family chauffeur and stalwart retainer – and in September it fell to Jim to break the news to his mother that the doctors held out little hope and he could only survive a matter of months. She reacted stoically, remarking that she could not imagine life without him after forty-five years – at which Jim 'marvelled that she seemed to have forgotten those long wretched years when they were on the worst possible terms'. George himself remained cheerful, talking about buying a new racehorse and visiting the casino at Deauville; but on 29 November Jim learnt that he was dying, and rushed to Wickhamford. 'He was lying on Mama's bed, curled up on one side, his head twisted, almost unrecognisable. His head was wizened to a skull with skin stretched tightly across it, so shrunk and taut it was. His mouth seemed to have slipped to one side of his face and his tongue lolled out. The breathing was deep, wracked and intermittent. How he would have hated me seeing him in that condition . . . I felt infinite compassion . . . perhaps for the first time I loved him unreservedly.' The following morning Jim and his mother were with him when he died, aged sixty-nine.

Jim recorded his feelings with some frankness. 'It was a terrible, harrowing experience, yet one which nearly every human being has to undergo, once if not twice a lifetime . . . The worst things about death are the disrespect, the vulgarity, the meanness. God should have arranged for dying people to disintegrate and disappear like a puff of smoke into the air. There are many other scraps of advice I could have given him.' The cremation at Cheltenham two days later was another ordeal; but worst of all was the subsequent memorial service in Wickhamford church, a place which had meant so much to Jim in childhood, represent-ing a form of religion which, partly to scorn his father, he had since forsaken. He was 'full of remorse for not having been more understand-ing and kinder, for until recently my father and I did not get on. He never liked me from the start, for which I do not blame him, although I think he should have tried to be nice to me first. Ours was a case of biological incompatibility. Our hackles rose on the mere approach of the other. Yet within his limitations he was a good man, respected by strangers and loved by his friends and other people's children.' His piety towards his departed father was matched by exasperation towards his bereaved mother, whose most irritating qualities, fuelled by drink, were brought to the fore by her loss. When he joined her for Christmas three weeks later, he found her 'vague, argumentative and cantankerous', and reflected: 'I now know what made me hestitate after A[lvilde]'s slight irritation with me when abroad this summer. It was fear that if I married her she might nag me as Mama has nagged my father ever since I can remember anything. Now I must never forget that until I was thirty my mother meant everything to me. We were as one. All things change and relationships turn topsy-turvy . . .'

George's estate was valued at some £110,000, worth around £2 mil-lion in early twenty-first century values, though this was but a fraction of what he himself had inherited, and little of what remained of it after payment of death duties was due to come to Jim. This was not unex-pected, for it had been agreed during the 1920s that his brother Dick would be their father's main beneficiary, while Jim would ultimately inherit the estate of their childless Uncle Alec; in any case, most of the diminished fortunes of both Alec and George went to their widows for their lifetimes. Nor could Jim quarrel with his father's decision to leave his shares in the family business and his remaining Lancashire properties to Dick; for Dick was now running (as he would continue to do for the remaining twenty years of its existence) the cotton mill in Oldham, which Jim wanted nothing to do with. (In September, after visiting Dick in Lancashire to discuss their father's illness, Jim had expressed his horror of 'that district of soiled rain like stair rods, black tearing clouds across the blackest moors and scarlet cottages, and tall chimneys like prison warders at every corner one tries to escape from'.) Jim retained affection for his brother and sister (if not for their spouses), but recent family meetings had made him painfully aware of 'how far I feel from them all'; the only relation with whom he still felt much affinity was his Aunt Deenie, the incarnation of sweetness and benevolence.

Following his father's death and obsequies Jim returned, no doubt with some relief, to sorting out the problems in the way of his relationship with Alvilde. During the last weeks of 1949 he was given some reason to be optimistic about his chances of obtaining both a half-time job with the National Trust and a papal annulment of the Chaplin marriage. Regarding the job, he was asked to wait until the Gowers Committee had reported in 1950, a moment at which the Trust would in any case be reassessing its future; clearly, no one wanted to lose him. Regarding the Chaplins, he was advised by the eminent Jesuit Martin D'Arcy 'that if Anthony and Alvilde could establish that their marriage had never been taken seriously, an annulment was possible, notwithstanding that a child had been born to their union'. Alvilde, always one for having her cake and eating it, took the view that, until the annulment came through and she was able to marry Jim, she would rather not divorce Anthony, preferring to remain married to him and his title in the eyes of the world. This, however, failed to take account of the wishes of Anthony, who – having come into some money on his father's death and thus no longer being financially dependant on his wife – wanted to put an end to their sham marriage after seventeen years. On the last day of 1949 Anthony and Jim lunched together to discuss the situation.

> The occasion was as happy as could be. Anthony definitely wants A. to divorce him, but he will not marry Rosemary, he assures me. He merely wants to be free: of what, I asked him? Not of A., for he has been free from her ever since he married her? He agrees with me that I would make a great mistake to abandon the National Trust altogether. I told him that A. was depressed by the thought of a divorce. He said this was pure sentiment for, once the divorce was over, he would see as much of A. as before; and that I must try to make her happy. This should be the first objective of the years that remain to me. We parted in mutual piety.

That evening Jim and Alvilde went to the theatre and dined at the Savoy. He 'promised her that if Anthony goes I will live with her and marry her when I get the Church's consent. We went home to her flat before midnight and were together when the New Year came in.'

That was the last entry of the regular diary which Jim kept from 1942 to 1949. He had in fact considered giving it up the previous May, having come to regard it as 'a vice, an indulgence' which largely duplicated the daily letters he was writing to Alvilde while they were separated. Now that he had definitely decided to give up full-time work with the National Trust and live with her, he had further reason to discontinue it. In so far as it was intended to describe his visits to English country houses and their owners, these were going to be fewer in future; in so far as it dealt with his personal life and thoughts, he no doubt thought it wise, as he prepared for married life, not to leave such a record lying about for her or others to read. Apart from sporadic journals which he kept for short periods, some of which he later destroyed, he was not to keep a regular diary again for another twenty-one-and-a-half years. This is a pity, for as a diarist he vividly evokes the spirit of the 1940s (as he was later to do with regard to the last three decades of the century), and it would have been fascinating to read his contemporary accounts of the 1950s and '60s, which were certainly not lacking in incident and drama as regards his own life.

Nineteen-fifty was to be Jim's last year of full-time work for the National Trust. At its meeting of 13 December the Historic Buildings Committee 'agreed to recommend that a new part-time appointment of Historic Buildings Adviser should be created and held by Mr Lees-Milne . . . [to] take effect from 1 January 1951 and [be] reviewed after a year's trial'. Jim's successor as Historic Buildings Secretary, appointed on his recommendation, was Robin Fedden, a dashing mountaineer and writer who had been serving as custodian of Polesden Lacey since 1945 and as Representative in South-Eastern England since 1946. Though he was a different type to Jim – self-consciously brilliant and a great seducer of women (though married to a lesbian) – they liked and respected each other and always got on well. (Fedden's weakness was heavy drinking, though he managed to keep this under control during his twenty-three years in the job.) For the Trust, the great event in 1950 which concerned Jim was the report of the Gowers Committee in June, and the consequent discussions between the Trust and the Government. Among the important properties with which Jim was involved during his final year as Historic Buildings Secretary were the neo-Norman Penrhyn Castle in Snowdonia, accepted by the Government in part payment of death duties and offered to the Trust (which accepted it on Jim's recommendation despite some scepticism from the Committee), and two great houses in Derbyshire which the new Duke of Devonshire, Debo's husband Andrew, hoped to get rid of in order to meet the crippling taxes on his succession – Hardwick and Chatsworth (of which the first eventually passed to the Trust, while the second, at which Jim was to be a frequent guest, remained in the hands of the family and was managed by them with outstanding success both as a tourist attraction and a centre of local life). The other noteworthy event in Jim's professional life during 1950 was the completion of *Tudor Renaissance*, published by Batsford in July

1951, to be considered in the next chapter together with the rest of Jim's output as an architectural historian. Suffice it to say here that, while not without merit, it was one of his less successful books and received mixed reviews – a fact which undoubtedly dented his confidence soon after he had arranged to devote half his working life to his calling as a writer.

In 1950 Alvilde began divorce proceedings against Anthony, and a provisional decree (probably based, as most society divorces then were, on fabricated 'hotel evidence') was granted that year and made absolute early in 1951. Throughout the year of the proceedings Jim and Alvilde had to take care, owing to the then state of the law,* not to be seen together in public or give the impression of cohabiting or even intending to do so in future. This accounts for such absurdities as Jim's letter to Paul Methuen explaining the reasons for his resignation as Historic Buildings Secretary, which makes no mention of Alvilde (though Paul, as a man of the world and an admirer of women, would perfectly have understood Jim's situation and had probably been informed about it):

> It took a lot of deciding, because as you know the Trust had for the past 15 years been the better part of my life, and I am so devoted to it. In fact that was in a sense the trouble. It absorbed too much of me and I was find-ing the office work on top of everything else a strain. Unfortunately the insanity of the world one inhabits does not allow one to benefit in one country from a little money one may have in another, and so I am obliged to live (at least ostensibly) more than half the year abroad.

Once the divorce became final, Jim and Alvilde were at last able to live together openly and had to decide where to do so. In London the problem was solved by the benevolence of Jim's landlord Geoffrey Houghton Brown, who might have been expected to disapprove of Jim's new domestic arrangements but who in fact (like other masochistic homo-sexual men) rather liked Alvilde. (His attitude was different from that of Jim's other old admirer Ted Lister, who promptly rescinded his bequest to Jim of Westwood Manor.) Geoffrey proposed that Jim give up his ground floor flat at 20 Thurloe Square and take instead the top three floors, to give enough space for himself, Alvilde and Clarissa. This turned out to be an ideal solution; the new flat was converted, decorated and filled with their possessions during the summer of 1951, and 'Miss Emily'

---

*Under which a wife suing for divorce on the grounds of her husband's adultery was required not to be in an adulterous relationship herself; a public official, the King's Proctor, conducted 'investigations' into the private lives of plaintiffs in cases where 'suspicious circumstances' were brought to the notice of the court.

continued to look after Jim and his new family. As regards their continental life, both Jim and Alvilde wanted to spend their winters on the Mediterranean; and during the first half of 1951 she sold her property at Jouy to buy La Meridienne, a house with a vineyard in the picturesque village of Roquebrune, just outside Monte Carlo and a few kilometres from the Italian frontier. This purchase was inspired partly by the breathtaking situation of the new residence, on a steep hillside facing the sea, partly by the fact that many friends lived nearby, such as Daisy Fellowes and Rory Cameron, partly by the circumstance that, in 1949, Prince Rainier had succeeded his grandfather Prince Louis as ruler of Monaco and invited his exiled father, Prince Pierre, to return to live in the Principality.* Pierre – a Polignac by birth, and homosexual – was Princess Winnie's nephew-by-marriage and shared her passion for music (they had been jointly responsible for luring Diaghilev's Ballets Russes to Monte Carlo in the 1920s); now that he was living in Monaco again as the father of the ruler (establishing himself not in the royal palace but in a sumptuous apartment in the Hôtel de Paris), he carried on her tradition by setting up a music foundation and festival. Alvilde, who had seen much of him in Paris in the 1930s (in fact it was he who had originally introduced the Chaplins to his aunt), and again after the war, was drawn to the Monaco area† by the prospect of being on close terms with the local royalty, as well as of seeing the survivors of the Princess's musical circle. Jim and Alvilde moved into La Meridienne in August 1951.

There remained the problem of the papal annulment of the Chaplin marriage. Jim applied for this at the same time as Alvilde sued for divorce; but by the time the divorce came through, it was nowhere in sight. Moreover, although Anthony, to encourage Alvilde to proceed with the divorce, had assured her that he would not remarry until Jim had obtained the annulment, once divorced he had no hesitation in breaking his word, and married Rosemary in March 1951. This enraged Alvilde, who with her acute sense of social proprieties could not bear the thought of still

---

*Monaco underwent a succession crisis after the First World War, as neither the inhabitants nor the French authorities were willing to countenance the German cousin who was Prince Louis' legitimate heir. The Prince therefore legitimised his natural daughter Charlotte and married her off in 1920 to a French aristocrat, Count Pierre de Polignac. However, Charlotte turned out to be a nymphomaniac and Pierre a homosexual, and such was their behaviour that, a few years after the birth of Rainier in 1923, the marriage was annulled and both were banished from the Principality.

†Roquebrune, constructed around a mediaeval Monégasque fortress, had been part of Monaco until 1861, since when it had been in France just beyond the Principality's borders.

carrying Anthony's name while being upstaged by his new wife. She therefore pressed Jim to marry her, annulment or no. This caused Jim some soul-searching, for marriage under such circumstances would result in excommunication, as the Catholic Church did not recognise divorce and regarded second marriages, where former spouses remained alive, as bigamous. For some months he struggled with his conscience. However, in the autumn of 1951, there still being no sign of the annulment,* he fell in with her wishes: his faith was perhaps not what it had been, and the judgement of his Catholic friends was sympathetic rather than censorious. As his fellow convert Lennox Berkeley — Alvilde's friend from Princess Winnie days, who had since become, along with his delightful young wife Freda, a friend of Jim's — wrote to him:

> I know what a struggle it must have been for you to come to a decision. I feel sure that in the circs I should have acted as you have. As we were saying last night, the Church has to have these very strict rules, but I can't help feeling that there are cases where the only sensible solution involves breaking with strict observance. I think there have been many Catholics who have found themselves obliged to lead their religious lives 'en marge' for reasons similar to yours, but remaining true Catholics at heart.

Others thought it boded ill for the future that Alvilde had pressed him to marry despite his religious doubts: Vita feared that, during their first marital row, Jim would say to her, 'And to think that for you I was prepared to sacrifice my immortal soul . . .'

The marriage took place at Chelsea Register Office on 19 November 1951. Four witnesses were present: Harold and Vita (the latter making one of her now rare visits to London), Jamesey and Angus Menzies. Harold wrote in his diary: 'I stand on Jim's right, and Angus on Alvilda's [sic] left and the registrar reads out a formula which they repeat. Then they sign the book. It does not take more than five minutes. It is embarrassing and sad.' They all went for lunch to the new flat in Thurloe Square, where they were joined by Lennox and Freda Berkeley and Rick Stewart-Jones and his new wife Emma. (Rick had met, fallen in love with and married the young novelist Emma Smith earlier that year, giving no warning to any of his friends or relations, most of whom were rather surprised.) It

---

* Some years later an annulment was finally granted, enabling Jim and Alvilde to solemnise their marriage in an Italian church. It has not been possible to discover exactly when this occurred, though it seems to have been during the early 1960s – as Jim had certainly been 'readmitted' to the Church by the late 1960s when he served on both the Arts Committee of the Brompton Oratory and a Papal Commission to investigate the provenance of St Peter's Chair.

may have been some reassurance to Jim that all three husbands among the guests, as well as the two bachelors, were homosexual, three of the five being ex-lovers of himself. 'It is rather strained and uneasy,' wrote Harold of the lunch party. 'We do not know whether to pretend it is a sudden happy union or to take it wholly as a matter of course. The presence of a wedding cake makes it all the more awkward.' On their Ruby Wedding forty years later, Jim also remembered it as a 'rather dismal' occasion, and that the rest of the day was worse. In the afternoon they drove to Worcestershire to meet his mother and Aunt Deenie. 'Neither liked A.,' recalled Jim, 'which put me in an embarrassed mood, I not having the character to rise above such things. Then we stayed the night at the Lygon Arms in Broadway, whereas we should have gone abroad to some delectable Mediterranean shore. It was a cloud upon our marriage, one of several that I now prefer not to dwell upon.'

10

Married Life
1951–8

FOR THE FIRST eight years of his marriage to Alvilde, Jim lived a curiously fragmented life. It was spent partly in England, partly abroad; partly working for the National Trust, partly writing his architectural books; partly together with her, in an approximation of conventional married life, partly apart from her, in something of a continuation of his former, homosexually-tinged bachelor life. Their annual routine ran as follows. After celebrating Christmas together in England, they would spend the winter in Roquebrune. After Easter he would go alone to London to take up residence at 20 Thurloe Square and his duties with the National Trust; she, still able to spend an average of only ninety days of the year in England in order to preserve her French tax residence, would join him there during 'the Season' from May to July. At the end of August, after deputising for Robin Fedden during his summer holiday, he would rejoin her in Roquebrune. At some point in the autumn he would return to England, where she would join him for Christmas.

Despite its proximity to the bustle of Monte Carlo – and the fact that local life had only recently returned to normal after the entire population had been deported by the Germans for Resistance activity – Roquebrune retained a timeless character, far from the modern world. From Cap Martin, just beyond the eastern border of Monaco, a winding road mounted a steep hillside to the village *place*, three sides of which contained shops, cafés and municipal offices, the fourth side being a cliff-edge with a panoramic view of the coast. There one had to leave one's car, for the narrow, cobbled streets beyond were inaccessible to traffic. The village included an imposing mediaeval fortress, a beautifully decorated rustic church, and an agglomeration of ancient stone houses, the best of which faced the sea and included terraced vineyards running down the slopes. La Meridienne was one of the last of these at the eastern end of the village, near the mountain path which led to Menton and the Italian frontier and some half a kilometre from the *place* (from which Jim had to struggle with their luggage when they arrived for the winter). It was a simple, two-storey structure, little more than a peasant farmhouse, but Alvilde made it delectable with Regency furniture, chintzy decoration and pretty works of art, and transformed the vine terraces into a ravishing tumbling garden. The main room on the ground floor, dominated by a grand piano, opened onto a fragrant terrace overlooking the garden and sea where they had their meals whenever the weather permitted. There were two tiny outbuildings, a *grenier* which eventually became a snuggery and a pavilion known as 'the *wagon-lit*' which Jim used as his writing-room, also containing a divan and wash-basin for guests. A woman from the village, Walterine, came in daily and acted as caretaker in their absence, though requiring some instruction in the ways of civilised living – Jim recorded an occasion when their royal friend Pierre de Monaco, 'pompous and correct', paid an unexpected call, to be greeted by Walterine shouting from an upstairs window that '*Madame est au water!*'

Their life in Roquebrune was not one of total idleness and pleasure. Jim worked hard at his books (a steady stream of the works he needed to consult was sent out from the London Library and Heywood Hill), and went for long, ruminative walks in the mountain paths behind the village. Alvilde dedicated herself to her garden, and was involved, with her musical friends, in organising the annual Menton Festival. Their daily existence revolved around the local society. Roquebrune later became so fashionable as a retreat for the rich that the French authorities had to build a new village over the mountain crest to house the displaced native villagers; but in the 1950s most affluent local residents occupied modern villas along the road from Cap Martin to the *place* – these included Daisy Fellowes, the newspaper magnate Lord Iliffe, the Italian Princess Ottobone, the Gaullist hero General Billotte, and Lytton Strachey's sister Dorothy Bussy and her French artist husband. It was still considered rather daring and bohemian for sophisticated outsiders to live in the old village itself; apart from Jim and Alvilde, the only other notable couple to do so was the French novelist and diplomat Romain Gary and his wife, the English writer Lesley Blanch. (Alvilde and Lesley became great friends, but Jim did not care for Romain whom he found 'gloomy and morose'.) After her transformation of La Meridienne Alvilde became something of a local legend, particularly when it became known that she worked topless in her garden and cooked her own delicious meals; soon she and Jim knew everyone of consequence in the neighbourhood, and were receiving invitations from the many who were curious to visit the house. While keeping their distance from the villagers, they took care to cultivate good relations with their neighbour the *curé* and his housekeeper

'Mademoiselle Marie': after installing a telephone in 1956, they did not dare to complain when the wires became entangled with Marie's jasmine, so that their calls were interrupted by 'excruciating crackles and total cut-offs' in the early evening when she watered her plants.

Outside Roquebrune, the Lees-Milnes moved in the most sophisticated English society on the Riviera. Their friends included Alvilde's former lover Rory Cameron and his mother Enid Kenmare at La Fiorentina, and 'Willie' Somerset Maugham and his companion Alan Searle at the Villa Mauresque, both on Cap Ferrat; Lord and Lady Glenconner at their mountain retreat, La Baumette; the artist Graham Sutherland (an old friend of Eardley) and his wife Cathy at their house in the hills above Menton (found for them by Alvilde); and the millionaire art collector Douglas Cooper and his secretary John Richardson at the Château de Castille in Provence. They lunched with Winston Churchill (a sometime friend of Jim's grandfather and Alvilde's father) when he stayed at Lord Beaverbrook's villa, and got him to unveil a war memorial in Roquebrune. Through Alvilde's friendship with Prince Pierre they were also in touch with the Monégasque Court. In 1953 they were asked to lunch with Prince Rainier at the royal palace, 'a Ruritanian experience'; Jim found the ruler 'a good-looking young man, plump but not gross, a head somewhat like Napoleon's', and agreed with Alvilde that he would make a suitable husband for Clarissa. When in 1956 the Prince married Grace Kelly, the Lees-Milnes were invited to the wedding (though Jim resented donning white tie and tails early in the morning 'in order to stand in the transept of Monaco Cathedral until noon, then to consume éclairs and pink champagne at the palace until tea-time').

A steady stream of English friends came out to stay with them: Alvilde was a marvellous hostess, ensuring comfort and good food and organising amusing parties and excursions. Regular guests included Nancy Mitford, Lennox Berkeley, Eddy Sackville-West and Jamesey Pope-Hennessy. Nancy, now a celebrated novelist, had known Jim and Alvilde long before they had known each other. Lennox, one of the judges of Prince Pierre's annual composition prize, was a link with the world of Princess Winnie. Eddy used his frequent visits to sit for his portrait by Graham Sutherland, which the Lees-Milnes were the first to see. Jamesey, who was no longer close to Jim but developing a conspiratorial relationship with Alvilde, tended to stay with her in Jim's absence. Other friends visited them from nearby hotels, including the Oswald Mosleys: Jim had not seen Diana since Tom's death, and found her 'as beautiful as she was at seventeen'; Sir Oswald, though his conversation still resembled the 'harangue' Jim recalled from the 1931 election, seemed more 'balanced and sane'. They also received visits from Alvilde's French friends, such as Charles de Noailles (whom Jim admired as an exquisite aristocrat) and the artist-writer Philippe Jullian (a 'most lugubrious little man' whom he didn't like). One old friend of Jim who turned up unexpectedly was Hamish Erskine. As Jim wrote to their schoolfellow Michael Rosse (whose brother Desmond had once been Hamish's lover), 'he and I go for after-noon walks when he can escape from his new (and not very arduous) duties as confidential adviser to Daisy Fellowes! Can you imagine a less enviable job? It is awful that he should be reduced to such employment and worse still that he should seem quite contented.'

Clarissa often stayed at both La Meridienne and Thurloe Square. She was a few months short of eighteen when Jim married Alvilde, and preparing to come out as a debutante. She was a pretty and high-spirited girl but suffered from the spoiling and controlling attentions of her mother, and had few thoughts in her head except to have a good time. Jim did his best to be a good stepfather, but often found her irritating. He was relieved when she departed from Thurloe Square in July 1953 to visit her father, 'because I have a great deal to do without having to look after her. I get impatient with young girl frivolities, especially when her mother is away. To live with adolescents is really quite impractical and should not be suffered.' Jim and Alvilde both longed for her to make a suitable marriage. Failing Prince Rainier or a French duke, they had hopes of Hugh Seymour, 8th Marquess of Hertford, the handsome young owner of Ragley Hall, Warwickshire, and were disconcerted when she dismissed him as 'a pansy'. Evidently she was not going to take after her mother. Indeed, like many girls of her class she seemed to prefer a rougher kind of male, and Alvilde contrived to break up a number of unsuitable relationships. Doubtless to his relief, Jim saw less of her as the 1950s progressed. (In September 1956 he wrote to Eardley – who rather liked her – that she had spent the winter in America and was 'now in Spain, then has the loan of the house for three weeks for a party of friends, then perhaps London or Paris for a fortnight, then winter in the Bahamas – that's her life'.) In February 1954 Alvilde (then forty-four) felt unwell and thought she might be pregnant, a prospect which appalled them both; when it turned out to be a false alarm, Jim was 'so relieved that I forgot to worry about the possible worse consequences for A. I know many men are indifferent to children . . . but when [they have their own] a paternal instinct develops in them. Well, I am sure it never would in me, and that on the contrary I might hate mine.'

Jim's Roquebrune existence was unlike anything he had previously known – a life of modest luxury and ease, in a picturesque spot with a pleasant climate, providing tranquillity for work and a busy social life, but far removed from his usual friendships and interests. How did he take to it? The answer seems to be that he liked it in some ways and disliked it in others; but that the last year of this life was so painful to him (for reasons which will appear) that he later tended to remember the disadvantages rather than the advantages. As he wrote on hearing of Romain Gary's suicide in 1980, 'I hated Roquebrune, the isolation, the pentupness of our doll-like house and the claustrophobia of the village on a steep precipice betwixt mountain and deep blue sea'. He did not generally care for the French, whom he considered 'ferocious, mean and cruel'. He did not feel at home on the Riviera, that playground of the rich and idle. Some of their social contacts he enjoyed; others filled him with boredom and unease. At La Fiorentina, they would typically arrive to find 'luncheon at 2.30 and 20 persons assembled, having been assured by Rory there would be no one'; the rest would be a gang of good-timers – 'Barbara Hutton and her twenty-eight-year-old lover – she is quite pointless I think – David Hicks, the expensive, decorating *poule de luxe* – and one or two cock-teasing American young others by the bathing pool . . . reminding one of one's lost youth'. Nor did he enjoy the backbiting which was an inevitable feature of such a society. Cathy Sutherland was a brash and vulgar woman whose gossip led to both a temporary coolness in the Lees-Milnes' friendship with the Kenneth Clarks and a permanent rupture in their relations with Douglas Cooper. Daisy Fellowes was both malicious in herself and the cause of malice in others; when she had a heart attack, her neighbour Princess Ottobone ('an old cat – they all are out here') remarked to Jim that it was the first time in her life that she knew what it was to have a heart.

Yet there was also much to delight him, as his letters to Eardley make clear. 'Weather divine and this little house and garden the most perfect imaginable . . . divine walks straight out of this village into the mountains,' he wrote on first staying there in August 1951. In September 1956, when they received a visit from the Eshers, he reported a 'paradisal' dinner on the terrace, 'not a breath of wind, moon full, stars twinkling, jasmine smelling and crickets purring'. As late as February 1958 he wrote from what he called 'Lotus Land' that 'it is very nice here and I feel very content'. During 1953 and 1954 he kept a sporadic diary which also gives the impression that he was enjoying his Riviera life. He describes amusing meetings with Maugham and Sutherland, welcome visits from

Bridget Parsons and Peter Quennell, long walks in the mountains with views 'as lovely as anything on the Mediterranean', visits to French rustic churches which made him glad (even as an excommunicant) to be 'a participant in the universality'. Provided he had collected his source material, it was also an ideal environment for his writing. (In old age, on miserable English winter mornings, Jim sometimes dreamt of Roquebrune – 'around us the smells of brioches, coffee, pine trees, the clean early morning freshness of the sky; no birds singing, but in the distance the susurration of the sea and the hesitant piping of a shepherd's flute; the senses heightened, expectant of lovely future days without end . . .')

However, as Roquebrune was the main setting for his married life, his happiness there depended on the state of his marriage. Life with Alvilde, as he had foreseen, had its good and bad sides. On the one hand, she was a beautiful, elegant and accomplished wife who looked after him wonderfully and did everything – entertaining, gardening, running the house – superbly well; on the other hand, she tended to nag, fuss and sulk. Although he relished her sharpness, he also valued his independence, and he resented that, when they were together, she managed his life and allowed him little privacy. (The geographical claustrophobia of Roquebrune lent a certain emphasis to this aspect.) Judging from his sporadic diary, after two years of marriage he was still in love with her to the extent of being eager to see her after a period of separation. 'After this interval [of six weeks] I truly desire to be with A. again,' he wrote on 21 August 1953; arriving in Monte Carlo four days later – at dawn on a perfect morning fragrant with pine and citrus – he climbed the five miles to Roquebrune, rushed up to the bedroom in which she was still asleep, tore off his clothes and jumped in beside her. A week later he wrote that 'A. and I are extremely happy together and it is though we were having another honeymoon'. Yet his pleasure in rejoining her after they had been apart was mirrored by his relief on leaving her after they had been together. The fact that he spent at least three months of the year in England without her provided a safety valve in a marriage which he would otherwise have found stifling. Soon after arriving in England he would usually stay at Long Crichel; Eardley noted that, at the start of his visit, he would seem stiff, serious and preoccupied, whereas by the end of it he would be a different person, the jovial, impish, carefree Jim of yore.

Certainly the world Jim inhabited in England – of industrious aesthetes struggling both to maintain the cultural heritage and to lead a civilised existence in a society which increasingly favoured the values of the masses over those of the élite – was a million miles from the vacuous hedonism of the Riviera. During the 1950s he may be said to have had four overlapping circles of English friends. First, Long Crichel. Eardley was his closest friend and confidant; Eddy and Desmond he also dearly loved. It came as a slight shock when Eddy abandoned the ménage in 1956 to live in Ireland; but his replacement, Raymond Mortimer, was both an old friend of Jim and a Long Crichel habitué. Other regular house guests whom Jim cherished included Derek Hill, Patrick Kinross, Jack Rathbone, 'Pat' Trevor-Roper and the Cambridge don 'Dadie' Rylands. Secondly, there was Harold Nicolson, to whom Jim remained devoted; they regularly dined together, and when Harold began to suffer from mild strokes and was advised not to be alone at nights at his flat in Albany, Jim volunteered to stay with him in a rota with other friends. While recruiting new young protégés, some of whom Jim befriended, Harold continued to dote on Jamesey; and although Jim was increasingly exasperated by Jamesey's egotism and debauchery, he continued to put up with him for Harold's sake. Thirdly, there were his Catholic friends – for despite being under a religious cloud, he remained a believing if not a practising member of the Roman church; these included Lennox Berkeley, Richard Rumbold and Geoffrey Houghton Brown. Fourthly, Jim had by this time a huge professional acquaintance with men involved, in one way or other, with art and architecture, often associated with the National Trust as committee members, staff members, advisers or donors. Many of these were already old friends of varying degrees of intimacy, including John Betjeman, Anthony Blunt, Kenneth Clark, Alec Clifton-Taylor, David Crawford, Ralph Dutton, Oliver Esher, Robin Fedden, Peter Fleetwood-Hesketh, John Fowler, Derek Hill, George Howard, Christopher Hussey, Wyndham Ketton-Cremer, Ian McCallum, Paul Methuen, Ben Nicolson, Michael Peto, Michael Rosse, Sachie Sitwell, John Summerson and Gerry Wellington. In the 1950s he befriended a new generation of such men: these included 'Bobby' Gore, Christopher Wall, and Hugh, Earl of Euston (later 11th Duke of Grafton), eager young additions to the National Trust staff; the art dealer Giles Eyre, tenant of the Trust's manor house at Lytes Cary, Somerset; and John Harris, an appealing youth with a passion for old buildings who was 'discovered' by Geoffrey Houghton Brown and became the basement lodger at Thurloe Square. Friends removed by death during these years included Ted Lister in 1956 and Rick Stewart-Jones in 1957: though he had long ceased to be intimate with either, Jim wrote tributes to them both in *The Times*. Ted bequeathed Westwood Manor (formerly left to Jim) to the Trust; Rick, recently appointed a Trust representative, was only forty-three, driven to heart failure by overwork and over-indulgence in alcohol and tobacco.

Most of these men were homosexual or bisexual, the heterosexuals among them generally taking a benign view of the alternative; and clearly Jim's marriage did not greatly alter the fact that he existed in an atmosphere of homosexual friendship, sensibility and gossip. He still had homosexual longings too: on the Blue Train to London in April 1953 he flirted with a handsome fellow passenger ('he was everything I had desired in my most sanguine daydreams – tall, delicate, strong, sensitive, masculine, mature, young, arrogant, well-bred, mysterious, discreet, radiant, beautiful'), and was dismayed when the London telephone number slipped to him by the desire-object turned out to be false. He was envious of those friends who formed lasting male partnerships – including Eardley, who fell requitedly in love with the gorgeous Bulgarian picture-framer Mattei Radev. But although he enjoyed discreet flings when opportunities arose (which was too infrequently for his liking), there appear to have been no serious affairs: so long as his marriage seemed reasonably happy and meaningful, he refused to allow anything of the sort to develop. One might have thought that Alvilde, with her liking for gay men and her own lesbian interests, would have been unconcerned about his post-marital homosexual life, provided it was conducted discreetly; but such was her possessive nature that she tended to be suspicious of all his friends who were not also friends of hers. Some of his friends, such as Lennox Berkeley and Pat Trevor-Roper, were indeed older friends of hers, while others, such as Eddy, Geoffrey and Jamesey, admired her. On the whole, however, his friends tended to be wary of her and deprecate her influence on him. Harold Nicolson disliked her, as did Eardley and Raymond. Even those who generally enjoyed her company, such as Derek Hill and Burnet Pavitt, were often shocked by her nagging of Jim, not to mention the barbs she sometimes directed at them. (It goes without saying that all these men were perfectly charming to Alvilde when they met her, while Jim loyally played the role of a happy husband and confided his mixed feelings about his marriage to no one except Eardley.)

Alvilde was still less popular with Jim's women friends from his bachelor days, Midi Gascoigne, Anne Hill, Billa Harrod, Bridget Parsons and Anne Rosse, whom he continued to love dearly and see periodically. (Nancy Mitford, however, was closer to Alvilde than to Jim, who had tired of her prickly, facetious personality.) For his part, Jim did not always warm to Alvilde's female friends, such as Violet Trefusis and Diana

Cooper (though he came to be intrigued by the former and admire the latter). He did, however, form close friendships with two women whom he knew through Alvilde. The novelist Rosamond Lehmann was a pre-war friend of Alvilde from the Princess Winnie circle. Jim found her beautiful, fascinating and (for she was the vainest of women) slightly ridiculous, and was intrigued by her tendency to see all life in dramatic terms. Soon after meeting they began a flirtatious, confidential relationship which lasted for forty years. The exotically beautiful Freda Berkeley (*née* Bernstein) was twenty years younger than her husband Lennox, with whom she had fallen in love during the war when she had been his secretary at the BBC; he, who had been tormented by the conflict between his sexual nature and his religious beliefs, had returned her love, and theirs was a supremely happy union, blessed with three sons, in which she encouraged him to remain close to the homosexual friends of his bachelorhood. Jim was a little envious of their marriage, which seemed to possess an element of cosiness and mutual respect lacking in his own, and always found himself cheered and inspired by Freda, with her relish for good-natured gossip and her positive attitude to life.

Another problem in Jim's marriage was that he felt uncomfortable about his financial dependence on his wife. By going half-time with the National Trust in order to live with her, he took a substantial cut in salary – in 1953 the Trust paid him £700 a year, and it is unlikely that, on average, his writing brought in a much greater sum. At Roquebrune, she footed the bills; in London, Jim could only afford the (relatively modest) rent at Thurloe Square by letting out rooms to the children of friends. (Thus the sons of Michael Rosse often stayed there, as did Ben Nicolson and his wife Luisa at the outset of their short-lived marriage.) When they travelled together, she paid for first-class tickets and rooms in grand hotels; when he travelled on his own, he made do with the cheapest seats and hostelries. The only windfalls which came his way during these years were a modest legacy on the death of his beloved Aunt Deenie in 1952, which he used to buy the car of his dreams, a drop-head Rolls-Royce coupé, and the Heinemann Prize, worth £100, which he was awarded for *Roman Mornings* in 1957. He was also conscious of becoming dependent on her in other ways. As his friend Lady Dorothy ('Coote') Lygon recalled: 'As a bachelor, Jim was perfectly capable of looking after himself. After a few years of marriage to Alvilde, he seemed to have become helpless.'

Yet outsiders usually noticed nothing amiss. During the weeks she spent at Thurloe Square she ran the flat there as superbly as she did the house at Roquebrune; at meals, the guests were always well-chosen and the food delicious. They seemed a happy couple when they stayed in other people's houses. (They particularly enjoyed visiting the Buccleuchs at Boughton in the 1950s and the Devonshires at Chatsworth in the 1960s, two establishments which managed to recreate an element of pre-war ducal style.) Nor, beneath the surface, was all tension and gloom. Jim was proud of her accomplishments, enjoyed being coddled by her, and experienced (at least during the early years of their marriage) many happy moments with her. In a tradition which would last thirty-five years, they usually spent Christmas with the Garrett Moores (who became Earl and Countess of Drogheda in 1957) at Parkside, their house near Windsor. The charismatic Garrett, who earned fame and fortune as managing director of the *Financial Times*, was devoted to Alvilde, with whom he had been in love aged eighteen; during the war, Jim had become equally devoted to his pretty and amusing wife Joan. It was a musical household: Joan was a professional pianist, while Garrett was a trustee of the Royal Opera House and its Chairman from 1958; they were often joined by Burnet Pavitt, Jim's lover of 1948, another Covent Garden trustee and Joan's partner for duets. The Lees-Milnes both looked forward to these visits, and felt affection for the Droghedas' only child Dermot ('Derry'), born in 1937.

While based at Roquebrune Jim and Alvilde travelled on the Continent, especially in nearby Italy. They regularly stayed in Venice, where they knew many rich expatriates such as the Chavchavadzes, and Florence, where Jim's friend Harold Acton and Alvilde's friend Violet Trefusis owned magnificent villas. They visited the blind aesthete Percy Lubbock at Gli Scaffari near Lerici with its lovely garden overlooking the sea. Jim also travelled to research his architectural books. At first she accompanied him on these trips; but architecture bored her and he was increasingly left to make them on his own (which provided further breathing spaces in the marriage). While working on *Roman Mornings* in the mid 1950s he shared a house in Rome with Derek Hill, who painted his handsome, melancholy portrait of Jim during this time. At Gli Scaffari he befriended an art historian couple, John Fleming and Hugh Honour, with whom he made several excursions to study art and architecture, starting with Sicily and Calabria in 1956. Alvilde also travelled on her own, introducing Clarissa to various places and visiting friends with whom Jim did not care to stay (and eventually – as will be seen – descending on Sissinghurst for assignations with Vita); and so there developed quite early in their marriage a tradition (certainly welcome to Jim) of separate travels.

During the six months or more he spent annually in England, Jim worked as Architectural Adviser (as the post became known) to the National Trust. Apart from the miserable pay, the job ought to have given him some satisfaction. Though still in his forties, he was now the most experienced member of the Trust's staff, revered for his vast knowledge of country houses. The respect in which he was held by the Historic Buildings Committee – which mostly consisted of his friends and whose chairmanship passed in 1956 from Oliver Esher to Michael Rosse – meant that his judgements were rarely challenged. Few important houses offered to the Trust were accepted, or, once accepted, arranged for showing, without his advice being sought and usually acted upon. The administrative arrangements he had set up in the late 1940s, whereby 'representatives' responsible to the Historic Buildings Committee complemented the agents responsible to the Estates Committee, remained in place and seemed to work. The colleagues with whom he closely collaborated – Robin Fedden, Jack Rathbone, Joshua Rowley, Hugh Euston – he regarded as friends. As an adviser to a committee rather than its secretary, he was spared most of the paperwork which had irked him and was able to concentrate on touring country houses, an activity which he loved 'more and more as I get older and become more and more fascinated by persons, places and things'. His 1953–4 diary contains some memorable vignettes: seeing Ashburnham House, Sussex being emptied of family contents after the death of Lady Catherine Ashburnham, 'the last Ashburnham of Ashburnham'; stopping at Ugbrooke, Devon with Hugh Euston to get help with a puncture, where Lord Clifford shows them the original Secret Treaty of Dover negotiated for Euston's ancestor Charles II by the Clifford of the day; calling at Saltram near Plymouth to find the butler of the 'permanently drunk' Lord Morley sitting for his lordship's portrait in regimental uniform and Coronation robes; persuading William Esdaile of Cothelstone House, Somerset to divulge a notebook of unpublished poems by his ancestor Shelley ('you must understand that until the last few years Shelley's name was never mentioned in my family – he treated my great-grandmother abominably').

Yet he was not happy. 'I know I ought to leave [the Trust] altogether for my presence there is redundant and embarrassing,' he wrote in April 1953. 'Robin doesn't now need me. In many ways he is better [as Historic Buildings Secretary] than I was. It is awkward for him when I am about. It is always a mistake to hang about when one has resigned from a post. Yet what am I to do? I can't leave England altogether and give up the £700 a year which the Trust still pays me. Without it I have no regular income at all.' (He might have added that, had it not provided him with an escape route from Roquebrune, he would have gone mad.) These scruples were unnecessary, for he took care not to tread on the toes of his successor, who valued Jim's advice and found him a useful link with the Committee with which he was on such close terms. Another reason for his dissatisfaction was that the Trust was in the throes of change; the rapid growth of both its membership and holdings meant that, with every passing year, it less resembled the cosy, gentlemanly fraternity of dedicated amateurs which Jim had loved. The days when he would go out to a newly acquired property to 'arrange the rooms', accompanied only by Eardley or Robin, were coming to an end. While recognising such developments as largely inevitable, he was depressed by the Trust's 'bureaucratisation', its recruitment of a small army of professional experts and its progressive tendency to 'museumise' its houses. His continued presence on the staff did, however, enable him to palliate these trends to some degree. Soon after joining the Trust in 1956 as curator of its picture collections, Francis St John ('Bobby') Gore visited Stourhead with Jim and noticed, in the corner of a room hung with valuable paintings, a cheap lithograph of a cat; Jim insisted on this being kept where it was as an example of the taste of the former owners, and for years afterwards, whenever the house was mentioned, wanted to be assured that the cat was still there.

Meanwhile, wider changes were taking place which affected the National Trust's efforts to preserve country houses. The report of the Gowers Committee led to the setting up in 1953 of the Historic Buildings Council, which made recommendations (which were invariably accepted) for the award of Government grants to assist with the upkeep of historic houses, including those owned or being considered by the National Trust, as well as for the handing-over to the Trust of houses acquired by the Government (usually in lieu of death duties). As the Council had been largely his own idea, arising out of proposals he had put before Gowers on the Trust's behalf, Jim confidently expected to be invited to join it. As he wrote twenty years later: 'It is the only committee I have ever wanted to be on . . . I believed I could not be left out, and dire was my disappointment when I was, and some with a tithe of my experience [such as Hugh Euston] were put on.' Jim attributed his exclusion to the animosity of the Chairman, the Royal Private Secretary (and old friend of Harold Nicolson) Sir Alan Lascelles, who seemed to hold some obscure grudge against him. Maintenance grants recommended by the Council enabled the Trust to aquire several important houses which it would otherwise have been unable to accept owing to insufficient endowment, such as Hardwick. The 1950s also saw two contradictory trends which affected the survival of country houses. On the one hand, several owners of splendid properties who had earlier despaired of continuing to live in them, such as the Duke of Bedford at Woburn, the Duke of Devonshire at Chatsworth, the Marquess of Bath at Longleat and (Jim's stepson-in-law *manqué*) the Marquess of Hertford at Ragley, managed to make them pay by turning them into flourishing public attractions. On the other hand, a vast number of architectural treasures which were not ripe for such treatment bit the dust in an orgy of demolition. Jim offered advice to several owners who were opening their houses to the public, and played a role in a national campaign, which achieved fairly meagre results, to stem the tide of destruction. Two houses which he may be said to have saved from the wrecker's ball were the Jacobean Plas Teg, Denbighshire and the Georgian Claydon, Buckinghamshire. Plas Teg was the ancestral home of Pat Trevor-Roper, which had fallen into disrepair after Pat's cousin had been killed in the war. In 1952 Pat saw it mentioned in a magazine article entitled 'Houses You Will Never See Again', and begged Jim to help him save it; the two of them rushed up to North Wales and were just in time to persuade the auctioneer who had acquired it with a view to pulling it down to sell it to Pat (who subsequently spent a great deal more restoring it) for £1,000. Claydon, seat of the Verneys, was on the verge of dereliction when Jim urged its acceptance by the Trust, made possible thanks to a Historic Buildings Council repair grant of £40,000. Other houses which the Trust accepted on Jim's recommendation included Mottisfont Abbey, Hampshire and Nostell Priory, Yorkshire. (There were also a few houses which the Trust refused on his advice to its subsequent regret – notably The Grange, Hampshire, a neo-Grecian pile with an interesting picture collection.)

Jim's greatest friend on the National Trust staff was still Eardley; he always looked forward to the tour of West Country properties which they made together each May. Eardley was an easygoing amateur, who found himself out of tune with the Trust's increasingly bureaucratic ethos. Never the soul of efficiency, he was constantly landing in trouble because of minor oversights, and did not always get on with the sometimes dictatorial agents. Jim sympathised with his difficulties, which seemed to arise from developments he himself deplored. When Eardley came into some money and considered leaving the Trust to devote himself to painting, Jim did not discourage him. 'Much as I should hate you to leave,' he wrote from Roquebrune, 'I honestly believe you ought to. We shall never again get satisfaction out of the N.T. The days when we thought we were creating something out of it are passed and won't return.' Eardley replied from Long Crichel: 'I don't think you or I are waning in our emotions or enthusiasms. Just because the silly old N.T. has passed beyond us & is altered to adapt itself to the new age to which we do not belong – that is nothing. It means we devote ourselves to things more worth while to us. But I do agree with you that the battle for preserving the beauties we have loved is very largely lost.' When Eardley resigned in 1957 (he was in fact prevailed upon to stay on until the end of 1958), Jim wrote to him that only financial considerations prevented him from resigning himself; he referred to 'that love–hate for the National Trust which in my case is now more hate than love'. Early in 1958 he was given a pretext to quit when an immensely valuable book, an edition of Erasmus illuminated by Holbein which had been in Henry VIII's library, was found to be missing from Charlecote, having last been heard of in Jim's hands in 1950. 'Can't remember a thing about it,' he wrote to Eardley. 'People write saying how sorry they are for the hell of remorse and worry I must be going through, whereas I don't feel the least guilty and suffer nothing to speak of. However I thought it fitting to offer my resignation to the Committee and if they accept it I don't care a damn.' Needless to say it was refused, and Jim remained on the staff while continuing to mutter to friends such as Harold Nicolson that he longed to 'chuck the Trust'.

It is hard to avoid the impression that Jim's increasing disenchantment with the National Trust reflected a general disenchantment with life. One equally gets this impression from his fulmination against the degradation of the face of England which was taking place at this time, manifested by the replacement of historic town centres with brutal modern buildings and road systems, the uncontrolled expansion of suburbia, the unconsidered demolition of architectural landmarks both urban and rural, and the disfigurement of the landscape with motorways and pylons. Of course, the great majority of civilised and informed people, including probably all Jim's friends, deplored these developments, and he was far from alone in protesting against them and trying to do something to stop them. But Jim's protests were invariably delivered in a tone of angry despair; he was constantly firing off letters to *The Times* worthy of disgusted colonels in Tunbridge Wells. Most of these were not published, though one which was – criticising as 'feeble and shocking' the failure to prevent Lord Lansdowne dismantling the main block of his unmanageably sprawling house at Bowood, Wiltshire – caused offence both to Lansdowne himself and to various bodies which had laboured in vain to find a better solution. He also found himself quarrelling with the Georgian Group and other societies. As he wrote to John Betjeman in 1956: 'The Georgian Group makes me sick. They are hopeless, snobbish defeatists. All they can do is give parties for The Cake [the Queen Mother] at Burlington House. They need slating.' Betjeman, now the nation's favourite poet, was one of the most effective of the pundits who strove to stem the tide of philistinism; while applauding Jim's indignant outbursts, he began to mock him affectionately as 'the Worcestershire grumbler'. As will be seen, Jim's increasing dissatisfaction as the 1950s progressed was not unconnected with developments in his personal life.

Between 1947 and 1960 Jim achieved a modest celebrity with six illustrated volumes of architectural history – *The Age of Adam* (1947), *Tudor Renaissance* (1951), *The Age of Inigo Jones* (1953), *Roman Mornings* (1956), *Baroque in Italy* (1959) and *Baroque in Spain and Portugal* (1960). As the titles suggest, the first three deal with the architecture of England (with a brief nod at Scotland in the case of Robert Adam), the last three with that of Southern Europe. Each of the six runs to fewer than two hundred closely packed pages – for in Jim's view 'few books about architecture . . . are ever too short'. *Roman Mornings* is a different sort of book from the other five, being not a general historical work but a set of discursive essays on eight of the city's monuments. It is also the only one of the six not to have been published by Batsford, and got off to an unlucky start when the publisher Jim found for it, Allan Wingate, went bankrupt a few months after issuing it, the unsold copies being seized and 'pulped' by the firm's creditors. Despite this, it is the only one of the titles to have endured, having been reprinted in the 1980s and '90s. The subjects treated by the other five have since attracted much new research leading to numerous publications, so that they may all now be considered obsolete. At the time, however, they were regarded as pioneering works, as little other relevant literature then existed for the general reader. In later years Jim was pleased to be told by eminent aesthetes such as Sir Roy Strong that their interest in these subjects had originally been inspired by his work.

The architectural writer to whom Jim is most often compared is Sacheverell Sitwell (to whom he dedicated *Roman Mornings*): both were historians in the amateur tradition whose books amount to brilliant summaries of the information then available. Jim made modest claims for his work; in the preface to *The Age of Inigo Jones* he denied that he had produced a work of scholarship or even of literature, describing himself, in the words of Sir Henry Wotton, as 'but a gatherer and disposer of other men's stuff'. He did himself an injustice: while often basing himself on the researches of others, he made a point of never writing about an extant building until he had seen it; and his architectural descriptions usually contain personal touches which prevent them sounding like mere reference works. The books are interesting for what they reveal about the author as well as their subjects. They are all works of Catholic propaganda, which treat the Reformation as a disaster for society and for art. They show a disproportionate interest in any figures known to have had unorthodox sex-lives (such as the pioneer German art historian Winckelmann, murdered by 'rough trade' in 1768). And they constantly fulminate against the ignorance and neglect which has permitted the decay and destruction of so much Jim sets out to describe. As he writes of the partial dismantling in 1929 of Adam's Lansdowne House (now the Lansdowne Club) off Berkeley Square:

> No more Belsen-like treatment of a work of art by speculative Philistines was ever tolerated in the decadent inter-war period by a smug and cynical public . . . The drawing-room . . . may now be viewed by shamefaced British visitors to the Philadelphia Museum of Art . . . The disgraceful fate of Lansdowne House was only one instance of this country's breathless anticipation of the brave new materialism into which the Gadarene swine are today gleefully plunging.

Despite being peppered with such rants, *The Age of Adam* is an impressive first book, displaying an intimate knowledge of both architecture and architectural literature and possessing a quality of youthful enthusiasm even though Jim wrote it in his late thirties. He clearly regards Robert Adam as England's greatest architect and his eclectic neo-classicism as her greatest architectural style; he lovingly describes his principles and deals savagely with his critics. He shows how, at a time of controversy between the artistic champions of Greece and Rome, Adam incorporated the best elements of both traditions into his work. Judging by the good reviews and sales, his excursion into an era of great national confidence gladdened hearts at a time of austerity and political anxiety two years after the war. It was hailed as 'a masterpiece of combined biography and appraisal' and 'the art book of the year'. In *Country Life*, Christopher Hussey welcomed Jim to the ranks of art historians, 'for he can write with such feeling and knowledge that he almost succeeds in making the Scotch genius human'. Jim may have been put out by the fact that one of the few equivocal reviews was by Raymond Mortimer, who thought the book, while it succeeded in placing its subject in context, 'a little unpractised in its style'.

If Jim regarded Adam as representing the culmination of the classical tradition in English architecture, in his second book, *Tudor Renaissance*, he turned back two and a half centuries to what he called 'the dawn of English classicism'. In so doing he took a risk, for research into Tudor buildings and the craftsmen who worked on them was in its infancy, and he was often reduced either to 'shrewd guesswork and bold generalisation' or to parroting the questionable theories of others (including the author of the last book on the subject which had appeared fifty years earlier). As the academic expert John Summerson wrote in the *New Statesman*, Jim could only give 'a wobbly sketch of what he fancies may be somewhere near the truth . . . To say that he comes through with some credit is the least tribute one can pay to his perseverance.' The first part of the book describes how Henry VIII at first imbibed the new, classically-inspired art – which influenced, if not English architectural style, at least architectural decoration – only to spit it out again when he broke with the Pope and sent Italian artists packing. Jim depicts early Tudor England as a barbarous country whose artistic achievements were almost entirely the work of foreigners, and laments that 'Italian classicism could not get a hold . . . before the Dr Jekyll in the king turned to Mr Hyde'. One of the last splutterings of this interrupted renaissance was the rebuilding of Lacock Abbey, a house Jim knew intimately, by Sir William Sharington who had been awarded it at the Dissolution of the Monasteries. Jim presumed that the main classical influence on Elizabethan architecture came in a bastardised form from the Low Countries – a view contested by Summerson, who believed future research would attribute it to 'the Loire school and Fontainbleau'. Neither the sales nor the reviews of *Tudor Renaissance* were as good as those of its predecessor, though critics acknowledged its erudition and readability.

When pure architectural classicism finally became established in England in the 1620s it was largely due to one man, Inigo Jones (1573–1652), the subject of Jim's third book. Jones was a fascinating figure whose biography had last been written in the 1920s. As a young artist of humble origins he had managed to visit Italy, where he studied the architecture and writings of Palladio with its strict rules derived from Ancient Rome: this accident had the momentous consequence that English architecture during much of the seventeenth and early eighteenth centuries was dominated by a style (thought by some to be excessively rigid) which had been fashionable in Italy in the sixteenth. Before being appointed Surveyor-General of the King's Works and Buildings in 1615 he had been a producer of masques for James I's consort Anne of Denmark (who, Jim noted, 'never chided her unsatisfactory husband' and 'did not resent his unconventional peccadilloes'), which gave him a theatrical approach to architecture. The fact that Jones was a self-taught amateur and generalist made him particularly attractive to Jim, whose book contains interesting new insights. (For example, Jim discovered that the scenery of operas staged in Florence during the first years of the seventeenth century bore a remarkable similarity to Jones's masque designs at slightly later dates.) The book was warmly received by the critics, many of whom (including Clough Williams-Ellis, another self-taught architect in the classical tradition) seized on Jim's disclaimer that it was a work neither of scholarship nor of literature and insisted that it was triumphantly both. Harold Nicolson in the *Observer* wrote that what made Jim's books special was that he was never afraid to parade his prejudices. 'He dislikes Archbishop Laud and the entrancing chapel of Brasenose College. He likes King Charles I and the gateway to the Botanical Gardens at Oxford, now marred by idiotic flower beds . . . He is not sure that he approves of Rubens and is positive that he dislikes Sir Balthazar* and those responsible for the destruction of Coleshill House.'† Jim was delighted by the reviews, writing that 'for the first time in my life I have experienced a modicum of achievement'.

Jim's first three books were originally conceived as part of a panoramic survey of English classicism from the sixteenth to the eighteenth centuries; but though he had still to cover the period from 1650 to 1750, he was now sidetracked by his love of Italy. (He would partly plug the gap in the 1960s with his books on 'English Baroque' and the Palladian Earls.) The first result, *Roman Mornings*, is an idiosyncratic, almost unclassifiable book, which no doubt explains both its difficulty in finding a publisher and its enduring appeal. It is partly a treatise on aesthetics, partly a guidebook. (Jim insisted that it was never meant as the latter; but it is hard to make sense of it without visiting the monuments he describes, especially as he includes few illustrations on the grounds that 'architecture cannot be judged from photographs'.) Four of the eight monuments he selects for discussion belong to the great era of Roman building in the sixteenth and seventeenth centuries; this was clearly his main interest, and his essays on earlier buildings are designed to show that, during the thousand years

---

* Sir Balthazar Gerbier, a rival architect to Jones who was intensely jealous of him.
† A few months before Jim's book appeared, Coleshill, Berkshire, built by Jones's disciple Pratt, which had been due to come to the National Trust, had been seriously damaged by fire and its shell demolished. Jim, who described it in his text as the greatest seventeenth-century Classical house in England, cursed those responsible in a footnote.

which separated the Renaissance from Ancient Rome, the city owed her cultural survival to her fidelity to the classical tradition. (He does not place much value on anything built after 1700: the only eighteenth-century monument included is the Trevi Fountain, which he classifies as charming rather than artistically outstanding.) In his Introduction, he reflects that 'architecture must be judged by the requirements and standards of its own time'. Twentieth-century notions of government and morality

> were not shared by the great patrons of the Italian Renaissance or, for that matter, by the Roman Emperors. Yet they produced architectural master-pieces apparently far beyond our capabilities. We are shocked, maybe, by their love of splendour and power. They would be appalled by our indifference to the architecture of our own time, to the meanness of our twentieth-century monuments and the hideous vulgarity of our streets. In these respects they would consider us quite decadent. I think they would be right.

He takes a swipe at academic experts, insisting that 'in reaching a true assessment of architecture there are other values to be taken into account besides the purely documentary. Chief of them are the associative and aesthetic.' This, indeed, is the main point of his book, which mixes architectural description with 'associative and aesthetic' musings. Thus, before offering a technical analysis of the interior of the Romanesque Santa Maria di Cosmedin, he describes it as

> severe, uncouth, uncompromisingly mediaeval. The relief it offers after the relentless roar of motor traffic on the cobbles outside is heavenly indeed. On entry you step down quite literally into the refreshing auster-ity of the twelfth century. The chill air is rinsed in that charnel smell of must and damp which is inseparable from all mediaeval Catholic churches on the Continent, and which the initiated church-roamer . . . grows to love . . . this effluvium of stale incense, bones, decaying parchment, and sacramental oil. In early spring . . . you will for the greater part of the morning be the sole visitor, left to your own devices once you have satisfied the small boy with a shaven head and aloe eyes . . . who collects tribute to the maintenance fund either of the church or himself . . . Only occasionally will the screaming door open to let in a momentary gale of traffic din and maybe a hesitant Scandinavian art student . . .

This formula was not to everyone's taste, though the critics were gener-ally admiring. Cyril Connolly in the *Sunday Times* found it 'a stiff but rewarding read' which 'tries to bridge the gulf between the dilettante enthusiasts like onself and the technical expert'. Others praised it as a work which 'enlarges the sightseer's power to see' and 'sets out to transform, by its informal discursiveness and pointing out of key clues, innocent enthusiasm into more subtle appraisal'. Some found it too discursive; the *Listener* thought the 'atmospheric' parts of it the worst. Jim was consoled for its mixed reception (and the failure of its first publisher) when it was awarded the Heinemann Prize; as Vita Sackville-West wrote to Alvilde, 'It's just the sort of encouragement he needs, more than most people, isn't it?'

The title of Jim's next volume, *Baroque in Italy*, is slightly misleading, as it too deals mostly with the buildings of Rome; also, perhaps mindful of having omitted these subjects from *Roman Mornings*, he devotes the first part of it to Michelangelo and the Mannerist style which preceded the Baroque. It was timely, as Baroque art and architecture had suddenly become immensely fashionable, to the point that two other books on the subject appeared almost simultaneously with Jim's – Rudolf Wittkower's academic survey, to which Jim paid tribute in his preface as 'a comprehensive work of immense erudition', and Nicholas Powell's *From Baroque to Rococo*, which was reviewed together with Jim's book, invariably to the advantage of the latter. Critics praised it as 'an excellent introduction to the subject which combines scholarship with a light touch' and 'the kind of book that brings magic with it'. Sachie Sitwell, whose own *Southern Baroque Art* had first stimulated Jim's interest in the subject, wrote in *Time and Tide* that it was 'by far the best book that he has written' and gave him credit for several original insights – such as that the churches built by the architect-priests Guarini and Juvarra possessed a 'celibate' quality. The following year Sitwell, now writing in the *Daily Telegraph*, was equally praising of the companion volume *Baroque in Spain and Portugal*, the fruit of Peninsular holidays. He applauded Jim's belief that architecture needed to be assessed in a living context, quoting his advice to see the Escalera Dorada at Burgos at some brilliant ceremony 'while the organ booms and the servitors in their astonishing dalmatics of gold and silver damask and wearing long red wigs carry the silver basin and linen towel before the mitred Archbishop'. Elizabeth Young in the *Guardian* similarly opined that Jim excelled not so much at argument as description – 'the moist and splendid horror of the Royal Pantheon in the Escorial; the passioniate fluttering Cartuga Sacristy in Granada; the fabulous jovialities at Oporto – yes, I feel, I'd like to see that, I want to go there . . .'

Apart from his books, financial necessity obliged Jim to produce much architectural journalism during the 1950s. Some of his productions – such as profiles of houses for *Country Life*, and guidebooks to National Trust properties – are of high standard (though lack of time for documentary research meant that he tended to rely overmuch on hearsay); others, such as his monthly column 'Open to View' in the magazine *John Bull*, consisting of jaunty anecdotes about houses open to the public, were mere potboiling. This may also be the place to mention Jim's poetry. He wrote verse all his life and longed to receive some recognition as a poet, without ever succeeding in getting a single line into print. In 1956 he did, however, make a determined effort to have some poetry published; he gathered together what he considered to be his best work (the most recent example being a set of 'Shakespearean sonnets' in which 'Roquebrune' rhymed with 'swoon') and begged two friends who were recognised poets – Vita Sackville-West and John Betjeman – to read it. Although Jim was steeped in English poetry, and felt impelled to write it, it must be said that he lacked the gift of expressing himself in verse: he never developed a distinctive style, his meaning is often obscure, and the overall effect is usually awkward and artificial. Both Vita and 'Betj' were kind and encouraging. Vita wrote that the sonnets reminded her of 'Tennyson's brother' and she thought them 'jolly good and full of feeling'. Jim followed up Betjeman's suggestion that he send his narrative poem *The Moat* (written in 1950 and set in Emral Park, the long-demolished house in North Wales which had belonged to his half-uncle Crawshay Puleston) to John ('Jock') Murray, Betjeman's own publisher who had been at Eton with Jim. Murray returned it (as Jim wrote to Betjeman) 'with a tart little note that the narrative is not sufficiently sustained by the inordinate length', making Jim feel 'desperately squashed'. Nevertheless, Jim continued to write verse for the rest of his life, his best poems belonging to his last years when he achieved a greater fluency of technique.

One cannot be precise about the chronology, but at some point between 1953 and 1958 Jim ceased to be happy in his marriage – or rather, the unhappy aspects of it began to outweigh the happy ones. In September 1953 he could write that he and Alvilde were 'extremely happy together'; five years later he felt himself trapped in a union which had been a mistake. It has been noted that he became rather discontented generally during the 1950s, no doubt a symptom of middle age; and it is impossible to say how far this mood was a cause of his marital unhappiness, how far an effect. One fact is known. At some point during these years, Alvilde declined to have further sexual relations with him. As Jim remained a highly physical man, this put him in a difficult spot. He relieved his frustrations with transient homosexual affairs; but he was only able to engage in these when apart from her, and he was painfully conscious (as he wrote to Eardley) that the passing years made it less easy for him to find such consolations than in the past.

What lent a bizarre touch to the situation was that, while Jim was suffering from a lack of romantic and sexual fulfilment, Alvilde was abandoning herself to a passionate (if intermittently consummated) affair with Vita Sackville-West, whose husband Harold had been Jim's lover twenty years previously. The affair was conducted discreetly, and until it was almost over Alvilde said nothing about it to Jim. Nor did Vita mention it to Harold: they made a point of never discussing their respective homosexual affairs. However, Jim cannot have failed to be aware that something was going on, as he noticed letters from Vita arriving 'almost daily for several years'. Some three hundred of these letters are now in the Berg Collection at New York Public Library. (Vita does not seem to have kept Alvilde's replies.) While the Vita–Alvilde romance belongs to their own biographies, and Jim turned a blind eye to it, it nevertheless had a variety of effects on his own life; and since far more is known about it than about the day-to-day relations between Jim and Alvilde, it seems appropriate to give an outline of the story here.

At the time of his marriage Jim had known Vita for almost twenty years, being linked with her both as a protégé of Harold and a friend of Eddy. (And even before meeting her, he had admired her poetry.) Although, owing to her reclusive life at Sissinghurst, their meetings were relatively infrequent, they developed much respect and affection for one another. It was thanks to Vita that Jim heard about the vacancy at the National Trust in 1936; and he kept her tactfully informed about the Trust's decade-long negotiations to acquire Knole. (She had strong but confused feelings about her family seat and childhood home, resenting the fact that Eddy, whom she otherwise loved, was the heir to it and not she.) In June 1949, during the first rapture of his affair with Alvilde, he made an overnight visit to Sissinghurst where he had an 'ineradicable' talk with her. As he wrote in his diary:

> Vita is adorable. I love her romantic disposition, her southern lethargy concealing unfathomable passions, her slow movements of grave dignity, her fund of human kindness, understanding and desire to disentangle other people's perplexities for them. I love her deep plum voice and chortle. We talked of love and religion. She told me that she learnt only at twenty-five that her tastes were homosexual. It was sad that homo-sexual lovers were considered by the rest of the world to be slightly comical.

He confided to Vita the problems he then faced in his relationship with Alvilde, and she was consoling and encouraging. Two years later, when he and Alvilde were finally able to live together, he took her to meet Vita, who found her 'lovely'. A few months after that, Vita acted as a witness at their wedding – a sign (since she did not normally care to play such parts) of her affection for him and interest in her.

During the next three years a close friendship developed between Vita and Alvilde, inevitably carried on mostly by correspondence, though in the spring and summer Alvilde usually made several solo visits to Sissinghurst, while Vita organised her rare London visits so that she and Harold could lunch with Jim and Alvilde at Thurloe Square. (Alvilde was seventeen years younger than Vita, though this would hardly have concerned her as she had been forty-five years younger than Princess Winnie.) Apart from mutual physical attraction, three things drew them together. First, gardening, which had long been Vita's passion and was now Alvilde's: without seeing it, Vita advised on the garden at Roquebrune. Secondly, Alvilde wanted to start an English garden too and thought of buying a small country house within reach of London, and Vita reported on various properties for sale in Kent which might be suitable. Thirdly, Alvilde became Vita's principal source of news about her cousin Eddy, who stayed at Roquebrune several times a year.

By the middle of 1955, they were clearly much in love. 'Darling, my lovely, far-away, strange, exquisite Alvilde,' Vita began a letter to her that July, 'cut off from me by geographical miles & by ice-barriers of conscience and morality as unshakeable as the ice-floes round the polar north . . .' Both longed to give physical expression to their feelings for each other, but Vita hesitated to do so as 'honesty would forbid anything that would break Jim's gentle heart. I know you say that Jim wouldn't mind if it was *me*. I can't agree. He would mind, whoever it was: and I couldn't hurt Jim: it would be a sin against the Holy Ghost . . . You say that when love is true and deep it cannot be wrong . . . But if you hurt somebody else, then does it become wrong – Yes? No?' Another inhibiting factor was that Violet Trefusis, with whom Vita had had a wild affair thirty-five years earlier and who was a more recent lover of Alvilde, had started taking a suspicious interest in their friendship. However, Vita's resistance was clearly weakening by the day. 'It is sometimes a mistake to follow one's nobler instincts, if you know what I mean . . . I hate caution; I love recklessness.' Finally, at Sissinghurst on 26 October 1955, under a full moon, they consummated their love. 'I don't know what to write to you – my head & heart in a whirl, and not only my head & heart. You feel wobbly & odd, and so do I.' There was no immediate possibility of following up the experience, as Alvilde was about to sail for America with Clarissa; but she suggested that Vita fabricate some pretext enabling her to go straight to Sissinghurst from Southampton when she returned on 22 December. Vita was doubtful; her family were descending for Christmas, and 'won't Jim find it very odd if you come tearing down here without even seeing him?' However, as soon as the family party at Sissinghurst had dispersed Alvilde arrived there for another night of bliss.

During the preceding decade Vita had suffered a sharp decline in health (partly attributable to her fondness for the bottle) and serious 'writer's block', and (according to her biographer Victoria Glendinning) the affair with Alvilde both renewed her zest for life and inspired her to write poetry for the first time in years. Her letters began to be spiced with love-verses to Alvilde.

> Suspender-belts do drop around my waist
> And as they stretch elastic so
> Does my love elastically grow . . .

During the years 1950–5 Alvilde had usually taken her permitted ninety days in England in two longish stretches, from May to July and in November–December; but in 1956, starting in February, she made a larger number of shorter visits in order to carry on the affair (though as Vita wrote, 'what reason you will give Jim I do not profess to guess'). Yet for Vita, Alvilde's fascination lay in the fact that she continued to be mysterious. 'It's so very odd the way you and I have burst into each other's lives. We know so little of each other – and yet so much . . . We have taken short-cuts, like walking through the rides of a wood instead of going by the main road, and the rides tell us so much more of each other. They are sun-lit, and there are chestnut leaves, & foxgloves & bluebells & bracken – and you love the things I love – and we could be quite quiet in the wood, sitting on a log, couldn't we? – and then go back to find the golden angel, and all that the g.a. means.' (This refers to a gilded wooden statue in a niche above the bed in which they made love.) Apart from their amorous reunions at Sissinghurst that year, Alvilde accompanied Vita to study the National Trust garden at Hidcote, Gloucestershire (of which Vita had been commissioned to write the guide book) in July, when they stayed at the Lygon Arms, Broadway where Jim and Alvilde had spent their wedding night in 1951.

All this time, Jim and Harold were meeting regularly in London as usual. Harold and Vita wrote to each other daily when they were apart:[*] his letters mention his discussions with Jim about National Trust matters; hers refer to Alvilde's visits purely in gardening terms. Neither of them so much as hints at the affair; and Harold made no secret of his dislike of Alvilde. 'I was lunching with Alvilde [at Thurloe Square] but find a postcard telling me to lunch somewhere else,' he once wrote. 'Now I loathe being taken to luncheon with people whom I do not know and may not like. This is what I call Alvilde's crinkum-crankum[†] – a certain trickiness. I shall be very rude.' On another occasion Vita wrote to him: 'Poor Alvilde. Why do you dislike her? If you think she doesn't love and appreciate Jim, you are quite wrong. She fusses about him like an old hen.' Sometimes Jim came down to Sissinghurst to see Vita on his own; these occasions filled Alvilde with apprehension, but she need not have worried – no direct reference was ever made to the affair. 'Jim and I sat up talking until nearly 1 a.m. & he couldn't have been more charming,' Vita wrote to her after one such visit. 'When I went off to bed he accompanied me and we both looked up at the moon & said how odd it was to think of it shining on Roquebrune too . . . and I felt we were both linked by our love of you.' Twenty-five years later, Jim wrote that he 'always supposed V. and A. had a *Schwärmerei*' but 'didn't mind . . . for there was I, an inattentive husband'. He does, however, seem to have used the situation to obtain some modest advantages for himself. He put an end to Vita's house-hunting on Alvilde's behalf, making clear to her that he preferred their English base to remain in London where he could see his friends. As noted, he asked Vita to read and comment on his poetry. She also proposed him as a Fellow of the Royal Society of Literature, and may have had a hand in the award to him of the Society's Heinemann Prize for *Roman Mornings*.

Nineteen-fifty-seven began with Vita's passion for Alvilde apparently undiminished. As she wrote in a note accompanying a New Year present:

> How shall I thank her, she so dear, so wild,
> So much a mistress yet so much a child?

Harold and Vita went on a winter cruise to the East Indies; but as soon as they returned Alvilde spent a night at Sissinghurst, the first of several

---

[*]So did Jim and Alvilde; but their letters, unlike those of Harold and Vita, have not survived.
[†]'Crinkum-Crankum' became Harold's private nickname for Alvilde; it is defined by the *OED* as 'a crooked course, deviousness', and was also an old slang word for vagina.

that spring. Vita accompanied Alvilde to the Chelsea Flower Show ('it will be odd meeting in public . . . our eyes will meet'). However, once Alvilde had returned to Roquebrune for the summer, Vita's letters underwent a change of tone. In August, sending her a present for her birthday, she wrote mysteriously that she had reason to believe her letters were being intercepted, so would have to be careful what she said in future. In September she wrote: 'I am in rather a state about us . . . You know how much I always worried about Jim and now I gather there is a lot of talk . . . At the same time of course I want to see you: but I do hate all this business about not divulging [to Jim] your coming to England & all that.' On receiving this letter, Alvilde dashed off to Sissinghurst, a visit which briefly seems to have stilled Vita's doubts. But in October Vita returned to her theme. 'Jim was my friend before I ever knew you; & I cannot bear the thought that I shd have stolen you from him. I know you will say I didn't – but you know quite well what happened . . . You know that I resisted – how I resisted! But I think we must now cut out all LL [lesbian love]. Nothing will ever stop me loving you, deeply, tenderly . . . But I cannot bear the thought of acting caddishly to Jim. You see, he wd mind if he knew the whole truth . . . So this is a sort of goodbye to LL but not to the deeper tender love I bear you & always shall.'

Alvilde was so distressed to receive this letter that she threw two years of caution to the winds. She telephoned Jim in London, confessed her feelings for Vita (which can have come as little surprise to him) and begged him to try to patch things up between them. Jim duly wrote to Vita, who replied to him that she had been been 'dreadfully worried for some time past and there is nothing I should like better than to talk to you'. At Sissinghurst, where they 'talked without stopping from 6 till after midnight', Jim insisted that he really did not in the least mind whatever Vita had been getting up to with Alvilde, that neither of them need be concerned on that account. This was evidently not what Vita wanted to hear, for she next wrote to him: 'I don't wonder you are perplexed . . . Without going into tiresome details, I hate Sissinghurst getting a bad name, as I am sure you will understand. We are threatened with a police case of a criminal nature – absolutely *nothing* to do with me, it concerns a young farm-hand and another man – and now it is being said "Well, if Lady N. herself . . .", etc., etc. I leave you to imagine the rest. So I do feel I must be careful . . . and I feel that since A's name has been mentioned it would be better for her not to appear here for a bit. That is why I wrote to her as I did.'

The truth was, of course, that Vita was looking for some excuse to break off the affair. Such was her volatile, romantic nature (inherited, she believed, from her Spanish grandmother) that she was apt to plunge into passionate relationships with other women, only to break them off just as abruptly when a new interest came along, or she just got bored. Her past was littered with girlfriends who had similarly found themselves discarded after a couple of years. In her biography of Vita, Victoria Glendinning notes that her rejection of Alvilde coincided with two other events in Vita's life – the resumption of an old affair with the locally-living artist Edith Lamont (a woman Harold particularly detested); and the writing of a love-letter, the first for many years, to her ancient flame Violet Trefusis (who had until recently been in her bad books for 'intriguing' against Alvilde). Though desperately unhappy, Alvilde continued to correspond with Vita and send her presents – though Vita wrote to Harold in February 1958 that 'I think – and hope – she has given me up as a bad job'. When Alvilde was next invited to Sissinghurst in May, it was to come down with Jim to spend the day with Vita and Harold.

However, before this visit could be arranged a development occurred which briefly reunited the former lovers. Following a whirlwind affair, Clarissa, now twenty-four, suddenly announced her intention of marrying Michael ('Mickey') Luke, a raffishly good-looking Old Etonian a decade older than herself who worked (when he did) in the film world. His family was not undistinguished – his father Sir Harry Luke was an eminent colonial administrator and travel writer, while his brother Peter was to be responsible for a successful dramatisation of Corvo's novel *Hadrian the Seventh*; but Mickey himself was a feckless, heavy-drinking charmer who had once gone to prison for beating up a girlfriend (an episode of which the Lees-Milnes heard vivid accounts as the lady in question was Rosamond Lehmann's ex-daughter-in-law). The feelings of Alvilde, who had planned a fairy-tale marriage for her daughter, may be imagined. Vita was highly sympathetic, especially as she herself had just learned that the marriage of her son Ben was falling apart after three years. 'I wanted to write to you, having heard not very good reports of C's fiancé, but felt it might be impertinent to offer condolences rather than congratulations . . . Even though you & I may have our troubles & sorrows, there is a permanent bond between us, indestructible.' Alvilde begged to come down to Sissinghurst on her own to unburden herself to Vita. Harold urged Vita to keep her away. 'I don't trust Alvilde's truthfulness or honesty a single inch. She may be using Clarissa as a stalking mare, not that she is not sincerely wretched about the Luke business, but that she thinks she can resume contact with you over this bridge of personal distress, knowing how compassionate you are.' However, Vita felt she must see Alvilde as 'one should not fail one's friends when they appeal to one in real trouble'. The visit, though it did not lead to any serious resumption of their affair, was a loving reunion which helped Alvilde reconcile herself to the Clarissa situation. When, a few days later (25 June 1958), Clarissa was married from the house of Anthony and Rosemary Chaplin in Devon, Alvilde supported the bride and tried to make the best of things, while Jim, who felt sufficiently exasperated by a frivolous step-daughter without having to acknowledge a dissolute stepson-in-law, refused to attend.

In later years, those who thought they knew Jim and Alvilde well felt that their marriage bore some resemblance to that of Harold and Vita, and thought it fitting that Jim should have had an affair with Harold in the 1930s, Alvilde with Vita in the 1950s. As Jim himself wrote soon after Alvilde's death: 'Re-reading Victoria Glendinning's *Vita*, I begin to see in our marriage the palest reflection of Harold's and Vita's, with all its high tragedy and farce.' However, the Vita–Harold marriage was based above all on mutual tolerance. As Vita once wrote to Alvilde: 'We [she and Harold] have gone our own ways for about 30 years; never asked questions; never been in the least curious about that side of our respective lives, though deeply devoted & sharing our interests.' And tolerance was not one of Alvilde's outstanding virtues. It might be said that, while the Vita–Alvilde affair lasted, Jim, as a complaisant husband, enjoyed a certain freedom in his marriage (though he found few outlets for this freedom at the time). However, the ending of the affair led to a drastic curtailing of that freedom. Alvilde once told Vita that there were only three people in the world who really mattered to her – Jim, Clarissa and Vita herself. By the middle of 1958, both Vita and Clarissa seemed largely lost to her; and she began to concentrate her possessive attentions on Jim. A crisis loomed.

I I

Mid-Life Crisis
1958–66

———·———

A ROUND THE TIME of his fiftieth birthday in August 1958, Jim fell into a state of depression. He felt that he had achieved little in half a century of life, and had even less to look forward to. After seven years, his marriage to Alvilde was not going well, and he was finding her possessiveness increasingly irksome. Of the two institutions to which he had been attached for more than twenty years, the Roman Catholic Church and the National Trust, he felt rejected by the first and out of love with the second. Although his latest book had won a prize, his writing career had not brought him much fame or fortune, and his hopes of publishing poetry had been dashed. He owned no property, had managed to save no money. He was appalled by the desecration of architecture and landscape which he saw all around him. He felt little affinity with any of his family. Most of the beloved friends of his youth had either died or gone off the rails (usually due to drink). When he turned sixty-five, Jim told Eardley that he felt 'a failure as a son, brother, lover, husband, conservationist, friend, writer . . . everything really', that he 'hated the world which had passed me by' and 'would quite like to die now'. That, however, was at a time when his marriage was tolerably happy, when he had come into some money, when he had resolved his religious perplexities and when he had achieved some recognition as a man of letters. It is likely that, at fifty, such feelings were even more acute. As Alvilde was in France on his birthday, he went to stay with his old company commander from the Irish Guards, Simon Combe, and his wife Lady Sylvia (daughter of Lord Leicester of Holkham) at Burnham Thorpe, Norfolk: as his hostess reminded him when they met on his eightieth birthday thirty years later, he spent the day in tears.

In the past, whenever a new decade of life had appeared on the horizon, Jim's thoughts had turned to love. At twenty he had been infatuated with Diana Mitford, at thirty, with Rick Stewart-Jones. At forty he had 'awaited some devastating romance' – and found it a few months later with Alvilde. But what romance could he look forward to as an ageing, henpecked failure? 'If only one had "my friend",' he wrote to Eardley (whom he envied as one who lived both in a happy ménage of friends at Long Crichel and in a satisfying relationship with the Bulgarian Mattei). 'Oh dear, no hope now, and all those sorts of longings quite abandoned.'

One faithful friend to whom he remained devoted after a quarter of a century was Harold Nicolson. On 23 October 1958 Jim dined with Harold at the Travellers. Two other guests were present. One was Harold's son Nigel, who announced in the course of the evening that he and his partner George Weidenfeld were thinking of publishing Vladimir Nabokov's controversial erotic novel *Lolita*: Harold was clearly unhappy about this, and Jim also expressed disapproval. The other was John Kenworthy-Browne, a personable young man interested in the arts who had been introduced to Harold the previous March by the historian Michael Howard. John was eager to meet Jim, having been an admirer of his books ever since reading *The Age of Adam* as a schoolboy; and Harold wanted Jim to meet John, who he thought might be suitable for a new post which was then being advertised by the National Trust, taking over many of the responsibilities of both Rick (who had died a year earlier) and Eardley (who was due to retire at the end of 1958).

At twenty-seven, John was exactly the age that Jim had been when he applied for a job with the National Trust, and indeed had a great deal else in common with Jim at that age. He was boyishly handsome, with un-assuming good manners and a sensitive disposition. He had a passion, matched by considerable knowledge for one of his years, for architecture, sculpture and painting. (Unlike the young Jim, he was also interested in music, being a respectable amateur pianist.) Like Jim, he could claim to be 'lower upper-class', being a great-grandson of William Kenworthy Browne, the Bedfordshire squire who had been loved by the poet Edward Fitzgerald. But the family fortunes had dwindled; and John did not always get on with his parents, who owned a preparatory school in Hertfordshire where he had been brought up. One difference was that, whereas Jim was a convert to Roman Catholicism, John was the son of converts; whereas Jim had been to Eton, John was educated at Ampleforth. After reading PPE at Oxford, where he became Chairman of the University Art Club, and doing National Service with the Rifle Brigade, John longed to find a job in which he could make use of his knowledge of the arts; but his current employment, with a firm of estate agents in Berkshire, satisfied him as little as had Jim's at Reuters. Like Jim, he felt that a job with the National Trust might be the answer to his prayers.

Jim and John were immediately attracted to each other. Jim saw in John a reflection of his younger self, and felt that here was the responsive young aesthete whom he had longed to meet. Almost overnight, his melancholia turned to euphoria; not only did John revive his interest in life, but the prospect of their becoming colleagues at the National Trust reconciled Jim to that organisation from which he had been on the verge of resigning. John for his part regarded Jim in much the same light as Jim had regarded Harold in the 1930s – as a mentor and father-figure who might further his education and help him on his way. Encouraged by Jim (as Jim had been encouraged by Harold), he lost no time in applying to the National Trust; despite stiff competition (which included the future Foreign Secretary Francis Pym), he duly impressed the selection board with his qualifications and, no doubt helped by the recommendation of Jim and other friends, he heard in the second week of December that he had got the job.

By then, Jim and John had established a close friendship. Largely based on their shared literary and artistic interests, it was essentially platonic in character, and not sensual except incidentally. It bore much similarity to the earlier Harold–Jim relationship – save in one respect. Whereas Vita had been unconcerned by Harold's affection for Jim (for whom, indeed, she developed a warm esteem), when Alvilde learned of Jim's feelings for John, she hit the roof.

Alvilde became aware of John's existence shortly before Christmas 1958 when Jim invited them both to a performance of Monteverdi's *Vespers* at the Brompton Oratory. Jim introduced John as a prospective National Trust colleague (he was due to start work in February); but her natural suspicions were soon aroused. In January, Jim visited Lombardy to write articles for the *Sunday Times*, and took John with him as a research assistant. In February, when John spent a few weeks working at the Trust's London office before moving to his own headquarters in Gloucestershire, Jim (then in Roquebrune) invited him to stay at Thurloe Square. After steaming open a few letters, Alvilde found her suspicions confirmed. Jim had hoped to keep his relations with John private from her just as she had kept hers with Vita private from him; but once she had tackled him on the subject, he made no secret of the fact that he was in love with John and hoped to see much of him in future, an admission which led to terrible scenes. In March Jim, no doubt desperate for a breathing space, went to Spain to finish the research for his book on Iberian Baroque. Alvilde was meanwhile visited by Pat Trevor-Roper, who was staying with his parents in Menton; she told him that she had been shocked to discover that Jim had been leading a life of his own in London, and that she had accordingly decided to sell La Meridienne and return to live in England to keep an eye on him.

When Jim learned of these plans, he was appalled. Had she kept her own counsel, it is likely that he would have worked out a fairly satisfactory life, pursuing his friendship with John during the months that he was apart from her, and feeling happier in his marriage as a result. As it was, he had been exasperated almost beyond endurance during the past couple of years by her nagging, and the thought of being with her permanently in future, and prevented from meeting the person he most wanted to see, was more than he could bear. He told her that, if her idea of marriage was keeping him under constant surveillance, he would leave her. Feeling wretched, they dashed off letters to their respective confidants, Eardley and Vita, both of whom counselled patience and restraint. Eardley wrote to Jim that 'you must not feel that if your life has to be reorganised it will be too great a problem, for you are really & truly one of the most loved people I have ever known and the world is littered with people absolutely devoted to you'; he recognised 'the paternal basis' of Jim's love for John – 'it is wonderful to be looked up to & respected & listened to . . .' Vita wrote to Alvilde that 'there must be something behind this . . . [for] one seldom breaks up one's life for an infatuation – and anyhow in this case what good would it do? They can't go off and live together – at least not without initiating such a scandal that they would both have to give up their jobs, which I don't suppose they want.'

At the beginning of April Jim and Alvilde, still 'together' but barely on speaking terms, travelled from Roquebrune to London. Fortunately Alvilde had another interest to take her mind off her marriage, for on 13 April Clarissa gave birth to her first child, a daughter, Chloë. Meanwhile Jim was involved in helping John in his new job. John had now taken up residence at Dyrham Park, Gloucestershire, his headquarters as National Trust Representative for Wessex and Severn Region, and was not having an easy time. A handsome William and Mary house, the near-derelict Dyrham had been acquired by the Government on the recommendation of the Historic Buildings Council in 1956 and presented to the Trust, since when architects and builders employed by the Ministry of Works had been restoring the fabric of the building and converting those parts of it which were not suitable for showing to the public into flats. However, John arrived to discover that not only was the work well behind schedule, but the flat earmarked for himself was not yet habitable. In this chaotic situation he found himself having to deal with three difficult groups of people: the Ministry builders; the Blathwayt family, who had formerly owned the house and still owned most of the estate; and the two local agents employed by the Trust, who resented being subordinated to a representative. John naturally sought the advice of Jim, who also had the official task of 'introducing' him to many of the country houses owned by the Trust which were henceforth to be his responsibility, including Brockhampton, Coughton, Hanbury and Wightwick.*

Given Alvilde's preoccupation with her new grandchild and Jim's professional involvement with John, they managed to keep out of each other's way that month. Their discussions about the future seem to have been carried on mainly through the intermediary of Harold and Vita, who found themselves dragged into the marital dispute. Harold wrote to Vita that he felt some responsibility for the situation 'as it was I who introduced [Jim] to the Browne boy', but that he was sure that 'the cause of separation is more irritation at Alvilde's bossiness than any passion for another'. Vita wrote to Harold that 'I don't see why Jim should wish to break up their marriage entirely, unless he really can't stand living with her any more', and that 'they already spend so little time together in the year that I should have thought they could arrive at some compromise without an open break'. At the end of April Alvilde returned alone to Roquebrune, having received assurances from Jim that he did not mean to abandon her, but having nevertheless made up her mind to put La Meridienne on the market with a view to giving up it and her French tax residence at the end of 1959. (The aspect of this she most regretted was parting from her ancient pekinese Foo; as she was unable to bring him to England, she had him put down.)

For the next two years the marriage was in a state of simmering crisis. Alvilde was desperate not to 'lose' Jim; yet she could not help herself behaving in ways which were bound to exacerbate his irritation with her. Jim for his part was anxious to preserve his marriage, provided he could at the same time maintain his friendship with John (whom he was in any case only able to see occasionally owing to John's isolation at Dyrham); but there were times when he found her company hard to bear. As Harold wrote after seeing him at a particularly bad moment in July 1959:

---

*John's job, which resulted from a reorganisation, involved the southern half of the region formerly managed by Rick, and the northern half of the region formerly managed by Eardley. It was Eardley's task to show John the properties on his patch, Jim's to show him those formerly on Rick's.

He says that it is intolerable for him even to see Alvilde, since her reproaches and 'spying' drive him mad with rage and he is afraid of saying or doing something he might regret . . . Anyhow, he did promise me to do nothing drastic or to render impossible reconciliation with Alvilde. He still professes to be very fond of her and to suffer from causing her distress. But he contends that he was not made for marriage, that his freedom means everything to him, that he cannot stand being scolded or fussed or nagged at or bossed. In fact he is very miserable and the delights of knowing J.K.-B. do not make up for the miseries of self-reproach.

Meanwhile, at Dyrham, John was devoting himself with some success to his job; he was anxious to retain the affections of Jim, whose friendship was precious to him, but never encouraged Jim to think of leaving Alvilde. There were in fact moments during those two years when Jim and Alvilde seemed to be getting on reasonably well. They continued to travel together as husband and wife – to Bavaria and Austria in September 1959, Florence that Christmas, Venice at Easter 1960 and Asolo that summer – and Alvilde tried to make these expeditions comfortable and agreeable. After she had relinquished her French base they spent much of 1960 looking at English country houses together with a view to finding one they both liked (and which Alvilde felt she could afford) as their future matrimonial home. In October 1960 Alvilde unbent to the extent of inviting John to a tête-à-tête at Thurloe Square; during the same month John visited Sissinghurst to meet Vita, who reported to Alvilde her favourable impressions of him. ('Charm, yes; and very easy to get on with. Light in hand, and plenty to talk about . . .') However, just when it seemed that all would be well, Alvilde would start behaving again 'like a woman scorn'd', thus infuriating Jim and plunging the marriage back into crisis. As Harold wrote to Vita, 'Alvilde never gives it [Jim's affection for John] time to wither but waters it with her tears'.

The main problem was that, although Alvilde in her saner moments must have recognised that she had no right to a total claim on Jim's affections, that their marriage was only likely to prosper if he were given some leeway within it, and that John was no monster and wished her no ill (at any rate, these points were constantly made to her by Vita and other friends to whom she turned for advice), so consumed was she with jealousy that she could not bear the thought of Jim and John meeting or even corresponding with each other. As Jim wrote to Eardley from Vienna, where his holiday with Alvilde was otherwise going well, 'the mere sight of a postcard addressed to [John] causes deep hurt and anger in spite of Rory [Cameron]'s sound talk'. She made it her constant business to find out where they were meeting and what they were up to; not for nothing was she a first cousin of the spymaster Sir Stewart Menzies, head of MI6 from 1939 to 1952. Her habit of intercepting and steaming open Jim's letters became such a joke among his friends that they often included some salutation to her in their correspondence with him. ('Dear Alvilde,' wrote Eardley, 'take the kettle off the boil, this one is a perfect wash out.') It was not so amusing for John, who sometimes found that Jim never received his letters. Anyone who facilitated a meeting of Jim and John, or even passed a communication between them, incurred her wrath. She scolded Harold when she discovered (by opening a letter from Vita to Jim) that he had had Jim and John to stay at his flat in Albany, and refused to speak to him when they next met at a party. Jim once stayed at Long Crichel and was pleasantly surprised to discover on his arrival that John had been asked too; John's presence was not however a surprise to Alvilde, who (as Raymond Mortimer told Frances Partridge) 'got in her car and drove across country and made a scene'. After this painful incident, Jim wrote to Freda Berkeley:

> If you have any influence with Alvilde, do persuade her not to make herself wretched and everyone else when there is so little need. I came [to Long Crichel] to write. I did *not* suggest John coming here. Raymond when he heard I was coming invited him without my knowing. Anyway why should I make excuses like this all the time? I am fifty-two and have always been independent. I shall not change now, I fear. I am desperately sorry for Alvilde because she cannot be happy, but I have told her over and over again – if living with me is intolerable, then I will clear out. She must make up her mind and cease expecting me to act the part of Romeo . . . After all I am not contemplating running away with anyone, you know! And if Alvilde were to leave me you may be sure I shall never live with anyone else . . . But if [she insisted that] I should never go off for a week or more in the year with someone whom she disliked, or else there would be scenes, then I could not live with her . . . The attitude of tragedy queen she assumes is very distressing. I will always love A., but [her] constant nagging and demands do submerge my love from time to time. After last night, I don't know how I feel, except prostrated.

Another problem was that, whereas Jim and John were always discreet, and never gave anyone (apart from a few trusted friends such as Harold and the Long Crichel circle) to suppose that they were anything other than ordinary friends and colleagues, Alvilde complained about them freely to all and sundry and thus risked provoking scandal. This prospect caused particular dread to the National Trust Secretary Jack Rathbone, a timorous man who lived in terror of the exposure of his own homo-sexuality. He told Harold that he was 'distressed by the way Alvilde tells and retells the story to comparative strangers', and feared this might 'cause a stink' which would result in both Jim and John having to leave the Trust and bring the organisation itself into disrepute. When Jim and John visited Rome together in October 1959, Jack had sleepless nights lest the visit get to the ears of Lord Crawford, 'who, unlike Oliver [Esher], takes such matters very grimly'. Rathbone must have felt that his worst fears were about to be realised when Alvilde stormed into his office one day and demanded that John be sacked for interfering with her marriage; she also wrote letters to this effect to other leading Trust figures. Needless to say, no action was taken against John, whose conduct had been irre-proachable and who was doing his job well – but Alvilde's vindictiveness was not helpful to him at a time when he had other problems to contend with, mostly arising from friction with the local agents. At the end of the day, the only result of her representations was that, on retiring from the National Trust after thirty years of service, Jim failed to receive the CBE which he might otherwise have expected (a loss which rankled more with her than with him).

Some of their friends took sides (though Harold and Vita were so exasperated at being involved in the seemingly endless trouble that their affection for Jim and Alvilde was sorely tried and they merely longed for the couple, one way or another, to be reconciled). For some years after the Long Crichel incident, Eardley and Raymond refused to speak to Alvilde. At first Eddy and Jamesey sympathised with Alvilde, which affected their longstanding friendship with Jim. Jamesey kept Alvilde company during her unhappy last summer at Roquebrune in 1959, and on his return to London behaved snubbingly to John, provoking a furious letter from Jim about betrayal of confidence. However, Jamesey later acknowledged that Alvilde had been at fault, and apologised to John; while Eddy, with whom she stayed in Ireland when in need of solace, admitted to Harold that he found her trying. No one who was aware that, just a few years earlier, Alvilde had been conducting a passionate affair with Vita can have failed to remark her hypocrisy; as Jim wrote twenty years later (in connection with Victoria Glendinning's forthcoming biog-raphy of Vita), 'our friends will undoubtedly think badly of A. for having made such a tremendous fuss over my affair with J., which began after hers with V., about which I had remained quite mum.'

Few who were in the know at the time expected the marriage to sur-vive, and that it did so owed much to their discovery of a house they both adored. They had been house-hunting throughout 1960 without success, when early in 1961 they came upon Alderley Grange near Wotton-under-Edge, Gloucestershire, situated in glorious unspoilt country (soon to be officially protected as an 'Area of Outstanding Natural Beauty') at the foot of the Cotswolds overlooking the Ozleworth valley. Built of beautiful grey stone which changed colour in different lights, and belonging to various periods, it was a handsome, solid building of just the right size; the grounds included a George II coach house and stable block, and a walled garden. As the house was in a state of disrepair and the garden a wilderness, it promised to be their 'Sissinghurst' and keep them busy for years. The purchase was completed in March; they rented the house near Bath of the novelist L. P. Hartley (whose secretary Ursula Codrington was another former lover of Vita) while they supervised the basic work needed to make the house habitable, and moved in during August.

The house was by no means grand but had a history calculated to appeal to Jim. The original structure was Jacobean; it had been erected by the Hale family, local landowners, and was the birthplace in 1609 of the famous lawyer Sir Matthew Hale, Lord Chief Justice under Charles II, who mostly lived at the much bigger Alderley House nearby. (Together with the parish church, the 'big house' was rebuilt in the early 1800s in the neo-Jacobean style by the pastiche architect Vulliamy, and by the 1960s was a preparatory school.) The future Grange (then known as West End House) was left to Sir Matthew's daughter whose descendants sold it in the 1740s to a Bristol merchant named Springett. Desirous of transforming his modest residence into a smart gentleman's seat, Springett added a new classical front in the style of James Gibbs, including a central 'Venetian' window and an oak staircase of exquisite craftsmanship; in 1810 his descendants extended this with ground-floor bays, thus creating two spacious Regency-style rooms, each thirty feet long, on either side of the staircase hall. Alderley became something of an intellectual centre in the late nineteenth century, when the Grange (as it had become known) was occupied by the eccentric orientalist Brian Houghton Hodgson, the big house by two bachelor Hale brothers, retired soldiers with literary interests, and Mount House in between by the traveller and artist Marianne North, sister-in-law of the historian and poet (and early writer on homosexuality) John Addington Symonds. Houghton Hodgson added a wing to accommodate such features as a billiards room. Since the Second World War the house had housed a variety of institutions. Much needed doing to it, starting with the demolition of the Victorian wing which Jim considered an excrescence.

Although Alderley was bought and restored with Alvilde's money (Jim still had none), he assumed responsibility for a share of its running costs, which meant that he had to give up Thurloe Square, his London home for fifteen years. He was especially sad at parting from 'Miss Emily', the perfect housekeeper. For a while Jim rented a room in another house nearby but soon gave this up, exasperated that Alvilde kept telephoning his landlord to check up on him. After that he usually stayed with Eardley at his small flat in Belgravia. When he and Alvilde went to London together to attend parties given by friends, she usually stayed on her own with the Berkeleys in Little Venice; she could not prevent him associating with old friends such as Eardley who now wanted little to do with her.

It was quite another matter that Alderley was only twenty minutes' drive from Dyrham. Alvilde made it clear that she would not tolerate Jim 'nipping over' there whenever he felt inclined – though he and John regularly got together to visit other houses on National Trust business or just out of general interest. John had meanwhile worked hard and successfully, with some advice from Jim, to prepare the main rooms at Dyrham for opening to the public, and the opening ceremony took place in June 1961. This was attended by both Jim and Alvilde, as well as by Vita, who was afterwards taken by Alvilde to see Alderley and hear her plans for the garden. (Vita wrote to her appreciatively about 'the charming exterior, the well-proportioned rooms, the really beautiful views . . . and of course the garden so full of possibilities – all those grey walls which make a wonderful background to any colour'.) Jim and Alvilde also encountered John when they subscribed to the concerts which he later hosted at Dyrham. Alvilde's manner towards John on these occasions was polite but frosty, while Jim suffered acute embarrassment. Once Burnet Pavitt was staying at Alderley and John asked if Jim might drive him over to examine the Dyrham piano; Burnet came, but it was Alvilde who drove him, and she would not enter the house.

In October 1961, while the restoration work at Alderley was in full swing, Jim was driving one night through Berkshire when he was involved in a collision; his car was a write-off, and he was lucky to escape with a broken leg. He spent two weeks in Reading General Hospital with his leg in plaster; the fellow occupants of his ward were amazed to hear the snobbish matron announce a visit by the Duke of Wellington ('Gerry' lived nearby at Stratfield Saye). Other visitors naturally included both Alvilde and John, the former taking care not to coincide with the latter. Vita wanted to write to Jim, but having been shocked to learn that

Alvilde had opened her previous letter to him (which had alerted her to the fact that Jim and John were spending a night with Harold in London), wrote to him care of John. This missive was also intercepted by Alvilde, who angrily reproached both Jim and Vita for using John as a go-between. At this, the patience of Vita, who was herself far from well, finally snapped, and she wrote to Alvilde denouncing her 'unsavoury strategems' and asking 'why on earth can't you accept the situation . . . if you really love Jim'. This rocket from one to whom she had always looked for sympathy seems to have brought Alvilde to her senses and she created no further trouble for some time. Once she had got Jim back to Alderley, she nursed him devotedly back to health.

In May 1962 Jim's mother, whose health had been causing him anxiety, died in Evesham Hospital, aged seventy-eight. Since the death of his father in 1949, Jim had found her a trial. When she stayed at Roquebrune in February 1953 he admitted to his diary to being 'immensely irritated' by her. 'She has become extremely affected, gushing and unnatural . . . She brings every sentence round to herself. Then abuse of her children and children-in-law . . . I dare not look at her for fear that she will say something so silly that I shall be driven to snap. Then I feel miserably, bitterly penitent.' Even then, however, she was able to stir romantic feelings in men; later that same year she accepted a proposal of marriage from a Worcestershire neighbour younger than herself, Harry Horsfield, a widower and a veteran of the Royal Flying Corps. (George Lees-Milne would have turned in his grave at the thought that his wife's second husband was both a Roman Catholic and an art-lover, though such things meant little to her.) The marriage was not a success and after a few months they agreed to separate. Twenty years later, Jim asked Horsfield whether life with her had been unadulterated hell. 'Not unadulterated,' he replied. She spent her last years at Wickhamford, being looked after by Haines the chauffeur and his wife, and taking increasingly to the bottle. (As by the 1960s Clarissa's father was also a confirmed alcoholic, it is little wonder that Alderley became a rather 'dry' household, where few drinks were offered except for wine at meals.) For all the difficulties he had had with her, Jim was inconsolable at her death; he wrote to Jamesey from Alderley that 'nothing can ever hit me so hard again . . . I sit about in this lovely place . . . and nothing seems to have any substance at all.' Just two weeks later Vita died, aged sixty-nine, a loss keenly felt by both Jim and Alvilde; Jim was anxious for Harold, who seemed devastated.

Jim was helped to survive the traumatic years 1959–61 by his absorption in a book. Long in the planning and ambitious in scope, it was a study of five early eighteenth-century earls (Bathurst, Pembroke, Burlington, Oxford and Leicester) whose fascination with architecture and landscape gardening led them to create five masterpieces (Cirencester, Marble Hill, Chiswick, Wimpole and Holkham). The earls knew each other and had much in common: all when young had done the Grand Tour on a grand scale; all were influenced by William Kent, and knew Alexander Pope who immortalised them in verse. There were also important differences: Pembroke, Burlington and Leicester were Whigs who pioneered a revival of the Palladian style first introduced to England a century earlier by Inigo Jones, while Bathurst and Oxford were Tories nostalgic for the Stuarts and the architecture of Wren and Vanbrugh. Jim's thesis was that their creations could not be understood without some appreciation of their lives and tastes; as he wrote in his preface, 'architecture wholly unleavened with historical association is unpalatable stuff'. In the course of research he not only familiarised himself with the five properties but consulted the surviving papers of the earls and discussed their work with their descendants (in the case of Lord Burlington, the descendant was Andrew Devonshire and the papers were at Chatsworth). Much of the book was written in the summer of 1960 at Asolo where Alvilde rented the house of the explorer Freya Stark, whose library had a famous revolving desk enabling a writer to have his sources at his fingertips. The title, *Earls of Creation*, was suggested by John (to whom it would probably have been dedicated but for the likely domestic consequences); it had some trouble finding a publisher but was finally brought out by Hamish Hamilton in the autumn of 1962 to excellent sales and reviews: forty years later, it remained in print.

Jim was already at work on his next book, a slim volume on his native Worcestershire for the Shell Guide series edited by John Betjeman. (Jim and 'Betj' had resumed their close friendship of the 1930s, Jim attending the first reading of Betjeman's autobiographical poem *Summoned by Bells* at Chatsworth in 1959.) Wishing to benefit from an extra pair of eyes, Jim took John Kenworthy-Browne with him on his motoring tours around the county, and these were among the happiest times they spent together. Though a conventional gazetteer, the book contained many characteristic and nostalgic touches. Before 1918, as Jim recalled, the county was

> a fertile garden, uneventful if you like, and heavily wooded. Its rutted lanes, shrouded in oaks and elms, threaded their way through interminable orchards enlivened with meandering brooks. In the springtime a dense mist of pink and white blossom descended upon acre upon acre of apple and plum trees. In the autumn months the air was laden with the

drowsy scent of hops and cider. The black–and–white farmhouses, barns
and cottages of the villages and the damson brick terrace houses of the
small market towns looked as though they had grown out of the lush
landscape, which still crept up to them on all sides . . . Within the past
forty-five years terrible toll has been taken of the rural landscape [as] the
tentacles of industry and the rash of building development [spread] farther
and farther from the towns . . .

Unfortunately Jim's manuscript ran into trouble which delayed its
publication until 1964: his unflattering remarks about petrol stations were
not acceptable to Shell, the series sponsor, who also required him to
remove his attacks on the Air Ministry, one of their best customers. On
libel grounds he was also asked to modify a passage suggesting that
Worcester had been more comprehensively wrecked by its own philistine
Corporation than by the Roman, Saxon, Danish, Welsh and Roundhead
armies which had sacked it and the German planes which had bombed
it.* Otherwise Betjeman was delighted with it. 'Let me, dear boy, say at
once how SPLENDID it is . . . There is so much delicious affection and
grumpiness in it . . . I feel it is a great act of kindness and generosity on
your part to have done it. Ta ever so.'

Jim's spat with Shell inspired him to do something to draw public
attention to the spoliation of the landscape. Through the good offices
of his friend Lord Archie Gordon (later 5th Marquess of Aberdeen),
formerly on the staff of CPRE and now Director of Talks at the BBC, he
gave a radio broadcast in 1964 entitled 'Who Cares for England?':

I suppose no country, not even Italy, was in its special way lovelier than
England . . . Yet the actual country is disappearing at an alarming rate.
Newbury is already practically a suburb of London . . . The centres of
the old towns themselves are being bought up for astronomical sums by
giant commercial syndicates [which] without the slightest regard for the
wellbeing of the inhabitants demolish buildings scheduled as historical
monuments, and replace them with hideous and shoddy substitutes . . .
Soon every town in Great Britain will lose its particular identity and
look cheap, vulgar and commonplace. There will be nothing but a church
or two to tell one whether one is in Worcester or Sheffield, Truro or
Newcastle . . . Every day further inroads are being made upon the
dwindling beauties of this country: and who really cares? For years, it is

---

*Jim had some reason for his fury. In *Britain's Lost Cities* (Aurum, 2007), Gavin Stamp
ranks Worcester as the worst example of a town in which the authorities took advantage
of relatively minor war damage to devastate a historic centre in the interests of
'planning'.

true, bodies like the National Trust . . . have gallantly been saving a slice
of land here or an old building there . . .

Jim pleaded for conservation legislation, to empower not 'a roving army
of minor officials . . . totally ignorant of nature, architecture and aesthetics' but 'regional panels of disinterested men and women who really care
and know about such matters', and also for education to raise public
awareness – 'I should like to hear preached from every clergyman's pulpit
and taught from every schoolmaster's desk the sanctity of historic buildings and beautiful scenery, a reverence for nature and wild life . . .'
Patriotism, he concluded, properly consisted not in thinking one's nation
superior to others but in loving the fabric of one's country, and 'if all its
towns are to be dominated by supermarkets and car-parks, and its farm-
lands by caravan sites and pylons, then why should we love it any more?'
The broadcast stimulated an enormous public response and was published
by popular demand in *The Listener*, which was one of several journals to
devote a leading article to his 'cry of protest'. CPRE made a film with
the same title, featuring readings by Michael Redgrave. Had he been
willing to make regular appearances in the broadcast media, Jim (like his
friend Alec Clifton-Taylor) might have built up a considerable popular
reputation as a conservationist pundit; but extreme diffidence deterred
him from going very far down this path.

During the early 1960s, perhaps as a result of his domestic traumas, Jim
seems briefly to have abandoned his religious faith. In April 1964, on the
thirtieth anniversary of his becoming a Catholic, he wrote:

> Within the last two or three years I have given up the pretence of believ-
> ing. I am utterly without faith, and am irritated by rather than sympathetic
> towards Catholicism. I don't think I ever really believed, even thirty
> years ago. I merely wanted to believe, and looked upon the Church as a
> necessary rock in a disintegrating world of materialism. Now that the
> world has disintegrated I can no longer maintain the fiction.

In fact, Jim had originally been drawn to Catholicism not just as a 'rock'
but also for aesthetic reasons, for he loved the old Latin Mass and the associated ritual and symbolism – and within two years of his writing the above
words, all this was put in jeopardy by the outcome of the Second Vatican
Council (1962–5). Paradoxically, his dismay at the prospective disappearance of these hallowed practices had the effect of re-igniting, for a few
years, his Catholic fervour; so long as it seemed possible to save them, he
felt they were worth fighting for. (In this he was encouraged by Geoffrey
Houghton Brown, a passionate upholder of the old ways and a stalwart of

the Latin Mass Society founded to defend them.) Another paradox was that around this time the papal annulment of the Chaplin marriage for which he had applied in 1950 finally came through, enabling him to be formally readmitted to the Church after more than a decade of excommunication and to solemnise his marriage to Alvilde in an Italian church (though he seems to have said little about this to his Catholic friends, many of whom were unaware of his readmission). Outward signs of Jim's Catholic 'rebirth' were his acceptance of a place on the Arts Committee of the Brompton Oratory, and his decision to embark on a history of St Peter's, Rome.

During the early 1960s Jim carried on as the National Trust's Architectural Adviser. Although far fewer properties were accepted than in the past, mostly owing to the cost of endowment, several houses which he had long nurtured came into the Trust's possession. These included Anglesey Abbey, Cambridgeshire, transferred by the sybaritic Lord Fairhaven in 1962, nineteen years after he had first discussed the matter with Jim, and Hanbury Hall, which fell to the Trust the same year after the death of Lady Vernon (through tact and patience, Jim and John had also succeeded in acquiring for the Trust much of the contents and surrounding land which had been left to her enemy, the late Sir George's adopted daughter). Jim also set the ball rolling with regard to several important properties which were only taken on by the Trust long after his departure. One such was Stowe, Buckinghamshire, whose splendid park (then owned by Stowe School which did not have the means to maintain it) was not to be acquired for another thirty years, but about which Jim, after visiting it with John, wrote to Eardley in 1961:

> When one thinks of the N.T. accepting for permanent preservation stockbrokers' herbaceous gardens in Surrey and botanical specimen gardens in Cornwall, with only an occasional pixie sundial or Swiss chalet as an ornament, and then contemplates Stowe rapidly falling into decay, one supposes something is wrong. Stowe far excels any garden I know – there are millions of temples, columns, bridges, urns, fountains, screens, lodges and extravaganzas tumbling into ruin, and the serpentine contours of Kent and Brown disappearing for lack of skilled attention. Surely the Trust could hold the gardens and let the silly school go on using the place for nothing?

Another property remarkable for its garden was Sissinghurst, offered by Nigel Nicolson who had inherited it from Vita: with her strong proprietary sense, Vita had held back from donating it during her lifetime, but Nigel, having no funds with which to maintain it, saw no alternative to the Trust's ownership except 'its gradual reversion to the fields and cabbage patches from which it had emerged'. Surprisingly, both the

Historic Buildings Committee and the Gardens Committee were in two minds about accepting it; but Jim certified the importance of the buildings while Alvilde, now sitting on the Gardens Committee, made an impassioned plea in favour of the garden in which she had experienced so many romantic moments with Vita. (After it had been accepted in principle, its transfer was delayed until 1967 owing to difficult negotiations with the Treasury over death duties, since when it has been one of the Trust's most visited gardens and greatest money-spinners.)

Although Jim derived satisfaction from such individual cases, he was increasingly depressed by the general direction in which the Trust was moving. With the steady growth in both membership and holdings (by 1965 there were some 160,000 members and 330,000 acres), the trend towards professionalisation, bureaucratisation and museumisation, so deprecated by him during the 1950s, became ever more marked. A turning point in the Trust's history occurred in 1961, when Lord Esher retired as chairman of the strategic General Purposes Committee and was succeeded by John Smith, a brilliant but abrasive banker. Smith was determined to rid the Trust of its surviving amateur character and turn it into an efficient business. On grounds of both personality and policy he found himself at loggerheads with the easygoing Jack Rathbone, a clash which dismayed Crawford and other leading Trust figures. The upshot was that in 1964 Rathbone suffered a nervous breakdown, following which Smith was made to resign his chairmanship (though he remained influential in the Trust). However, during his three years in charge, Smith succeeded in railroading through one particular reform. When, after the war, Jim had created the system of regional representatives acting in tandem with regional agents, Esher had agreed with him that, in any dispute between an agent and a representative on a matter which involved an aesthetic dimension, the representative should prevail. This rule held until the 1960s (despite the fact that agents had come to be paid more than representatives); under Smith, it was reversed. One of the victims of the new dispensation was John Kenworthy-Browne. Since becoming a representative in 1959 he had suffered endless trouble from his local agents, especially the one in charge of the southern part of his area, who behaved like the squire of his domain and resented having to accept instructions from anyone else on his patch (Eardley had similarly had trouble with him, as would John's successor Tony Mitchell). Already overworked, and suffering from Alvilde's vindictive attentions, John felt unable to serve under the new regime; he resigned early in 1965 after six productive but not altogether happy years in his post.

Jim's inclination was to leave at the same time, but he agreed to stay on for another year to see through various matters. He had been appalled by the Smith reforms and much else, and saw that worse was to come. One of his few remaining consolations was that the Trust was still largely run by friends of his who were cultivated and public-spirited aristocrats. In fact, like the Palladian movement of the 1730s, the National Trust in the 1960s was dominated by earls. The Earl of Rosse chaired the Historic Buildings Committee; Earl de la Warr chaired the Estates Committee; when the Earl of Crawford retired after twenty years as National Trust Chairman in 1965, he was succeeded by the Earl of Antrim. However, one of the questionable services which Smith (himself the brother-in-law of the Earl of Euston, now chairman of the Trust's East Anglian Regional Committee) had rendered before relinquishing office was to engineer the appointment of Commander Conrad Rawnsley, grandson of the Trust's co-founder Canon Hardwicke Rawnsley, to run Enterprise Neptune, a campaign to acquire for the Trust large stretches of the United Kingdom's coastline. Even before the campaign's official launch in May 1965, Rawnsley, who had a chip on his shoulder and whose self-importance amounted to megalomania, had quarrelled with Antrim and others and started publicly denouncing the Trust as 'an institution of feudalism, a protégé of the old landowning class' which had been 'bedevilled since before the war by the stately-home [sic] scheme' whereas it ought to exist 'for the man in the street'. A showdown loomed: in the autumn of 1966 Rawnsley would be sacked, whereupon he would try to stir up the membership against the 'self-perpetuating oligarchy' of decadent aristocrats and homosexuals which, he claimed, had diverted the Trust from its original purposes.

Jim did not wait for this volcano to erupt. In March 1966, thirty years to the month since his appointment as Country Houses Secretary, he resigned from the staff. Though he left amid glowing tributes, it was not a happy departure – as he wrote to Michael Rosse, it was 'like being divorced from someone you have lived with for thirty years'. He was invited to join the Historic Buildings Committee, but said he would need some time to consider this. 'The truth is I don't yet know whether or not I want to make a complete break. My feelings about the Trust are very mixed. I look back upon my thirty years as a long, losing battle (a lost battle really) against ugliness, philistinism and agents. I feel I have shot my bolt – to use a military term which you will understand – as far as the National Trust is concerned.'

12

Alderley
1966–74

B Y THE TIME of Jim's resignation from the National Trust, he and Alvilde were well-established at Alderley Grange. In the five years since they had acquired it, the business of repairing it, decorating it, improving it and managing it had provided them with an abiding common interest and helped shore up their marriage at a difficult time. She, having a flair for such matters, had made most of the decorative decisions, while he, with his National Trust experience, had arranged the rooms. On the walls, portraits of Jim's Puleston and Thomson ancestors jostled with paintings by artists they had known such as Graham Sutherland and Paul Methuen; the heavy Victorian furniture which Jim had inherited contrasted with the delicate French furniture which Alvilde had collected. Many contents spoke of their past associations – the sketch of Stravinsky which his son had done for Alvilde; the looking-glass which Ivy Compton-Burnett, teasing him for his vanity, had left Jim. Although it was not large by country house standards, it provided them with enough space to stay out of each other's way. Of the two noble rooms off the staircase hall, one was Jim's library and inviolable sanctum; he retreated there after breakfast and often remained there, working in seclusion, for most of the day. Alvilde's private space was not the big drawing room opposite (generally used only when they had guests) but her cosy sitting room in the old part of the building, filled with French furniture, pictures and books. However, her main 'territory' was her garden, created since 1961 but already one of the most admired in the neighbourhood – 'a glorious success,' wrote Frances Partridge, 'proliferating up walls, cascading, abundant, making blue pools round the feet of trees' and 'permeated by her love and care for often rare and unusual plants'. In summer it was 'fragrant with roses which clamber over every wall and intoxicate the senses'. An alley of lime trees planted in 1962 was starting to come into its own.

Since their move there, Jim's circumstances had changed in one notable respect. Three deaths in rapid succession – of his mother in 1962, his rich

Scottish cousin Neale Thomson in 1964, and his pipe-smoking Aunt Dorothy in 1965 – had brought him (along with many possessions, the best of which he kept for Alderley) some capital for the first time in his life: conservatively invested in the stock market, it produced an income of several thousand pounds a year. This was timely, as Alvilde was feeling less rich than in the 1950s: her abandonment of her French domicile had exposed her to swingeing British taxes, and since her feckless son-in-law rarely earned much money, she felt obliged to support her daughter and four grandchildren (who led a peripatetic existence in France and Italy). The costs of running even a medium-sized country house mounted alarmingly from year to year, and Jim was glad to be able to bear his share. Their greatest expense – as well as their greatest headache – was staff. Eventually they found a couple to live in the converted stables, of whom the husband, a former German prisoner-of-war, became the gardener, while his English wife cleaned the house; they were a surly pair, but at least they stayed. A cook–housekeeper was also needed to live in the house itself, but it seemed impossible to find anyone to stay in this job for more than a few months: no doubt this was a sign of the times, though several departing housekeepers made it clear that they had been driven away by their mistress's exacting demands and autocratic manner.

By the mid 1960s the Lees-Milnes had many friends in the locality. Their closest neighbours were Jim's old friend Midi Gascoigne and her husband Derick, who had moved (with encouragement from Jim) into the eighteenth-century Mount House in Alderley village soon after the Lees-Milnes had moved into the Grange. They were on excellent terms with the local landed gentry, the Harfords of Ashcroft; Colonel Harford was a conventional figure, but his wife Joanie was an enlivening presence, loved by all. While they had little in common with the local great aristocrats, the Duke of Beaufort and his semi-royal Duchess at Badminton, who were mainly interested in hunting, they became great friends with the Duke's cousin and heir, the art dealer David Somerset, and his wife Caroline, daughter of Lord Bath of Longleat, who lived in Badminton village. Other nearby couples with whom they exchanged hospitality included the art-collecting squire Basil Barlow and his wife Gerda at Stancombe Manor, the Rolling Stones' manager Rupert Loewenstein and his wife Josephine at Biddestone Manor, the novelist Isabel Colegate and her husband Michael Briggs at Midford Castle, the architectural historian David Verey and his wife Rosemary (another noted gardener) at Barnsley House, the inventor Jeremy Fry and his wife Camilla at Widcombe Manor, the engineer Andy Garnett and his journalist wife

Polly at Bradley Court, and the clothes designer Peter Saunders and his American wife 'Didi' at Easton Grey. (Fry, Garnett and Saunders, a generation younger than the Lees-Milnes, were close friends, another of their circle being Lord Snowdon, Anne Rosse's son by her first marriage who had married Princess Margaret in 1960.) The single men they saw included Paul Methuen, now an eccentric widower in psychic communication with his late wife; Leslie Hartley (Jim admired his novels and was pleased to be consulted about a house for the film of *The Go-Between*); Ian McCallum, now curator of the American Museum near Bath; and Bob Parsons, an American architect who became the tenant and restorer of Newark Park, a National Trust house near Alderley. They also knew several interesting widows: Diana, Countess of Westmorland, daughter of the eminent Edwardian Lord Ribblesdale, at Lyegrove; Eliza Wansbrough, granddaughter of the Victorian solicitor Sir George Lewis, at Broughton Poggs; Sally, Duchess of Westminster, illegitimate half-sister (as she was not anxious for her friends to discover) of the writer Joe Ackerley, at Wickwar Manor. Alvilde, who loved the social round, generally took the initiative in meeting these people; Jim enjoyed their company, but left to himself would have led a more reclusive life. He had, however, a few local friends whom he generally visited on his own, including two exuberant bachelors, the inventor Alex Moulton of The Hall, Bradford-on-Avon, and Hiram Winterbottom of Woodchester Priory, a businessman of German-Jewish origin who lived with his ex-guardsman servant Ball.

Jim loved going for long walks (like many writers, he found that striding stimulated the mental processes); and there was wonderful walking in the coombs, valleys and woods around Alderley. His invariable companions on his daily expeditions were their beloved whippets, Fop and Chuff. He was rarely accompanied by Alvilde, who was not a walker and preferred to work in her garden, but quite often by Midi, with whom he exchanged confidences as of old. In the mid 1960s two other writers came (independently) to live near Alderley – the poet and university lecturer Charles Tomlinson, and the art expert and archaeologist (later travel writer and novelist) Bruce Chatwin – and Jim often walked with them singly or together. Jim was both fascinated by and wary of the ambitious, anarchic and narcissistic Chatwin, who was still in his twenties but already something of a legend with his alluring looks, flamboyant behaviour and travels in remote places. He was then under contract to write his first book, *The Nomadic Alternative*, which he talked about endlessly but never produced. Though married to the American heiress

Elizabeth Chanler, his basic nature was clearly gay; he discussed sex on his walks with Jim, who managed to resist his flirtatious charms. ('I have seldom met a human being who exudes so much sex appeal with so comparatively little niceness. What does this boy want?') Another walking companion, with whom Jim felt more at ease, was John Harris, the former protégé of Geoffrey Houghton Brown and basement lodger at Thurloe Square who was now a distinguished (and happily married) architectural expert, and who secured (with help from Jim) a weekend cottage on the Ashcroft estate. Harris later recalled that Jim, though he could walk long distances (he regarded ten miles as a satisfactory amble), was not one for getting his shoes muddy, and tended to avoid cross-country routes and stick to roads and paths.

At weekends they often had friends to stay. Regular guests included the Berkeleys, the Droghedas, John Betjeman and his paramour Elizabeth ('Feeble') Cavendish, Diana Cooper, Rosamond Lehmann and Desmond Shawe-Taylor. An occasional guest was the Bloomsbury Group survivor Frances Partridge, famous for her wise perceptions, who recorded several visits to Alderley in her diary. She thought the house and its surroundings very beautiful, and felt that 'Jim has achieved what he most desires – I could see no sign anywhere of the modernity he detests . . . Tea on the lawn as in a past age, silver kettles, swooping white doves.' She reported that the food was delicious, that she met interesting people, that they drove around looking at churches. She found the garden full of delights. Yet to her mind, something was not quite right. She was 'subtly aware of alien values . . . it is all just a little too conventional and safe'. (She was of course aware that the Lees-Milnes did not share her left-leaning outlook – but she probably meant more than this.) Much as she admired Alvilde's gardening talents, she found her cold – 'any other gardener would have given me some flowers to take to London and I would have asked any other hostess to let me pick some'. Her hosts were 'outwardly loving, "darlings" fly back and forth', yet somehow this did not ring true.

What was the state of their marriage? It was probably not very different from that of many couples who, within a decade of matrimony, undergo a traumatic crisis involving mutual recrimination, but decide to stay together. On the positive side, they were united by their love of their house, their dogs and their common friends, as well as by a shared interest in nature and a similar outlook in social and aesthetic matters. They also had their absorbing separate interests – his writing, her gardening – which took them out of themselves while giving them pride in each other's achievements. (Jim modestly wrote that 'she has created something which, if ephemeral, is a work of art. It is more than I have yet done.') As at Roquebrune and Thurloe Square, she ran the house beautifully and looked after him wonderfully; and although the property was hers and not his, he played with distinction the role of literary squire. On the other hand, the factors which had bedevilled their marriage during the years 1959–61 had not gone away. She continued to resent his ongoing relationship with John Kenworthy-Browne and association with friends who disliked her, notably Eardley. He continued to be exasperated by her possessiveness, her habit of steaming open his letters and listening-in to his telephone calls, and her tendency to fuss, nag and sulk. However, they both made some effort if not to overcome these feelings at least to restrain them; and it would be fair to say that, with every passing year, the pain lessened and the marriage became happier. Indeed, as things settled down, they may both have come, subconsciously, to enjoy something of a role-playing fantasy, whereby he periodically 'escaped from mother' to play with friends she disapproved of and was consequently 'punished' in small ways. Frances Partridge was correct in her perception that their marriage was not the cloudless union presented to the world; but by and large, it worked.

It did so because Jim was able to get away. Several times a year he managed to take a holiday with either John or Eardley, or go off on his own on National Trust business or for historical research; she also took occasional separate holidays, usually going to stay with one of her upper-class gay bachelor friends such as Rory Cameron at Cap Ferrat, David Herbert in Tangier or Micky Renshaw in Cyprus. The need to attend committees of the National Trust and other bodies, exchange books at the London Library, and see publishers, agents and other contacts also gave Jim a pretext to go to London most weeks for a night or more. As they had many common friends who lived in or near the capital (the Berkeleys, the Droghedas, etc.), she sometimes accompanied him; but they stayed in separate places, and it was accepted that, if they dined with friends, he would not see her home. She usually stayed with the Berkeleys in Little Venice (where a number of their other friends also lived, including Diana Cooper and Patrick Kinross). Jim usually stayed with John, who now worked for Christie's and owned a substantial terrace house in Fulham. In fact, after John left the National Trust in 1965 and ceased to be their 'neighbour' at Dyrham, Jim saw much more of him on these London visits. At first Alvilde, who soon became aware of the situation through her prying, objected. As Jim wrote to Eardley in July 1965 (a few months after John's departure from Gloucestershire):

Your previous letter . . . implied that A. was sensible now and all was well between us. That has been so for long spells especially when we are alone here. But every now & then, especially when there is someone staying who knows all about things, she has to manufacture a scene. Such a one has happened this week-end with Rosamond [Lehmann] staying. Elizabeth Cavendish & [the conductor] Raymond Leppard too. It should all have been such fun. On Saturday we went to Raymond's concert at Dyrham, where we saw [John] with a friend he was staying with in Bristol . . . And I naturally spoke to him and introduced him to Rosamond. Whereupon A. behaved like a perfect Dragon. She was rude and odious . . . Back here A. told Rosamond that I was living in flagrant sin with John in London and she was not going to stand for it. Would Rosamond pass this on to me? . . . Now the guests have gone and the grandchildren have arrived. I feel so shaken that I can neither work nor speak. I shall have to have it out with her because I cannot bear it any more, this being treated like a chattel.

Fortunately this turned out to be something of a final performance, and Alvilde resigned herself (albeit with some bitterness) to Jim seeing John in London. Jim's feelings for John did not greatly alter with the years. More than a decade after they had met, he wrote that he still loved him 'deeply and devoutly, though the first fine careless rapture has passed . . . A measure of my love is that, when I have not heard from him for a week, I get anxious and unhappy.' He regarded him 'like my son'. He valued John's comments on his work. 'John's criticism is always sound . . . In fact he is an extremely perceptive person, because he is super-sensitive.' They often spent evenings together at the theatre or cinema, and sometimes visited Sissinghurst to see Harold Nicolson, who following Vita's death sank into a dotage from which he was released in 1968.

With Jim's departure from the National Trust staff in March 1966 he became a full-time writer, and immediately plunged into working on an ambitious book which he had been planning for some years – a history of St Peter's, Rome. Hamish Hamilton had agreed to publish this back in 1962, after their success with *Earls of Creation*. However, George Rainbird, who had invented the concept of 'packaging' – designing lavishly illustrated books with a view to bringing out similar editions in different markets all over the world – got to hear of the project, and it was finally with Rainbird that Jim signed his contract (the edition for sale in UK bookshops appearing under the Hamilton imprint). Towards the end of 1965 Rainbird had an audience with Pope Paul VI, who declared that the appearance of such a book was 'providential and opportune', that he wanted it to come out in 1967 (St Peter having traditionally been martyred under Nero in AD 67), that he would give every facility for photography, and that he wanted two thousand specially bound copies for himself. Soon afterwards Jim himself visited the Vatican with Rainbird's (Catholic) managing director George Speaight, where they discussed the project with the Pope's private secretary Monsignor Macchi and supervised the photography by the Italian art photographer Mario Carrieri. The Second Vatican Council (held in the basilica's nave) had recently ended; and Rainbird urged Jim to be 'tactful' in his text, as 'although as you said it is almost impossible to avoid satire in writing about the modern church . . . Papal approval is worth a mass'. The speed with which Jim wrote it was astonishing: in February 1966 he undertook to produce 100,000 words; by October these had not only been delivered but had received the Papal '*imprimatur*' and '*nihil obstat*'. It was published in the UK in July 1967, American, Italian, Spanish and German editions following later in the year.

Saint Peter's is an impressive work, regarded by many as Jim's *magnum opus*. It is readable, erudite and concise. It is clear that long before he wrote it he had explored every corner of the great building and mastered most of the vast literature on the subject, as well as doing documentary research in the Vatican Library. Most of it is devoted to the period 1450–1700 during which the present basilica was built; but it also deals in a broad sweep with the life of St Peter, the history of early Christianity, and the basilica of Constantine which endured for a thousand years. It combines architectural history with the history of the Papacy itself. The illustrations, it goes without saying, are sumptuous. It has however two shortcomings. Jim did not quite know how to adapt his style to a popular work designed for mass circulation. His attempts to sound demotic (for example, by addressing the reader in the second person) tend to jar. He originally conceived a book which mixed fact and anecdote; but as he admits in his preface, the factual narrative finally took up most of the allotted space and so 'many picturesque incidents which came to light during my prolonged studies have had to be sacrificed to drier data'. Secondly, bearing in mind Rainbird's exhortation, he virtually ignored the recent Council, merely saying that it was 'too early to judge its effects', that it had promulgated no dogmas and condemned no heresies, but that it had resulted in 'permissive use of the vernacular in parts of the Mass' and a gesture in the direction of Christian unity. Jim concludes that St Peter's cannot be regarded as sublimely beautiful in itself, being 'a hotchpotch of great warring components . . . the mixed-up children of frustrated geniuses', but that 'its primary beauty is to be looked for

in a historical context . . . in the living continuity of Christian worship
on this site, the sublimity of symbolism, and the everlasting thanksgiving
it renders to the Prince of the Apostles'.

Although Jim made more money out of *Saint Peter's* than any book he
wrote – about £7,500 – its progress was disappointing. Rainbird's, who
a year earlier had made a fortune for both themselves and Nancy Mitford
with *The Sun King*, her life of Louis XIV, proved unable to repeat the
trick with Jim. This was partly due to the fact that Jim, unlike Nancy,
could not quite catch the easy, racy style which a Rainbird book required,
but mainly because it simply came out at the wrong moment. At a time
when Catholics everywhere, both traditionalist and progressive, were
digesting the momentous implications of 'Vatican Two', few were disposed to buy an expensive history of their headquarters church which
barely mentioned it. Indeed, the *Tablet* criticised Jim for writing 'as if John
XXIII and Vatican II never happened'. (Jim would probably have done
better had he dispensed with papal approval and written a heretical book.)
There were few other reviews, though a number of Jim's friends, such as
Alan Pryce-Jones and Peter Quennell, gave it admiring notices. Large
printings were sold at a discount through book clubs in Britain and
America; but by December only 7,000 copies had been taken by UK
bookshops, with the prospect that some of these might be returned after
Christmas. Rainbird's nevertheless considered the enterprise worth-
while; Speaight wrote that 'although we are bitterly disappointed in some
ways, it is quite untrue to dismiss your book as a flop'. This was little
consolation to Jim, who was depressed that the result of years of thought
and investigation had brought almost no response from serious critics.

The Pope, however, was delighted with it; he handed it out to important visitors at audiences, and it was largely at his insistence that a trans-
lation appeared in Italy, where no publisher was very keen to do it. This
papal favour had a somewhat bizarre consequence for Jim. In the summer
of 1968 he

> received a letter from the Cardinal Secretary of State couched in the most
> flattering terms, addressed to L'Illustrissimo Professore, etc., telling me
> that the Pope had set up a small Commission of six persons to investigate
> the authenticity of St Peter's Chair, kept inside Bernini's great bronze
> cathedra at the far west end of St Peter's. I answered that I was greatly
> honoured to be so invited, while pointing out that I had few qualifications
> to assess this most precious relic. I thereupon received a slightly tart reply
> that His Holiness had made the selection himself, and it became me to
> accept without further ado . . . So I could do nothing but agree to serve.

The Commission – consisting of two Monsignores, a Jesuit, an Italian professor, a German professor, 'and the Englishman, J.L.-M., professor of nothing' – assembled at St Peter's in November. Jim described in humorous terms the business of extracting the chair from the place high up in the Basilica where it had rested undisturbed for three hundred years; he was glad to note that, of the commission members, he alone, just turned sixty, was able to scamper up and down the ladders placed for them with speed and agility. They then spent two fruitless days staring at the chair and deciding what to do next. 'Very revealing how Italians behave during committees. They all talk and gesticulate at once. No one listens to anyone else.' Jim's main feeling was of surprise at the crudity of the chair, 'how roughly, rudely put together it is'. In the end, their deliberations were pointless as carbon testing definitively dated the object from the 880s, eight centuries after St Peter's death, suggesting that it had been made for the coronation of the Emperor Charles the Bald by Pope John VIII.

Although Jim was content to lend his name to this exercise to demythologise a sacred relic, he was appalled at the general effect of the decrees resulting from the Vatican Council, which became especially apparent during 1969. Among his papers there is a draft of an undated letter to Pope Paul which was probably written that year, expressing 'disquiet' about 'the reforms or – as I prefer to term them – changes of Catholic ritual since the Ecumenical Council'. The abandonment of the use of Latin had caused the Mass to lose 'much of its mystery and a great deal of its solemn beauty. Its celebration today has made it almost indistinguishable from the services of the Protestant denominations.' This change had been accompanied by what could only be described as 'acts of iconoclasm'. In England there were no historic Catholic churches which had been in continuous use; but in France, which he had recently visited, he had been dismayed to find that 'many high altars which are works of great artistic value are being taken down and even broken up; the side chapels dedicated to individual saints are being dismantled; ancient statues and images are being scrapped; holy water stoups are frequently no longer filled; incense is used less and less . . . Everywhere in Europe the tendency is the same – to discredit the traditional rituals and practices, and so to reduce the Catholic Acts of Faith to those of the Reformed creeds.' He concluded: 'May I, as a person who has made some study of Catholic history and pondered deeply over the traditional symbolism of the Church, beg Your Holiness with the utmost humility to prevent the Latin Mass as ordained by St Pius V from totally disappearing, and to safeguard those ritualistic practices which are part of our Catholic discipline and belief.'

It is possible that Jim never sent this letter (or only did so as a favour to his old friend Geoffrey Houghton Brown who was prominent in the campaign to save the Latin Mass); for by this time he had become disillusioned with Roman Catholicism for other reasons. He was incensed by Pope Paul's encyclical *Humanae Vitae* of 1968 reaffirming the Church's ban on contraception, which he considered madness at a time of rampant overpopulation. Over the next few years the IRA violence in Northern Ireland, which he believed the Church to be covertly encouraging, completed his alienation. Meanwhile he had started attending the Anglican parish church at Alderley. It was a pretty building of 1810; he liked the vicar; the service used was still that which he had known as a child at Wickhamford. It gave him satisfaction to participate in one of the rituals of village life, and to worship with Alvilde, a lifelong Anglican. He no longer believed in the Catholic doctrine of consubstantiation. 'Now I regard Holy Communion as commemorative, a sort of pledge of betterment, a swearing-in of allegiance to God . . . but I no longer believe that Christ is in that wafer.' There was no actual moment that Jim resigned, so to speak, as a Catholic, and rejoined as an Anglican. In 1972 he attended the annual Mass (still in Latin) at the Brompton Oratory for St Philip Neri, and at the ensuing dinner was presented to the Archbishop of Westminster, Cardinal Heenan (though recording the event in his diary he wrote that the Cardinal 'would be shocked if he knew of my lapse from *our* faith . . . Although intelligent and awfully jolly these Catholics are unreal. There is a pretentious sexlessness about these people . . .'). During the next couple of years various events indicated that he had effectively completed his reversion to his original faith. In May 1973 he was sworn in as a churchwarden at Alderley; he thought the officiating Archdeacon 'a splendid old boy, so humorous, clever and holy, just what a high-up dignitary of the English Church should be, a true descendant of a Trollopian cleric'. A few months later the Lees-Milnes entertained the Bishop of Gloucester when he preached at Alderley. And in March 1974, after he had published a letter in *The Times* attacking the papal attitude to birth control, Jim heard from Father Michael Napier accepting his resignation (which he had not offered) from the Oratory Arts Committee and coldly thanking him for his past services. Jim relinquished this final connection without regret; during the next few years his disenchantment with the Roman creed turned to positive hostility. (In 1979, after attending the funeral of the son of his old Catholic patroness Mamie de Navarro, he wrote: 'In that Broadway church I did not experience one second of spiritual devotion . . . Just irritation and revulsion . . . I am really quite anti-Catholic now. How my great-aunt Katie would smirk.')

A hangover of Jim's Catholicism was a history of the Stuarts in exile, to which he devoted three years of work from 1970 to 1973. Much had already been written on this romantic subject, but Jim did new research in the Vatican Library and elsewhere (though he was refused access to the Royal Archives), as well as visiting Scotland to see places associated with Bonnie Prince Charlie in 1745–6. He was dismayed when the book was rejected by publishers on the grounds that another biography of Prince Charlie had just appeared. However, Jim's book also dealt with two lesser-known figures who were also fascinating in their way – Prince Charlie's estranged wife, known as the Countess of Albany, who outlived him by almost forty years, and his younger brother the Cardinal Duke of York, James II's last legitimate descendant, who 'reigned' as Henry IX from 1788 to 1807. In both cases there was sex interest: the Countess had a string of passionate love affairs, notably with the poet Alfieri, while the Cardinal King, as Jim was intrigued to discover, was gay.

> It is as clear as day that he was, poor man, homosexual. He had infatuations for young, handsome clerics. The Pope was surprised, but thought there was nothing criminal in it . . . But his old father was very upset, and gave the lovers the sack. There were sulks, non-speakers and the Cardinal flounced off twice . . . Yet there it is, and no book has suggested it that I am aware of, until muck-raker Milne comes along.

At the suggestion of his new friend in the publishing world, the formidable Norah Smallwood of Chatto & Windus, Jim attempted to rewrite the book as 'the Countess and the Cardinal'; but he had now lost enthusiasm for the subject, and the result was unsatisfactory. He put the work aside, hoping to publish it another day.

After *Saint Peter's*, Jim wrote one more book on architecture: it dealt with English country houses of the so-called 'Baroque' period, 1685–1715, and was one of a chronological series in quarto format published by Country Life Books (a subsidiary of Hamlyn), the volumes on the preceding Caroline period (by Oliver Hill) and the succeeding Early Georgian period (by Christopher Hussey) having long since appeared. It was an easy task, as he had already written articles for *Country Life* on most of the houses to be included, resulting in the photography with which the book was eventually illustrated. The project brought Jim into contact with John Cornforth, the new architectural expert on the staff of *Country Life*, whose erudition he admired, while regarding him as stuffy and unattractive. (On the other hand he was much taken with the 'frisky' Giles Clotworthy, the young editorial assistant with whom he worked at Country Life Books.) The book (for which he was paid a fee of £800) was written in 1968, published in 1970, and acclaimed by the critics as one of the best in the series; Cyril Connolly in the *Sunday Times* described it as 'a labour of love written with wisdom, charm and learning'.

Jim had long been familiar with most of the twenty-eight Baroque houses he described. Some were National Trust properties, such as Dyrham and Petworth; others he had stayed in, such as Biddesden and Boughton. Of them all, the one which undoubtedly meant most to him was Chatsworth.

> Few English houses so dominate their surroundings as Chatsworth. The vast palace is set at the eastern foot of a great basin of hills on the left bank of the river Derwent. It commands wide views over a vast park, beyond which the savage moorland rolls away in all directions. Everything about it is ample and generous. It looks, and virtually is, the capital of a principality.

Jim had been a frequent guest at Chatsworth since the Devonshires had moved into the house in 1959. He was slightly intimidated by the moody and heavy-drinking Andrew, but adored Debo, who cherished him as an old family friend. Sometimes he stayed there with Alvilde: they were present in June 1963 when President Kennedy made a surprise visit by helicopter to visit the grave of his late sister (who had been married to Andrew's late brother). Often he went there without her, especially when Debo had her sisters to stay. (Debo was given a perfect excuse to ask Jim on his own when they were both appointed, in the late 1960s, to a committee to advise on the redecoration of nearby Sudbury Hall, a recent acquisition of the National Trust; the committee was in no hurry to complete its deliberations which continued for some fifteen years.) Jim had boundless admiration for the dedication and flair with which Debo managed the house and estate.

> Before dinner I walked with Debo. She visited the cows, the bulls, the stallions, the new additions to Rowsley Inn, the gardens, the farm, talking to all and sundry and giving instructions. I said to her, 'How are you able to cope with all this?' She said, 'It is my passion. Stupid, I know.' I said, 'It is far from stupid. It is marvellous, and right.' . . . Here they still are surrounded by works of art of the greatest rarity, living in this enormous house, with old retainers, servants and butler and footman, and private

telephonists on duty all day and night; and providing access to the public practically the whole year round. Long, long may it last.

Baroque Country Houses was to be Jim's last book on an architectural subject for many years. He now sought to establish himself as a general man of letters. The result was *Another Self*, written in 1968–9 and published by Hamish Hamilton in 1970 against an advance of £300; it was dedicated to Rosamond Lehmann who had suggested the title. Although it purports to tell the story of his life up to his early thirties, it contains (as has been observed in the first chapters of the present work) many touches of fantasy. It is in fact a hybrid book, part memoir, part novel. As such, it belongs to a long tradition of such works, some of which present themselves as autobiography (such as the memoirs of Osbert Sitwell), some as fiction (such as the novels of Nancy Mitford). Jim – who had already drafted two unpublished works of an autobiographical nature, his pre-war 'sketches' and his 1941 novel *Dust and Ashes* – claimed that the main inspiration for it was Harold Nicolson's celebrated collection of autobiographical essays *Some People* (1927). The two works are similar in one respect: both describe, in humorous terms, a series of curious personalities and bizarre incidents which confront the bewildered narrator, dealing with which helps shape him as a man. In other respects they differ. Nicolson, unlike Jim, does not purport to give a narrative of his life, merely to relate a series of random episodes. He is detached, whereas Jim freely gives his (often heated) opinions on such varied subjects as the neglect of architecture, the morality of Britain's declaration of war on Germany in 1939, and the degeneracy of 1960s youth. And while Nicolson's writing is dry and spare, *Another Self* is an uproarious romp, recalling comic scenes from silent films. Having written it, Jim was always reluctant to discuss it. (When, shortly before his death, he gave permission for another reprint, he hoped he would not live to see it lest he have 'to face the inevitable question, "Is it true?"') However, some clue as to his intentions is suggested by a quotation from Aldous Huxley with which he originally thought he might preface it:

> At the risk of seeming confused and digressive, I shall stick as closely as I can to the complex realities of the autobiographical process – a process that supplements facts with pseudo-facts, inference and rationalization, because it is not the truth, but an elegantly streamlined falsehood . . . Every life is a set of relationships between incompatibles. To get to know oneself, one must get to know all the disparate fields of which, at any moment, one is the centre.

Whatever Jim's purpose in writing *Another Self*, its critical reception was rapturous. Anthony Curtis in the *Financial Times* praised his 'superb skill as a raconteur', and wondered 'through tears of laughter' whether it could 'all really have happened quite like this', whether he had 'something in him which attracts the bizarre'. Similar thoughts occurred to the *Daily Telegraph* reviewer: 'Farcical encounters break repeatedly upon the reader, who sees himself being ushered towards some bizarre climax, but does not discover its most improbable details until the last moment. Mr Lees–Milne, an eccentric by heritage, seems to have attracted oddities as an old coat does moths.' Patrick Kinross in the *Sunday Telegraph* thought that out of the humorous narrative there emerged 'a serious philosophy of life'. The *TLS* agreed, suggesting that the book might be subtitled 'Self-Portrait of a Non-Believer in the Gods of the Twentieth Century'. Frank Giles in the *Sunday Times* found it 'a delightfully outrageous book . . . delightful because Mr Lees–Milne writes with such felicity of style and sustainment of interest . . . outrageous because of the tallness, the almost Munchausen quality of some of his stories'. Even the poet Geoffrey Grigson, a former Communist who thought Jim 'a partisan of almost everything I detest except good buildings', found it 'open and endearing'. Almost overnight *Another Self* transformed Jim's literary reputation, causing him to be regarded no longer as a mere architectural specialist but as a writer of great power and originality. (Reprinted in every succeeding decade, the book has survived to become a classic: the film rights were sold in 2008.)

After *Another Self*, Jim never looked back. He was almost sixty-two; and during his remaining twenty-seven years he would produce no fewer than twenty-two volumes for publication, not to mention contributions to multi-authored works and a prodigious quantity of journalism. Jim was one of those engaging personalities (rather more common in the thespian than the literary world) who come into their own in later life; only in his mid eighties was there some falling-off in both the quality of his work and its rate of production. He was (as he wrote on his fortieth birthday) a slow developer; as a writer, he carried on 'developing' until near the end.

Jim's first thought after *Another Self* was to write a novel, which he completed by the end of 1970 and entitled *Heretics in Love*. All his life he longed to be recognised as a novelist; but his excursions into fiction, while eloquent and ingenious, somehow failed to capture the public imagination, perhaps because they never quite succeed in suspending disbelief. They do however reveal much about the man: many of the persons, places and situations he describes are drawn from his own experience; and his bizarre and gothick plots, set in decaying country houses whose inmates are prey to romantic obsessions, give an insight into his imagination. As he wrote of his last novel in the 1980s: 'I got so worked up during the writing that the characters became real to me. It was like writing autobiography, although totally fictitious. Of course all novels must be wish fantasies.'

Heretics in Love – which takes its title from a line of Donne – concerns twins, Augustus and Augusta ('Gus' and 'Star'), who are as alike as a boy and a girl can be and the last of an ancient noble line. Their parents are dead and they are brought up by their adoring, eccentric and piously Catholic grandmother Donna, Baroness Fitzpoudell (to whose title Gus is the heir) at Wribbenhall, a rambling house in a rambling estate, where they lead an isolated existence. They are inseparable; and on reaching adolesence they have sexual intercourse and Star gets pregnant. The child, a boy, is duly born (there is no question of 'getting rid of it' in this Catholic household), and foisted on Donna's butler and maid who are sworn to secrecy and given a comfortable annuity to treat it as their own. The problem of what to do with the twins themselves is solved by the outbreak of the Second World War. As a wartime country house owner, Donna suffers terrible privations and soon dies. Star is killed in the course of war work. Gus becomes a prisoner-of-war and survives, latterly as a fugitive in the Vatican. After the war he cannot bear to return to England, now bereft of his sister, and remains in Italy. However, during the 1950s he must go back to Wribbenhall to decide the future of the estate. (The house is now an uninhabitable ruin.) On arrival, he enters the family vault and opens Star's coffin; while in the throes of a necrophiliac swoon, he is accosted by a handsome youth. This is Norman, his son, who is of course unaware of his true origins. He strikingly resembles Star, being the age at which Gus last saw her; but his manners and outlook are those of 'the lower orders', and he is a sly, mentally unstable fiend. Gus is bewitched by Norman, who ruthlessly exploits the infatuation. In the end Gus loses everything except the two things Norman cannot take from him, his noble title and his religious faith. It is not made explicit that Gus and Norman have homosexual relations; but this is implied by the words of the latter – 'After all I've done for you!' – on making the horrific discovery of the origins which have been concealed from him.

The incestuous twins were inspired by two sets of siblings whom Jim had known intimately and who (though not twins or even only children) were unusually alike and close – Tom and Diana Mitford, and Desmond

Jim with the West Brompton detachment of the British Red Cross, 1939

West Wycombe, Buckinghamshire, seat of the Dashwoods, to which the National Trust was evacuated in 1939 (its offices were on the ground floor on the left), and where Jim went to live and work in 1941. The Trust accepted ownership of the estate in 1943, soon after returning to London

Eardley Knollys (*left*) and Desmond Shawe-Taylor (*right*) at Long Crichel, Dorset, a house which became 'almost a second home' to Jim after the war

Alvilde Chaplin with her Pekinese, Foo, at Jouy-en-Josas in 1949, the year she and Jim fell in love

Jim's portrait by Derek Hill, 1954

Jim and Alvilde dining in the South of France

The view of Monte Carlo from Alvilde's garden in Roquebrune

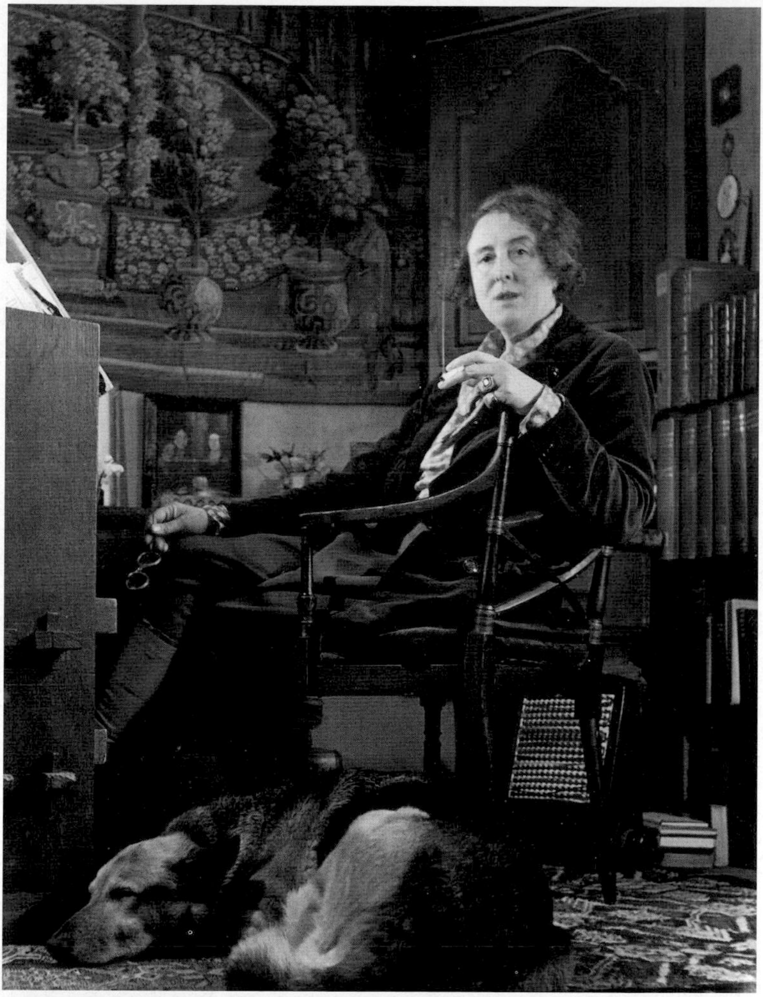

ight: Vita Sackville-
'est, with whom
lvilde had a
mpestuous affair
the 1950s

low: John
nworthy-Browne

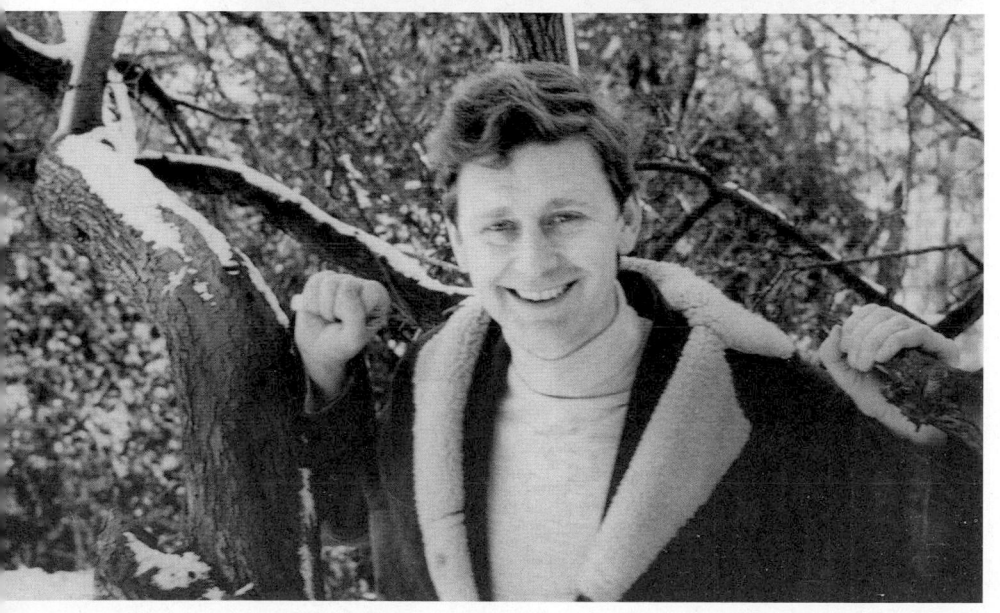

Above: Alderle
Grange,
Gloucestershire
Jim's and Alvil
'Sissinghurst',
where they live
from 1961 to

Left: Strolling
the lime alley

20 Lansdown
Crescent, Bath,
where Jim
worked for
twenty years in
the library
created by
William Beckford

Essex House, Badminton

Jim and Alvilde reconciled in old age – 'I have grown to love her so deeply for her goodness to me . . .'

and Bridget Parsons. 'Donna' is based (at least as regards her eccentricities) on Jim's old patroness Con Ismay; the genealogy of the Fitzpoudells, changing their surname in each generation as the title descends through females, recalls that of Gerald Berners. 'Wribbenhall' is Ribbesford, Jim's grandmother's house where he spent much of his childhood, with a slight touch (in its Catholic aspects) of Pixton; the servants are based on his grandmother's (as Jim's sister recognised). Jim draws on his personal knowledge of the tribulations experienced by country house owners before, during and after the war, as well as of expatriate life in Rome, where Gus spends the postwar years. He also uses the novel to vent his spleen on three categories of people he dislikes – lawyers (the bane of the twins' existence is their middle-class uncle-by-marriage, a bumptious solicitor), land agents (the one who manages Wribbenhall during Gus's long absence is both haughty and devious), and officials of the Ministry of Works (who succeed in wrecking what is left of the house). When asked about the meaning of it, Jim explained that it was a morality tale, a parable on narcissism: Gus twice falls in love with his own reflection, and pays the price.

Jim had some difficulty finding a publisher for the novel: the literary agent who normally acted for him, David Higham, refused to handle it, and it was turned down by both Hamish Hamilton and John Murray ('I know of no greater agony . . . the pain, humiliation and disappointment are always devastating'). Finally it was accepted by Norah Smallwood at Chatto against an advance of £250. ('Blessed be God for being good to me. And about time too.') As he contemplated publication, Jim began to have cold feet. He 'suffered from terrible *Angst*, a gnawing in my vitals and a terrible dread . . . Am I too insecure to write about incest, homo-sexuality, bestiality, necrophilia, coprophilia and the divers nasty little habits that flesh is heir to?' Alvilde told him she found it revolting, and thought their latest housekeeper, if she got to read it, was sure to leave. Even Leslie Hartley (who spent his last years enslaved to a succession of 'rough trade' servants) thought it 'unpublishable because of the subject'. On publication day in February 1973 Jim felt so nervous that he 'skulked to avoid friends' in the London Library, and had to sit in St Martin's Church to calm himself before lunching with the publishers. He dreaded the reviews, which were mostly disdainful. One critic mocked his 'patri-cian sentiments' and 'elaborately insouciant fantasies'; another detected 'a strong smell of death about the whole enterprise, as if the manuscript had been exhumed from some neo-gothic tomb'. More flatteringly, com-parisons were drawn with Edgar Allan Poe, Evelyn Waugh and *Le Grand*

Meaulnes. One of the few critics to understand Jim's intentions was Isabel Quigly in the *Financial Times.* 'Style and landscape are beautifully at one . . . The story is bizarre and not meant, I think, to be strictly credible or realistic . . . Both the book's worlds, the inner and the outer, the imagined world of its action and the mind of its creator, are strongly individual . . .' The book sold a respectable 2,000 copies in England – though it had huge paperback sales in America, where it was marketed as a work of pornography. Its operatic quality made it of passing interest to several film-makers, including Losey and Visconti.

Although Jim's second novel, *Round the Clock,* was not written and published until the late 1970s, it is set at Alderley and so may be considered here. Jim makes things easy for the reader by explaining his intentions in a prefatory note.

> The moral of this tale is a simple one. The object of over-demonstrative affection is apt to recoil from the lavisher thereof . . . Worse still, he, she or it is apt to expend a similar doting affection upon someone or something else. A chain of unreciprocated lovers will thus be created until the last link attempts to fetter itself upon the first. Hence within a mere twenty-four hours an inordinate amount of misunderstanding and disillusion can be engendered in a seemingly modest household.

It is a 'stream of consciousness' novel in the manner of Virginia Woolf, each of the eight chapters describing what runs through the mind of one of the eight characters. The first of these is a dog, the whippet Nero (based on Jim's own whippet Fop whose evanescent mental processes he had carefully studied). Nero loves the younger son of the house, Jaspar; Jaspar loves his sister-in-law, Adda; Adda loves her father-in-law, Adolphus; Adolphus loves his grandchild, Emily; Emily loves her grandmother, Lois; Lois loves her elder son, Dolly; Dolly loves the housekeeper, Mrs O'Grady; Mrs O'Grady loves the dog, thus completing the circle. Each treats the one that loves it cruelly and is so treated by the one it loves. The setting is 'Amberley', a house which is Alderley in all physical respects except that its grounds include a lake. It is the ancestral seat of the St Clairs, who have been faced with the prospect of leaving owing to the difficulties of finding a housekeeper, a subject on which Jim writes with some feeling. 'Lois . . . was sick of training untrainable Italian, Spanish, Portuguese and Filipino peasants, all of whom having promised to stay at an agreed wage for an agreed period gave notice before six weeks elapsed . . . Sicker still was she of being cheated by English housekeepers with excellent forged references, who turned out to be alcoholics, lunatics, Nazis, Communists, thieves or other delinquents.' At last, they have been blessed with apparent good fortune as a model housekeeper has appeared in the form of the hardworking, cheerful and seemingly devoted Mrs O'Grady. They all love her. However, she is about to bugger them all as she turns out to be working for the IRA, laying the ground for a burglary by 'the boys'. An interesting touch is that Jim, aged sixty-eight, transposes himself into the handsome eighteen-year-old Jaspar, an aspiring poet and novelist. (There are strong physical resemblences; and Jaspar's bedroom, described in detail, is Jim's at Alderley.) Published by Chatto in 1978, this ingenious literary experiment attracted little attention, except from dog-loving old ladies who wrote to Jim to lament the fate of Nero, stolen by Mrs O'Grady's evil confederates along with the family treasures.

At the same time as he embarked on his not altogether successful career as a novelist, Jim was contemplating another literary role which was to win him enduring fame – that of diarist. The fact that *Another Self* takes his life almost precisely up to the point where he began keeping a regular diary in 1942 suggests that he always meant to follow it by publishing the latter. It is not clear when he began transcribing his wartime journals. (As noted in the Preface, some of them were kept in the form of shorthand notes which required writing up – though as he subsequently destroyed the original manuscripts, it is impossible to tell how far these differed from the versions he eventually submitted to publishers.) In January 1972, thirty years after starting it, he re-read his 1942 diary, and reflected:

> How immature I was then in spite of my 33 years, how censorious and absurd. I have forgotten so much that happened to me. Yet I find it difficult not to believe, irrationally perhaps, that all the experiences of my past life . . . have not been to some purpose to be gleaned in a later time.

He dithered for another two years. Suffering from the usual lack of self-confidence, he showed his 'edited' diaries for 1942 and 1943 to Rosamond Lehmann, a writer on whose literary judgement he often relied. Rosamond was encouraging, assuring Jim that 'you have the perfect equipment for a diarist – a light, intimate touch, marvellous eye for detail and ear for gossip; above all sympathy and wit, the latter sly and deliciously turned against yourself as well as others'. He then submitted them to Norah Smallwood at Chatto, who wrote to him in April 1974 that she and her colleagues were 'mad about them' and eager to publish them, provided they were 'a little pruned' and occasionally altered to avoid libel. The contract which Jim signed soon afterwards stipulated an advance of

£1,500 (as compared with the £250 he had been given for *Heretics* two years earlier). Ian Parsons, Chatto's managing director and a fan of the diaries, suggested the final cuts, and publication was fixed for the summer of 1975. As usual Jim looked forward to the event with mixed feelings, writing on the last day of 1974: 'Oh God! am I making another dreadful mistake?'

Meanwhile, thoughts of diaries had inspired Jim to start keeping one again: on 1 July 1971 he resumed the journal which he would keep regularly for the remaining twenty-six and a half years of his life. A month after he had begun it, he wrote in it that, whereas in 1942 his reasons for keeping a diary had been 'in part, at least, a contemptible, vain desire for immortality', his present motives were different. He was going 'to keep this diary only for six months, just to see if I can make a book out of . . . everyday events, thoughts, nothing much, nothing at all perhaps', his main purpose being 'to keep . . . the fingers flexed, and the mind'. He recalled that Harold Nicolson had kept a diary (which had been published in the 1960s and brought him renewed fame) as part of his daily routine when Jim had lived with him at King's Bench Walk in the 1930s. On 1 January 1972 he decided to continue for another six months. On the diary's first anniversary, 1 July 1972, he wrote that it 'has not turned out the kind I meant. It is too factual, too gossipy, too introspective, and lacks cognition.' But he carried on with it. A year after that, he wrote that 'the reason one keeps a diary is the compulsion to write something, anything', and that 'all writers are advised to keep diaries for practice, like playing scales. No doubt diary-writing is also a kind of vanity. One has the sauce to believe that every thought that comes into one's head merits recording.'

The first years of Jim's later diary may certainly be described as consisting of 'every thought that came into his head'. It is a spontaneous mixture of scenes from country life, tales of a writer's lot, character sketches of friends, gossip and anecdote gleaned at first or second hand, fulminations against the modern world, descriptions of art and architecture, accounts of travels at home and abroad, religious ruminations, nature observations, and musings on the past. It abounds in reflections on human nature, his own as well as others'. It shows the contrasting influence of the two diarists he most admired, Harold Nicolson, who recorded noteworthy conversations and events, and Francis Kilvert, whose journals, edited by Jim's friend William Plomer, dealt with the small incidents of everyday life and the thoughts they inspired. It is not wholly candid and unrestrained. He rarely mentions his love (which still dominated his emotional life) for John Kenworthy-Browne. Equally, there is little about the irritations of life with Alvilde (though he writes with a touch of envy about husbands such as John Betjeman, Bruce Chatwin and Lord Snowdon who refuse to allow their marriages to interfere with the rest of their lives). Though marital tiffs still occurred from time to time (as his letters to Eardley show), only one is described:

> Last night before going to bed I had a blazing row with A. who insisted that I was going to London next Monday instead of Tuesday because I wanted to enjoy myself. I lost my temper, stamped, threw my slipper on the floor because I could not throw it at her, and cursed and swore. Anyway, why the hell shouldn't I want to enjoy myself? Slammed the door and went to bed without saying goodnight . . . This morning I went to her room, apologised profusely, and we embraced tenderly.

He writes disingenuously that Alvilde seems to have 'telepathic intuitions' about what he has been up to and with whom, whereas he well knew that her methods of discovery (opening letters and so on) owed little to psychic powers. When he rails against marriage, it is usually in general terms. 'God, there is something maddening about the assumption that husband and wife are to be regarded as interchangeable. How I sympathise with Vita who, devoted as she was to Harold, hated being called Lady Nicolson because she claimed to be a person in her own right.' Yet it is also clear that he loved Alvilde dearly, that she cared for him devotedly, that their marriage was happy on the whole. When she was suddenly taken ill with temporal arteritis, a treatable but potentially life-threatening condition, he was beside himself with anxiety. On her birthday he wrote, 'I think with dread of the awful possibility that she may die before me' – though on reflection, he concluded that he could probably manage on his own rather better than she, because he possessed the art of making and keeping friends.

Indeed, one of the joys of Jim's diary is his descriptions of his friends, who are presented so vividly that the reader almost has a sense of personal acquaintance. He has the gift of evoking them, with all their quirks, in a few words. From John Betjeman there pours out 'confidences, fun, folly, tears, wisdom, recitation, readings of extracts from the *DNB*, *Burke's Peerage*, shouts of laughter, jokes about Irish peers, his friends, fear of the after-life and God's retribution, total disbelief in the whole thing, genuine deep devotion to the Church, hatred of Papistry . . . What torments he suffers, what enjoyment he extracts from life.' David Somerset is 'moody and restless' despite being 'heir to a dukedom, rich, handsome, successful, courted, blessed with a heavenly and beautiful wife and four children' and possessing 'charm, that often fatal gift of the gods'. Diana Cooper 'must be, no *is*, the centre of attention and she will talk so much'. Desmond Shawe-Taylor is 'the sweetest fellow, entertaining, funny and extraordinarily quick . . . But his fussiness is a disease.' Freda Berkeley 'unwittingly makes mischief because she attracts confidences. All her friends ring her up about her troubles, which she delights in sorting out. Afterwards the sympathy she exudes for poor So-and-So cannot be contained.' Rosamond Lehmann, who 'indulges in grief', will be 'undergoing an orgy' on the death of her former lover Cecil Day-Lewis. Charlotte Bonham-Carter misses Paul Methuen's funeral at Corsham but turns up for the tea, 'tucking into a huge meal, saying she had not eaten since dinner the previous evening'. Harold Acton's 'charm is limitless and his wit is contagious', whereas John Pope-Hennessy 'has little natural charm and when he endeavours to exhibit this exiguous quality attains it more readily than ordinary people from whom one expects a modicum'. Jim's waspish descriptions are not confined to friends. Meeting (rather to his alarm) Lord Snowdon, Prince Charles and Princess Margaret at a dinner party, he finds the first 'full of vitality and cheer', the second 'very charming and polite', and the third 'far from charming, cross, exacting, too sophisticated, and sharp'.

Jim had a lifelong fascination with death, and constantly anticipated his own. As he approached sixty-five (when he still had twenty-five years to live), he wrote: 'At my age dread of death governs all thought. Each fresh symptom of my decay, physical and mental, and the passing of contemporaries, are clockwork reminders of annihilation.' A feature of his diary is the recording of the decline and deaths of friends. Two passings which affected him particularly, though they were of people to whom he had not been close for years, were of Nancy Mitford in 1973 and Jamesey Pope-Hennessy in 1974. He had known Nancy for half a century, but since the war he had found her rather insincere and callous, and she had been Alvilde's friend rather than his. Yet her struggle against agonising, undiagnosed illness affected him deeply. He marvelled that she could write him jolly letters while *in extremis*. When she died, he found it 'difficult to imagine that bright spirit silenced'. Her funeral was 'a very harrowing experience', at which he wore dark glasses to conceal his tears; as he gazed at her tiny coffin 'the utter nullity of existence and fame overwhelmed me'. Much to his surprise, he was invited by Diana Mosley, Nancy's literary executor, to write her biography; but after reflecting that he would find it difficult to write about her in a way which would avoid upsetting her sisters, he declined the offer, to Alvilde's disappointment. As for Jamesey, Jim had barely spoken to him since, largely out of mischief, he had posed as Alvilde's shining champion in 1959. When, as a gesture of reconciliation, he was invited to spend a weekend at Alderley in 1967, the result (as recorded by his fellow-guest Frances Partridge) was disastrous: emboldened by his seduction of a guardsman on the train, he got drunk and set out to provoke Jim, declaring that he 'was in favour of what the Russians were trying to do, put an end to class', and 'wanted to get rid of the Royal Family, they were no good to man or beast'. 'He's a fiend, always has been,' a fuming Jim told Frances after Jamesey's departure, 'and now the worm has turned.' They never met again, though Jim heard reports of his progress from Cecil Beaton – generally of his going downhill, though sometimes of his literary success. Then, in January 1974, came the horrifying (if not wholly surprising) news that Jamesey had been done to death at his flat in Ladbroke Grove by 'rough trade'. Jim wrote:

> The police station is opposite Jamesey's flat, a thing I have often wondered wryly about, I mean whether they were aware of the strange comings and goings. But this is a hideous tragedy. My first fears are about what may be disclosed . . . Although I have not seen James for seven years . . . yet I always loved him, albeit I did not wish to see him again . . . Lately he has been much in my thoughts because in 1942 and 1943 [for which years Jim had been editing his diary] I saw or spoke to him practically every day. We were inseparable. He was one of the most brilliant creatures I have known, but alas, he was a bad friend.

Though he shared few interests with most of them, Jim remained fond of his family. He kept in close touch with his sister Audrey and brother Dick and showed brotherly concern for them at vital moments – when Audrey was widowed in 1972, when Dick, who had retired with his wife to Cyprus following the liquidation of the family cotton mill in 1970, was caught up in the fighting on the island in 1974. He was an affectionate uncle to Simon, Dick's son (who shared his father's and grandfather's passion for motor cars), and Dale (Mrs James Sutton), Audrey's daughter by her second marriage (who inherited her mother's and grandmother's love of nature). Audrey's daughter by her first marriage, Prudence, had married Ted Robinson, a rich landowner and a regimental comrade of her father Matthew (now 3rd Baron Glenarthur); they lived at Moor Wood near Cirencester, a house half an hour's drive from Alderley which Jim often visited. The Robinsons had three strapping sons, Henry, Nicholas and Richard, all of whom attended Winchester; these brothers were the relations of whom Jim was fondest – especially 'Nick', who, aged sixteen and a half, was 'about the handsomest boy I have ever seen . . . A sidelong smile has taken the place of a rebarbative scowl . . . He clearly is the intellectual of the three. I tremble for him on account of his superlative looks.' When Nick came to lunch at Alderley, accompanied by Henry, Jim found him 'better looking than words can describe'. The two boys expressed an interest in visiting Rome, where Jim took them in April 1973. This was not a total success.

> The boys most strange. Sweet they were and polite, but never expressed enthusiasm for anything. Never read the guidebook I gave them, seldom knew what they were looking at. Everything I told them was greeted with 'H'm!'. Nick moderately interested in paintings, but Henry not apparently interested in anything . . . At meals when well oiled with wine they unfolded a bit, but I did not get beyond polite terms with them . . . [Their] scruffiness unbelievable . . . Yet Nick's beauty undeniable. Faultless features, eyes, nose and hair (unbrushed, the pity of it). Aged only eighteen, he may improve.

Jim 'loved [Nick] dearly and longed to become intimate with him', but knew this would take time. 'He is an exceedingly clever boy which should make our companionship easy; yet with someone of two generations' difference it is hard to click in a hurry . . . Clearly the more we see of one another, the easier we shall become . . . If only he would not chain-smoke, and dress like a tramp.'

The diary details Jim's involvement in voluntary work. A year after leaving the National Trust staff in 1966 he accepted Michael Rosse's invitation to join the Historic Buildings Committee, which in 1970 was merged with the Estates Committee to form the Properties Committee. Jim found the proceedings of this body, which met monthly in London to consider lengthy reports, rather tedious, but enjoyed his membership of the Trust's Arts Panel which visited historic houses to make aesthetic recommendations *in situ*. While there was much about the Trust that depressed him, he derived satisfaction from being able to influence decisions in the right direction, and had great respect for colleagues: on a visit to Uppark with the Arts Panel, he reflected that his fellow panel members were 'some of the most understanding, cultivated, earnest men of good sense and taste it were possible to find'. He was on excellent terms with Bobby Gore who succeeded Robin Fedden as Historic Buildings Secretary in 1973, and admired younger staff members such as Martin Drury, Merlin Waterson and the architectural expert Gervase Jackson-Stops. Although he continued to deplore ever-increasing bureaucracy and museumisation, he 'didn't mind in the least . . . that every house of the National Trust that I had arranged had already been rearranged, every guidebook I had written had been scrapped . . . In the nature of things it has to be.' Other charitable bodies on which he served included the Bath Preservation Trust, whose committee he joined in 1971, and the Mutual Households Association, which saved country houses by converting them into flats. He also sat on the Wotton Planning Committee and the Alderley PCC, and became a trustee of the Corsham estate (which put him in the unfamiliar role of acting on behalf of a frustrated National Trust donor).

He continued to rail against the ruination of both architecture and nature. He shocked Alvilde by remarking that he would 'betray my best friend and go to any lengths short of murder if I thought he proposed desecrating the landscape or an old building'. On learning that the local authorities had sanctioned 'an enormous cow factory' near Alderley, he wrote: 'Let us face it, beauty of landscape is absolutely at a discount in England and the world. The most beautiful country of northern Europe in my youth will before I am dead be irredeemably ruined, damned and finished.' Touring Worcestershire in 1973, he was shocked to see the changes which had taken place since he had written his *Shell Guide* a decade earlier. 'I know that people say change is always resented by the old. But never, never has there been such devastating change as during my lifetime, change always for the worse aesthetically, never for the better. The public *en bloc* are blind to hideous surroundings. I prefer to stay at home in my ivory tower and never go on expeditions rather than be affronted at every familiar turn with a substitute architectural monstrosity.' He was also an environmentalist who had served on the founding committee of the UK's pioneering 'green' organisation, the Conservation Society. As he wrote: 'Our earth is like an apple being eaten by maggots. The maggots increase by devouring the apple which then falls to pieces, hollow and empty. The maggots then die for lack of sustenance. The sun sees to the remains. This is happening to us.'

In expressing views in his diary, Jim often appears in the guise of Colonel Blimp. 'The thugs of this world cannot be checked by light sentences and comfortable cells, but only by being executed, got rid of . . .' 'I was right about the danger of the intellectuals flirting with Communism in the Thirties, right about favouring Munich in 1938, right in knowing that Communism was a worse evil than Fascism, right in deploring Churchill's insistence upon unconditional surrender . . .' Equally often, however, he comes over as unusually broad-minded for one of his generation. He was indignant when Lord Lambton and Lord Jellicoe were made to resign from the Government in 1973 after disclosures about their private lives. 'What the hell does it matter to anyone on earth that these men have slept with whores?' He dismissed as 'a lot of old fogies of the dreariest description' his fellow members of the Society of Antiquaries (which he had joined in order to use the car park at Burlington House). Jim was an inveterate grumbler, and deplored many of the changes that had occurred in his lifetime, but it would be a mistake to see him as a mere stuffy reactionary. Bruce Chatwin recognised him as a fellow anarchist. The architectural writer and broadcaster Alec Clifton-Taylor, himself a conventional figure, said to him: 'You may appear to strangers to epitomise the conventional; but you are thoroughly unconventional. This is what your friends discover.'

When they moved to Alderley in 1961, Jim and Alvilde planned to remain there for the rest of their lives. However, three factors during 1971–4 not only caused them to leave, but ensured that they did so with relief rather than regret. First and foremost was the difficulty of finding and keeping suitable staff. All too often they were without a housekeeper, at which times Alvilde was worked to the bone, especially when they had guests. Their German gardener was often unwell, and Jim found his writing outrageously interrupted by having to mow the lawns and weed the drive. His diary shows him suffering the repeated agony of interviewing prospective housekeepers who, if engaged, rarely stayed more than a few weeks, and the even worse agony of confronting the gardener's wife, their charwoman, after she had been caught stealing (he did not dare sack her and risk losing her husband's services altogether). 'The terrible truth is that one cannot trust anyone today. One is suspicious of them all. They have no loyalties, no morality, no gratitude, no decency . . . They think only of themselves and of money, and more money, and employers are "they", to be rooked, tricked and deceived.' In April 1973, while Jim was in Rome with his great-nephews, the house was burgled; Alvilde surprised the intruders, who only got away with some porcelain displayed in the dining-room, but the incident added to their sense of domestic insecurity.

Secondly, they lost their most cherished local friends. Midi's husband died in 1972, and a year later she sold Mount House and moved to London. Joanie Harford died in 1973 – 'undoubtedly our most intimate friend round here, whom we would see without prearrangements, who had tea with us in the kitchen, or in the summer on the lawn, who belonged, who knew everyone, and everything about everyone, who was kind and good'. Nineteen seventy-three also saw the deaths of their adored whippets Chuff and Fop who had been with them since they came to Alderley. 'While carrying [Fop's] special basket from the library I burst into tears. Alvilde was angelic, comforting and sensible. I recovered quickly, and now merely have the ache of sadness at losing the companion of twelve years, day and night. The house is cheerless without the two dogs and their departure marks the end of an era . . . *Eheu!*, you darling old friends.'

The determining factor, however, was the situation in the country. Like most people who relied on fairly static incomes, the Lees-Milnes were increasingly worried during the 1960s by high taxes, inflation and strikes. Their hopes were briefly raised by the election of a Conservative government under Edward Heath in 1970; but inflation continued to rise and industrial unrest to mount. In the late autumn of 1973 the nation was plunged into crisis when, with a fuel shortage looming in the wake of an Arab oil embargo, the National Union of Mineworkers began industrial action. Sachie Sitwell, who claimed to be in the know, warned Jim 'that "we" have only three months to clear out of England'. While deeply anxious, Jim extracted a certain grim humour from the situation.

> Diana Westmorland . . . was blazing with fury against the Trades Unions, and Mr Gormley [the miners' leader] in particular, for saying over the air that he did not care a damn about the inconvenience he was causing the public, and he was going to have a jolly good Christmas. She wanted to write him a letter. What should she write? I said, 'The Dowager Countess of Westmorland presents her compliments to Mr Gormley and begs to inform him that he is a shit.' Her retort was, 'No. I will write, "Fuck off to Russia!"'

The first weeks of 1974 saw the introduction of emergency measures including a three-day industrial week, the declaration by the NUM of an all-out strike, and Heath's decision to call a snap election on 28 February to decide 'who governs Britain'. 'Never have affairs been worse in my lifetime,' wrote Jim. 'I think it very possible there may be fighting within four months.' He was not reassured by the prognostications of the people he met: Lord Camrose, proprietor of the *Telegraph*, thought 'that anything might happen overnight, like a Communist takeover', while a stockbroker told him that 'the City . . . expects a complete economic collapse any day, when we shall be in the same condition as Germany in 1923'. The day after the election, which resulted in stalemate between the main parties (and thus a humiliation for Heath who had sought a mandate to deal with the crisis), Jim wrote: 'We are finished. We may as well pack up. We have left it too late. We were warned we had three months to clear out of England. That was three months ago. Labour has got in. The consequence is a victory for the Unions who are the dictators of the Labour Party. I see nothing but total disaster ahead.'

The Lees-Milnes now panicked. The servant situation had already caused them to wonder how long they could face staying on at Alderley; the penal taxation introduced by the new Labour Government (whose post-election budget raised marginal tax rates on unearned income to 98 per cent) made them feel they could no longer afford to. They had little grasp of politics and none of economics, but the (often second-hand) gossip they heard in the apparently well-informed circles in which they moved made them fear the worst. Lord Rothschild told David Somerset 'that this government is determined to finish off the capitalists'. At the annual Garter Service at Windsor which they attended as guests of the Droghedas, Field Marshal Sir Gerald Templar told Garrett 'that the revolution would undoubtedly come before twelve months had elapsed'. They learnt that several of their rich friends were salting money abroad. Rupert Loewenstein advised them to sell their stocks and shares and hold only cash. It was in fact a moment for keeping one's nerve and staying put, for holding on to one's country house and shares, whose values were plunging but would soon rise. However, the Lees-Milnes, already finding the running of their house an unwonted expense and strain, began to feel that the moment was approaching when no one would be able to live in such houses, that their best hope lay in moving to much smaller premises without delay. The day after the election they (jointly) made an offer for the ground floor and basement of a house in Lansdown Crescent, Bath, which was sold to them two months later for £38,000. Originally they saw this as a bolt-hole; but in May they made up their minds to leave Alderley. 'The last straw was to be told by the nice woman who puts her cows in our paddock that [the gardener and wife] told her they intend to leave in September.'

Alvilde had few regrets at selling the house she owned, but Jim initially felt 'positively sick with sadness' and 'wept at the prospect of parting from this place'. He hated the prospective buyers who came to view the house, regarding them as 'desecrators'. When the Filipina housekeeper, who had promised to remain with them until they left, suddenly announced her departure, he cursed their faithless servants. 'I hope unemployment leaps to astronomical proportions, and that they are humiliated and come begging cap in hand for work. I shall be prepared to undergo every personal deprivation for the satisfaction of seeing them reduced to starvation.' However, when during August Alvilde found highly suitable young purchasers, he shared her sense of relief. The new owners (who paid £102,500 for the property) were Camilla, daughter of Lord Howard de Walden, one of the richest men in Britain, and her husband Guy Acloque, an expert on antique furniture: she was a great-granddaughter of one of Alvilde's godmothers; he was a keen horticulturist who undertook to maintain her garden. 'I am no longer heartbroken,' Jim wrote. 'Had we waited three months longer we might not have sold at all . . . As things are, we shall not be certain that the deal is clinched until contracts are exchanged, documents signed and money handed over. The financial situation is so dicey that a complete national collapse might occur within the next few weeks, and the purchasers not [be] able to pay.' (While Jim's attitude seems in retrospect to be ludicrously alarmist, it undoubtedly reflects how many people in their position felt at the time.)

They had three months to move to their Bath maisonette. This involved getting rid of 'seven-eighths of our beloved possessions', and Jim had a depressing time carting objects to London auction houses (it was of course the worst moment to sell anything) or depositing them with friends and relations who had the space to keep them. On 22 November they 'said goodbye to Alderley for good, having removed the last remaining objects in the house. Left it quite empty, and vastly melancholy . . . [A] pang of intense sadness struck because this moment was the final break with the house, which I dearly loved and in which I had hoped to end my days.'

13

Bath and Badminton
1974–81

JIM HAD KNOWN Bath since childhood. His Lees-Milne grandmother
had an unmarried sister, 'Aunt Iny', who lived at 5 Royal Crescent
with a cook, parlourmaid and housemaid on £600 a year. (Jim marvelled at these economics fifty years later, when it cost him and Alvilde
several thousand a year just to run their Lansdown Crescent maisonette
with a daily help.) While staying at Ribbesford during and after the
First World War he had often accompanied his grandmother to visit this
aunt. He was unimpressed by Bath. The houses looked identical and
dull. His aunt's house, though large, was gloomy, stuffy and cluttered.
The meals they ate were washed down with disgusting 'Bath water'.
But he became quite fond of his aunt, who encouraged his interest in
literature by sending him, while he was at Eton, cheap editions of the
classics into which she sometimes inserted ten-shilling notes. When she
died in the 1930s, he and the three servants were the only mourners at
her funeral.

In adult life Jim, as a devotee of classical architecture and co-founder
of the Georgian Group, naturally came to appreciate the uniqueness of
Bath, nearly all built in the eighteenth century in a variety of classical
styles by a series of gifted architects using the same beautiful stone, but
took its existence somewhat for granted. When he joined the National
Trust he was required to visit Bath, as the Assembly Rooms, designed in
1769 by John Wood the Younger and long out of use, had been rescued
and presented to the Trust in the early 1930s by the philanthropist Ernest
Cook. Jim usually combined his inspections of this monument (which
the Trust gradually restored with the help of the SPAB) with visits to
country houses near the city, such as Corsham, Westwood, Great
Chalfield and Lacock. During and after the Second World War he also
visited Bath with Eardley, whose mother had a house in the Circus. In
April 1942 the Germans bombed Bath in retaliation for an Allied raid on
Lübeck. The Assembly Rooms were burned and gutted. Jim wrote in
his diary:

It has upset me dreadfully that so beautiful a building, hallowed by Jane Austen and Dickens, should disappear like this in a single night. Eardley, who was staying the weekend with his mother, came in for the full brunt. He says the Circus has a crater in the middle of the grass, and all its windows are blown out. Two houses in Royal Crescent are burned out, the Abbey windows are gone, and the fires and destruction have been devastating.

When Jim went to live at Alderley, about twenty miles from Bath, the National Trust were restoring the Assembly Rooms for a second time; the work, jointly supervised by John Kenworthy-Browne as the local Representative and Jim as Architectural Adviser, was completed in 1963 and judged a success.* Elsewhere, however, terrible things were happening to Bath. The city corporation promoted the restoration of famous landmarks such as Royal Crescent, the Circus and the Paragon and their conversion into flats; but large areas of humbler Georgian dwellings, many of them exquisite and all part of the original Bath plan, were scheduled for demolition on the specious grounds that they had become 'unfit' and would cost too much to repair. As streets and squares came down, horrors went up such as the Technical College, designed by the architect of Heathrow Airport. In 1965 a new traffic plan was proposed which would have involved the construction of a tunnel under the historic centre; although this was eventually abandoned, extensive 'clearances' designed to facilitate it went ahead. The high tide of demolition took place during the years 1969–71. Until then Jim, while appalled at the destruction, had not protested much against it; he could do little on his own, and had scant confidence in the main local conservation organisation, the Bath Preservation Trust (BPT). By September 1970, however, he could contain himself no longer; with fuming sarcasm he wrote to the editor of *The Times*:

> Your readers may be interested to learn that we are getting on quite nicely with the demolition of the centre of Bath. This year alone we have swept away several acres between Lansdown Road and the Circus. The whole southern end of Walcot Street (including the nineteenth-century burial ground with tombstones) has already gone. We are just beginning on Northgate Street, and have only knocked down two or three houses in Broad Street this month. But New Bond Street's turn is imminent. All the houses are (or were) Georgian, every one.

---

* It was leased to Bath Corporation, which used it partly for civic receptions, partly to house a costume museum; it now pays its way as a venue for private functions and a location for 'period' films.

Jim was far from alone in crying out: a great chorus was now clamouring for the demolitions to cease. Meanwhile the BPT had been revivified under a vigorous new chairman, Sir Christopher Chancellor, former head of Reuters,* and had already won several minor victories. When Jim resumed his diary in 1971, one of the first entries described his joining the committee of the BPT ('not without embarrassment, for in the past I have been very critical of this Trust and even resigned my membership'). During the next couple of years, he played an active part in the campaign to save Bath. He published an article in *The Times* explaining, more in sorrow than in anger, how the city's character was being destroyed by the clearances. He was instrumental in persuading a number of celebrities to visit Bath and lend their support, including Lord Snowdon, who published photographs of threatened buildings, and John Betjeman, who penned appropriate verses:

> Goodbye to old Bath. We who loved you are sorry
> They've carted you off by developer's lorry.

The campaign was successful: early in 1973 the Government offered new money for the conservation of Bath while providing that all demolition should cease pending the consultations of a working party consisting of representatives of the Corporation, the Department of the Environment, the BPT and the Georgian Group: these consultations have effectively continued to the present day, during which time little of importance has been demolished. What had been lost was lost; but the rest was saved. (Subsequently the BPT was riven by terrible rows, as a result of which Chancellor resigned as chairman in 1975 and Jim left the Architectural Committee soon afterwards; but the main object had been achieved.)

Given his recent concern for its architecture, it was natural that Jim and Alvilde, faced with moving in 1974, should have chosen to go to Bath. Lansdown Crescent, created by John Palmer between 1789 and 1792, was one of the last great Georgian building projects there; from its high situation it had superb views south over the city. The ensemble was remarkable for its concave–convex undulations, inspired by the Italian architect Borromini and following the contours of Lansdown Hill. The houses were noted for their patinated stonework and wrought-iron lampholders. No. 19, where the Lees-Milnes bought the ground floor and basement from Lord Strathcona, was at the west end of the Crescent's

---

*He and Jim were united by a common dislike of their former boss Sir Roderick Jones, whom Chancellor had succeeded.

main sweep. Its claim to fame was that the eccentric writer, builder and collector William Beckford (1760–1844), a personality by whom Jim had long been fascinated, had lived there during his last years. In fact when Beckford moved to Bath in 1822, forced by debt to abandon his neo-Gothic extravaganza thirty miles away at Fonthill, he had first bought No. 20 next door; he then acquired the house on the other side, 1 Lansdown Place West, which he joined to No. 20 (from which it was separated by a lane) with a (still-surviving) bridge. He spent the next few years building his famous tower one mile to the north, and buying up and beautifying the intermediate land: once this project was completed, he would ride out from Lansdown Crescent most mornings, cross his deserted garden, and spend the daylight hours in his tower, reading and contemplating the landscape. In 1836, however, No. 19 came on the market and the hypersensitive Beckford, who had meanwhile sold 1 Lansdown Place West, snapped it up for fear that new neighbours might disturb him with 'the ticking of some cursed jack, the jingling of some beastly piano, horrid-toned bells tinkling, and so on'. He commissioned H. E. Goodridge, the local architect who had executed his tower, to design a 'Grecian library' for him there: the result was a noble room in which bookcases and doorcases of red mahogany were divided by yellow scagliola pilasters with arched recesses between them for busts. Despite some post-war restoration necessitated by bomb damage, this room survived into the 1970s roughly in its original state, the only Beckford room so to do.

Jim was thrilled at the prospect of working in Beckford's library. The property had one further advantage: their friend Jeremy Fry,* a great life-enhancer, who had sold Widcombe at the same time as they had sold Alderley, was their neighbour, having bought the top flat of the house. Otherwise it had little appeal. Behind the big library was a dark, north-facing room which became Alvilde's bedroom and sitting-room. The (rather damp) basement contained a dining-room, kitchen, Jim's bedroom and a tiny guest room. There was 'a pocket-handkerchief of a garden'. As soon as they had bought it, Jim wrote that 'neither of us wants to go there in the least' and that he was 'overcome with guilt . . . for it is my selfishness which has pushed [Alvilde] into the project. Beckford's library is what got me. I think she hates the beastly place already.' However, they subsequently decided that they could 'make it quite cosy'. Their main feeling on moving there in November 1974 was of relief at

---

* His wife Camilla had left him a few years earlier.

being spared the expense and worry of running a country house requiring three servants; Jim wrote to Norah Smallwood that 'we are delighted with our new little dump . . . and have already found a heavenly daily'.

In January 1975, just as Jim, 'as pleased as punch', was adding the final decorative touches to Beckford's library, he was asked if he would write a short biography of Beckford to coincide with a forthcoming exhibition about him. At first he refused, having just accepted a lucrative commission to write part of a coffee-table book on Great Architecture of the World ('such rot'). But he quickly changed his mind. 'Then I thought, to hell, if someone else can do this book, which cannot be good no matter by whom within so short a time, why not I? Besides, I am interested in Beckford.' Having agreed to deliver 40,000 words in six months against an advance of £500, he felt 'rather thrilled, yet apprehensive. I have not yet written a biography . . . and much will depend on how I acquit myself.' (Jim was being unduly modest, as his *Earls of Creation* and *Later Stuarts* are in effect multiple biographies, while his works on Adam and Inigo Jones are largely biographical, even if their focus is architecture.) He set himself to read the vast literature on the subject. After ten weeks he noted: 'I am so steeped in Beckford that I identify myself with him – a horrid character, it cannot be denied.' When he began writing in mid May his problem was 'to abbreviate': he felt it would be easier to produce a book of 200,000 words than 40,000. By August it was finished – though abbreviate as he might, he could not reduce it to fewer than 50,000. Published in 1976 by Michael Russell (who would reissue the complete series of Jim's diaries in the next century), it proved a success with the exhibition visitors and was well received by the critics.

Jim worried that his book was inadequate and had little original to say on the subject; but it is fascinating for two reasons. First, he managed to capture the essence of this extremely complex, elusive and long-lived man. Secondly, he found that in writing about many aspects of Beckford, he was writing about himself. Of course Jim entirely lacked Beckford's wealth and the opportunities it gave him; many of Beckford's qualities he could not claim (or would not wish) to share. But in describing his hero's moody and contradictory personality, his sensitivity, his passion for beautiful artefacts, his propensity to fantasy, his longing for seclusion, his constant analysis of both himself and others, and the effect that his homosexuality and the problems associated with it had on his character, Jim (to use a modern expression he would never have employed) 'knew where he was coming from'. In dealing with matters as diverse as Beckford's fascination with archaic religious rituals, his distaste for blood-sports, and his decision, towards the end of his life, to publish a 'titivated' version of diaries he had kept decades earlier, Jim was writing to some extent from personal experience, and revealing something of himself. As one might expect, the most interesting parts of the book concern Beckford's infatuations and love affairs (notably his early passion for William 'Kitty' Courtenay which ruined his life), and his two great architectural creations – Fonthill Abbey, which survived in innumerable descriptions both literary and pictorial, and Lansdown Tower, still standing just twenty minutes' walk from Jim's front door. Those who wish to be introduced to Beckford might do better to read Jim's concise and perceptive monograph than the several weighty biographies which have appeared since.

The completion of *William Beckford* coincided with the publication by Chatto of *Ancestral Voices*, Jim's diaries for 1942 and 1943. They proved a *succès d'estime*: although they had sold fewer than 3,000 copies by the end of 1975, the reviews were almost uniformly ecastatic. John Betjeman found them 'funny and touching, honest and personal, prejudiced and tolerant' and 'full of strangely riveting anecdotes'. A. L. Rowse thought them 'entrancing' and 'a contribution to the social history of the age'. Terence de Vere White thought that 'of the many diaries that have appeared in recent years, none seems to me more likely to appeal to future generations than this journal of the last war'. Alistair Forbes, in a review which was not untinged with malice, concluded that Jim was almost as much a national treasure as the houses he described, 'and these diaries too, for their contribution to our knowledge of the past, deserve the Preservation Order he has slapped on them'. Among the volume's fans (so Jim learnt from various sources) were Christopher Isherwood, Artur Rubinstein, and the Queen Mother. Some of those pictured within were less enchanted. Two figures from the past with whom Jim was still in touch, Helen Dashwood and Stuart Preston, were hurt by the mildly satirical way in which they were presented. Stephen Spender objected to a reference to his homosexuality. Osbert Sitwell's former lover David Horner considered suing for libel as he had been described as 'epicene', prompting Jim to remark to Harold Acton 'that D.H. ought to be flattered, because to be called epicene implied that he had the qualities of both sexes, whereas . . . only those of the female sex pertained to him'. The heirs of country house owners who had received Jim as a representative of the National Trust were not invariably pleased to read what he had written about their parents and properties. Some of the Trust's stuffier luminaries, notably Hugh, Duke of Grafton (formerly Jim's colleague the Earl of Euston), thought the whole thing a shocking breach of confidence and taste, as a result of which Jim's diaries – though extracts had first appeared in the Trust's magazine, and they unquestionably constitute the greatest work of literature to have emerged from the Trust's history – were banned from sale in National Trust shops (an interdict which appears to remain in force more than thirty years later). Notwithstanding this setback, the publishers were delighted at the book's reception, and called for the next volume. Jim's own reactions were characteristic. He affected to be far more upset by the objections than pleased by the excellent reviews. In November 1975 he referred to 'those accursed diaries', and wrote that the criticisms he had received had plunged him into a state of depression. However, by the end of the month he was forging ahead with the next volume, *Prophesying Peace*, covering 1944 and 1945, having meanwhile destroyed the manuscripts on which *Ancestral Voices* was based.

Although the Lansdown Crescent property was easy to run, and Jim derived endless delight from Beckford's library, the Lees-Milnes did not enjoy living there. Apart from the library, it was cramped and claustrophobic. It was not convenient either for entertaining guests to meals or for having them to stay. Alvilde found it 'like living in a hotel'; the tiny garden, though she did her best with it, provided little scope for her talents. Jim missed his rural walking. By a stroke of luck, they had only been living there a month when a solution presented itself. Among their good friends were David Somerset and his wife Caroline, who lived at The Cottage, Badminton (in fact a substantial village house). Although the Somersets were twenty years younger than the Lees-Milnes, the two couples shared a similar sense of humour and (for Badminton was just five miles from Alderley) had spent many jolly evenings together. David was the heir to his cousin the 10th Duke of Beaufort, owner of the Badminton estate; and the Somersets had for years been telling the Lees-Milnes that, if they ever wished to move from Alderley, a house near to their own in Badminton village, known as Essex House, might soon become available on the demise of its elderly female tenant. The old lady proved more durable than expected; but just before Christmas 1974 David telephoned to say that the house was now vacant, and Jim and Alvilde could have it if they wished.

'We are in a great quandary,' wrote Jim. Alvilde was 'madly keen' on Essex House, especially as it had a garden; Jim was less keen, not wishing to abandon his beloved library, and fearing that, living in a village, it would be difficult to 'preserve anonymity'. (Alderley had been a mere hamlet; and Jim recalled Roquebrune with a shudder.) A month later they

inspected the house, which they found riddled with damp. This, however, proved to be no great problem as the estate employed excellent
workmen able to put it right. Finally they decided to rent Essex House as
soon as it was ready, and treat it as their main residence, but to keep the
Bath maisonette and divide it up: Jim would continue to use Beckford's
library for his work (a daily 'commute' of fourteen miles from Badminton),
and eat his lunch in the back room, while the basement would become a
self-contained flat. As the combined cost of running the Bath and
Badminton properties promised to be about the same as that of Alderley,
they realised that they had been somewhat hasty in abandoning the latter.
But the basement could be let to naval officers from the Admiralty establishment in Bath, enabling them to recoup some of their expenses. And
the plan for Jim to work away from home proved an ideal arrangement:
perhaps he was inspired by the example of Beckford, setting out each
morning to spend the day in the seclusion of his beloved Tower. Their
move to Badminton took place in October 1975, less than a year after
their move to Bath.

Essex House (which Alistair Forbes was to dub 'Bisex House') was a
pretty dwelling of yellow-washed local stone. It probably dated from the
reign of the first Duke of Beaufort, who died in 1699. Its basic plan was
simple, 'two up, two down'. The room on the left of the small entrance
hall became Jim's study, that on the right, Alvilde's sitting room. Above,
they had their respective bedrooms. At the back was a large kitchen, in
which they ate; above it were bathrooms. They managed to squeeze two
guest rooms into the attic. There was a patch of garden in the front, and
an acre at the back. Over the front door and the front gate were the arms
of the Duke of Beaufort, landlord of the house, the village, and a huge
swathe of surrounding territory. The gates to his palatial residence,
Badminton House, 'the grandest seat in Gloucestershire', stood directly
opposite Essex House. By settling at Badminton, the Lees-Milnes did not
merely acquire a comfortable new home in picturesque surroundings
(with a ready-made set of local friends from Alderley days); they found
themselves caught up in the operetta of life on one of the grandest estates
still in private hands, run along old-fashioned lines. Jim's initial doubts
were largely (though never entirely) overcome by the charm of the place.
'Badminton is a village isolated from the present,' he wrote in his diary.
'All the cottages are inhabited by people working on the estate. They are
all friendly, contented and respectful. All the men say, "Good morning,
Good night, sir", as of old.' From the late tenant they inherited a treasure
of a 'daily', Peggy Bird, who would continue working at Essex House

until Jim's death; anything that went wrong in the house could be repaired by her husband Gerald, a handyman on the estate. Jim wrote to Anne Hill that 'A. is delighted to be in the country again and I must say it is heaven to sleep in a bedroom that does not look out on a well below ground level and to hear the cocks crow and the vixens bark, not to mention those hounds baying. Even so I don't feel I belong to Badminton . . . The D. of Beaufort throws me into fits of shyness.'

Henry FitzRoy Somerset, the 10th Duke, was then seventy-five and had succeeded to his title and estates more than half a century earlier. He was not just one of England's greatest aristocrats, but arguably her leading sportsman. He lived for foxhunting, having been known as 'Master' since the age of nine and served for long years as MFH of 'the Beaufort'. He was also a prominent equestrian, who had founded the Badminton Horse Trials in 1949 and served three sovereigns as Master of the Horse. His wife Mary, born Princess of Teck, was a descendant of George III, a niece of Queen Mary (who had spent the war at Badminton) and a first cousin once removed of Elizabeth II. The Beauforts were popular with the Royal Family, who came to stay annually for the Trials. The Duke, whose wife had been unable to give him a child, a fact which rankled with him, was also a great Lothario: his many mistresses, all of them keen huntswomen, included the Lees Milnes' friend Sally, Duchess of Westminster, and Peggy, Viscountess De L'Isle, widow of Jim's cousin Lord Glanusk. He was a public-spirited man who took the keenest interest in his duties as Lord-Lieutenant of the county and patron of innumerable organisations, and in the welfare of his estate employees and their families. He was also a philistine who took not the slightest interest in the many priceless works of art with which his house was stuffed.

As former local residents and friends of the Somersets, the Lees-Milnes had already seen something of the Beauforts, mostly on formal occasions. Jim admired 'Master' for the decorum with which he acquitted his ceremonial duties (such as investing the long-standing custodian of a National Trust property with the British Empire Medal), and his sense of *noblesse oblige*, but otherwise regarded him, given his obsession with field sports and contempt for the arts, as a grotesque figure. (No doubt he was reminded of his father.) He got on far better with the Duchess, who was funny and friendly and enjoyed historical chat. While Master, in Jim's estimation, was fundamentally stupid, she, though uneducated, was not: she came out with remarks which were as shrewd as they were eccentric – that she hated Oliver Cromwell more than Harold Wilson; that her cousin the Duke of Windsor reminded her of Bonnie Prince Charlie. Jim was also fascinated by her recollections of her pre-1914 royal childhood, such as of visiting the Emperor Franz Josef at Schönbrunn. After the Lees-Milnes had settled in, the Beauforts occasionally had them to lunch and dine at 'the House'. Jim was at first intrigued to observe them at close quarters. 'She has a funny little-girl manner of speaking, and is often sharp and to the point.' 'The Duke has a limited charm, and his manners are almost the best I have encountered.' The thrill of these ducal invitations soon wore off. By June 1976 he was writing: 'Dinners here are sticky, and the food is disgusting. The grey parrot in the Raglan room is a help after dinner, for he does say the most amusing things.' Soon he was describing such evenings as 'torture', only made bearable by the richly comic details they supplied for his diary.

> Leaving church this morning Mary Beaufort asked us to dine tonight; old Horatia Dunant [a relation of the Duke] staying. We were told to arrive at 7.45 because they wanted to look at a film about Lily Langtry. After a rushed drink of sherry we were bustled into the dining-room. I sat next to Horatia with no one the other side of the huge table. Mary was opposite me behind a pot plant. Dinner eaten with great rapidity. No waiting. We choked over soup, fish, fruit salad; hardly time to toss down a glass of white wine. Master stacked the plates. Hustled back to the panelled room. Master turned on the telly and for a quarter of an hour we watched a film about naval privateers in Regency times in which a whore was being tossed from hammock to hammock. 'Unlike Lily,' Master growled. Then I ventured to suggest that it was not the Lily film, but another, as it proved to be – viz., *Mutiny on the Bounty*. Hurriedly we switched on to the right film. Therein Lily made to go to bed with a young man for a diamond necklace. Raped another called Sir George Arthur. Mary did not see for she was asleep. Neither Master nor Horatia made a comment. At nine the News came on. When it was over, we rose, and left . . . A purposeless occasion, surely.

Every spring the Horse Trials took place and huge crowds descended on Badminton, along with the Royals. Jim hated this event, and was shocked that the normally deserted parish church, which the Royals attended on Sunday, was 'filled to the brim' with 'gapers'. Once, when a friend of the Royal Family was staying with the Lees-Milnes to see the Trials, they were invited to a birthday party for the Queen given at the House.

> Mary Beaufort had hired a 'funny man', as she called him, from Bristol. It was rather painful . . . This little man was no Ruth Draper, and signally unfunny. Only the Royals in the front row were holding their sides, whether out of pity, good manners or enjoyment, who can tell. Twice the

performer called for assistance from the audience. Each time Prince Andrew and Prince Charles volunteered to go forward. Both very good, unshy, and the Prince of Wales was frankly funnier than the 'funny man' in his clowning. A ghastly party, and we had drinks afterwards in the dining-room . . . I did not speak to one Royal.

While increasingly anxious to avoid his company, Jim enjoyed hearing about Master's eccentricities. Though vastly rich he was obsessively mean. To save fuel bills he stopped turning the central heating on in winter, and burned electric fires. When the Queen Mother complained that the stairs to her room were uncarpeted, a strip of red carpet appeared on one side of the staircase only. His philistinism was mind-boggling. Jim was once shown his room: 'Huge portraits of nineteenth-century Beauforts on horseback with hounds, all chairs and sofas draped with scruffy blankets for dogs, foxes' brushes mounted and plastic models of foxes littered around.' When he published his memoirs, it turned out that 'not only had he not written them, he had not read them'. His prejudices were archaic. 'When engaging servants today,' David Somerset told Jim in 1978, 'Master asks them what their religion and politics are. If they are foolish enough to disclose that they vote Labour they are of course not engaged. If they admit to being Roman Catholic, that is worse.' He ran his estate autocratically and all who worked for him were terrified of him. One of the few who stood up to him was the Vicar. Tom Gibson, a splendidly bewhiskered former RAF pilot, had been appointed to the living at Badminton shortly before the arrival of the Lees-Milnes, who soon befriended him and his South African wife Gloria. While approving of his ducal patron's traditional approach to the liturgy, he repeatedly felt obliged to point out that his writ did not extend to anything that happened inside the church. He was not entitled to ask bishops to preach at Badminton, which was the Vicar's prerogative; nor was he entitled to sell a valuable Grinling Gibbons monument which graced one of the tombs, even if it had been given to his grandfather by Queen Victoria. The Vicar enjoyed a good gossip, and contributed to Jim's fund of ducal stories.

> [I]t was traditional for an annual meet to take place in honour of [Master's] birthday. One year the birthday fell on Good Friday, and the Vicar told him he could not possibly have a meet that day. Whereupon the Duke took up the telephone and put through a call to Buckingham Palace. He asked for the Queen, who came on the line. 'Our Vicar tells me . . .', he began, and told the story. Then a long pause, and the Vicar heard him say, 'Well, if you really think so, Ma'am. That's what the Vicar advises. Seems

incredible to me.' He put the receiver down, and said not a word. There was no further question of it.

As Badminton residents, the Lees-Milnes harboured a deadly secret: they were unenthusiastic about blood-sports. Though both had hunted in their extreme youth, they had since acquired such a reverence for nature that they hated to think of living creatures being killed for pleasure. (Their thoughts on the subject were slightly ambivalent, however, for they enjoyed the ceremonial side of hunting, and abominated hunt saboteurs.) They kept their views to themselves: otherwise they risked eviction. Even in his diary, Jim kept his criticisms *sotto voce*; on hearing that the hunt had had 'a super day' and 'killed five and a half brace of foxes', he merely commented: 'A massacre.' Master, to be sure, had his suspicions. As he remarked to David Somerset: 'What is the *point* of those Lees-Milnes? They don't hunt, they don't shoot, they don't fish.' Sooner or later an 'incident' was inevitable; and the wonder is that it did not come until May 1979, three and a half years after they had moved to Badminton, when their two whippets (the late Fop and Chuff having been replaced by Folly and Honey) were caught chasing a vixen.

> I took the dogs round the village. Crossing the recreation ground they bolted towards Vicarage Wood. I heard furious yells. Stalked cautiously round the entrance gates and saw the Duke with a pair of binoculars. I retreated, coward that I am. Alvilde very boldly decided she must look for the dogs; ran into the Duke who was beside himself with passion. He had been watching his cherished vixen and cubs. He was almost apoplectic. Said he would not have our bloody dogs on his land. Bloody this and bloody that. He would get his gun and shoot them. A. kept her head and temper, apologized and said what a good idea. Then he called at the house. I went to the door. Again he ranted. He sent the keeper after the dogs; keeper called and also said he would shoot them if ever again they were seen loose. Duke then telephoned, abused A., and slammed down the receiver. All for a trivial cause, in concern about some cubs which his hounds will tear to pieces before the autumn is through. Ghastly values, ghastly people. How I hate them. I shall never set foot in the big house again, in the unlikely event of being asked, and shall never speak to the hell-hound again beyond a curt good-morning if I pass him on the road.

Six months later, there was a hilarious sequel.

> Such a Trollopean scene today. Sally Westminster asked us to luncheon to meet the Beauforts and the Weinstocks [the tycoon Sir Arnold Weinstock and wife]. The first idea that we should make it up with the Duke and be

friends again. Second idea that it would be an uplift for the Weinstocks to meet the Duke and Duchess and learn what real aristocrats were like . . . In the middle of luncheon, Master said to Sir Arnold, 'Nice coverts you have got in the place you've just bought'. Sir Arnold replied, 'I refuse to let the hunt come near me. They make such a mess. And they are so rude. You as doyenne [sic] of the hunting world ought to teach them manners is all I can say.' Master went scarlet in the face and didn't say a word more. The peccadillo of our dogs chasing his vixen last May paled beside this enormity.

Reasonable relations were thus restored between the Lees-Milnes and their landlord; but the diaries record no further entertainment at the House during Master's reign.

By the middle of 1976 Jim had settled agreeably into his shuttlecock existence of living in Badminton and working in Bath. His novel *Round the Clock* had been accepted by Chatto. He had also sent them his second volume of wartime diaries, *Prophesying Peace*; he had edited this carefully to avoid causing offence to the living, and feared it lacked 'the spontaneity and sparkle' of *Ancestral Voices*, though his agent David Higham assured him it was just as good, and compared him to Pepys. He now had to find a subject for his next book. Meanwhile he had been asked to write the entry on Harold Nicolson for the *Dictionary of National Biography*. Soon after Harold's death in 1968, Jim and Alvilde, as former lovers of Harold and Vita, had been consulted by Nigel Nicolson over his plans to write a book about his parents dealing candidly with their homosexuality. At first they were rather shocked, but eventually they both came round to the view (which was not shared by most of those who had known the couple) that so much had already appeared on the subject, notably in Quentin Bell's biography of Virginia Woolf, that there could be no objection to such a book. When it was published in 1973 as *Portrait of a Marriage*, Jim thought it 'very well done' and likely to enhance the reputations of both Nicolsons, though he felt Nigel had over-romanticised his father. It was naturally to Nigel that Jim now turned for information on Harold for the *DNB* entry, especially concerning his diplomatic career. In June 1976 Nigel duly replied with the requested details, adding, 'Why, dear Jim, don't you write Harold's biography?'

This was just the sort of absorbing project Jim had been seeking; yet he greeted the invitation with 'indecision, perplexity and wonder'. He knew Harold too well in one sense, too little in others. 'I know nothing about diplomacy and politics. And do I find Harold, whom I loved and revered, quite my sort of subject? I like romantic figures, Beckford,

Byron, and H. was never this. Vita was. Oh Lord!' He consulted other old friends of Harold, such as Eardley and Raymond Mortimer, but concluded that 'no person can give one advice. One must make up one's own mind.' What finally decided him to accept was that both Nigel and his older brother Ben seemed so genuinely keen that he should do it. The brothers made an odd pair. Jim found Nigel (now editing the letters of his mother's great love Virginia Woolf)

> affectionate, fair, honourable, just, dutiful, extremely hard working, a first class writer, an exemplary parent, an aesthete, exceedingly clever yet modest. At the same time is he quite human? . . . He speaks didactically, in a precise, academic manner. He is a cold man who wants to be warm, and cannot be. Nigel told me that he was in love with James [Pope-Hennessy] at the same time as his father was. I know more about this than he thinks. For Jamesey told me he was in love with Nigel and used to lie with him, though without touching. That has always been Nigel's failing, the inability to make close contact.

Ben (with whom Jim had briefly been intimate after the war) was by contrast a rebel and a bohemian who immersed himself in his calling as an art historian and cared nothing for the world's opinions; he may have reminded Jim of Rick Stewart-Jones. (Like Rick, he drank and smoked to excess and was destined for an early grave: he never saw Jim's biography, dropping down dead in Leicester Square underground station in 1978 at the age of sixty-three.) Jim marvelled that both brothers 'talked about [the sex-lives of] their parents dispassionately as if they were persons of ancient history, nothing to do with them'. Nigel, now the National Trust tenant at Sissinghurst where Jim periodically visited him to discuss the project, 'gaily' entrusted his father's voluminous papers to him with the words: 'It wouldn't matter much if they were lost. I have read through them all; and you will do the same. And I don't suppose anyone else will ever do so.'

Harold Nicolson occupied Jim longer than any other book. He reckoned it would take him three years but it finally took him five; and (apart from his diary) he produced no other significant work during that time (though Chatto brought out *Prophesying Peace* in 1977 and *Round the Clock* in 1978). It was a labour of love; but his intimate acquaintance with the subject over thirty-five years was a dubious advantage: every time Jim visited the London Library and met the eyes of the rather foxy photograph of Harold (the Library's Chairman from 1952 to 1957) on the stairs, he had an uneasy feeling of being quizzed from beyond the grave. The project presented him with a number of problems. First, Harold, like Jim himself, had led an unusually varied life. He had been a diplomatist, novelist, essayist, diarist, historian, biographer, critic, gossip-columnist, parliamentary politician, wartime minister, broadcaster, lecturer, gardener, a noted clubman and society figure, one half of a highly unusual marriage, and a mentor of young men. All these aspects had to be treated: Jim had hoped to be spared going into much detail about the diplomacy and politics, subjects which interested him little, but Nigel insisted they be 'dealt with fully'. Secondly, the extent of the source material was immense. Harold had kept a regular diary from 1919 onwards, only a tiny part of which had been published. He wrote to Vita every day they were separated, which was most days during almost fifty years of marriage. He wrote innumerable other letters, which (though he did not keep many letters himself) were frequently kept by recipients who were eager to show them to Jim. The Public Record Office contained thousands of his diplomatic despatches, Hansard hundreds of his parliamentary speeches. Jim felt he had to read and analyse all this material, not to mention more than thirty books Harold had written and a mass of high-quality journalism. Then there was Harold's sex-life. Though Jim had criticised Nigel for 'romanticising' this, it was difficult to tell the whole truth – that Harold was an over-sexed individual who sought a homosexual experience at least once a day well into middle age; that these experiences were mostly unromantic and fleeting; and that he patronised a series of discreet young men willing to oblige him in this regard. Several of Harold's lovers who were still alive were anxious that Jim should say nothing about his homosexuality – or no more than had already been disclosed by Nigel in his *Portrait* (which disclosures they regarded as unforgivable). The architect Claud Phillimore

> begged me not to analyse Harold's relations with men, and merely leave them to the imagination or interpretation of the reader. I said I intended to do this, yet was faced with the difficulty of withholding truth. After all, if the subject of one's biography loved women one would be bound to say so. Yes, he said, but don't elaborate on whether they went to bed together. I said I would never do that unless I had proof positive, and unless the action had a distinct influence upon the story.

Raymond Mortimer, the one man with whom Harold had been madly in love, asked Jim to remain silent about their affair, which had lasted for most of the 1920s: at his age, he said, he would not be able to stand the attendant publicity. Jim 'promised to be discreet' – though when Raymond died in January 1980, aged eighty-four, Jim, who was about to return the corrected proofs of his Volume I, 'inserted a few things about him which I would not have included had he lived'. When it came to Volume II (which opens in 1930), one friend Jim hardly mentioned was himself. He makes just three fleeting appearances – in connection with his first visit to Sissinghurst in 1932, his trip to Paris with Harold in 1934, and his tour of National Trust properties with Harold and Vita in 1947. Of the fact that he had lived with Harold for several years there was not a word.

Jim got round these problems by writing a book which might almost have been entitled 'The Life and Times of Harold Nicolson in His Own Words'. Harold was a writer of outstanding elegance and descriptive power; and few men have written more (or more entertainingly) about themselves. It was possible to produce an account of his life largely consisting of paraphrased extracts from his diaries, letters and autobiographical writings; and this Jim skilfully set out to do. Those aspects of his life which Harold had not written about were hardly mentioned. Comment was kept to a minimum. The result was a vivid, entertaining and richly detailed narrative, following Harold's progress from month to month and concentrating on his impressions rather than his achievements. There were two problems with it, however. First, having chosen this method, Jim produced a book which was very long. Even after extensive cutting it required two volumes, which in the view of Chatto, who rather reluctantly agreed to publish it, was more than the subject's reputation warranted and risked prejudicing its chances of commercial success. Secondly, it was uncritical and took Harold at his own estimation (though Jim's editorial selection of material often implied a certain wry commentary). Jim did not, for example, seek to question the success of the Nicolsons' marriage – though his own experience must have suggested to him that it was not, perhaps, quite as happy as they both claimed it to be. (After Volume I had appeared, Nigel suggested that Jim introduce more of his own opinions into Volume II – which had the unfortunate effect of interrupting the autobiographical flow with apologetic passages in which Jim sought to defend his subject against charges of snobbery and having been an ineffective public figure.) On its own terms, it could not have been better done; it is a brilliant read, and a fascinating source-book on the times; but it left room for the more critical (if less readable) biography which appeared a quarter of a century later.

Jim's study of Harold's life gave rise to various reflections which he recorded in his diary. Reading Harold's wartime letters he was 'struck by his intense patriotism, and Vita's too, the very polarity of Bloomsbury's contempt for such an attitude. Does anyone under fifty have these feelings today?' The discovery of 'powdery fresh' ash between the folded leaves of a 1930 letter provoked thoughts on mortality – 'even cigarette ash can be preserved longer than the flesh and blood of a genius'. The diary also records many meetings with people who had known Harold (whose recollections did not generally add much to what Jim already knew). Harold Macmillan (who pretended to be senile but was in fact alert and mischievous) said that Harold Nicolson, his parliamentary friend of the 1930s, was 'a decent character, easy to get on with, kind to colleagues . . . but he lacked push and virility, was too soft and sentimental for politics'. When Jim asked if the former Prime Minister had been aware of Nicolson's 'propensities', Macmillan seemed 'aghast', explaining that he did not think 'anyone' knew, and if they did they would never have discussed it because 'thirty-five years ago . . . nearly all in the House were gentlemen'. Another politician to whom Harold Nicolson had been close was the raffish Bob Boothby. 'Boothby showed me several letters he had received from Harold . . . They disclosed that H.N. was homosexual, Lord Boothby remarked to me. I thought they disclosed that Boothby was too, or H.N. would not have written to him recommending a harbour in Greece where pretty sailors were to be seen drinking and smoking.' Jim drove to Devon to see Harold's elder brother Lord Carnock, still alive in a nursing home in his mid nineties, who opined that Harold was a liar and a coward and not worth a biography. 'No man is a hero to his valet, or to his family, it seems,' sighed Jim, who was also irritated by those who dismissed Harold as a 'lightweight'. 'For who are the heavy-weights? – Churchill, Lenin, Hitler, I suppose, men of no one perfected distinction to their credit, whereas Harold was a writer of rare quality.'

When he had finally sorted out his material and got down to writing, Jim worked fast as he always did: each of the two volumes, running in their unedited state to more than a quarter of a million words, was writ-ten in about six months. Volume I appeared in the autumn of 1980, Volume II a year later. Many of the reviewers were old friends of Harold, who were generally delighted with it. ('If there has been a better biog-raphy in the past fifty years,' wrote Michael Howard in the *Sunday Times*, 'I would like to know which it is.') It was, however, a grim time for British publishing: both volumes were held up by printers' strikes and distribution problems; Chatto produced it cheaply to save costs. Sales were disappointing, and no publisher could be found at the time to issue it in paperback (though Hamish Hamilton did so a decade later). Though Nigel assured Jim that he had done a marvellous job, and it was awarded the Royal Society of Literature's Heinemann Prize (which Jim had already received twenty-five years earlier for *Roman Mornings*), Jim's main feeling as he neared the end of his literary marathon was inevitably one of depression.

> Now that I have divested myself of Harold . . . I am at a loss. Feel bereft, with no purpose in life. I understand how Virginia Woolf had a break-down when she finished a book. Only she didn't have hers returned, underscored, or larded with requests to rewrite. Non-writers don't under-stand how writers feel like emigrants in an alien new world, having left forever the shores of yesteryear.

Jim was in the midst of *Harold Nicolson* when he reached his seventieth birthday in August 1978. This was another occasion for moaning and groaning. 'Dear God, how could you do this to me?' he wrote, later remarking that 'let's face it, we are all of us dying over seventy, though some of us are not yet in the terminal stage'. In fact Jim was unusually fit for his age, both physically and mentally. He thought nothing of walking fifteen miles with Eardley (six years his senior but equally fit), along the Kennet Canal or over the Berkshire Downs, or of spending a week on Mount Athos, where he made the first of four fascinatingly documented pilgrimages with Derek Hill in September 1977, hiking and enduring the discomforts of monastic life. *Harold Nicolson* shows him at the height of his literary powers: on a good day, he could produce five thousand words of faultless prose. He prided himself on reading well over a hundred books a year ('not including articles, or parts of books'). He kept up a huge correspondence with friends. (It is typical of Jim that several of his regular correspondents were 'pen friends' whom he did not meet: these included Stanley Baldwin's niece Monica, who spent most of her life as a nun, and various fans of his books who never stopped writing to him and to whom he never stopped replying.) His busy life included weekly trips to London and much travel at home and abroad: during the autumn of 1978 he visited Cyprus and Istanbul with Alvilde, and Rome with John Kenworthy-Browne.

Indeed, he could feel himself to be a lucky survivor. He had already outlived most of his friends of his own generation. The great loves of his youth, Tom Mitford, Desmond Parsons, Rick Stewart-Jones and Jamesey Pope-Hennessy, were all gone. Many old friends (some of them younger than himself) had recently died, including Ran Antrim, Cyril Connolly, Hamish Erskine, John Fowler, Patrick Kinross, Angus Menzies and Ben Nicolson; several others, such as Michael Duff and Michael Rosse, were 'on the way out'. Though he mourned the passing of friends, there was a hint of truth in Alvilde's accusation that he 'got kicks' out of seeing them in the obituary columns. A less guilt-inducing pleasure was to meet people who had treated him disdainfully in his youth and discover that they were now doing considerably less well than himself. At the theatre he saw Graham (now Viscount) Monsell, the local MP's son who had shamelessly bullied him as a boy in Worcestershire.

> He held my hand and said how delighted he was to see me and would so much like us to meet and talk over old times. Old times, my foot! I was terrified of Graham as a boy. At children's tennis tournaments he used to bash his racquet over my head so that I looked like a clown peering through a broken drum . . . At Oxford he was . . . excessively supercilious, rich and disdainful. Now he is bent, blind, sallow, dusty and diffident. How the late worms change places with the early birds.

If one compares Jim's 1970s with his 1940s diary, one sees that the list of those to whom he was close at forty, and who still played a significant part in his life when he was seventy, was not long – Eardley, Raymond Mortimer, Desmond Shawe-Taylor, Harold Acton, Johnnie Churchill, Burnet Pavitt, Geoffrey Houghton Brown, Midi Gascoigne, Billa Harrod, Anne Hill, Derek Hill. (The Berkeleys and Droghedas were really friends of Alvilde whom he came to know well after his marriage to her.) On the other hand, one of the joys of later life was re-establishing contact with friends of early youth. During the late 1970s Jim resumed the threads with two loved ones of his adolescence whom he had hardly seen for fifty years – Diana Mosley and Rupert Hart-Davis. Meeting Diana (now living at Orsay near Paris with Sir Oswald) at the seventieth birthday of her sister Pam in 1977, Jim wrote that 'she retains for me the same ineffable magic. The same Mitford jokes – which require tuning in to . . . I think of her, as it seems yesterday, that radiantly lovely Botticelli Venus aged 17, sitting on a Cotswold wall, whom I, her elder by two years, worshipped.' He wondered if he would see her again; but after this meeting they became regular correspondents, and Debo often invited Jim to Chatsworth when Diana was staying there. Following his fourth marriage and his retirement from publishing, Rupert had become a recluse in Yorkshire, where Jim visited him in 1978. 'I had misgivings about seeing him again after so many years . . . It was a great success. He was so affectionate . . . We talked non-stop for hours.' A famous editor and proof-reader, Rupert insisted on Jim sending him all his future books for 'correction', which Jim gratefully did.

Jim's marriage to Alvilde now seemed very happy. 'I have grown to love her so deeply for her goodness to me,' he wrote in January 1978. Writing about the marriage of Harold and Vita had the effect of drawing him closer to her: he found it painful to consider the last years the Nicolsons had spent together, which brought home to him 'the little of the life . . . to be left to them. And it follows – how little is left to A. and me.' Indeed, in a sense Alvilde was a better wife to Jim than Vita had been to Harold, for she devoted herself to his well-being and spared him all domestic worries. After twenty years, she had reconciled herself to his relationship with John Kenworthy-Browne. Jim continued to stay with John in London, and remained in love with him to the extent of being jealous of John's patron in the art history world, the great museum director Sir John Pope-Hennessy (brother of the late Jamesey and known as 'the Pope'): when John, after visiting Rome with Jim in November 1978, went to stay with the Pope in New York, Jim felt miserable not hearing from him for several weeks. 'It is absurd that after twenty years and more I should mind as much as I do. I miss him when we are out of touch. I just long for him to telephone and say he is glad to be back, and did not enjoy his visit much; and above all that John Pope-Hennessy was hell to him.' Apart from Eardley, still Jim's greatest confidant and principal companion on holidays and expeditions, the other person who meant most to him was his great-nephew Nick Robinson. After reading Art History at Cambridge Nick considered a career in publishing, and Jim, who knew the editor Denys Sutton, got him a job on the art magazine *Apollo* at £3,000 a year. This was not a success – Sutton complained that Nick never came into the office before 10.30 and only seemed interested in field sports, and sacked him after six months. Norah Smallwood, who had met Nick with Jim, then employed him at Chatto, which gave Jim a welcome pretext to look in on him when he called on his publishers. (Nick, who had some private capital, soon set himself up as a successful independent publisher and eventually became chairman of Constable, that distinguished firm with which Jim had vainly sought a job in 1935.)

To those who met him, Jim appeared a sprightly septuagenarian with a touch of boyish eagerness. He carried himself tall and erect, with a spring in his step. He dressed carefully: though a grey suit was his invariable London uniform, there was something of the dandy in his choice of shirts and ties, shoes and socks. He was attached to such accessories as his father's Brigg umbrella and the silver pencil given to him by Vita Sackville-West. Beneath a quiff of sparse white hair, his expressive face had a chameleon quality, able to switch in an instant from the grave and earnest to the jovial and impish. He spoke with precise diction, and both his intonation and choice of words seemed old-fashioned even for a person of his class and generation. His manners too were those of another age, and he was exquisitely courteous, concentrating his whole attention on his interlocutor.

One of the pleasures Jim began to experience during the 1970s, especially after publishing his diaries, was that he became an object of fascination to the young. Many eager and talented young people – largely male, and gay – knew of his work for the National Trust, and were thrilled to read his witty and poignant accounts of visits to wartime country house owners and his tales of bisexual adventures during the Blitz. They also found that he was delightful to meet, that they could talk to him on equal terms, that the age-gap of forty or more years was no bar to friendship. Thus in his late sixties Jim got to know several clever, attractive and amusing aesthetes in their twenties. These included his successor as the National Trust's architectural adviser, the baby-faced Gervase Jackson-Stops (known as 'Jerks-and-Stops' on account of his stammer); the writer Simon Blow ('highly intelligent and sympathetic, albeit neurotic'); the beautiful baronet Tatton Sykes (nephew of Jim's old friend Christopher); two budding art historians, John Martin Robinson and Colin McMordie (who first visited Jim in 1973 as Oxford postgraduate students); another art historian and expert on the Bloomsbury Group, Richard Shone ('charmer of all time'); the artist Glynn Boyd Hart (who drew Jim in his library); and a domestic partnership consisting of the early music enthusiast Julian Berkeley, younger son of Lennox and Freda, and the BBC music presenter Tony Scotland. ('I can't get out of my head those two boys, so beautiful both with their long, dark, curly, glossy hair, and both so nicely dressed and spruce. There is no concealment of their relationship . . . It is wonderful that today these situations are just accepted.') Of these youthful fans, the one who became fondest of Jim seems to have been Colin McMordie, a fair-haired Northern Irishman with striking if slightly effeminate good looks. He visited Jim in Bath, dined with him in London and invited him to Oxford. Jim was touched that Colin was so keen to meet him and discuss his emotional problems (which centred on the fact that he hated being beautiful), but found him 'rather precious'. Much as he liked Colin's company, he wished he were not always so intense and serious, and 'would have preferred less talk about literature and art, and more fun and jokes'. As with that other beautiful but neurotic figure, Bruce Chatwin, he held back from the intimacy which beckoned; as he wrote to Eardley (to whom he was unrestrained in his confidences),

'Oh, Colin, Colin, how lovely you are like a magnolia in bud before it gets blowsy and how attractive you look in those absurd trousers with legs as wide as skirts and tight little you-know-what seen from behind. And I am not in love with you a bit.' By 1979 Colin, with help from a rich patron, had become an art dealer in Paris (where Stuart Preston, also now a Paris resident, fell unrequitedly in love with him), and Jim saw little more of him before his tragically early death in 1985, aged thirty-six.*

Another young friend Jim valued was the writer and genealogist Hugh Montgomery-Massingberd. (He does not quite belong in the above paragraph because, though scarcely older than the names listed therein, he combined a schoolboy outlook with a middle-aged appearance; and though given to hero-worship, he was basically heterosexual.) Hugh was a great-nephew of Field Marshal Sir Archibald and Lady Montgomery-Massingberd, the donors of Gunby, and a nephew of Jim's Eton friend Peter Montgomery with whom he had lain half-naked in the Piccadilly Hotel during the Blitz. In the 1960s he abandoned the prospect of a university education to join the staff of Burke's Peerage, meeting Jim when the latter wrote a preface to the final edition of *Burke's Landed Gentry* in 1969. He admired Jim for his romantic love of the squirearchy, and for some years they considered writing a book together on the subject. Hugh (who as obituaries editor of the *Daily Telegraph* in the 1980s was to become a brilliant sender-up of the recently dead) also found Jim a man after his own heart for his love of fantasy and anecdote, and his combination of charming manners with waspish mischievousness. When *Another Self*, followed by the wartime diaries, appeared in the 1970s, they immediately became some of Hugh's favourite books (which he would help immortalise after Jim's death by using them as the basis for a successful play).

I now come to my own part in this story; unlike Jim in writing about Harold, I cannot indulge in the luxury of leaving myself out of the narrative, if only because Jim has written so much about our association in his diary. When we met in February 1979 I was twenty-five and working on a doctoral thesis (which was never presented) at St John's College, Cambridge, where I had been in residence since 1971 as an undergraduate and postgraduate. A friend of mine in publishing, Charles Orwin, had drawn my attention to Jim's two volumes of diaries, which I had devoured with fascination. I longed to meet the diarist, and found an excuse to do

---

* As Jim, on hearing of his death on 3 August 1985, recalled him lying beautifully naked like Onslow's Shelley Memorial, the friendship was not, perhaps, totally platonic.

so when the 'Albany' column of the *Sunday Telegraph* (compiled by Jim's friend Kenneth Rose) announced that he was writing Harold Nicolson's biography. For I was then contemplating a biography of Philip Guedalla (1889–1944), a pre-war author of stylish historical works who had known Harold, if not well. I found Jim's addresses (confusingly, two of them, in Badminton and Bath) in *Who's Who* and wrote to him, asking if we might meet to compare notes on the two historians. He replied charmingly, doubting if he could help me much (though he had once heard Guedalla lecture) but inviting me to lunch at Brooks's. I remember that I was late owing to a delayed train, and I see from Jim's diary that our lunch was rather a hurried one, as Alvilde was meeting him at Brooks's at 2.30 to return with him to Badminton (they had just visited Berlin together, where Harold had served at the British Embassy in the late 1920s). However, from the moment we met, we 'clicked'. I thought he was quite simply the most wonderful person I had ever met. On the one hand, he seemed a fascinating figure from another age and world; on the other, I had never met anyone of an older generation it was so easy to talk to, or who seemed so interested in my unworthy self. Among his engaging qualities was an eagerness to establish a sense of complicity with those he felt might share his tastes. The Ayatollah Khomeini had just taken power in Iran, and Jim said to me, with a conspiratorial look, that he was glad to have visited Tehran (where Harold had also served in diplomacy) a couple of years earlier, as men of his persuasion might not be so welcome there now. Before we parted we found a reason to meet again when he offered to introduce me to Rosamond Lehmann, who had known Guedalla.

We began exchanging letters. His to me were marvellous, full of entertaining descriptions of his doings, and avuncular advice; mine to him (most of which he returned to me before his death) were jejune and artless, if open and affectionate. Within a few weeks, a close friendship had sprung up between us. We did not see much of each other (which would have been difficult, more than a hundred miles separating Cambridge from Badminton and Bath). It appears from his diary that, after our initial encounter, we met on six occasions up to the end of June. In March he invited me to dine with Ros Lehmann at an Italian restaurant in London; in April he visited me in Cambridge, spending a night in a guest room at my college; later that month I had him to dine at my flat in Bayswater to meet Charles Orwin; in May he asked me to two meals at Brooks's, at one of which we were joined by his schoolfriend Alan Pryce-Jones; in June he again visited Cambridge, this time staying two nights. Each time I saw him I felt a rush of delight, which he seemed to feel too. But the essence of our relationship was that we communicated regularly while meeting infrequently. In this respect it was similar to other relationships in his life – with Diana Mitford in the 1920s, Anne Gathorne-Hardy in the 1930s, the mystery telephone voice in the 1940s (as related in the last pages of *Another Self*), and doubtless others. And like those relationships, it was platonic.

Looking back after thirty years, I find it easy to see why I fell for him, but am still slightly puzzled as to what he saw in me. After all, during the past few years there had been no lack of personable young admirers who were eager to have his friendship, at least one of whom had thrown himself (so to speak) at his feet. And these young men mostly came from similar backgrounds and had similar interests to his own. This was not the case with me. I was the son of a factory owner in Northern Ireland,★ where I went to the local grammar school; my ancestors were Polish Jews. True, I was fascinated by history (though at Cambridge I had read law); but my knowledge and appreciation of art and architecture were sketchy, a fact which Jim, when he thought about it, found curious.

> Strange how he is not much interested in art or artefacts. I showed him a ravishing pair of ormolu candlesticks in a shop and he did not register. Said possessions meant little to him. When I asked if there was any object in my library he would like to have, he said he did not think he would have anywhere to put it. I take it for granted that my friends are interested in the arts, but I suppose such people are a minority.

Perhaps my attraction lay in the fact that, like him, I was a bit of a fantasist, lost in a world of dreams, and felt myself to be an outsider. Perhaps it was simply that Jim, having just entered another decade of life, was ready to fall in love again, and I happened to come along at the right time. He wrote in his diary that I reminded him of various friends he had known in the past; but I think these associations arose out of his imagination once he had taken a liking to me. After our first meeting he wrote that my 'large luminous eyes' reminded him of Brian Howard (said to have been the principal model for Anthony Blanche in *Brideshead Revisited*), though I was 'not chi-chi like Brian'. A couple of months later he wrote: 'He reminds me more and more of Jamesey [Pope-Hennessy], without the bitchiness.' He also compared me to 'nephew Nick'.

★While I made no secret to Jim about my family's textile business, it was not until we had known each other for about a decade that he mentioned his family's cotton mill to me.

(Although Nick Robinson and I were in most respects quite unlike, and did not meet for many years, we were, Jim wrote, 'the two young I am most fond of'. Towards the end of 1979 Jim commissioned his artist friend Derek Hill to paint portraits of us both – though in the end my portrait was not painted owing to objections from Alvilde, while Nick's was a disappointment to Jim who found it 'hardly recognisable'. At the same time he drew up a new will, appointing Nick his executor and me his literary executor.)

I was of course aware that Jim reciprocated my feelings for him; but it came as rather a shock to discover, twenty years later, how intense and indeed painful were his feelings for me, aspects which he took care to conceal from me at the time. Even when we had met just once, and were writing each other mildly amorous letters, he seems to have been working himself up into rather a state. In June 1979, when he was due to visit me in Cambridge, he was presented with a dilemma as two good friends he had known since Eton, Michael Rosse and the artist Reynolds Stone, were at death's door. 'Supposing Reynolds dies, supposing Michael Rosse dies and the funeral [coincides with] my visit to Cambridge next week, I shall make every excuse and endeavour to go to Cambridge . . . So here is inconstancy, disloyalty: putting someone I have known for a few months before old friends of a lifetime.' (Fortunately both held out just long enough to spare him the choice.) A month later he wrote: 'How long am I to suffer? The last spell endured 15 years at least, and is not entirely over today. Does this mean I shall be eighty-five before I have recovered from this one? In other words, are all my remaining years to be spent aching, waiting for the post, the telephone call, the fleeting meeting, the mild jealousies, the angst?' ('The last spell' refers, of course, to John Kenworthy-Browne; it is an indication of Jim's ability to keep his friend-ships separate that, although John continued to see Jim regularly in London and have him to stay, he and and I were scarcely aware of each other's existences until Jim introduced us in 1987.)

A complicating factor was that Alvilde had now found out about us. (Jim did not tell her about me; but some helpful friend – I think it was Burnet Pavitt – saw us together on a couple of occasions and reported this to her.) She asked to meet me; and I was invited to dine with them both at Brooks's at the end of July, along with John Betjeman and Elizabeth Cavendish. I was tremendously excited to meet the Poet Laureate, having read his *Collected Poems* so often that I knew most of them by heart, so I don't suppose I attended to Alvilde much: she seemed very handsome and distinguished, as well as rather haughty and snubbing, but I was terribly naïve and just imagined that this was how all women of her class behaved to whomever they met. Jim wrote that 'I think A. liked M., though she finds him looking, as she says, unhealthy'. Six weeks later, when she was in France visiting Clarissa, he wrote to her from Badminton:

> M.B. has, I suppose, disturbed the hitherto acquired equanimity of my old age. My feelings for him are such as I have never experienced before. I have never had an emotional relationship, reciprocated too, on a totally platonic plane. For some curious reason the intensity of it seems thereby intensified [*sic*]. How wonderful too that I can now talk to you about it, and you can be so wonderfully understanding and sweet, and not resentful. Even so, I don't want to discuss it much. It is locked away, and I hope it will abate with time. You have been an angel of forbearance . . . and I am so deeply grateful. I feel deeply penitent if I have caused you any heart pricks. There is absolutely no cause, for as I have said to you over and over again, you are the only person who is the permanent love of my life.

In November, Alvilde invited me to spend a weekend at Essex House. Should I accept, I asked Jim? Yes, he said (though Eardley told him he was 'mad to allow it'). I enjoyed the visit, and was fascinated to meet people such as Frances Partridge who was also staying, and the Anthony Powells who came to lunch, though I was slightly overawed by the whole experience, and aware that Alvilde did not like me much and Jim was not very comfortable with my being there. Indeed, he wrote in his diary that it was 'agony' for him. 'There is a tense suspicion, and a shyness on M's part which does not make hostmanship easy . . . I did not enjoy this weekend and do not want him and A. to meet often, because I have a nasty suspicion that she wishes to break up the relationship by any means.' A fortnight later he wrote: 'A letter this morning from M. I droop when I am out of contact like a lily yellowing at the edges. No wonder A. who misses nothing resents these moods which are beyond my control. I wish I could snap out of them for it is ridiculous.' Soon afterwards he saw Freda Berkeley, who 'told me how unhappy A. was being made by me. I told Freda how unhappy this was making me, but asked her next time A. consulted her to impress upon A. how little cause she had for unhappiness. I could not help being in love, but my love was platonic and surely no harm to anyone but myself.' By this time I had received a hostile letter from Alvilde, hinting at dire consequences if I did not leave Jim alone. I did not mention this to Jim, but sought the advice of Rosamond Lehmann who was a friend of them both. She dictated the reply I sent – to the effect that I was not behaving in a way which could possibly harm her marriage and saw no reason not to continue seeing Jim. When Alvilde again invited me to stay at Badminton in July 1980 she apologised for the letter, explaining that she had 'almost lost' Jim twenty years earlier and 'couldn't bear to go through that again'. (This affair of the letter had an unhappy sequel. In November 1981, two years after I had received it, Rosamond told Jim about it. Alvilde, with her talent for discovering things, soon found out that Jim had been enlightened in this way, and refused to have anything more to do with Rosamond, her friend of almost fifty years, during the remaining decade of their mutual lives.)

In fact, during the years 1979 to 1981 the Lees-Milne marriage went through something of a re-run of the crisis of 1959 to 1961. I represented no more of a threat to it than John had; but Alvilde could not bear to see a letter from me on the breakfast table, and complained about me to her friends in much the same terms as she had complained about John. Meanwhile she constantly reproached Jim for his 'infidelity'. In April 1980 he recorded that she

> left with my luncheon packet a note to be read and digested. Such a sad note and so accusatory that I can hardly bear to refer to it. Even suggesting that it might be better if we separated. But oh dear, what cause? Not my purely socratic friendship with M. Not the charge that I, aged seventy-one, am not attentive enough. In the evening we discussed the matter calmly and affectionately, and embraced, and agreed to let it pass. I am still riddled with guilt – and yet I am guiltless, surely?

Another echo of the past was that, just as Jim found it difficult to meet John after the latter had gone off to Dyrham in February 1959, I too became physically isolated from him when I went to Paris in February 1980 to work for Maître Suzanne Blum, the Duchess of Windsor's formidable octogenarian lawyer. (The job, which involved writing books based on papers entrusted to the Maître by the Duchess, was originally to be for six months, but in the event lasted almost a decade.) So our relationship became more than ever an epistolary one. I was always thrilled to receive his letters, and our occasional reunions seemed to make him as happy as they did me; that spring he visited me in Paris, where we spent one evening with Stuart Preston, another with the Mosleys. (Jim had given me introductions to both 'the Sergeant', who became a great friend, and Diana, who was very kind to me: when Sir Oswald died in December 1980, I had the rather odd task of representing the Duchess of Windsor at his funeral.) However, his diary shows that, while he was delighted to see me when he did, at other times I was the unwitting cause of some agony.

At one moment he might be chatting to me 'with oh what ease and affection', feeling 'very happy indeed about this relationship, free of passion and deep-seated on both sides'. At another, he could write that 'my dependence on M. is such that I can honestly say I wish I had never met him. In some dreadful way I almost wish he would die so that I could thereby possess him totally. At times I feel I am going mad.'

However, time calmed these disturbances, and by the end of 1981 our relations had settled down to a happy literary friendship which no longer caused him much guilt or anxiety. He gave me much help and encouragement over my first book, which appeared in 1982, and asked me to read and comment on his own manuscripts, paying too much attention to my immature suggestions. We discussed the books we were reading; and he continued to send me letters worthy of Lord Chesterfield, full of sympathetic advice on every subject and affectionately chiding me for my indolence, frivolity and other shortcomings. Meanwhile Alvilde (whatever her feelings) showed me much friendliness. In May 1982 she asked me to stay at Essex House again to meet a new friend of both hers and Jim's, the 'delicious' Selina Hastings, who was writing Nancy Mitford's biography (and would later undertake Rosamond Lehmann's). A few weeks later, at her suggestion, I was included in a small dinner party in London to celebrate Jim's receipt of the Heinemann Prize for *Harold Nicolson*. She once sent me a touching letter asking if I could help Jim find a subject for his next book.

14

Struggling On
1981–8

———◆———

MORE THAN EVER, Jim lived for his writing. Having completed *Harold Nicolson* in 1981, he plunged into a frantic series of literary projects. In the space of about eighteen months he completed no fewer than five books and contributed to a sixth. (All the while, of course, he was keeping up his diary.) Two of these books were compilations which gave him little trouble – an anthology of writings about country houses for Oxford University Press, and a third volume of diaries, covering 1946 and 1947. Jim thought the latter 'far less entertaining than the previous diaries', but Chatto were keen to publish them, which they did in 1983 as *Caves of Ice*. (As usual, Jim was more embarrassed by the occasional offence they caused than pleased by the mostly favourable reviews. 'Wish I had never published these bloody diaries,' he wrote soon after publication. 'Can't think what came over me.') The third book was an iconography of Bath in a limited-edition series published by Bamber Gascoigne (son of Midi). This too was an easy task, especially as Bamber provided him with a handsome picture researcher, the American David Ford, 'a nice young man indeed'. The fourth book was *The Last Stuarts*, which, to Jim's delight, Chatto's agreed to publish eight years after originally rejecting it. In the course of revising it he substantially rewrote it, with the advantage of access (denied him in the 1970s) to the Royal Archives at Windsor. Though it combined scholarship and readability and told a fascinating, little-known story, it attracted scant attention on publication, to Jim's distress. The fifth book was a novel, provisionally entitled *Innocence*, about a 'sex-starved' German count, a prisoner–of–war in England in 1917, who seduces first an English schoolboy, then the boy's mother. Jim had been mulling over the plot for some years (it was inspired by the film of *The Go-Between*), but wrote the first of its many drafts in a matter of days; he considered it one of the best things he had done, though it is manifestly inferior to his two previous novels and was rejected by every publisher to whom he submitted it. (One is reminded of Evelyn Waugh, who thought his best book the ludicrous historical novel *Helena* in which the mother of the Emperor Constantine talks and behaves like one of the Bright Young People of the 1920s.) The sixth book was *Writers at Home*, a collection of essays edited by Gervase Jackson-Stops on the 'literary shrines' owned by the National Trust, to which Jim contributed a lengthy introduction which proved more of a struggle than any of his other recent works. He concluded with an arresting reflection:

> As the English countryside dwindles from year to year, the tentacles of Metroland stretch further from the hub of the metropolis, and the provincial city centres become eviscerated by developers, the little shops and dwellings bulldozed, to be replaced by supermarkets and car-parks, the shrines of the writers of the future are less and less likely to be either urban or rural. They will not be brought up in the Queen Anne rectories of Cotswold villages, or in the half-timbered rooms projecting over the narrow streets of market towns, or even in those neat Regency terraces on the edge of industrial cities, now denominated slums. They will be brought up . . . either in cement tower blocks poised between earth and sky or in chains of semi-detached, chimneyless boxes of pre-constituted stone along by-pass roads, totally divorced from community life and nature. It will be interesting to see what nostalgic effects these cradles of authorship have on their writing.

This astonishingly prolific output, all of high quality (except perhaps for the novel) and produced between the ages of seventy-two and seventy-four, shows that Jim was at the height of his powers as a writer, and had become something of a literary celebrity. He was 'besieged with requests to write books from literary agents and publishers', including a biography of Cyril Connolly and a survey of great architecture to tie in with a television series, both of which he turned down. He did not, however, wish to spend the rest of his working life potboiling, and longed to get his teeth into some serious new work. One little-known figure who interested him as a possible subject was William Bankes (1786–1855), a Beckford-like personality whose promising political career was cut short by a homosexual scandal, obliging him to live abroad. He was a great traveller and art-collector, and a friend of Byron. His country house – Kingston Lacy, Dorset – had recently been bequeathed to the National Trust by its last Bankes owner together with its huge estate and entire contents, including numerous works of art acquired by Bankes (mostly during his exile) and his papers. Jim joined a queue of art historians wishing to read the papers; when he finally saw them, he was disappointed to discover that they contained few documents referring to Bankes's proclivities and disgrace, having presumably been 'weeded' by sub-sequent generations of the family.

Jim was wondering whether there was enough material for the book he had in mind* when another biography was proposed to him – that of Reginald ('Regy') Brett, 2nd Viscount Esher (1852–1930), father of Oliver, 3rd Viscount, who had been Jim's boss and mentor at the National Trust. This extraordinary figure had been a confidant of all three sovereigns under whom he had lived, as well as of every prime minister from Rosebery to Lloyd George. Though offered a host of exalted posts by both political parties, from Secretary of State for War to Viceroy of India, he only ever held two minor offices, in the Civil Service as Secretary to the Office of Works and in the Royal Household as Deputy Constable of Windsor Castle. He shunned the limelight for two reasons – because he believed that power is best exercised from the shadows; and because he feared the lime-light might draw attention to the fact that, although married with four children, he was romantically interested, from his Eton schooldays onwards, in adolescent boys. Ever since the death of Oliver Esher (who had hated his father) in 1963, his son Lionel, the 4th Viscount and a distin-guished architect, had been trying to find a biographer for his grandfather. As in the case of Harold Nicolson, there was a huge archive of letters and diaries: this included a mass of vaguely compromising material about his relations with various boys and young men which his son and grandson, unlike the Bankes family, had preserved *in situ*. Lionel had already approached at least half a dozen historians with the subject, promising them complete access to the papers along with an eager publisher in the form of Lord Longford of Sidgwick & Jackson; three distinguished names – Philip Magnus, Michael Howard and Max Egremont – had accepted in turn, only to change their minds. Rather to Jim's surprise, as they had quarrelled a decade earlier over the redevelopment of Bath,† Lionel, meeting Jim at a concert in July 1982, offered the book to him. Jim (who had already heard about the project a year earlier from another author who had been approached, Frances Donaldson) was in two minds. 'How much do I want to tackle this man's life? He is not romantic. He is an establishment figure

---

*After thinking about the project for most of the 1980s, Jim finally decided not to write about Bankes. A biography by Anne Sebba, *The Exiled Collector*, was published by John Murray in 2004.

†Much of the demolition in Bath (actual and proposed) had been in accordance with plans drawn up the architect Sir Hugh Casson. Lionel Esher, a friend of Casson, had defended his proposals in the correspondence columns of *The Times*, provoking furious replies from Jim.

with a skeleton in the cupboard.' On the other hand, he was intrigued by the mysteriousness of both the private life and the public influence. In October he visited Cambridge, where he spent three days going through Regy's papers, which Lionel had deposited at Churchill College ('a beastly building, like an enormous public lavatory . . . surely Churchill would be even more appalled by the college named after him than he was by Graham [Sutherland]'s portrait of him'). Finally Jim agreed to write the book on condition that he could have the papers in Bath and use the Royal Archives. It took time to get permission for the latter, as the Queen had to be consulted; but by the end of the year the Royal consent was forthcoming, and Jim 'cleared the decks' to get down to Regy in 1983.

Jim proceeded with Regy much as he had with Harold, spending almost two years working methodically through the vast corpus of papers and taking copious notes. He also did research in the Royal Archives and other collections, spoke to the few ancient individuals who remembered Regy (from whom he learnt little of value), and visited places connected with his subject. Among the people he consulted was Sir Philip Magnus, one of the historians who had 'chucked' the project. Magnus – the ultimate closet queen, who had known Harold Nicolson and been in love with James Pope-Hennessy – confirmed that it was Regy's proclivities which had deterred him from proceeding, and warned Jim that he would find Regy's official work very boring and would be so fascinated by the private life that he would 'concentrate on that to the exclusion of all else'. This proved to be not far from the case: whenever Jim uncovered evidence of Regy's peccadilloes, he was like a pig who had found a truffle. (To be fair, however, he was also interested in Regy's relations with the sovereigns he had served; and although bored by Regy's political activities, he nevertheless spent countless hours compiling notes about them.) Two discoveries excited him particularly. He found that a schoolfriend of Regy and fellow protégé of the great Eton housemaster William Cory (who was ultimately sacked for becoming too intimate with boys in his care) was his own great-uncle Fred Lees. And whereas Regy's relations with his highly intelligent elder son Oliver (Jim's future boss) were mutually mistrustful, his feelings towards his rather dim younger son Maurice were positively incestuous: when Maurice went to Eton, Regy wrote him frank love-letters, addressing him as 'Molly' and encouraging him to write back with details of sexual frolics with schoolfriends. (The relationship may have had a physical dimension: as Regy reminded 'Molly', then aged nineteen, in 1901, 'I was almost certainly the first human being who kissed you at all, and quite certainly the first who kissed you passionately.') For Jim, the big difference between Harold and Regy was that he did not find the latter sympathetic, though he was intrigued by him – indeed, 'intrigue' of various sorts was the main thing about him.

A bizarre paradox was that, whereas Jim earned fairly modest sums from his writing in the 1980s, Alvilde, who had never been much of a reader let alone a writer, was responsible in her seventies for a series of best-selling books. She had now won some renown as a gardener (since they had settled at Essex House she had created another superb garden there); and with a fellow gardener, Rosemary Verey, she compiled a volume entitled *The Englishwoman's Garden*. The formula was suggested by the publisher Sebastian Walker: forty women, most of whom might be termed upper-class, wrote about the gardens they had created, which were illustrated with sumptuous photography. Published by Chatto in 1980, it proved a runaway success for the Christmas market. *The Englishman's Garden* followed in 1982. (Whereas half the 'Englishwomen' were titled, half the 'Englishmen' were gay.) Alvilde and Rosemary then fell out and ended their collaboration; but Alvilde, now with Derry Moore as her photographer, continued producing books according to the same winning formula – *The Englishwoman's House* in 1984; *The Englishman's Room* in 1986; *The New Englishwoman's Garden* in 1988. Jim wrote that she was earning huge sums from these works, far more than he had ever earned from his; but he was not the least envious – on the contrary, he was delighted for her. And her success did not end there. Having read *The Englishman's Garden*, Mick Jagger asked Rupert Loewenstein, his manager and a friend of the Lees-Milnes, if she would lay out the garden of his recently acquired *manoir* at Amboise on the Loire. This commission proved a boon for both parties: it gave Alvilde an absorbing occupation for the rest of her life, while Jagger, used to receiving the adulation of women, was fascinated by this bossy upper-class matron who treated him like a naughty child. Before long she was inundated with requests from other eminent people to design or advise on their gardens, and able to command high fees. This new influx of wealth was welcome, as she was finding the maintenance of her daughter Clarissa and four Luke grandchildren an increasing drain on her resources: indeed, in the month *The Englishwoman's Garden* appeared she became a great-grandmother when her eldest grandchild, Chloë, aged nineteen, 'produced an infant' (as Jim expressed it).

The contributions to *The Englishman's Room* included one by Jim on his Bath library, which is self-revealing. He wrote that the presence of Beckford was 'keenly felt by me. It is my belief that presences of the dead, or ghosts if you will, can only survive in rooms which have not been structurally tampered with and redecorated, as is the case here.' As the library faced south, it attracted sunlight; Jim used blinds to restrict this, creating 'what Horace Walpole called "a Gothic gloomth" which suits my splenetic temperament'. In describing the possessions with which he had furnished the room, including portraits of his undistinguished ancestors, he admitted that 'on the whole I prefer the dead to the living, and things to people. I adore my possessions, perhaps because they are so few and comparatively valueless.' As for books, 'I simply worship them'; one of his greatest regrets was having had to part with most of his library on leaving Alderley; above all he loved works of reference, which comprised 'the profoundest thoughts and most beautiful words of the greatest men and women of the world encapsulated within one's reach'. He loved routine, aiming to arrive at his library for work and leave again at the same time every day; if his dogs accompanied him, they were trained to recognise the clock-chimes and expect their dinner at midday and their walk at three. Returning to Beckford, Jim was 'not quite sure how much he likes having me here. At times he makes me feel an interloper. But he has got to put up with me for a little while longer. Meanwhile my library is a private retreat to which human visitors are admitted on sufferance.'

It was still part of Jim's routine to go to London for a night each week. By 1983, when he gave up most of his committee work, these visits tended to follow an established pattern. He usually aimed to see, however briefly, two beloved friends who were older than himself, Eardley and Rosamond, and two younger friends, John Kenworthy-Browne and (when I was in London and not in Paris) myself. (Jim remarked that John and I – we had still not met and hardly knew of each other – provided contrasting company, John, in his early fifties, thoughtful and melancholy, I, in my late twenties, full of evanescent enthusiasms.) He also conscientiously visited friends who were ailing, such as John Betjeman. He haunted three establishments which were a short walk from each other and where he ran into many old friends: Brooks's, where he now generally stayed; the London Library, where he looked up references and changed books; and Heywood Hill's bookshop, where he exchanged social and literary gossip with the manager, John Saumarez Smith. Also nearby were the galleries where he saw the latest exhibitions, and the offices of Chatto and of his literary agent Bruce Hunter (of whom he became increasingly fond).

He continued to travel energetically. Most years he went abroad with Eardley, when they walked and talked. (Alvilde, who was excluded from this friendship, once asked Jim what they talked about. 'I said what do oldest friends talk about on walks? Everything. Non-stop. Politics, the world, friends, his painting, my writing, our loves, sex, God.') In 1982, aged seventy-four, he again experienced the spiritual delights and physical hardships of Mount Athos with Derek Hill. He also accompanied Alvilde on three intercontinental journeys – to Australia in 1980, South Africa in 1983 and the United States in 1985. In each of these countries they were made a great fuss of by the grandest people, especially in Australia where Alvilde still had many friends from the days of her father's governorship in Adelaide. Jim was interested to see the flora, fauna and architecture of these distant lands, but was worn out by the endless round of entertainment, and extremely bored by having to meet and be polite to people he felt he had little in common with. At Washington's National Gallery they attended the opening of the great loan exhibition *Treasure Houses of Britain*, organised by Gervase Jackson-Stops: while quite enjoying this event and the associated festivities, Jim counted the days until their return.

An aspect of Jim's life in the 1980s which provided material for his diary was that he quite often found himself meeting royalty. This was by accident rather than design: he rarely enjoyed these encounters, and had 'no wish to be taken up by royalty or move in royal circles'. Presented to the Duke of Gloucester, 'an undistinguished youth, badly dressed in a sloppy city suit', at Montacute on the fiftieth anniversary of its donation to the National Trust, he found the conversation, as usual on such occasions, 'clipped, awkward and pointless'. The Duke tactfully enquired whether Jim still wrote books. ('I suppose I looked old and gaga.') After their banal exchange, Jim reflected: 'It must be agony for "them". I fancy one should be tremendously jolly and crack jokes. That is what "they" like.' At least the Duke tried to be agreeable, whereas Princess Margaret, whom Jim met at a charity event, 'was not gracious and a little brash . . . How I hate meeting royalty. One gets absolutely nowhere.' On the other hand, Jim got a voyeuristic kick out of observing royalty. He was intrigued to see them lined up in St George's Chapel when he and Alvilde accompanied the Droghedas to the Garter Stalls on Christmas Day. ('Queen wearing hideous turquoise blue dress. Prince of Wales with scar on left cheek. Duke of Edinburgh shorter than I supposed, and lined. Princess Pushy of Kent, as they call her, in hideous hat. Prince Michael's beard a mistake. Princess of Wales sweet. Old Duchess of Gloucester a sweet, shrunken old lady.') He also enjoyed hearing inside gossip from friends at Court such as Fortune Grafton (Mistress of the Robes) and

David Herbert's sister Patricia Hambleden (Lady-in-Waiting to the Queen Mother). (He learned some interesting things about the royal attitude regarding the Duchess of Windsor and Maître Blum, which he passed on to me.)

Meeting the Prince of Wales at drinks with the Queen's Private Secretary at Windsor, Jim did not find him very bright or well-informed (he asked whether Jim had 'started' the National Trust), but thought he had 'the best complexion of a young man I have ever seen' and was impressed by his interest in preservation. Subsequent experiences confirmed his impression of the Prince's earnestness and good manners. Meeting the Queen Mother at a reception of the Keats–Shelley Committee (mercifully, Badminton provided a subject for conversation), he found the encounter 'artificial and profitless', though he was impressed by her stamina. 'For an hour and a half she stood . . . talking to total strangers and making herself agreeable.' In 1982 he was presented to the Queen at Hatchards' Authors-of-the-Year Party.

> She said, 'Are you an author? . . .' I said, 'Yes, I suppose I can call myself one, Ma'am.' 'And what books, what are you . . .?', she began. So . . . I explained that I had recently written a biography of Sir Harold Nicolson. 'Such an interesting man,'[*] she said, 'but it must have been an uphill struggle?' 'It wasn't so much a struggle as rather onerous,' I replied, 'because of the quantity of letters the Nicolsons wrote to each other . . .' Then we talked about letters. She asked if I kept them. I said I kept a great many . . . 'But do you re-read them?' I said I seldom did because I found it sad work. 'Oh, I don't find it sad,' she said. And I, rather cheekily, 'Well, Ma'am, you are so much younger than I am. But most of the letters I have kept are from dead friends.' Then a few more *politesses* and she passed on. But . . . far from being stuffy or awkward, she was bright, extremely natural, and rather funny. I would far prefer to sit next to her than the Q. Mother. There is none of that sugary insincerity in the Queen. She is absolutely direct. V. dignified notwithstanding. Face to face she is good-looking, with that wonderful complexion.

Interestingly, the royal with whom Jim made the greatest hit was the black sheep of the family, Princess Michael of Kent. Meeting Jim in 1979 at a charity concert, she declared that she was a fan of his books and longed to have a proper talk with him. Jim took this with a pinch of salt, and was surprised when, four years later, she asked him and Alvilde to

---

[*] She had invested him as a KCVO in 1952 after he had written the official biography of her grandfather George V.

dine at Nether Lypiatt Manor (a house Jim had known in the 1940s when it was owned by another man-eater, Violet Woodhouse). Once the guests had assembled – received by the Prince, 'a poor, but very gentle and courteous little mouse' – she made a theatrical entrance. 'With a rush as of Pentecostal wind, *She* appeared, like a gigantic Peter Pan fairy alighting on the stage at the end of a wire, large, handsome, Valkyrian, blond hair over shoulders in straight Alice in Wonderland rays.' When Jim rejoined the ladies after dinner, the Princess

> took me by the arm and hand and led me into a corner. Most intimate and cosy. Is flirtatious. I tried not to press her hand back, lest *lèse-majesté*. She told me how these last few years have taught her never to believe anything in the newspapers . . . Told me her mother was in prison when pregnant with her, just before end of war. Was released for birth of child. I said, 'Oh Ma'am, but how romantic it would have been for you to be born in prison.' Remark not favourably received . . . Was very saddened by the death of her favourite brown Persian cat. Knocked over by a car on road, it tried to walk home but died en route. She said with tears in her eyes that this cat's death meant more to her than the deaths of most of her friends and relations. She is writing life of Queen of Bohemia, but said she had too little time, and must resort to an assistant. At this I trembled, but said nothing . . . It is impossible not to like this un-royal princess, with her beauty, vitality and friendliness.

On parting, the Princess said how much she hoped to see Jim again; but it was another four years before she next issued an invitation – by which time her book had appeared and been savagely criticised for plagiarism.

> The truth is one cannot dislike the Princess. She is extremely friendly, anxious to please, does please, and makes one feel interesting. Also she enjoys conversation and has a poor opinion of the English, calling them the stupidest nation in Europe. She particularly dislikes their false modesty, which she finds hypocritical. They must always deprecate themselves. At that moment, one of the guests . . . asked me across the table, 'Which of your books do you think the best?' I at once replied, 'They are all pretty bad.' 'There you go!' said H.R.H. 'What did I tell you?' She is aggrieved over the reception of her book here. Said she had frankly confessed in her preface that she had done no original research and derived her opinions from other learned historians whose names she quoted . . . 'Anyway,' she said, rubbing her hands, 'all the beastliness has given me much publicity and I have sold 60,000 copies so far, with American sales still to come.' I congratulated her heartily, telling her that no book of mine had sold 6,000. She makes it very clear by innuendo that she dislikes the Royal Family . . .

One occasion attended by the entire Royal Family was Master's funeral at Badminton: he died in February 1984, aged eighty-three, from a heart attack after hunting. He had been the local 'royalty' and his passing was regarded as an event of mystical significance, attended by omens: the night before the funeral, his hounds kept up a continuous baying. Even Jim, not Master's greatest fan, felt a certain awe. The ceremony, witnessed and recorded by Jim, was stark in its simplicity: the bearers of the coffin were estate servants, including Gerald, husband of the Lees-Milnes' daily Peggy; following behind were huntsmen in full rig; the Last Post was played by a bugler of the Gloucestershire Hussars. A pathetic note was provided by Mary Beaufort, now so vague as to be unaware of the purpose of the proceedings. Jim was moved, though glad that the occasion gave rise to a few jokes. Selina Hastings wrote to him: 'Honey and Folly [the Lees-Milnes' whippets whom Master had once threatened to shoot] must be very happy little dogs. Will they be having a party to celebrate?' Derry Moore suggested that 'the late Duke's mistresses ought to have been parked, like nuns behind a grille, in the gallery of the church during the funeral . . . How they would have hated each other.'

Master's death heralded a big change in the Lees-Milnes' lives at Badminton, for their friends the Somersets succeeded as the reigning Duke and Duchess. Happily, David Beaufort (as he now was) had already made a substantial fortune as an art dealer, so was able to pay death duties without having to sell off too much of the estate, and undertake a thorough restoration of the house and its art treasures. (On the other hand, he was only moderately keen on hunting, and inevitably dispensed with many of the traditions which had been kept up by Master.) Whereas Master had barely tolerated the 'pointless' Lees-Milnes, they were now treated as friends of the family. The Beauforts sought Jim's advice over their improvements to the House, and had him as their first dinner guest (Alvilde being absent) when they moved in a year later. ('David kept asking how I liked what they had done, which is indeed in the best possible taste.') Henceforth Jim and Alvilde were regularly entertained at the House, especially when there were other interesting guests, and joined the family for Christmas lunch at Badminton. (Whereas Alvilde adored their being the Beauforts' 'friends in the village', Jim, while enjoying it, did not feel entirely comfortable with it. There was a jet-setting element to the lives of the Beauforts and their four children which was alien to him. He found David 'charming yet ruthless, apparently highly sensitive to one's feelings, yet he would probably not care tuppence if one dropped down dead at his feet'. David and Caroline led independent lives which must have reminded him of his parents' in the 1920s, and he was embarrassed, for Caroline's sake, when David installed his mistress Miranda in a house on the estate.)

In August 1983 Jim had turned seventy-five. 'One is aware of one's utter insignificance' was his typical diary comment – though he was also aware that he had entered the pantheon of national figures. His birthday was now mentioned in *The Times*. He was invited to be a guest of honour at Foyles Literary Luncheons (though mercifully not to speak at them). Faber & Faber were about to publish paperback editions of *Another Self* and his three volumes of diaries. His retirement from the National Trust Properties Committee was marked by a dinner in his honour at one of the houses he had 'saved' – Fenton House, Hampstead.

Apart from arthritis in his right shoulder and some sight-weakness in his left eye, he seemed in good health for his age. In 1982 a check-up had revealed that he had suffered 'a small coronary attack' which he had been unaware of; but this had not prevented him from visiting Mount Athos with Derek later that year. However, in March 1984 he learned that he needed an operation on his prostate. He wrote resignedly in his diary:

> What are my feelings? Of course dreading the worst. But not so shaken as I would have been twenty years ago, for I am approaching the natural term of my life. I don't want poor darling A. to be worried and unhappy. I don't want to leave her. But apart from abandoning her to wrestle alone, without very intimate friends and with that irresponsible and demanding Luke family, there is no one else but M. I regret leaving. And he being so young cannot miss me for long. One thing I dread, and that is recovering from this operation to be told I have got cancer, and dragging on, operation after operation, drug after drug, being a perfect nuisance to others and an abject misery to myself. In that event I would prefer to die under the anaesthetic. But I would like to finish Regy, my novel, and tidying up my remaining [1940s] diaries. I have no other ambitions.

The operation revealed that Jim was indeed suffering from cancer, and required further surgery to remove his testicles. He thought of his father, who had died in agony of bladder cancer, aged sixty-nine. At the same time he could find a grim humour in the situation.

> Motoring into Bath yesterday I found myself behind a small car in the back window of which was a printed label FLASH YOUR LIGHTS IF YOU FIND ME SEXY. I could only see the driver's head. It did not make a sensational appeal. Now, ten years ago I would have flashed for the fun of the adventure. Alas, I thought, I have a mere three days left in which I remain a man, and even so, the experience is out of the question.

As he faced up to cancer and a second operation, he drew close to Alvilde, who offered just the right combination of breezy optimism, no–nonsense practicality and sympathetic care. 'My one overpowering desire now', he wrote, 'is to be with A.' Henceforth there were to be few clouds upon their marriage.

She did not mind when he asked me to spend a night at Badminton just before he went into hospital, saying he wished to consult me as his literary executor. I found him in a state of serenity. He wanted my views on which of his three current writing projects he should concentrate on in the possibly limited time left to him. I gave him the obvious advice: that if he only had a short time to live, he wouldn't be able to finish Regy anyway; that his novel had already been written, and just needed revising; but that he was most likely to be remembered for his diaries and that he alone could edit the next volume (covering 1948 and 1949), especially as it concerned the delicate matter of his courtship with Alvilde. (He showed me the originals of these diaries, a combination of engagement books and bundles of loose notes held together with rubber bands, many of them in shorthand.)

The operation was a success, and Jim was to experience no recurrence of cancer for almost four years – though this was not immediately apparent, and for some weeks he experienced persistent bleeding and felt he might be dying. When he realised that, for the moment at any rate, he was better, he experienced a sense of rebirth. He was untroubled by the absence of sexual feelings, which brought 'enhanced detachment'. He was however saddened at this time by the deaths of two men who had meant much to him. His brother Dick, two years his junior, died in Cyprus, of an illness possibly caused by the cotton dust he had inhaled during the twenty-five years he had struggled to run the family mill in Lancashire. Hearing that he was sinking, Jim felt 'as if part of my own life is draining away with him, as though we were twins. Yet we drifted apart in life, without a jot of mutual dislike, just through sheer difference of environment and interests, coupled with the fact that [his wife] Elaine never let us have a moment together.' And John Betjeman, who had been suffering from Parkinson's disease, died in Cornwall. Though still weak from his operation, Jim attended the funeral, which took place in the tiny and romantically isolated church of St Enodoc during a dramatic storm, with drinks afterwards at the cottage which John had shared with Elizabeth Cavendish. It was a slightly uncomfortable occasion, being attended by the deceased's wife (Penelope), mistress (Elizabeth) and former fiancée (Billa Harrod). 'Anyway, I have paid my respects to the best man who ever lived and the most loveable . . . The poignancy of sitting on John's little death-bed with Archie the teddy bear and Jumbo the elephant propped against the pillow.'

Back in the land of the living, Jim edited his diaries (published by Faber in 1985 as *Midway on the Waves* – Jim no longer felt loyalty to Chatto following the death of Norah Smallwood), rewrote his novel, and then returned to Regy. As with *Harold*, he produced this enormous and complex biography at furious speed. Having finished his research, he began writing it on 1 November 1984 and completed a first draft, running to some 300,000 words, in April 1985. Before showing it to the publishers he had to have it approved by Lionel Esher, and obtain royal approval for those parts of it which derived from the Royal Archives. Lionel was pleased with it (or at least relieved that the biography had finally been written), though he asked Jim to remove some 'smutty' references to 'Regy's vicarious enjoyment of his son [Maurice]'s affairs at Eton'. The Queen, who, to Jim's amazement, read the submitted extracts herself, was also rather shocked by some of the things they contained, such as that Lord Esher had had a crush on her great-uncle Edward, Prince of Wales (the future Duke of Windsor) – though she requested no changes. In December 1985 Jim took the revised manuscript to London to deliver it to Sidgwick & Jackson. He found himself in a predicament familiar to many authors, as the people in the firm with whom he had originally dealt (the Chairman Lord Longford, and his editor Margaret Willes) had now left, it being far from certain that their successors would regard the book with the same interest or enthusiasm. Jim's description of the long-anticipated moment of delivery is poignant.

Carried my Regy typescript to Sidgwick & Jackson, having telephoned last week to forewarn Mr Robert Smith, my new editor. Hateful dealing with new people who know not my ways, probably not my name even. I reached the door on which a notice directed me to another entrance in Museum Street. I suppose I was looking around while walking, for I stumbled on the pavement and fell headlong into the gutter. Lay there a few seconds, assessing situation. Decided I was not badly hurt, and picked myself up. Contents of my pockets were strewn in the gutter, but not so my typescript, which remained in its cardboard box. Arrived shaken, hands cut, clothes torn, face dirty. Surprised lady directed me to lavatory. No concern. When I indicated the typescript, she said coolly, 'Just put it down there, will you.' After four years' intensive labour, the precious thing was accepted as though it might be an unwelcome Christmas card. God knows if it will even reach Mr Smith. How I hate Regy. Fed up with

him. And the more I revise, the more corrections I find to make. I hope
to spend the next month without hearing of him. But when I do, no doubt
it will be to be asked to cut the book down by a third.

In the event Sidgwick, though daunted by the book's length, liked it, and
the changes they proposed were not as drastic as Jim had feared. It
was published in October 1986 as *The Enigmatic Edwardian* to admiring
reviews – though as a biography of someone few had heard of its commercial prospects were limited, and some outrage was expressed at Jim's
exposure of Regy's paedophilia, notably by the descendants of the adored
Maurice. The book is a substantial achievement for a writer in his late seventies, and probably comes as close as is possible to demystifying its subject,
dealing delicately (if pruriently) with Regy's private life and giving a comprehensive account of his relations with leading figures and various public
activities (though Jim barely conceals his boredom with such subjects as
army and navy reform). Its weakness is that, after ploughing through such
a mass of material, Jim sometimes could not see the wood for the trees: he
missed, for example, the fact that Regy, who at the Office of Works was
responsible for organising such occasions as Queen Victoria's Diamond
Jubilee and King Edward VII's Coronation, effectively invented modern
royal ceremonial. Taken together, *Harold Nicolson* and *The Enigmatic
Edwardian* paint a fascinating picture of British high politics and society
from the 1870s to the 1960s, as seen by two men who were able to view them
with a certain detachment owing to their unconventional sexual natures.

Apart from Regy, Jim's other literary achievement in the mid 1980s
was his diary, which conveys a strong flavour of the times. He recorded
the arrival of the AIDS epidemic ('I hope I am immune'), which eventually carried off several of his friends – Rory Cameron, Ian McCallum,
Bruce Chatwin, Gervase Jackson-Stops. He was fascinated by Mrs
Thatcher, of whom he heard accounts from those of his friends (such as
Derry Moore and Selina Hastings) who met her, mostly to the effect that
she 'was like a steamroller' who talked and rarely listened. His admiration
for her fearlessness in standing up to the unions and other 'enemies' at
home and abroad knew no bounds. At the same time, he was disturbed
that her regime seemed to be creating greater extremes of wealth and
poverty. When, in 1987, he wrote a book on Cotswold country houses,
he was concerned to discover that much of the countryside was being
taken over by a new class of metropolitan spivs.

This was Jim's first 'architectural' book since *Baroque Country Houses*
two decades earlier, after writing which he had rather lost interest in

architecture. In 1980 he shocked Desmond Shawe-Taylor by remarking
that

> I was no longer the least interested in the National Trust, or in architec-
> ture. Why, he asked? Well, I think it may be because I have given up the
> battle of conservation. The world is ruined, and that's that. Besides, having
> looked after the N.T's buildings for so many years, my interest has just
> evaporated, and that's all there is to it. But it shouldn't be, he said. Are you
> no longer interested in the buildings of Venice or Rome? You were never
> in charge of buildings in those two cities. I am not interested in them from
> a scientific point of view, I said, only from a general aesthetic one, or for
> associative reasons. The intricacies of architecture bore me now.

However, during the 1980s his enthusiasm both for the Trust and for
architecture revived somewhat. He was touched by the tributes he
received on his retirement from the Properties Committee in 1983, and
early the following year defended the Trust when it was attacked by
Roger Scruton in *The Times*. (Scruton argued that for a house to fall to
the Trust amounted to the 'dead hand' of nationalisation; Jim riposted
that, in many cases, the only alternative was literal death and demolition.)
He was glad to be invited to stay on as a member of the Trust's Arts Panel,
and excited to see and advise on new additions to the Trust's portfolio of
country houses (they were few in number, but mostly spectacular) such
as Canons Ashby, Northamptonshire and Calke Abbey, Derbyshire. He
developed a warm friendship with Dame Jennifer Jenkins, who became
the Trust's Chairman in 1986.

Despite this reviving interest Jim, who was again thinking of writing
a biography of William Bankes, might have turned down the proposal
that he write a book on Cotswold houses had not the proposer, David
Burnett of the Dovecote Press, been 'an utterly charming man . . . tall,
strong, handsome and sensitive'. When David offered to drive him
around the houses which might be included in the volume, Jim could not
resist. In March and April 1987 he enjoyed half-a-dozen 'blissful'
reconnaissance expeditions in David's company, finding him

> a perfect companion. Treats me as though I were Dresden porcelain.
> Always solicitous as to whether I am not too cold, too tired, etc. He leaps
> from the wheel to ask directions and questions while I sit like Buddha
> wrapped up in front seat poring over the map. We eat deliciously in pubs,
> make jokes and laugh. He has the sort of humour that I appreciate.

'It is a long time since I have driven round the counties and looked at
houses with a critical eye,' Jim wrote. On the whole, he was happy with

what he saw of the great mansions which remained in the hands of the families which had built them, such as Cirencester and Stanway, or of houses which continued to have traditional owners, such as Sezincote. These were mostly well kept up, with care and taste. What shocked him was the condition of the many lesser houses which had been bought by rich commuters. 'The village people don't like these fly-by-night, new rich, suburban-minded, totally non-country folk, who bring their middle-class friends and cocktail bars for a few days and are of no use to the community.' Such owners invariably 'tarted up' their properties with unnecessary alterations, and their taste was usually execrable. 'No one stays long. Each owner undoes what the previous one did. No owner leaves well alone.' Even worse was the condition of large houses which had been bought by developers. The spectacle at Northwick Park, which Jim had known in the 1930s, was

> horrifying. There stands the great house in the middle of the erstwhile park, a mile from Blockley village in an area of outstanding natural beauty. It was unapproachable, for one drive was blocked up, the other so churned by tractors and tree-felling vehicles that we could not get up to it. A long row of hideous garages with blue doors newly erected; pegged strips in the park where new residences will be built. Northwick, where George Churchill lived surrounded by precious pictures and works of art, can henceforth be erased from the memory.

Some houses were being converted into flats, which was 'a good idea in principle, but the conversions are seldom sympathetic'. Jim was depressed by so much evidence of degradation, though he produced a charming book dealing with twenty-eight houses which could still be considered beautiful, concentrating on their historical associations and general aesthetic effect rather than their architectural details. He wrote it with his usual speed, and David Burnett also showed extraordinary efficiency in getting it out before the end of 1987. 'How sad I am', Jim wrote, 'that my association with this adorable man is coming to an end.'

Almost simultaneously with *Some Cotswold Country Houses* Jim wrote *Venetian Evenings*, a belated sequel to *Roman Mornings*, having been pressed to do so by Collins, who published it (together with a reprint of the earlier work) in 1988. He spent ten days in Venice selecting and studying the monuments he wished to include, hardly speaking to a soul. Yet he admitted to his diary that he felt little of the inspiration which had moved him to write *Roman Mornings* thirty years earlier ('my love affair with Venice ended years ago'); nor did he enjoy the visit much ('the terrible scourge in Italy today is the schoolchildren and undisciplined teenagers who swarm like locusts, making shrines disgusting with their litter, their transistors, their rudeness, their mere presence'). He dedicated it 'to Alvilde, who is always in a hurry' – a tribute which did not please her, especially as, when the book was printed, her name was wrongly spelled.

For some years Debo Devonshire had been urging Jim to undertake a biography of her hero the 6th Duke of Devonshire (1790–1858), known as 'the Bachelor': he was a great art-collector who beautified Chatsworth, patron of the gardener and architect Joseph Paxton, and a Whig statesman who became Lord Chamberlain to William IV. After Jim had finished with Regy she pressed him more strongly, knowing he was at a loose end. In February 1987 Jim visited Chatsworth to discuss the project with her and see the Bachelor Duke's papers. The latter were voluminous, and Jim 'soon discovered what I had feared, that his handwriting is appalling and gets worse as his life progresses – or as it ebbs, as mine is doing'. However, Debo dismissed his objections, insisting that it was the ideal subject for him and bound to interest a publisher.

> There was sex (which seems to amount to his having kept a mistress . . . like any other aristocrat); there was royalty (true, relations with George IV and William IV may prove interesting); he was one of the greatest collectors of books, pictures, furniture and, above all, sculpture; and he was a great builder and gardener, with Paxton. Friendship is another quality Debo emphasizes. So I find myself in the predicament of trying to respond to D's immense enthusiasm while having grave doubts – about my ability to read his writing, about my having to spend months here (for I don't suppose they will let me take the papers away), and about my state of health, for I doubt if I can summon the strength to embark on another long book of this sort.

On at least one of these points Debo was able to reassure him: though she hoped he would spend much time at Chatsworth, there was no problem with his having the Bachelor's papers in Bath. Jim gave in, and agreed to write the book. In October, having finished his two architectural volumes, he visited Chatsworth again and took away four boxes of the Bachelor's diaries. After struggling through these ('the handwriting still strikes me as appalling'), he wondered what he had let himself in for.

> He knew everyone in London and cosmopolitan society, and had hundreds of guests to stay at Chatsworth and Devonshire House, where he entertained more lavishly and exclusively than any other nobleman. Yet seldom does he give any description of these endless acquaintances and his meetings with them. I am seizing upon any straw to suggest that he is an

interesting character, but so far I don't think he is a character who will appeal to the readers of today, who are not interested in dukes merely because they are dukes and have left lists of encounters with their peers. He had his mistress; but what duke did and does not? That is of no interest unless scandals and domestic complications ensue, and being a bachelor he had no wife to take exception. He was highly neurotic, writes of his health on every page, was always gripped by some cold or fever, and always tired. I suspect he suffered from depression, and drank. I dare not tell Debo that I don't really think he is the material for a biography; nor do I wish to concentrate on his great works at Chatsworth and Bolton and Hardwick, about which too much has been written already. Oh dear!

Jim suspected (and doubtless hoped) that his new subject, with his sensitivity as a connoisseur and restless disposition (not to mention his lack of inclination to marry), might be sexually ambiguous like the previous two; but there was not much to go on, except that the Bachelor had something of a crush in his youth on the future Emperor Nicholas I of Russia (said to be the handsomest man in Europe), and in later life became quite attached to one of his nephews.

Since his brush with cancer in 1984 Jim had been in reasonable health, except for eye trouble which necessitated a cataract operation. Shortly before Christmas 1987, however, he became aware of a 'swelling on the right side of my face'. His doctor was concerned, and arranged for him to have a biopsy. Jim was resigned to bad news. 'After all, my life is almost done, cancer or no cancer, and my working life finishing. I wish, oh how I wish it had been more successful.' When he was told that he was suffering from a malignant growth inside his cheek, and ought to begin a course of radiotherapy without delay, he at first said he 'would rather not, as the sooner I died the better'; but on being informed that this death might be slow and messy, he agreed to have the treatment. It lasted a month, and was painful and debilitating ('truly, I don't remember ever suffering such agony as I am now undergoing'), but it did the trick – though Jim took some time to get over it, his sense of taste and smell were impaired, and the whole experience aged him.

Such is the unfairness of life that, while Jim was undergoing and recovering from this cancer treatment, he had to endure the climax of a ghastly year-long drama. Since moving to Badminton in 1975 he and Alvilde had let the furnished basement of their Bath property to a succession of naval commanders from the nearby Ministry of Defence establishment. The rent was modest, £160 a month; in return, the tenants undertook to look after the small garden. This arrangement worked satisfactorily for a decade or so, until a departing commander asked if a girlfriend who had been living with him there might succeed him as tenant. Jim soon regretted agreeing to this: the girl created much disturbance, neglected her duties with regard to the garden, and fell behind with the rent. In May 1987 Jim asked her to leave, out of kindness giving her six months' notice instead of the three stipulated by their informal (but signed) agreement. However, as the months passed, it became clear that she would not budge; and the Lees-Milnes' solicitors informed them that the only way to get rid of her was either to put in motion a slow and costly legal process, or to pay her a large sum (she asked for £10,000) to quit. Jim was incensed, especially on learning that the girl's parents were selling a house behind Lansdown Crescent for £750,000. 'The law is not just an ass – it is a fiend.' The drama struck a gruesome note in February 1988, when Jim was in the midst of his radiotherapy.

> Just before I left Bath for my treatment in Bristol, the telephone rang. It was Miss X., the frightful basement tenant we are trying to get rid of, to say her bedroom had been flooded. I suggested she either contact my solicitors or call a plumber. Five minutes later the doorbell rang, and I was confronted with an unknown middle-aged woman. 'I am Miss X's mother,' she said. 'You must come down and do something about the water.' I declined. 'But this is my daughter's home and she is not well,' she continued. This raised my ire. 'Your daughter is a squatter in my house,' I retorted. 'It is not her flat at all. She is remaining there in flagrant breach of our agreement.' Woman then turned very nasty. 'She has every right to remain,' she hissed, 'as you will find out when the case comes up.' I then told her that her daughter had no sense of honour, adding, 'And she is a little bitch.' That was a mistake. I rang Alvilde to tell her of the encounter, and drove off to Bristol.

Not until August 1988 did the Lees-Milnes manage to get her out – and then only after paying her £1,000, settling a solicitors' bill for a considerably greater sum, and resigning themselves to the wreckage of their garden and their furniture. However, as a writer Jim turned the experience to account. Not only did it provide colourful material for his diary, but he published an article about it in the *Spectator*, reprinted in the local press, which put heart into many people who had been experiencing similar trouble.

15

Grand Old Man
1988–97

'**A**LL MY LIFE I have been a slow developer,' wrote Jim on his fortieth birthday; and certainly his fame was a slowly developing quality. As he approached eighty, he could feel that he had at last 'arrived'. He was seen as a fascinating survivor of his generation, a grand old man of letters and architectural conservation. There was widespread appreciation of the fact that he had been responsible for preserving some of England's greatest country houses. He was besieged with requests to appear on radio and television. His 1940s diaries were recognised both as a masterpiece of literature and a contribution to social history: Patrick Garland proposed to produce a one-man play based on them, featuring Paul Eddington, famous for his appearance in the television series *Yes, Minister*. (The project was thwarted by Eddington's declining health – though after Jim's death another distinguished actor, Moray Watson, would delight audiences with another dramatisation of the diaries, devised by Hugh Massingberd.) His eightieth birthday in August 1988 was marked by lavish press tributes: in the *Telegraph*, Hugh Masssingberd described him as 'a veteran in the war against the philistines' who had 'almost single-handedly saved much of what we now take for granted as the "national heritage"'; in the *Spectator*, John Martin Robinson wrote that 'his many friends and admirers have found his work a constant source of inspiration, solace and encouragement'.

Recognition certainly meant much to Jim, and he noted these develop-ments with satisfaction in his diary. But his attitude, as always, was ambivalent; while craving the world's attention and praise, he also shunned it. His main thought at the time of his birthday was to disappear and avoid all celebrations. (He and Alvilde went to stay in Norfolk with Billa Harrod.) Though 'very gratified' that his diaries might be drama-tised, he felt that he 'could not possibly attend a performance'. He was 'appalled' to be offered the Life Achievement Award of the National Art Collections Fund, involving attendance at a public dinner. He turned down an invitation to be photographed by Lord Snowdon. When he heard that friends were lobbying for him to receive an honour in overdue recognition of his conservation work, he begged them to desist. (They were encouraged by Alvilde – a nice irony, as the main reason Jim had not been honoured on his retirement from the National Trust staff in the 1960s was the fuss she had made over his friendship with John Kenworthy-Browne.) When in November 1992 he was offered a CBE in the forthcoming New Year's Honours List, he had no hesitation in refusing. As he wrote in his diary:

> At my age, I can't face up to all the bother – the congratulations from all and sundry, the letters to be replied to, the investiture ceremony and celebratory dinner. It is too late. I am not interested, and quite content to be just plain me. I daren't tell A., for she might press me to accept. It might have been different had I been offered a knighthood in which she could have shared, or one of the honours in the personal gift of the Queen. The CH is the only honour I really covet, but that would be beyond my deserts.

By then he had received a mark of recognition which meant more to him than any 'gong', having become a John Murray author. The current head of England's oldest publishing dynasty, John Murray VI, known as 'Jock', had been with Jim at Eton; but since the 1930s he had rejected every manuscript Jim had submitted to him, also giving short shrift to his poetry in the 1950s. Jim was amazed to hear from him in August 1989 that he wanted to publish *The Bachelor Duke*. 'A thrill to be published at last by this Rolls-Royce of publishers,' wrote Jim six months later, after delivering the finished work to the famous Murray premises at 50 Albemarle Street. Jock's belated eagerness to recruit Jim to his stable was presumably unrelated to the prospects of the book, which was elegant and erudite but (as Jim admitted) 'lacked sparkle' like its subject. Rather it arose partly from Jim's new-found celebrity, partly from the influence of Debo, who had assured Jim that the Bachelor would find a suitable publisher, and who was 'Queen' of the John Murray world. (Her close circle included top Murray authors such as Patrick Leigh Fermor; and the son of her great friend Kitty Mersey was married to Jock's daughter.) Jim, of course, had 'done' the Bachelor largely to please Debo, and the delight of doing it was that he saw much of her during the three years that he was engaged on it, at Chatsworth and two other Devonshire residences which the Bachelor had haunted, Lismore Castle, Ireland and Bolton Abbey, Yorkshire. As he wrote after staying with her at Lismore:

> I consider Debo the most remarkable woman I know. Because she is a Duchess? Largely yes, because this status has brought out her astonishing

Mitford qualities. I feel that, in any crisis, she would come out top, organise, keep her head, show her innate courage and self-assurance. As it
is, her charm, her 'unbending' (for she does have to unbend from her
Olympian height), and her dignity never fail to captivate.

When Murray published *The Bachelor Duke* in March 1991, Jim's satisfaction was tempered by alarm that they proposed to mark the occasion
with a party at Albemarle Street. This prospect was 'like a rat gnawing
at my vitals. I have nightmares of being hemmed in by a multitude of
faces, recognising no one, hearing nothing, panicking'. However, when
the dreaded day arrived, he

> actually enjoyed it. Numerous friends old and new, plus critics and celeb-
> rities. Everyone enthusiastic about the book and congratulating. Many
> came with book in hand asking for signature. One woman asked me to
> write, 'To Jacqueline Onassis from J.L.-M.' Instead I put, 'For J.O. and *by*
> J.L.-M.' Much photography, I suspect for *Tatler* . . . Certainly I have never
> before been fêted in this way. At nine Jock gave a dinner at Brown's Hotel
> for eight, Devonshires, Murrays, Ariane [Bankes, J.L.-M's editor],
> Gervase [Jackson-Stops] and L.-Ms. I praised God that it was all over and
> had been without embarrassments, feeling rather pleased with myself.

Something which gave Jim almost as much pleasure as the publication
of *The Bachelor Duke* by Murray was the publication of the novel he had
written (and rewritten) during the 1980s by his great-nephew Nick
Robinson, now a successful independent publisher: originally entitled
Innocence, it finally appeared as *The Fool of Love*. That it had been rejected
by at least a dozen other publishers to whom it had been submitted is
perhaps not surprising in view of the plot. The hero, Rupert, is an English
schoolboy who during the First World War has his first sexual experience
with Ernst, a handsome and aristocratic German prisoner who works as
a gardener at the family seat in Staffordshire. Nine months later Rupert's
mother gives birth to another son, Peregrine (whose father is assumed to
be her husband, whom she has in fact not seen for more than a year but
who, returning from the war, does not bother to disclaim the paternity).
After the war Rupert goes cycling in Germany with a view to paying
Ernst, by whom he remains obsessed, a surprise visit. Arriving at Ernst's
castle, he is devastated to find his mother and Ernst *in flagrante delicto*;
cycling away, blinded by tears, he is killed in a road accident. Twenty
years later Peregrine, now a young officer, falls in love with and marries
a German girl, Ernst's daughter, unaware that she is his half-sister: of the
two people who might have warned him, his mother has gone mad and
an elderly, omniscient servant (based on the parlourmaid at Wickhamford)

is rendered speechless by a stroke on hearing the news. The Second World War then breaks out, during which Peregrine is captured by the Germans and executed on the orders of Ernst, who is both his father and his father-in-law. The novel contains some good dialogue and descriptive passages, and is interesting as social history, drawing on Jim's memories of country house life in 1917. What seems strange is that, having been assured by almost everyone who read it that the story simply would not do, Jim remained determined to foist it on the world; he even wrote that he would never forgive any of the rejecting publishers, and was 'out for revenge'. Possibly there were Freudian reasons which impelled him to air the themes of lost innocence, love betrayed, and incest (already aired in *Heretics in Love*). Seeing that it meant so much to him, Nick offered to publish it out of affection. Jim, who loved Nick more than any of his relations, was thrilled; the offer struck him as 'almost incestuous' (though Nick drew the line at the incestuous part of the novel, asking Jim to conclude it with the death of Rupert). Jim then went through much the same psychological process as he had with *Heretics*: as publication (set to coincide with his eighty-second birthday in August 1990) drew near, his delight at its impending appearance gave way to dread. He need not have worried: despite Hugh Massingberd doing a feature on it for the *Telegraph*, it sank without trace.

Jock was meanwhile anxious to get another book out of Jim without delay. He suggested a biography of the recently deceased Sachie Sitwell – but Jim could not face writing another life of a long-lived individual who had left voluminous papers. Instead he took up a suggestion made to him by his 'clever and civilised' cousin Jamie Fergusson, obituaries editor of the *Independent*, that he 'write a book about what he called "my babies" – that is, those houses which the National Trust acquired largely through my efforts'. This project absorbed him throughout 1991. Out of some forty houses he might have written about (which came to the Trust while he was 'running' the Country Houses Scheme from 1936 to 1950), he selected fourteen almost at random – Attingham, Blickling, Brockhampton, Charlecote, Cotehele, Gunby, Hanbury, Hatchlands, Knole, Little Moreton, Smallhythe, Stourhead, Wallington and West Wycombe. Most of these he had not seen for decades, and he was fascinated to revisit them all, some in the company of local friends such as Hugh Massingberd (Gunby), Nigel Nicolson (Smallhythe) and Billa Harrod (Blickling), others under the wing of the National Trust's regional representatives, for whose knowledge, enthusiasm and good taste he conceived much admiration. (His own local representative, Tony

Mitchell, John Kenworthy-Browne's successor at at Dyrham, had become a good friend.) On visits to London he also spent countless hours reading files at the National Trust's Headquarters in Queen Anne's Gate, where he was treated with reverence by the current Historic Buildings Secretary, Martin Drury.

The result, published by Murray as *People & Places*, is an extraordinary book: mostly written in his eighty-fourth year, it is regarded by some as his best work. One might say it is five stories rolled into one: a history of the houses, with a view to evoking in each case its particular flavour and worthiness of preservation; a work of anecdote, both poignant and amusing, on Jim's dealings with the owners; an account of the (often long and tortuous) processes by which the houses were transferred into the Trust's ownership; a survey of the difficulties which the Trust, once it had taken possession of the houses, experienced in maintaining them and showing them to the public; and a personal assessment of the houses today. It is Jim's National Trust testament, a reappraisal, after half a century, of the work he had done for that body in his thirties. The reader is made particularly aware of three facts. First, that the Trust, which by the 1990s had become a huge bureaucratic empire with a staff of thousands and a membership of millions, had in Jim's day been cosy, amateurish and happy-go-lucky to a degree later difficult to conceive. Secondly, that many acquisitions would not have been accomplished but for his patience and tenacity in dealing with the owners or with various authorities (including his own committee) whose co-operation was required. Thirdly, that the original purpose of the country houses scheme was to preserve the buildings not as museums but as living houses in which the donor families continued to reside – though in the majority of cases that was not how it worked out in the end. In fact, by the 1990s only three of the fourteen houses Jim describes (Charlecote, Knole and West Wycombe) were still treated by the families as their homes. Jim's evident regret at this development is emphasised by the fact that his chapter titles refer to the families rather than the houses; but he was nevertheless realistic: he recognised that, for various reasons, many families had little interest in maintaining a connection with their old homes; and certainly the 'museums' which most of the houses had become were magnificent show-pieces, restored and arranged by expert hands, of a sort which could hardly have been imagined before the war. Indeed, he had to admit that Blickling and Cotehele, Stourhead and Wallington were far better kept than in his time, while those few houses which were lucky enough to have found wealthy tenants with good taste from the old gentry class – such as Hatchlands, let to the Anglo-Irish artist and collector of old musical instruments, Alec Cobbe – were not only 'alive' but had been restored to a glory not seen since their heyday. However, while the book's message was essentially positive, there was a lingering note of sadness. Jim recalled a remark Lord Crawford had made in the 1950s, that 'not one person of the next generation will have a clue how country houses were really lived in before the war'. As he wrote after seeing the redecorations at Hanbury, which, unable to attract a suitable tenant, had just been restored by the Trust as a high-class conference and banqueting centre,

> somehow the new curtains seem too sumptuous, the pelmets too swank-ily draped, the wall hangings too vivid, the William and Adelaide Gothick wallpaper in the upstairs corridor (although copied from a fragment found under layers of later paper) almost too imperial, the whole air of well-being too exquisite for Counsellor Vernon [who built the house around 1700] in his old wig and bands, even for the coquettish Emma [a late eighteenth-century heiress] and her adolescent Lord of Burghley, and certainly for homely Sir Harry and his reprobate heir [the twentieth-century donor], to have felt comfortable among such pretension. God knows Hanbury was shockingly neglected by Sir George and has with sweat and tears been rescued from perdition. So why not be intensely grateful and shut up? It is cavalier to complain. And yet, and yet . . . Is Hanbury wholly real inside? Can an ancient squirearchical house be quite the same after such tremendously drastic treatment? Is it not bound to look glossy and almost new? And just very faintly suburban?

People & Places was published by Murray in October 1992. Although the National Trust initially distinguished themselves by refusing to sell it in their shops or even have it reviewed in their magazine,* the press showered it with praise. Apart from uniformly glowing reviews, *The Times* published a feature by its editor Simon Jenkins (destined sixteen years later to become Chairman of the National Trust) paying Jim the unusual compliment of calling him a 'masterly confidence trickster', one of 'a small band of enthusiasts' who 'took it on themselves to induce first a handful, then dozens, then hundreds of grandees to part with houses and estates that had been in their families for generations'. Faced with the eccentricities of the owners Jim encountered,

> most public officials would run for the door and send the local solicitor a form in triplicate. Lees-Milne smiles tolerantly, meeting self-pity with

---

* They relented after Jock's son and others had written in protest to the Chairman and Director-General.

sympathy. I believe Lees-Milne is stating some fundamental truths about all public administration, not just the custodianship of historic houses. His approach was based not on organisation and authority but on simple trust between individuals . . . Each deal was fragile. In less sensitive hands all these negotiations might have foundered. Without trust, owners would have despaired and handed over their estates to the auction houses, the ever-present vultures of the tale . . . What emerges from Lees-Milne's account is the importance of touch. He . . . worked by knowing when to leave well alone, when to delegate . . . It was the finest hour of the old boy network. I believe the aristocracy of Britain yielded up its finest possessions because it rightly believed it was yielding them into the care of like-minded guardians.

Jim was delighted to receive such notices, writing that 'at moments euphoria has wafted me to such heights of confidence that I feel I can still write almost anything'. In fact, though he continued writing for another five years, *People & Places* was (apart from his diary) effectively his literary swansong.

Jim never felt very well in his eighties, though he struggled on and managed to 'hold desperately on to my wits as a man holds on to his hat while crossing a desolate moor in a whirlwind'. He coped with deteriorating eyesight and hearing, neither of which deterred him from continuing to read and enjoy social life on a fairly heroic scale. From time to time he suffered further outbreaks of malignancy, and reluctantly submitted to treatment. ('You see, Jim,' explained his doctor, 'you are still worth patching up. In other respects you enjoy reasonable health . . . and your brain is still functioning.') For a few years he kept up his customary routine, driving the fourteen miles from Badminton to Bath and back most weekdays, and making regular overnight visits to London. He continued to travel, if not so far afield as before: in 1989, apart from staying with various friends in England, he visited Ireland with Debo, Scotland with Eardley and Germany with Derek. One difference was that he no longer went for very long walks, especially after the death of his beloved whippet Folly in 1991: though bereft (their other whippet, Honey, had died five years earlier), the Lees-Milnes did not feel able to start with new dogs in their eighties.

Many old friends died (Sachie in 1988, the Droghedas in 1989, Rosamond in 1990, Midi in 1991), their passing often provoking a flood of nostalgic reminiscence. This was not invariably benevolent. On the death of Helen Dashwood in 1989, he wrote: 'She was a spoilt, snobbish and vulgar woman who had to be invited to every lighted candle, though

few of the lighters cared for her. She was horrid to the humble and meek.'
When Bruce Chatwin died of AIDS the same year, aged only forty-eight,
he wrote: 'A grievous loss to literature, the papers say . . . You would
suppose Lord Byron had died. Does he deserve it?' Two deaths, however,
filled him with remorse. When his sister Audrey died in October 1990,
having suffered a stroke two years earlier, he wrote:

> I was often unkind to Audrey; she irritated me and I snubbed her, an
> unforgivable thing. She was as good as gold, and never harboured an
> ungenerous thought or did a mean thing, which cannot be said of me. And
> let's face it, goodness is greatness; nothing else counts for much in the sight
> of God. I am now the last of the Wickhamford family, and feel like a plant
> torn out of the earth.

And when Eardley died of a sudden heart-attack in September 1991,
he wrote:

> How beastly I was when he stayed last month [at Badminton, during
> Alvilde's absence] . . . He was without doubt my best friend these fifty
> years . . . All those wartime and postwar years when we visited properties
> together, laughing, gossiping; he forever patient and tolerant, someone I
> could always turn to in moments of near-desperation; and we went abroad
> together year after year. Latterly a change in us both, no doubt. Old age
> and bad temper. I already miss E. There is no one who possesses my entire
> confidence now.

Jim had drawn close to Alvilde. Her possessive qualities, which had in
the past been an irritation to him, were now a consolation (though when
she went away he still experienced 'an unaccountable feeling of release,
a sense of relief that I can now, not indulge in wickedness any longer, but
lie back and collect my thoughts'). He took pride in her gardening
achievements. (Following her success with Mick Jagger, those who
sought her horticultural advice included Valéry Giscard d'Estaing and
the Queen of Jordan.) He joyfully celebrated her eightieth birthday in
1989, and their fortieth wedding anniversary in 1991. They loved their
life at Badminton, where they continued to be on close terms with the
Beauforts. Although many of their local friends had died or moved away,
they had made attractive new ones of a younger generation: these
included John Julius Norwich (son of Diana Cooper) and his wife Mollie,
Duff Hart-Davis (son of Rupert) and his wife Phyllida, the local MP Sir
Charles Morrison and his wife Rosalind (last of the Lygons, the family
which had inspired *Brideshead Revisited*), and the publisher Desmond
Briggs and his handsome boyfriend Ian Dixon. The only cloud upon the

marriage was Jim's exasperation at the demands made on Alvilde, and
intermittently on himself, by her daughter Clarissa and four grandchildren. Clarissa had now left her unsatisfactory husband Mickey Luke and
was living with an 'extremely good-looking and stupid' man named
Billy, twenty years younger than herself. They were constantly short of
money, and eventually moved into the basement flat at Lansdown
Crescent which had been vacant since the departure of the nightmare
tenant. Alvilde doted on her three granddaughters, by whose modern
ways Jim was sometimes irritated. He himself did his best with his step-
grandson Igor. This youth had 'Christ-like looks' and was 'guileless
and good', but 'gormless'. Conversation with him was difficult. He did
not seem to be qualified for anything. His ambitions – to be a tennis
champion, an officer in the Brigade, a foxhunting squire – were
unrealistic. The humble jobs it was possible to find for him (such as that
of gardener to Diana Mosley in Orsay) usually ended in disaster. Jim felt
affection for him, but found him an anxiety.

Alvilde had looked after Jim devotedly, especially during his cancer
episodes. (When, after an exasperating day in Bath grappling with
plumbers, he told her that he sometimes wished he lived in a 'home'
with no responsibilities, she sharply replied, 'You are living in one now,
with minimal responsibilities.') Now, however, their roles were to be
reversed. In 1990 she began suffering from fainting fits and was told she
needed a hazardous operation to replace a heart valve. In the face of this
she was breezily calm, while Jim was beside himself with anxiety. On
hearing that the operation had been a success, he experienced 'an odd
feeling as though of disappointment, can't understand why'. She remained
easily tired, and Jim took on a greater share of domestic duties. At first
she resumed a fairly normal life, accepting a commission to design a new
garden at Cornbury House, Oxfordshire, and going abroad with Jim to
Venice and Egypt. Then, in March 1992, she collapsed and fell into
a coma, the doctors holding out little hope of recovery. Jim suffered
'agonising worry . . . the worst misery I have ever endured'. Amazingly,
she pulled through, though severely weakened and disabled. Jim wrote
that he henceforth intended to devote himself completely to looking after
her. However, when she was discharged from hospital at the end of May,
he found caring for her a strain.

> I have to recognise that I am no longer an independent being. My day
> begins at 7.15 when I rise, draw back her blinds, empty her commode,
> descend to fetch her orange juice. Having shaved and dressed myself I boil
> her egg, lay tray, carry her breakfast up to her in bed. I confess there are

moments when the devil gets into me and I am tempted to take revenge on her in little ways. I lack all intellectual stimulus, and physical exercise apart from endless climbing of stairs. I am miserable at not being able to get down to work.

Fortunately their devoted daily Peggy was a great resource, and Alvilde partially learnt to cope with her disabilities, so that after a few months Jim was able to resume a reduced version of his former routine, getting away to Bath for a few hours in the middle of the day and to London (now usually a day trip) from time to time. He lacked the energy and concentration for sustained writing, but was kept busy with articles and reviews. He also kept up his diary; and as Murray wanted another book from him, he began editing his post 1940s diaries for publication. Sometimes Clarissa came to stay and he was able to go off for a few days to visit friends. Eventually Alvilde was able to drive short distances, go out to meals, even stay away. They spent Christmas 1992 at Chatsworth, visited Mick Jagger's French *manoir*, where Jim was able to admire the garden she had created, and had a holiday in Morocco. Her frailty was evident, however, and as 1994 began he asked himself sadly, 'how long shall I have A. for? How long shall we remain united?'

  Her end, when it came ten weeks later, was traumatic for Jim. Friday 18 March was a rainy day. At 4.45 in the afternoon, having done 'a good day's work' at Lansdown Crescent and then the shopping, he returned to Essex House to be greeted by the sight of her lying face-down on the wet flagstones of the garden path, car keys in hand and legs and walking-sticks askew. She had gone out to have her hair done, slipped on the path on her return, fallen headlong and succumbed to heart failure. 'Sudden, I am sure – but what is "sudden" at the time of death?' After getting through the nightmare of her funeral, he felt desolated.

> Time has somehow ceased. The evenings alone are agony. I go in and out of her bedroom. The whole house is full of coffee cups – her notes, diary, telephone book, every single thing is redolent of her.

He was also tormented by remorse.

> I am haunted by my lamentable unkindness to A., particularly in two respects. First, I never tried hard enough to understand and share her love of gardening. She put plants into the earth with her own hands, nurtured them, watched them grow, and when they were blossoming, looked not merely at them but into them. Secondly, I was often horrid about her descendants, so that she was reluctant to discuss with me all the worries they caused her. I find it hard to forgive them; yet I behaved very ill.

Even at this time, however, his sense of the ridiculous did not desert him.

> At four, the undertaker called. He bowed from the waist and asked solemnly if I was prepared to receive the urn, which he held out like the Archbishop offering the orb to the Queen. He added a few words, 'If I may presume on such an occasion', etc. I asked him if he was sure the ashes were A's. He appeared to be shocked by the question. 'Perhaps in the big cities misadventures may occur.' Laughing and crying, I carried upstairs the large, brown, nondescript plastic urn, embraced it, and put it inside the large blue-and-white bowl above my clothes cupboard. I don't find it macabre; on the contrary, a comfort to have her remains so near me while I sleep.

Many people showed kindness to Jim in his bereavement. He was covered with filial affection by Nick Robinson and his brothers Henry (a farmer) and Richard (a banker), who having lost both their parents cherished him as their *paterfamilias*. His local friends were solicitous towards him, especially Desmond Briggs and Ian Dixon, who had adored Alvilde as much as they admired Jim. The Devonshires invited him to become their permanent guest at Chatsworth, while the Beauforts told him that he need no longer pay rent on Essex House. Jim was touched by these offers, but refused to accept them, valuing his independence; his income was sufficient to pay the costs of Essex House, and Peggy continued to look after it (and him) as Alvilde would have wished. He was shocked and saddened when soon after Alvilde's death Caroline Beaufort, still in her mid sixties, was diagnosed with a fatal and inoperable tumour: she made the most of her remaining months, showing much desire for the company of Jim (who also befriended David's mistress and future wife, Miranda Morley).

While Jim missed Alvilde sorely, her loss was also a liberation: not only did he no longer have to look after her, but whereas during their marriage any going off on his own had involved delicate negotiation, he could now do as he pleased. Thus in the nine months following her death he made three visits to Chatsworth, spent a week in Venice, had a holiday in Argyll, and stayed with friends in Norfolk and Buckinghamshire. Others whose hospitality he enjoyed during his remaining years included the Edmund Brudenells, who gave 'beautifully staged' house parties at Deene Park, Northamptonshire; Rosalind Morrison, who 'took on' Madresfield Court, her ancestral home in Jim's native Worcestershire; Owen Lloyd George, a splendid advertisement for the aristocracy which his grandfather had excoriated; and Diana Mosley, who was always delighted to see Jim at Orsay, regarding him as her oldest friend. He also enjoyed revisiting the scenes of his past. He was welcomed at Wickhamford Manor by its current owners, Jeremy and June Ryan-Bell, who were 'eager for any information on its days of yore'. Equally welcoming were the Acloques at Alderley, where Jim was 'bowled over by the beauty of the garden' which had been created by Alvilde and faithfully maintained by them. Another house he visited after a long interval was Long Crichel, now inhabited (following the death of Desmond Shawe-Taylor, the last of the original tenants) by Pat Trevor-Roper and Derek Hill. In March 1995, on the first anniversary of Alvilde's death, he visited the French Riviera for the first time since she had sold La Meridienne in 1959, staying at Menton in the company of three women to whom he felt close – Freda Berkeley, Billa Harrod and 'Coote' Heber-Percy. He made 'a pious pilgrimage' to Roquebrune during which, 'although rather sad with thoughts of A.', he 'did not feel sentimental'. He considered scattering Alvilde's ashes there, while Freda considered scattering Lennox's ashes in Nice, where his grandfather had been British consul. However, so distressed were they both to see the degradation of the coast that they finally retained the remains of their respective spouses with a view to these being mingled with their own when the time came.

When not absent on these visits or meeting friends and relations, Jim continued to dedicate himself to his writing. With a heavy heart he gave up his beloved library at Lansdown Crescent, his place of work for twenty years: the daily journey to Bath was becoming too much for him, and he gave in to pressure from Clarissa, who had inherited her mother's interest in the property, to be allowed to occupy the whole of it.* Most of his books were sold at Heywood Hill, the proceeds used to endow a library at one of Jim's favourite National Trust houses, Gunby; those he kept, including his collection of reference works, filled a 'book-room' which he created out of Alvilde's bedroom at Essex House. During his last years Jim edited his diaries for the years 1971–8, published by Murray (who also reprinted the 1940s diaries) in three volumes – *A Mingled Measure* (1994), *Ancient as the Hills* (1997) and *Through Wood and Dale* (1998). The

---

*Jim eventually bequeathed to Clarissa his own interest in the maisonette on the condition that, when she came to sell it, the Bath Preservation Trust should have first refusal. Unfortunately, by the time Clarissa sold, the BPT could not raise the money to buy it. Happily the purchasers, civilised antiquarians of whom Jim would have approved, restored the library, which Clarissa had converted to a modern drawing-room, to its former condition.

manuscripts of these diaries, which he sold to the Beinecke Library at Yale together with most of the rest of his papers, show that his 'editing' was light, mainly consisting of removing or modifying references likely to offend the living. (He sometimes slipped up: in 1973, Hugh Massingberd told him that an elderly landlady who had been in love with him had, upon his recent marriage, behaved like a hell-cat towards his wife; it turned out that the lady was still alive in her nineties in 1997, when the story appeared in *Ancient as the Hills*.) A great selling-point for these diaries was that Alan Clark, whose own diaries of his years as a minister in the Thatcher government, also dealing with his colourful private life, caused a sensation on their publication in 1993, declared that Jim was his favourite twentieth-century diarist. (Jim only partly returned the compliment: while admiring Clark's loyalty to Mrs Thatcher, and finding his style 'vivacious' and his descriptions 'arresting', he found him 'difficult to like', and was put off by 'too many acronyms, initials and filthy words used as adjectives'.)

Apart from a regular stream of journalism, and a not very successful ghost story which was dutifully published by Nick Robinson, Jim wrote one further book, a collection of fourteen 'sketches' (as if to complement the fourteen houses he had treated in *People & Places*) of departed friends. It is a very uneven work. For a start, the choice of subjects was odd. He included one person (Everard Radcliffe) he had known well but not much liked, and another (William Plomer) whom he had greatly liked but hardly known. He included Vita but not Harold, the lugubrious Paul Methuen but not the sparkling Oliver Esher. Some of the sketches consist mostly of personal memories, others of rather banal biographical data; there was much recycling of what he had already written by way of diary entries, obituaries and memorial service addresses. Nor was he particularly frank in revealing his subjects' foibles. Still, the collection contains flashes of inspired original writing, and at least one of the sketches was considered by a biographer to be an invaluable resource. One of the best things about the book was the title he originally chose for it, 'Straight and Bent' (seven of the fourteen subjects being gay or lesbian); but he got cold feet, and it was finally published by Murray in 1996 as *Fourteen Friends*. It was given an easy ride in the review pages by living friends. (Jim might have done better to write another book he had in mind, about 'places which have coloured my life', starting with Wickhamford and Ribbesford, Eton and Magdalen, George Lloyd's house in Portman Square and Harold Nicolson's rooms in King's Bench Walk.)

However, Jim's main literary achievement during his last years was the continuation of his diary up to the month before his death. As its admirer David Sexton has written: 'The endless curiosity about other people, the unsparing honesty about what he feels as he voyages into old age, the ceaseless noticing of the condition of his fellow travellers, make it weirdly compelling reading.' In a sense his diary kept him going: it was both a safety-valve, which enabled him to release his feelings on matters which exercised him, and a spur to leading an active life – even at moments when he least felt like going about, the prospect of obtaining 'copy' for his journal helped him overcome his inertia.

It deals candidly with matters which are not often mentioned by men in their eighties, including Jim's changing attitude towards sex. His sexual psychology was always rather complex. He was certainly no misogynist. In childhood and adolescence, he had worshipped his mother; and throughout his adult life he delighted in the company of sympathetic women. (In his youth, the women he admired were often of an older generation; in later life, they were often younger – thus in his seventies he had a penchant for attractive women in their thirties, such as Selina Hastings, Rosalind Morrison and Ariane Bankes.) He had enjoyed heterosexual affairs before his marriage; and he was certainly in love with Alvilde during the earlier and later stages of their life together. However, apart from Alvilde (who was herself a rather masculine personality), it is clear that most of the emotional attachments in his life were to men. As with many of his generation, his homosexuality involved feelings of ambivalence. He was obliged to lead a double life; he had a horror of those who flaunted their proclivities; he sometimes referred disparagingly to 'buggers' and 'homos'. However, not only were his inclinations predominantly homosexual, but he got a thrill from belonging to a clandestine society, and the narcissistic, mischievous and duplicitous elements in his personality tied in with his preferences. He was also pruriently fascinated to learn of others who shared his tastes, in the past as well as the present. After he lost his testicles in 1984, Jim ceased to have overt sexual feelings; but for some years afterwards his interest in homosexuality did not abate. In writing his biographies of Lord Esher and the Bachelor Duke, he made the most of the homoerotic strands in their lives; and whenever he met a dazzling youngish man, such as the opera producer Freddie Stockdale, the *Country Life* editor Clive Aslet, or the publisher David Burnett, a wave of infatuation overcame him.

However, in the early 1990s, as the diary shows, his feelings underwent a change. Friends who had previously entertained him with homosexual gossip began to notice that this no longer amused him. In December 1992 he noted that he now far preferred the society of women to men, and wondered whether, were he 'still to have a propensity to sex', he would be 'predominantly heterosexual'. By October 1993, he no longer had any doubts. He

> thought how curious it was that I, as an old eunuch, am now totally heterosexual. I am drawn exclusively to the mystique of the female persona, whereas the male physique revolts me and the male persona has little allure. I suppose that, by a tilt of the scales, a nudge from the tip of an angel's wing, I would have been wholly 'normal' from adolescence onwards.

In 1995 he described himself as 'one hundred per cent hetero-platonic'. Moreover, he now regarded homosexuality with 'distaste' and dismissed it as 'a mistake'. Whereas in 1990 he had revelled in the publication of a novel with gay themes, in 1995, in writing about his seven gay subjects in *Fourteen Friends* (at least four of whom had been his lovers), he either did not mention their proclivities at all or did so (notably in the case of Jamesey Pope-Hennessy) only to deplore them. A few months before his death, meeting gay fellow-guests at a lunch party given by Julian Berkeley and Tony Scotland, he wrote: 'Their mannerisms, their social contacts, their sharp little jokes are the same the world over. How is it they do not recognise that they are artificial, shallow, slick, sophisticated, absurd?' It seems probable that this development in Jim's psychology – which co-incided with Alvilde's breakdown in health and consequent death – was connected with irrational guilt-feelings that he had 'betrayed' her through his homosexual associations. One result of the realignment of his preferences was that he ceased to feel so close to either John Kenworthy-Browne or myself, though he remained a generous friend to us both. (In my case, he wrote that I would probably 'end up like Jamesey', and that he was having second thoughts about making me his literary executor.)

Although Jim had never been much interested in politics, his late diaries contain some interesting reflections on the subject. He thought Thatcher's successor John Major 'an honourable and decent man', but wanted to tell him that 'he can't both go "back to basics" and have "a classless society". For basic politeness and civilised behaviour are the attributes of a gentleman, nurtured in country houses and on the playing fields of Eton.' He was

> bitterly opposed to the bloody Maastricht Treaty. I foresee the European Community becoming like the Soviet Republics, governed by a distant,

unknown, unseen force of rulers. It will produce lack of competition, lack of will to work, corruption, inefficiency, disunity and anarchy. Then we shall have a reaction in the form of tribalism, such as we now see in the former Soviet Union and the Balkans and every African nation state.

He disapproved of Serb generals being arraigned for war crimes at The Hague. 'No doubt they are responsible for ghastly atrocities; but war itself is a crime, and all who engage in it must be regarded as accomplices to some degree.' When New Labour came to power in May 1997, Jim, while shedding few tears at the demise of a Tory administration containing 'far too many spivs', was 'appalled at the jubilation, the ringing of church bells, as though Great Britain had been delivered from Hitler, Stalin or President Mobutu [a recently deposed African dictator] rather than good, honest, wise Mr Major who has improved the lot of the working classes'. Looking to the future, he feared 'not so much extremist socialism as the insidious liberalism which will overlook the appalling scandals of bogus social security claimants, kowtowing to the IRA and all criminals, encouraging rather than limiting more coloured immigrants, and the general descent into American-style vulgarity and yob culture'.

It must not, however, be supposed that Jim towards the end of his life was a snobbish reactionary. On the contrary, during his eighties he railed more than ever against the vacuity and arrogance of the idle rich. As he wrote after a Badminton dinner party: 'What a lot they are, redolent of the worst aspects of the Edwardian age. A crowd of arrogant, fatuous drones, waited on by a regiment of servants. It is so archaic as to be barely true.' Lunch at another Gloucestershire country house was 'two hours of sheer banality, during which I never heard a single remark worthy of remembrance. It is ghastly that I . . . spend so much time with these idiotic society people . . . How rich the rich are today . . . Is "society" on the edge? Can it last – and should it?' A few weeks before his death, he was 'revolted' to see the television adaptation of the novel sequence (of which he had never been a great fan) of his friend Anthony Powell. 'The snobbery, hauteur, stupidity, insolence of the young people was ghastly – except for Widmerpool, who was supposed to be ghastly, but seemed good. I felt ashamed to have grown up in the 1920s and been a young adult in the 1930s. Thank God that generation is now extinct.'

Among the people Jim got to know in his last years was the Prince of Wales, who had become a close friend of both Debo Devonshire and Derek Hill. Jim was staying at Chatsworth in January 1992 when the Prince made an impromptu visit. The conversation at dinner consisted of the usual banalities to be expected when royalty was present; but the following morning, when Jim breakfasted with the Prince and the Devonshires, they had 'a jolly talk'.

> I feel this very sweet man is deadly serious and worries more about the devastation caused to the world's face than any other problem. He says he feels John Betjeman's mantle has fallen on his shoulders. This is rather touching, but alas he is too ignorant, groping for something which eludes. I somehow feel that all his interests and commitments and speeches and writings are too much for him, that he may have a breakdown. And the sadness of his marriage. No one to share thoughts with.

The breakdown of the Prince's marriage to Diana was much in the news at the time, and he often retreated to Chatsworth to seek solace from Debo, who also provided a sanctuary for the pursuit of his friendship with Camilla Parker Bowles. Jim was appalled to see the Prince's television interview with Jonathan Dimbleby in June 1994, in which he admitted to adultery. 'This idealistic middle-aged man struggled to get the words out and writhed with intellectual deficiency, wrinkling his forehead and making grimaces. I was left with the feeling that he is not equipped to be a leader, and certainly not to wrestle with clever minds.' When, the following year, the Princess got her revenge by the same medium, he thought it 'an astonishing performance . . . She did not criticise Prince or Family directly, yet left watchers with no doubt that she hated the lot. I don't know that I like her more than hitherto, and I am not particularly taken in by her professions of love for ordinary people, but I respect her for her candour and for so boldly confronting millions.' In November 1996 he was taken by Derek to lunch at Highgrove: the naturally shy Prince seemed to relax in the company of Derek, by whom he allowed himself to be teased. Jim (then eighty-eight) enjoyed the experience, chatting easily with the Prince, mostly on architectural subjects, and expressing suitable appreciation of the house and its pictures. His verdict on his host was sympathetic.

> What a sweet man. Heart bang in the right place. Earnest about his charities, and writhes in misery at the destruction of the world. Not very clever in spite of praiseworthy intentions. Lays himself open to criticism because he contends with intellectuals and specialists in fields of which he can inevitably have only superficial knowledge. He deserves all our encouragement and support. A figure of tragedy with abundant charm.

Jim experienced a revival of interest in conservation during his last years. He was 'jubilant' when a letter he wrote 'to all and sundry' led the National Trust to acquire seven hundred acres of wonderful parkland at

Croome Court in an unspoilt corner of his native Worcestershire. In 1996 he was 'fascinated' to visit Barrington Court, Gloucestershire, seat of the reclusive Wingfield family, to which he had been trying to gain access for sixty years; the occasion reminded him 'of my wartime visits to remote country houses and harassed owners', and he wrote a diary entry worthy of that time. A few months before his death he was given a privileged look at the National Trust's latest country house acquisition, the Jacobean Chastleton, Oxfordshire, and amazed the Trust officials by revealing that he had attended children's parties in the house and played hunt-the-slipper in the long gallery. Religion was also a great consolation to him as the end drew near. His friend Tom Gibson had retired as Vicar of Badminton in 1993 and moved to Bath, but on days when Jim felt rotten Tom would sometimes admit him privately to one of the small churches on the Badminton estate and administer Holy Communion, which always had a revivifying effect on him. It was, of course, the Anglican liturgy of his childhood which Jim loved; rather surprisingly, as he had shown much hostility to Roman Catholicism since his 'reversion' in the 1970s, he experimented, soon after Alvilde's death, with a weekend retreat to the Benedictine Abbey at Downside, but decided it was not for him. ('A feeling of intense loneliness here. Memories of private school rise within me. I feel the moment they can get away the brothers will indulge in every diversion known to man.')

On his eighty-ninth birthday on 6 August 1997, Jim lunched with his nephew Henry Robinson and his family at Moor Wood. He then 'paid respects' at the grave of his sister Audrey, and joined a Georgian Group visit to Rousham (making no comment in his diary which would lead one to suppose that his desire to preserve architecture had been born there). Several of the party congratulated him on his diaries for 1973–4, recently published as *Ancient as the Hills*. Two weeks later he underwent a major cancer operation. He was now extremely frail; but he did not lose either his desire to carry on or his interest in life. He continued to keep his diary (writing by hand as typing had become too great an effort). When, just after his discharge from hospital, Princess Diana met her death, he thought 'the tragedy seemed pre-ordained' and 'would be recognised as a mercy in the long run'. He spent a week at Chatsworth, driven there and back, revelling in its comforts and Debo's ministrations but feeling 'languid and dotty'. He continued to receive a steady stream of visitors at Essex House. A BBC man came to record a radio interview (broadcast after his death and showing him in sparkling form), and Fiona MacCarthy came to discuss her biography of Byron, Jim finding her extremely attractive. On 29 October he greatly enjoyed a long-planned day-trip to Windsor and Eton, being shown the Royal Library and the College Library by their respective librarians, Oliver Everett and Michael Meredith.

On 4 November he set out with Debo for his annual visit to Diana Mosley at Orsay, travelling on the Eurostar. He was in good form that evening; but the following day he was taken ill, and on the 6th he returned to England, accompanied by Diana's daughter-in-law Charlotte, going straight into the Royal United Hospital in Bath. It was there that he wrote the last entry in his diary, showing that, even *in extremis*, he had not lost either his human sympathy or his sense of humour. He gives a chilling vignette of a blunt doctor telling a newly admitted patient about an unpleasant operation he was to experience; and he describes how, 'elated' after a talk with Debo on the ward telephone, he returned to the wrong room and was about to get into 'what corresponded with my bed by the window . . . when a terrified lady gave a yelp of horror'. His final diary words were, 'My handwriting is very shakey [*sic*]. Damn it.' There was not much more the doctors could do for Jim, who was moved at the end of November to Tetbury Cottage Hospital. This was just a few miles from Highgrove, and Prince Charles, hearing from Debo that he was there, made several visits to his bedside. These surely gave him pleasure, though he characteristically told other visitors that it was 'rather a strain' having to pull himself together for the heir to the throne. He gradually sank into a morphine-induced twilight, and died in the early hours of Sunday 28 December.

Publishing History of
James Lees-Milne's Diaries

THE DIARIES OF James Lees-Milne were originally published in twelve volumes, with titles deriving from Coleridge's *Kubla Khan*. The first seven were edited by the diarist during his lifetime (the last of them appearing posthumously), and are listed below with their original publishers and years of publication.

> *Ancestral Voices*, 1942–3 (Chatto & Windus, 1975)
> *Prophesying Peace*, 1944–5 (Chatto & Windus, 1977)
> *Caves of Ice*, 1946–7 (Chatto & Windus, 1983)
> *Midway on the Waves*, 1948–9 (Faber & Faber, 1985)
> *A Mingled Measure*, 1953–72 (John Murray, 1994)
> *Ancient as the Hills*, 1973–4 (John Murray, 1997)
> *Through Wood and Dale*, 1975–8 (John Murray, 1998)

After publishing *Midway on the Waves*, Faber reissued the previous three volumes in paperback; after publishing *A Mingled Measure*, John Murray reissued the 1940s diaries in two hardback double volumes. The remaining five volumes of the diaries were edited by Michael Bloch after James Lees-Milne's death, and published by John Murray, paperback editions appearing in the years following the hardback editions, the dates of which are given below.

> *Deep Romantic Chasm*, 1979–81 (2000)
> *Holy Dread*, 1982–4 (2001)
> *Beneath a Waning Moon*, 1985–7 (2003)
> *Ceaseless Turmoil*, 1988–92 (2004)
> *The Milk of Paradise*, 1993–7 (2005)

Since 2003 the first nine of the twelve volumes have been reissued by Michael Russell in the Clocktower Paperback series. In April 2009 Penguin published a selection of entries from the 1940s diaries in their English Journeys series, under the title *Some Country Houses and Their Owners*.

John Murray have published an abridged three-volume edition of the complete diaries, edited and introduced by Michael Bloch.

Diaries, 1942–1954 (2006)
Diaries, 1971–1983 (2007)
Diaries, 1984–1997 (2008)

Notes

'JLM' refers to James Lees-Milne
'Diary' refers to the diaries of JLM
'Beinecke' refers to the papers of JLM in the Beinecke Rare Books and Manuscripts Library at Yale (GEN MSS 476)
'*AS*', '*FF*' and '*P&P*' refer to JLM's memoirs *Another Self* (1970), *Fourteen Friends* (1996) and *People & Places* (1992); all works cited for whom no author is given are by JLM

PREFACE

xi. JLM described as 'one of the best prose writers': Diary, 19 January 1987
xii. JLM's destruction of manuscripts: Diary, 18 August 1975, 24 November 1975, 5 July 1984, 10 September 1984

CHAPTER 1: THE DREAMING BOY

1. 'Sport and Booze': JLM to Simon Lees-Milne, 2 February 1991
2. Nimrod, Ramrod and Fishing Rod: Diary, 21 October 1981
2. Lees family and Winston Churchill: Diary, 21 July 1954
2. grandfather refuses baronetcy: Diary, 5 June 1992
3–4. correspondence of Bailey grandparents cited in Diary, 23 April 1996
4. courtship of JLM's parents: Helen's diary (Mrs James Sutton)
4. John Nuttall: Diary, 9 August 1990
4. George buys Wickhamford: Diary, 27 May 1990
5–7. Helen's diary (Mrs James Sutton)
7. 'everyone in the village automatically assembled': *AS*, ch.1
8. vicar treated 'abominably': Diary, 22 April 1946
9. LM children learn village dialect: Diary, 6 March 1947
9. 'a cissy child': *AS*, ch. 2
9. 'desperately wished I were a girl': Diary, 14 August 1974
12. 'When we went shopping': JLM to Alexander Robinson, 16 February 1986

13. 'nursing the wounded': *AS*, ch. 2
13. 'the decadent aristocrat': Diary, 19 December 1973
15. dates of JLM at Lockers Park: D.R. Lees-Jones (headmaster) to the author
16. 'If only my Uncle Robert had lived': Diary, 21 August 1990
17. Lockers Park: Ruth Bardens, *A History of Lockers Park School* (1999)
17. involved in editing school magazines: Diary, 4 April 1945
18. 'a lovely nineteenth-century illustrated book': Diary, 11 August 1983
18. 'that sarcastic brute': Diary, 4 February 1972
18. JLM plays little part in House: information from Sir Wilfred Thesiger
18–20. Julian Hall, *The Senior Commoner* (Martin Secker, 1933), pp.72–9, 93–5, 142, 345
20. 'flashing across the nave confidential smiles': Diary, 1 March 1942
20. 'on Sunday eves before Chapel': Diary, 20 July 1980
20–1. engaged in trysts: Diary, 9 August 1983
21. 'No subsequent escapades': Diary, 20 May 1973
21. JLM's schoolfriends appear to him in dreams: Diary, 21 May 1985
21. secret club at the Cockpit: Alan Pryce-Jones, *The Bonus of Laughter* (Hamish Hamilton, 1987), p. 5
22. 'whom I knew at Eton as Hobart': Diary, 3 July 1947
24. 'sitting with a pile of books under the mulberry tree': Diary, 5 September 1990
24–5. 'We . . . rode over on our ponies': Diary, 15 June 1983
25. 'he used to bash his racquet over my head': Diary, 9 May 1975
25. 'Bare moorland, windswept, cloudswept': Diary, 30 December 1992
26. poem about Emral: *The Moat* (1950), MS in author's possession
27. 'he made us read Byron': Diana Mosley, *A Life of Contrasts* (Hamish Hamilton, 1977), p. 4
28. The child was stillborn: JLM to the author; Diary, 26 March 1987

CHAPTER 2: FURTHER EDUCATION

30. JLM reads *Don Juan*: Diary, 15 August 1942
31. 'Last night in London': Diary, 7 April 1976
33. Nancy's letter to Tom, 25 February 1928 in Charlotte Mosley (ed.), *Love from Nancy: The Letters of Nancy Mitford* (Hodder, 1993)
33–4. The sisters' version of Jim's contretemps with Lord Redesdale in Jonathan and Catherine Guinness, *The House of Mitford* (Hutchinson 1984), pp. 291–2
34–9. Diana Mitford's letters to JLM in Beinecke; JLM's letters to Diana shown by her to the author in 2000, and now at Chatsworth
39. 'I was terrified of W.C.': Diary, 7 January 1975

39. Diana Churchill to JLM, 18 January 1928 (Beinecke)

39. 'she was the most divine adolescent': Diary, 16 June 1945

39. 'all my inhibited love for Diana': Diary, 3 March 1972

41–2. JLM's admission file in Magdalen archives kindly made available by Robin Darwall-Smith

42. 'delighted you have got in all right': Sir Herbert Warren to JLM (Beinecke)

43. JLM unable to remember who had taught him: Diary, 20 October 1993

45. 'I'm drunk with love': Johnnie Churchill to JLM (Beinecke)

45. JLM officiates at mock marriage ceremony: Diary, 18 June 1984, 20 April 1986

45. JLM teaches Clarissa to write sonnets: Diary, 15 October 1978; Clarissa Eden, *A Memoir* (Weidenfeld, 2007), p. 7

46. '[Hamish] had the most enchanting looks': Diary, 19 December 1973

46. Randolph and Basil waste talents through drink: Diary, 4 April 1945

47. 'I *know* you will like him': Diana Mitford to JLM, 17 November 1928 (Beinecke)

48. 'with him I slept more than once': Diary, 20 March 1983

48. 'For six weeks I was infatuated with him': Diary, 7 March 1981

49. 'particularly green, very provincial': *FF*, p. 41

49. 'All my life I have been a slow developer': Diary, 6 August 1948

49. drawing classes at Ruskin School: Diary, 28 August 1942

49. 'fostered secret . . . ambitions to write': Diary, 10 August 1971

50. JLM on Little Moreton Hall: *P&P*

50–1. Maurice Hastings at Rousham: see Bevis Hillier, *Young Betjeman* (John Murray, 1988), ch. 13

CHAPTER 3: PATRONS AND PATRONESSES

54. 'both took to their beds': JLM interviewed by Richard Robinson, January 1988

55. 'going from house to house in the back streets': *FF*, 'Vita Sackville-West'

58. 'cables constantly come through': JLM to Desmond Parsons, 18 December 1928 (Birr Castle)

59. 'in perpetual trouble for small peccadilloes': Diary, 19 April 1983

59. 'You have been very good to me these last 3 years': George Lloyd to JLM, 'Sunday' (Beinecke)

60. JLM tongue-tied while Hobhouse sparkles: *FF*, 'Vita Sackville-West'

60–1. JLM visits Sissinghurst, August 1932: Diary, 27 January 1948; *Harold Nicolson: A Biography*, Vol. II, p. 31

61. 'God! How I wish you could have come to Paris with me': Harold Nicolson (HN) to JLM, 13 December 1933 (Beinecke)

61. 'He was a superlative guide': *Harold Nicolson*, Vol. II, pp. 43–4
61. 'I found that Jim Lees-Milne was going to Paris': HN to Vita, 4 February 1934, in Nigel Nicolson (ed.), *Harold Nicolson: Diaries and Letters, 1930–1939* (Collins, 1966)
61. 'for having been so charming to me': HN to JLM, 4 February 1934 (Beinecke)
62. 'It is possible to be affectionate': HN to JLM, 11 February 1934 (Beinecke)
62. 'Yes, but he did not fall in love with me': Diary, 26 June 1976
62. 'an almost unassuageable appetite for clever and beautiful young men': Adam Nicolson, *Sissinghurst: An Unfinished History* (Harper, 2008), p. 267
63. JLM stays with Eddy at Knole: Michael de la Noy, *Eddy: The Life of Edward Sackville-West* (Bodley Head, 1988), pp. 108, 154–5
63. 'I remember him typing his diary': Diary, 13 August 1971
64. 'Today I understand there is to be a hostile demonstration': JLM to Desmond Parsons, 5 February 1933 (Birr)
64–5. 'Paul and I went to a Russian film': JLM to Anne Gathorne-Hardy, 27 September 1935 (Beinecke)
65. 'Think twice before becoming a Catholic': Diana Mitford to JLM, undated, from Swinbrook House (Beinecke)
66. 'proprietory, boozy, gluttonous and dirty': Diary, 3 May 1997
66. Father Napier-Hemy drunk: Diary, 26 April 1981
66. 'Irish Catholicism is like a vice': Diary, 2 May 1948
66. JLM and *Humanae Vitae*: Diary, 9 February 1977
67. 'What I need is a twilight atmosphere': Diary, 5 September 1943
67. Chesterton and Knox: see Joseph Pearce, *Literary Converts* (Harper Collins, 1999)
67. Greene and Waugh: Diary, 15 March 1943, 13 December 1975, 3 April 1991
67. D'Arcy and Martindale: their letters to JLM, 1932–3 (Beinecke)
67–8. JLM's father denounces his 'apostasy': *AS*, ch. 7
68. 'one misplaced word': Diary, 22 February 1979
68. For Jean, Lady Hamilton's patronage of JLM, see her diaries in King's College, London
69. For Kathleen Kennet's penchant for gay men, see biography by her granddaughter Louisa Young, *A Great Task of Happiness* (Macmillan, 1995)
69. Kathleen Kennet's visit to Switzerland with JLM in December–January 1936–7 described in her diary in Cambridge University Library
70. 'Today a young person of modest means': *FF*, 'Vita Sackville-West'
70. 'He once made advances to me': Diary, 20 March 1983
70. Chavchavadze 'transports' JLM: Diary, 30 June 1983

71–2. 'What you do not say or probably even realise': Midi O'Neill to JLM, 28 February 1933 (Beinecke)

CHAPTER 4: ANNE

73. 'a dreadful man called Professor Joad': JLM to Desmond Parsons, June 1933 (Birr)

73. 'She had camellia-like skin': *FF*, 'Patrick Kinross'

74. Anne's brothers not entirely heterosexual: see Jonathan Gathorne-Hardy, *Half an Arch* (Timewell Press, 2005)

74–5. 'She is truly one of the world's worth-while women': Diary, 27 February 1943

75. Jean Hamilton's dismay in her diary, July 1935 (King's College, London)

75. 'behaved like a housemaid': Anne Gathorne-Hardy (AGH) to Gerald Hochschild, 1957 (Gathorne-Hardy MSS, Lilly Library, Bloomington, Indiana)

75–6. 'my father has been the damndest fool in the UK': JLM to AGH, 16 September 1935 (Beinecke)

78. I really don't know when I have been so unhappy': *ibid.*, 11 September 1935

78–9. 'The worst about sensitive and therefore sexless people': HN to JLM, 10 September 1935 (Beinecke)

79. 'if you have not found someone else': JLM to AGH, 16 September 1935

79. 'How I adore Harold': *ibid.*, 10 September 1935

80. 'such an enjoyable evening with Hamish': *ibid.*, 24 September 1935

81. 'Tonight I am dining with Eddy West': *ibid.*, 25 October 1935

81. 'Dinner with Mrs Cooper': *ibid.*, 1 November 1935

81. 'I dined with John Sutro': *ibid.*, 12 December 1935

81. 'The Connollys are marvellous people': *ibid.*, 20 December 1935

82. JLM 'rather in love' with Heywood: JLM to Anne Hill, 18 April 1970 (Lilly Library)

82. Anne upset that no mention of her in *AS*: see John Saumarez Smith (ed.), *The Bookshop at 10 Curzon Street: Letters between Nancy Mitford and Heywood Hill, 1952–73* (Frances Lincoln, 2004), pp. 144–5

85. 'whenever I like for as long as I like': JLM to AGH, 11 December 1935

85. 'What a wonderful thing is a country house': *ibid.*, 9 January 1936

85–6. 'more upper-class than it is possible to conceive': *ibid.*, 12 January 1936

86. 'I have as you know always looked upon him with the utmost veneration': *ibid.*, 9 January 1936

87. 'there was a time in the mid-thirties': Diary, 12 November 1987

87. 'an ugly bore': JLM to AGH, 7 January 1936

88. Anne hoped they would remain the best of friends: her letter does not survive but it is possible to glean its sense from JLM's grateful reply sent from Haselbech on 22 January 1936 (which together with other letters she received from JLM after the breaking-off of their engagement are among her papers in the Lilly Library)

88. Angela went off with another admirer: see Angela Culme-Seymour, *The Bolter's Granddaughter* (Writersworld, 2003); also *FF*, 'Patrick Kinross'

88. 'hardly spoke to me at all but looked stern and cross': JLM to AGH, 4 February 1936 (Lilly Library)

89. 'a good, facetious picture of English country life': *ibid*.

CHAPTER 5: THE NATIONAL TRUST

90–3. For the historical background to the National Trust's Country Houses Scheme, see Peter Mandler, *The Fall and Rise of the Stately Home* (Yale, 1997), ch. 7; for its early progress, see Jennifer Jenkins & Patrick James, *From Acorn to Oak Tree: The Growth of the National Trust, 1895–1994* (Macmillan, 1994), ch. 4. The files of the Office of Works in the National Archives – HLG/126/65–67 – tell the story from the official point of view. The files of Paul, 4th Baron Methuen (Box D50) in Corsham Papers, Wiltshire Record Office, and of Oliver, 3rd Viscount Esher at Watlington Park, Oxfordshire (consulted by kind permission of the present Viscount), are the most illuminating private records. Owing to archival turmoil, the only sources it was possible to consult among the records of the National Trust (NT) were committee minutes, a file of JLM's early reports on his country house visits, and a bound volume of 'Architectural Notes' – though judging from Jenkins & James, who had access to them, the other records would not add much to facts already known

93. JLM job interview at NT: *P&P*, 'Introduction'

95. 'raw and ignorant': *ibid*

96. 'Until about 1930': 'Landed Proprietors and Properties' in 18th edition of *Burke's Landed Gentry*, Vol. II (1969)

96–7. First meeting of Country Houses Committee: NT minutes

97. Life at Buckingham Palace Road: *P&P*, 'Introduction'

98. 'a shrewd, genial, irreverent and witty man': *ibid*

98. JLM on Methuen: Diary, 25 November 1989; *FF*, 'Paul Methuen'

98. Copies of lists drawn up by sub-committee in NT minutes, Office of Works files, Methuen papers

98. JLM's preparatory work for sub-committee: Matheson to Esher, 24 March 1936 (Watlington)

98. 'misgivings about this hastily compiled list': *P&P*, 'Introduction'
99. Copies of memorandum sent to owners (in various stages of drafting) in NT minutes, Methuen papers, HLG/126/66
99. 'the most enjoyable summer of my existence': *P&P*, 'Introduction'
99–102. Consultation exercise summarized in 'Report on the Progress of the Country Houses Scheme', 10 October 1936, in HLG/126/67
100. 'Sir Henry Fairfax-Lucy, military, dapper and arrogant': Diary, 18 July 1942
100. 'old Lord Bath': *P&P*, 'Introduction'
101. 'They were surprisingly unreserved in explaining': *P&P*, 'Attingham'
101. JLM on Knole and Little Moreton Hall in *P&P*
102. 'the finest kind of live, unmuseumy house': report on visit to Mrs Baker Baker at Elemore Hall, 4 August 1936 (NT)
102. JLM's father's attitude to NT in *P&P*, 'Brockhampton'
102. the 'surviving scheme' did not start 'with a bang': *P&P*, 'Introduction'
102–4. JLM on Wallington, Hatchlands, Stourhead, West Wycombe, Hanbury and Smallhythe: *P&P*
103. for National Trust Bill of 1939 see Mandler, p. 305
105. 'very little altered since the great Lady Holland's time': report on visit to Lord Ilchester at Holland House, 21 October 1936 (NT)
105. 'I rely on instinct sharpened by years of experience': Diary, 25 March 1945
106. 'the manner which used to endear me to owners': Diary, 7 April 1983
106. 'It would happen that an enthusiastic owner': *P&P*, 'Introduction'
107. JLM's 'Red Books' in possession of John Kenworthy-Browne
107. 'sweeter and funnier than anyone on earth': Diary, 4 January 1944
108. 'Dear old John': JLM to Betjeman (undated) in Betjeman Papers, University of British Columbia
108–9. For JLM and Byron, see James Knox, *Robert Byron* (John Murray, 2003), pp. 228 ff; *FF*, 'Robert Byron'
109. For Georgian Group, see Knox, pp. 376 ff
109. 'kept very busy from 9.30 to 5.30': JLM to Michael Rosse, August 1937 (Birr)
110. 'Harold is completely caught up in the Mother of Parliaments': JLM to Desmond Parsons, 24 November 1936 (Birr)
110. Nigel Nicolson in love with Jamesey: Diary, 26 June 1976
110. JLM's letter to Jamesey (undated) in Pope-Hennessy Papers, Getty Research Institute, California; Jamesey's letters to JLM in Beinecke (some of them also quoted in Peter Quennell [ed.], *A Lonely Business: A Self-Portrait of James Pope-Hennessy* [Weidenfeld, 1981])
111. 'Our friendship did not slowly develop': *FF*, 'Richard Stewart-Jones'
111–12. For Rick see Elizabeth Pulford (ed.), *Richard Stewart-Jones* (1980)
112. JLM's 'flirtation' with Ursula Brocklebank: Diary, 9 March 1982

113. 'It is not that the summers were always fine': Fred Oppé in Pulford, p. 26

113. JLM's letter to Rick in Beinecke

114. 'he was something of a saint': Diary, 31 October 1975

114. 'He was one of the chief loves of my life': Diary, 23 June 1972

114. JLM moves in with Byron: Knox, p. 416; *FF*, 'Robert Byron'

115. Report on visit to Wootton Lodge, 11 December 1936 (NT)

115. Listens to Abdication broadcast with Diana Guinness: Diary, 7 June 1972, 28 March 1978

115. 'Goodnight, regicide': Nicolson diary, 9 December 1936

115. Anne 'couldn't be in love with him again': Patrick Balfour to JLM, 8 February 1937 (Beinecke)

115. 'the sequel turned out wonderfully for you in marrying Heywood': JLM to Anne Hill, 24 May 1996 (Mrs Simon Frazer)

116. 'Palladio's Vicenza' in *Architectural Review*, February 1939; 'Spanish Architecture' in *Architects' Journal*, 9 February 1939

116. Doreen Baynes advises JLM: her letter to JLM of '4 October' (Beinecke)

116–17. JLM's early memories of Brooks's: 'The Second World War' in Philip Ziegler and Desmond Seward (ed.), *Brooks's: A Social History* (1991)

117. 'I am always happy in this stuffy, dingy Victorian library': Diary, 17 June 1944

117. JLM and George Chettle: *P&P*, 'Introduction'

117. Records of exchanges with *Demeures Historiques* in Methuen Papers, Box D50, Vol. 2; Kathleen Kennet's account of Belgian tour in her diary, 7–13 July 1939 (Cambridge University Library)

118. 'Whatever may happen, I have known and still know one perfect thing': Stuart Preston to JLM, 29 August 1939 (Beinecke)

CHAPTER 6: SOLDIER BLUE

119. JLM's reaction to outbreak of war: Diary, 3 September 1989

119. JLM to Esher, 31 August 1939, on evacuation of NT offices (Watlington)

119–20. JLM's pacifism: see correspondence with Lord Clonmore, 1936 (Beinecke)

120. JLM persuaded to support war: HN to JLM, 4 September 1939; Byron to JLM, 27 September 1939 (Beinecke); Diary, 6 September 1942

120. For Federal Union Club, see Knox, pp. 423–7

120. Rick's breakdown: Pulford p. 41

121. 'rather splendid and awful': Diary, 16 April 1953

121. Correspondence of JLM and Rosse, February–May 1940 (Beinecke and Birr)

121. JLM's hopes for exemption from military service discussed in correspondence with Lloyd, May–July 1940 (Beinecke)

122. 'I do think our comments on military life': JLM to Rick Stewart-Jones, 27 June 1940 (Beinecke)

122–8. JLM's letters to Rick Stewart-Jones, June–November 1940, in Beinecke

125. 'gay, amusing, amused, very bright and clever': Diary, 27 December 1981

128. 'The damage inflicted is appalling': JLM to Rick, 23 October 1940

128. incident in Hyde Park Square: *AS*, ch. 8

129. 'saw Robert, who was fairly cheerful': JLM to Rick, 16 November 1940

130. 'go rather easy for a year or so': JLM to Eddy Sackville-West, 12 August 1941 (Beinecke)

130. For JLM's fear of mental instability see letter from Midi Gascoigne, November 1940 (Beinecke)

130. JLM's dismay at Soviet alliance: *AS*, ch. 8; Diary, 14 March 1981

130. 'I should be untrue to you if I told you': Eddy Sackville-West to JLM, 23 August 1941 (Beinecke)

130. 'anyone reading the book might jump to the conclusion': Helen Lees-Milne to JLM, 19 May 1941 (Beinecke)

130. Byron's death: HN to JLM, 10 April 1941 (Beinecke)

131. JLM's last meeting with Byron: *AS*, ch. 8

131. 'Oh how I wish I had seen her': JLM to Nigel Nicolson, 2 November 1994 (Nigel Nicolson papers)

131–2. 'Wickhamford Diary', August–September 1941, in possession of Nick Robinson

133. 'quite conscientiously return to the Trust': JLM to Esher, 14, 30 October 1941 (Watlington)

CHAPTER 7: 'THE MAN WHO SAVED ENGLAND'

134. 'West Wycombe Park is a singularly beautiful': Diary, 1 January 1942

134. 'the true sock': Diary, 8 February 1942

135. 'My house is settling down': Diary, 23 January 1943

136. 'I have been sitting for an hour': Diary, 17 August 1943

136. JLM visits Avebury with Eardley: Diary, 2 April 1942

138. Ministry of Works to consider each property on merits: minutes of Country Houses Committee, 18 March 1941 (NT)

138. Spencer to Esher on endowment: quoted in Jenkins & James, p. 97

138. JLM's views on endowment: Diary, 22 February 1942

139. 'preposterously large' endowments: Diary, 17 May 1942

140. Trevelyan praises JLM: Diary, 14 March 1942
140. 'Esher said he had no quarrel to make': Diary, 10 March 1943
140. 'pretty confident that Esher . . . will agree': Diary, 3 February 1945
140. JLM's loyalties 'first to the houses': Diary, 18 March 1943
141. 'true county squirearchy': Diary, 18 May 1944
141. 'They are such dear people': Diary, 25 March 1943
141. JLM saves Gunby: *P&P*
141. 'overjoyed that the Trust has been instrumental': Diary, 11 November 1943
141–3. Stourhead, Charlecote and Knole: *P&P*
143. 'a thoroughly romantic house': Diary, 15 September 1942
143. 'diddled out of his inheritance': Diary, 9 May 1945
143. 'a perfect specimen of a Disraelian Gothic mansion': Diary, 13 June 1942
143. 'a fiendish old imbecile': Diary, 3 February 1943
143. 'a pompous old ass with a blue face and fish eyes': Diary, 19 July 1945
144. 'decided to stress on the feudal, reactionary Lord L.': Diary, 22 June 1945
144. 'an elderly, delicate, hot-housey lady': Diary, 22 December 1944
144. 'It is nice being loved so much': Diary, 15 January 1946
144. 'The man who saved England': *Daily Mail*, 1 August 2007
144–5. 'The lengths to which I have gone': Diary, 1 June 1945
145. 'failed to make friends': Diary, 15 October 1943
145. 'to adjust myself to different sorts of people': Diary, 30 March 1944
145. 'a sort of Edwardian stage peer': Diary, 15 May 1942
145. 'pompous, courteous': Diary, 13 June 1942
145. 'breezy and good-natured': Diary, 20 June 1942
145. 'the first woman chairman of the LCC': Diary, 25 September 1942
145. 'an astonishing nineteenth-century John Bull': Diary, 12 October 1942
145. 'rather an absurd, opinionated man': Diary, 25 January 1943
145. 'a little ponderous': Diary, 25 March 1943
145. 'a tall, ungainly, exceedingly coy woman': Diary, 26 May 1943
145. 'a slightly absurd, vain man': Diary, 10 September 1943
146. 'a short old man with white hair': Diary, 18 September 1943
146. 'a handsome and forbidding woman': Diary, 28 October 1943
146. 'courteous and charming': Diary, 21 February 1945
146. 'what my father would call "effeminate"': Diary, 13 June 1942
146. 'photographs of smiling choirboys': Diary, 6 January 1942
146. Edith Craig's lesbian entourage: Diary, 26 March 1942
146. one notorious peer: Diary, 9 July 1944
146. 'puts his arm round one's waist': Diary, 15 September 1945
146. 'ample opportunity of circulating scandalous gossip': Diary, 9 October 1949

146. 'I thought how enviable their ménage': Diary, 26 April 1944

146. Lord Berwick's belief in ghosts: Diary, 8 July 1943

146. Lady Sibyl's tree house: Diary, 17–18 March 1944

146. Lord Brocket 'beams, bows': Diary, 20 June 1942

146. 'haunt him until his dying day': Diary, 15 April 1943

147. 'reduced to eating rats': Diary, 12 October 1942

147. 'inwardly vows there will never be a next time': Diary, 25 September 1942

147. incident at Polesden Lacey: Diary, 4 November 1942

147. 'certified for descending . . . stark naked': Diary, 11 February 1943

147. 'they put God before their country': Diary, 24 July 1944

147. 'climbs to one of the castle towers': Diary, 28 January 1944

147. 'The world is too much for him': Diary, 25 November 1943

147. 'their day is done': Diary, 23 December 1943

147. 'at his wits' end': Diary, 4 May 1944

147–8. 'for people in their position': *P&P*, 'Stourhead'

148. 'one indoor servant only': Diary, 28 April 1943

148. 'whereas Lord Curzon thought he was pigging it': Diary, 26 May 1945

148. 'slaved all these years single-handed': Diary, 21 November 1944

148. 'a nervous breakdown brought on by the anxiety': Diary, 19 June 1947

148. 'the moment one leaves the room': Diary, 22 September 1943

148. lunch with Spencers: Diary, 19 March 1943

148. lunch with FitzAlans: Diary, 23 January 1944

148. lunch with Sir Edward: Diary, 22 February 1943

148. dinner with Lord Fairhaven: Diary, 10 September 1943

148–9. Lord Astor's taxation: Diary, 6 July 1942

149. 'does not receive sixpence from each pound': Diary, 19 March 1943

149. Lord Bradford's taxation: Diary, 22 September 1945

149. Duke of Wellington's taxation: Diary, 19 January 1944

149. 'very indifferent ironwork': Diary, 24 February 1942

149. JLM saves gates of Stourhead: *P&P*

149. JLM saves railings of Brooks's: Diary, November–December 1942

149. 'out of devilry': Diary, 14 May 1942

149. sarcophagi forced open: Diary, 5 August 1942

149. Barnardo children: Diary, 4 July 1944

149. door-handles stolen at Kedleston: Diary, 26 May 1944

149. damage at Picton: Diary, 13 April 1945

149. 'the park is cut to pieces': Diary, 25 November 1943

149. 'caused much damage': Diary, 29 May 1943

150. 'extraordinary how quite intelligent people': Diary, 5 October 1942

150. 'How splendidly proportioned': Diary, 2 April 1942

150. 'a misleading, fakey sort of house': Diary, 30 March 1943

150. 'a hideous red brick edifice of 1860': Diary, 23 April 1943

150. Charlecote 'drastically altered': Diary, 31 May 1945

150. JLM's *Horizon* article published June 1945

150. 'It is completely surrounded by a moat': Diary, 24 March 1945

151. pub-crawling in disreputable districts: Diary, 16 October 1943, 1 July 1944

151. 'so engaging . . . I forgive him all his trespasses': Diary, 28 May 1943

151. 'write a book and join us': Diary, 17 May 1944

151. 'as easy as falling off a log': Diary, 13 June 1942

151. Lady Victor Paget: Diary, 17 April, 11 May, 20 August 1943

152. 'Lord Q. was . . . full of solicitude': Diary, 7 February 1943

152. 'The whole of London congregates': Diary, 1 March 1943

153. 'treating it all as a great joke': Diary, 20 January 1944

153. 'an unreprentant Nazi': Diary, 27 August 1944

153. 'for he does not wish to go to Germany': Diary, 6 November 1944

153. 'jumping up and down in his chair': Diary, 4 January 1944

153. 'damnable and devilish': Diary, 28 April 1943

153. 'a young RAF sergeant . . . of ineffable beauty': Diary, 12 October 1942

153. 'I would write to him if I knew where': JLM to Eddy, August 1941 (Beinecke)

154. 'Every day I have a letter': Diary, 20 March 1943

154. 'ravishingly beautiful with her long, arrogant neck': Diary, 18 April 1943

155. removal of diary references to mystery voice: Ian Parsons to JLM, 2 September 1976 (Chatto & Windus papers, Reading University)

155. 'Words flew, as of old': Diary, 29 August 1942

156. GBS's 'very ugly' cottage: Diary, 9 February 1944

157. 'hell-bent on collecting scalps': Diary, 28 January 1942

157. 'out of curiosity': Diary, 7 August 1943

157. a woman 'out of the common run': Diary, 29 September 1945

158. JLM and 'Princess Winnie': Diary, 13 May, 22 July, 3 November, 24 November, 26–7 November 1943

158. JLM's 'cyclothymia': Diary, 7 September 1989

159. 'had the most enviable life': Diary, 6 October 1942

159. JLM and the Pope: Diary, 6 May 1944, 10 March 1945

159. 'the moment reason takes over, faith flies out': Diary, 5 December 1943

160. 'the worst sins are the most enjoyable': Diary, 10 December 1943

160. 'no matter how much we kick against the pricks': Diary, 22 December 1943

160. Sir Vere's snobbery: Diary, 12–13 August 1942

160. Derek Jackson's Nazi sympathies: Diary, 27 June 1942

160. 'if we could . . . once a month . . . invite the Poles': Diary, 8 May 1945

160. JLM the anarchist: Diary, 22 November 1943, 20 February 1946
160. 'would make a fine Piranesi ruin': Diary, 28 January 1942
160–1. 'like wandering around in Pompeii': Diary, 14 March 1942
161. 'empty blankets of snow': Diary, 5 February 1942
161. Holland House: Diary, 5 February 1942
161. 'Both raids are sheer barbaric bloody-mindedness': Diary, 28 April 1942
161. 'they will make a point of bombing English country houses': Diary, 30 April 1942
161. 'the heraldic beasts': P&P, 'Knole'
161. 'It was beautiful but shameful': Diary, 23 February 1944
161. 'The Palace front sadly knocked about': Diary, 24 February 1944
162. 'They think about 20,000 books are lost': Diary, 27 February 1944
162. 'like an H. G. Wells story': Diary, 16 June 1944
162. 'For sheer damnable devilry': Diary, 18 June 1944
162. 'Another fearful night': Diary, 20 June 1944
163. 'Women sang into the harsh microphone': Diary, 1 July 1944
163. 'The V-2 has become more alarming': Diary, 5 January 1945
163. 'I do not see how they can fail to get most of us': Diary, 8 January 1945
164. 'mesmerised like a rabbit by a stoat': Diary, 4 April 1945
164. 'stress the Trust's opposition to museumisation': Diary, 22 March 1945
164. the 'satanic' Charles Fry: Diary, 20 February 1945
165. JLM meets Diana Mosley: Diary, 16 June 1945
165. 'I rushed up and he threw his arms around me': Diary, 6 July 1945
165. 'we have waited and suffered too long': Diary, 1 May 1945
165. Geoffrey offers accommodation: Diary, 21 October 1944, 16 May 1945
165–6. JLM at Blickling: Diary, 23 June to 8 July 1945

CHAPTER 8: A NEW WORLD

167. 'missed it like an old friend': Diary, 6 January 1946
168. JLM meets Dalton: Diary, 30 July 1947
168. HN joins Labour Party: Diary, 14 March 1947
168. 'A whole social system has broken down': Diary, 16 June 1947
168. 'worthless society people': Diary, 13 April 1946
168. 'pre-war good-timers': Diary, 19 April 1946
168. 'staleness and futility': Diary, 3 May 1946
168. 'I believe my generation': Diary, 3 February 1948
169. 'I have very strongly urged': Diary, 7 July 1948
170. Mallaby's views: Diary, 9 January, 16 January 1946
170. 'not a bureaucratic team of experts': Diary, 14 June 1946

170. 'well out of his depth': Diary, 20 December 1946
171. 'only plumbers': Diary, 29 July 1942
171. Esher approves creation of representatives: Diary, 29 October 1946
171. Uppark: Diary, 12 January 1946
172. Upton: Diary, 1 March, 11 July 1946
172. Cotehele: Diary, 8 May 1947
172. 'deliciously hideous': Diary, 26 March 1944
172. 'fascinating as the shrines of great men': Diary, 23 November 1949
172. 'a pathetic shoddy little place': Diary, 20 September 1945
172. Lamb House: Diary, 17 August 1948
173. 'the enemies of the human race': Diary, 7 April 1988
173. Westwood Park: *P&P*, 'Epilogue'
173. 'I foresee all families leaving these anachronistic white elephants': Diary, 8 February 1949
174. 'the Ministry lacks taste and sensitivity': Diary, 17 June 1946
174. Harewood House: Diary, 26–7 November 1947, 16 March 1948
174. opening ceremony at Charlecote: *P&P*
174. visitor numbers quoted in Jenkins & James, p. 162
175. showing of Gunby, Hatchlands, West Wycombe, Knole: *P&P*
176–7. 'that is precisely how he wheedles things out of old ladies': Diary, 16 May 1947
177. arrangement of Stourhead: *P&P*; Diary, 18 September 1947, 9 December 1947, 25 June 1948
177. 'the dearest and best companion': Diary, 26 June 1946
177. 'more fun being with Eardley than anyone': Diary, 9 May 1947
178. 'no one . . . with whom I have shared more cherished moments', Diary, 30 January 1948
178. 'We had to start from scratch': Diary, 9 December 1947
178. 'Eardley, Desmond and Eddy lead a highly civilised existence': Diary, 18 January 1947
178. 'greeting me like three big affectionate dogs': Diary, 27 May 1948
178. 'the gayest, sweetest-tempered, most informative person': Diary, 19 February 1947
178. 'the inmates . . . are angelic to me': Diary, 6–9 January 1948
179. 'wicked and amusing': Diary, 1 February 1948
179. 'rather traded on his generosity': Diary, 4 February 1993
179. 'my respect for her kindness and gallantry': Diary, 14 March 1946
179. 'I admired her for her lightning perception': Diary, 11 July 1948
180. Tony Gandarillas's opium-smoking: Diary, 10 October 1946
180. 'Such a flavour of Edwardian London': Diary, 12 December 1946
180. 'a jolly talk about sex problems': Diary, 9 March 1947
180. 'true love can only exist': Diary, 12 November 1949
180. 'Oh, lust *is* a jest': Diary, 2 July 1948

180. 'Eddy maintained that born homosexuals': Diary, 19 February 1947
181. 'sometimes I am in the arms of God': Diary, 1 July 1947
181. 'he scarcely requires sex these days': Diary, 9 May 1946
181. 'He reminded me of an old, spruce hen': Diary, 13 July 1947
181. 'His conversation very strange': Diary, 17 June 1948
181. 'drunken, dissolute and destructive': Diary, 29 January 1947
181. 'the worst and most depraved man I know': Diary, 25 April 1947
181. 'lust . . . is uninteresting': Diary, 31 December 1981
182. 'there is too little of it left': Diary, 11 April 1946
182. 'a grubby house-painter': Diary, 15 June 1949
182. JLM and Stuart Preston: Diary, 6 June 1948; letter from Stuart to JLM
     dated 'Monday' (Beinecke): 'I am thoroughly ashamed of my absurd,
     rude and histrionic behaviour on Saturday night . . .'
182. 'Her beauty is of a frail sort': Diary, 5 October, 8 October 1947
183. 'the sound of her voice again . . . made me jump to hear': Diary, 8
     February 1948
183. 'a dark gigolo with a scar': Diary, 2 December 1948
183. 'We discussed the cussedness of inclinations': Diary, 1 June 1948
184. 'when she got going on her writing': Diary, 15 June 1946
184. 'writing is a terrible effort for him': Diary, 14 August 1948
185. 'the surroundings unsurpassed': Diary, 1 August 1948
186. 'No one remembers anything like it': Diary, 6 March 1947
188. 'I do not like Ireland': Diary, 2 May 1948
189. 'like a startled kangaroo': Diary, 30 April 1946
189. visit to Sweden: Diary, June 1946
189. 'an ugly Greek prince': Diary, 5 July 1946
189–90. visit to Switzerland: Diary, July–August 1946
190. visit to Italy: Diary, September–October 1947
191. 'Then in came the great man': Diary, 12 October 1947
191. 'His fine classical features were illuminated': Diary, 16 October 1947
192. 'What we now want is some Protestant boys': Diary, 6 September 1948
192. JLM's papal audience: Diary, 14 September 1948
192. 'The shock is not too great': Diary, 6 August 1948

CHAPTER 9: ALVILDE

194. 'her beauty is proud, guarded, even shrouded': Diary, 17 March 1949
194. 'ecstasies of frustrated desire': Lord Drogheda, *Double Harness*
     (Weidenfeld, 1978), pp. 25, 30
194. For Menzies family, see Anthony Cave Brown, *Secret Servant: The Life
     of Sir Stuart Menzies* (Michael Joseph, 1988); for Bridges' career, see his
     memoirs *Alarms and Excursions* (1938)

195. Alvilde in Adelaide: information from Lady Downer, Mrs John Gosse and Mrs Leonie Matheson (daughter of Margaret Newlands); it was also they who recounted the story of how Alvilde got her name

196. Moyne's expedition to New Guinea described in his book *Walkabout* (1937)

196. Alvilde mystified as to how child conceived: Diary, 19 April 1949

196–7. Two biographies of Princess Winnie, Michael de Cossart, *The Food of Love* (Hamish Hamilton, 1978) and Sylvia Kahan, *Music's Modern Muse* (Rochester UP, 2003), touch upon her relationship with Alvilde

196. 'Alvilde . . . suffers dreadful remorse': *The Letters of Nancy Mitford*, p. 191

197. 'I'm not surprised she is hurt': Hon. Anthony Chaplin to Edith, Marchioness of Londonderry, January 1940, in Northern Ireland Public Record Office, D3099/3/2/695 (kindly brought to the author's attention by Richard Davenport-Hines)

197. 'the camaraderie among the crew': Diary, 1 December 1944

198. Alvilde loses possessions: Diary, 21 February 1985

198. Alvilde's affair with Duff Cooper: see *The Letters of Nancy Mitford*, p. 230

198. 'a seductive creature, just slightly affected': Diary, 11 November 1946

199. Alvilde's abortion: information from Rosemary Chaplin

199. 'this woman is dear to me': Diary, 28 April 1947

199. 'tormented by sex': Diary, 25–6 July 1947

200. 'My mind a turmoil': Diary, 14 March 1949

201. JLM spends Easter at Jouy: Diary, 14–19 April 1949

202. 'I having to make untruthful excuses': Diary, 28 April 1949

202. JLM accompanies A. to Clarissa's confirmation: Diary, 14–15 May 1949

202. 'a curious party *à quatre*': Diary, 4 June 1949 (see also 17 September 1986)

202. 'We realise this exchange is sentimental': Diary, 9 June 1949

203. 'it is middle-class to have financial scruples': Diary, 10 June 1949

203. 'Is it true that you are in love . . .?': Diary, 9 June 1949

203. 'bear in mind that you may be sacrificing': Diary, 23 August 1949

203. 'that he would chuck Long Crichel and his perfect life': Diary, 25 July 1949

203. 'He said that nobody else could do my job but me': Diary, 13 August 1949

204. 'I don't believe this': Diary, 8 August 1949

204. 'At times we had rows . . . some of them deep': Diary, 19 September 1949

205. 'A. and I have reached a happier and even high plane': Diary, 4 October 1949

205. 'when he does not come to talk to me': Diary, 15 August 1949

205. 'she seemed to have forgotten those wretched years': Diary, 24 September 1949

205. 'a terrible, harrowing experience': Diary, 30 November 1949

206. 'remorse for not having been more understanding': Diary, 2 December 1949

206. 'I now know what made me hesitate': Diary, 25 December 1949

206. George's estate: English probate records; Dick Lees-Milne to JLM, 7 August 1963 (Beinecke)

206. 'that district of soiled rain': Diary, 21 September 1949

206. 'how far I feel from them all': Diary, 19 October 1949

207. 'if Anthony and Alvilde could establish': Diary, 7 December 1949

207–8. JLM tires of keeping diary: Diary, 22 May 1949

208. Historic Buildings Committee 'agreed to recommend': Minutes (NT)

208. scepticism about Penrhyn: Jenkins & James, p. 178

209. 'It took a lot of deciding': JLM to Paul Methuen, 10 January 1951 (Methuen papers)

211. 'I know what a struggle it must have been': Lennox Berkeley to JLM, 18 November 1951 (Beinecke)

211. 'And to think that for you': Vita to Harold, 20 November 1951 (Lilly Library)

211–12. Harold Nicolson Diary (Balliol), 19 November 1951

212. 'Neither liked A.': Diary, 19 November 1991

CHAPTER 10: MARRIED LIFE

213. For information about Roquebrune, I am grateful to Lesley Blanch, with whom I had some fascinating talks around the time of her hundredth birthday in 2003, and to Mark Brockbank, who was my generous host when I visited the village in 2005

214. *Madame est au water!*': Diary, 29 March 1953

214. 'gloomy and morose': Diary, 6 December 1980

215. 'excruciating crackles': Diary, 13 September 1957

215. 'a Ruritanian experience': Diary, 9 February 1953

215. 'in order to stand in the transept of Monaco Cathedral': JLM to Eardley Knollys, April 1956

215. 'as beautiful as she was at seventeen': Diary, 31 August 1953

216. 'he and I go for afternoon walks': JLM to Michael Rosse, 26 January 1956 (Birr)

216. 'I get impatient with young girl frivolities': Diary, 22 July 1953

216. Lord Hertford 'a pansy': Diary, September 1953

216. 'I forgot to worry about the possible worse consequences for A.': Diary, 7 February 1954

217. 'I hated Roquebrune': Diary, 6 December 1980

217. 'ferocious, mean and cruel': Diary, 20 September 1949

217. 'luncheon at 2.30 and 20 persons assembled': JLM to Eardley, 2 September 1959

217. Cathy Sutherland: Diary, 18 February 1980, 25 July 1982, 13 May 1984

217. 'an old cat – they all are out here': JLM to Eardley, 2 September 1959

218. 'as lovely as anything on the Mediterranean': Diary, 20 September 1953

218. 'a participant in the universality': Diary, 6 March 1953

218. 'around us the smell of brioches': Diary, 6 January 1993

222. architecture bored her: Diary, March 1953, March 1954

223. 'more and more as I get older': Diary, 8 May 1953

223. 'the last Ashburnham of Ashburnham': Diary, 3 July 1953

223. incident at Ugbrooke: Diary, 5 August 1953

223. the 'permanently drunk' Lord Morley: Diary, 6 August 1953

223. 'treated my great-grandmother abominably': Diary, 19 June, 1 July 1953

224. 'the only committee I have ever wanted to be on': Diary, 26 July 1971

225. 'Much as I should hate you to leave': JLM to Eardley, 2 September 1956

226. 'waning in our emotions or enthusiasms': Eardley to JLM, undated (Beinecke)

226. 'that love–hate for the National Trust': JLM to Eardley, 13 February 1958

226. 'Can't remember a thing about it': *ibid.*

226. 'chuck the Trust': HN Diary (Balliol), 29 October 1957

226. 'feeble and shocking': *The Times*, 29 June 1955

227. 'The Georgian Group makes me sick': JLM to John Betjeman, 18 January 1956 (UBC)

227. 'Few books about architecture': *Baroque in Spain and Portugal*, 'Preface'

227. eminent aesthetes praise JLM's architectural works: Diary, 22 July 1971, 19 May 1988, 21 May 1989, 1 June 1989

228. 'No more Belsen-like treatment': *The Age of Adam*, pp. 113

229. 'Italian classicism could not get a hold': *Tudor Renaissance*, pp. 19–20

230. 'never chided her unsatisfactory husband': *The Age of Inigo Jones*, p. 73

230. 'a modicum of achievement': Diary, 17 January 1954

231. 'severe, uncouth, uncompromisingly mediaeval': *Roman Mornings*, pp. 53–4

232. 'just the sort of encouragement he needs': Vita Sackville-West (VSW) to Alvilde (ALM), 11 May 1957 (Berg Collection, New York Public Library)

233. 'Tennyson's brother': VSW to ALM, 8 April 1956

233. 'desperately squashed': JLM to Betjeman, 5 January 1957
234. 'almost daily for several years': Diary, 1 November 1979
234. 'Vita is adorable': Diary, 29 June 1949
235. 'my lovely, far-away, strange, exquisite Alvilde': VSW to ALM, 19 July 1955
235. 'honesty would forbid anything': *ibid.*, 3 August 1955
235. 'It is sometimes a mistake': *ibid.*, 9–12 July 1955
235. 'I don't know what to write to you': *ibid.*, 28 October 1955
236. 'won't Jim find it very odd': *ibid.*, 25 November 1955
236. Vita liberated from writer's block: Victoria Glendinning, *Vita: The Life of V. Sackville-West* (Weidenfeld, 1982), p. 381
236. 'Suspender-belts do drop': VSW to ALM, 5 January 1957
236. 'what reason you will give Jim': *ibid.*, 3 February 1956
236. 'It's so very odd': *ibid.*, 16 January 1956
237. 'I was lunching with Alvilde': HN to VSW, 18 December 1956 (Lilly Library)
237. 'Poor Alvilde': VSW to HN, 15 June 1956 (Lilly)
237. 'Jim and I sat up talking': VSW to ALM, 24 July 1956 (Berg)
237. 'V. and A. had a *schwärmerei*': Diary, 18 November 1982
237. 'How shall I thank her': VSW to ALM, 5 January 1957
238. 'it will be odd meeting in public': *ibid.*, 2 May 1957
238. 'I am in rather a state about us': *ibid.*, 4 September 1957
238. 'Jim was my friend before I ever knew you': *ibid.*, 6 October 1957
238. 'dreadfully worried for some time past': VSW to JLM, 17 October 1957 (Beinecke)
238. 'I don't wonder you are perplexed': *ibid.*, 29 October 1957
239. 'I think – and hope – she has given me up': VSW to HN, 20 February 1958
239. 'I wanted to write to you': VSW to ALM, 10 June 1958
239. 'I don't trust Alvilde's truthfulness': HN to VSW, 11 June 1958
240. 'one should not fail one's friends': VSW to HN, 10 June 1958
240. 'Re-reading Victoria Glendinning's *Vita*': Diary, 21 December 1994
240. 'We have gone our own ways': VSW to ALM (quoted in Glendinning, p. 383)
240. Alvilde once told Vita: VSW to ALM, 11 April 1958

CHAPTER 11: MID-LIFE CRISIS

241. 'a failure as a son, brother, lover': Diary, 19 September 1973
241. JLM in tears on birthday: Diary, 6 August 1988, 15 November 1996
242. 'If only one had "my friend"': JLM to Eardley Knollys, 1 October 1956

244. 'you must not feel that if your life has to be reorganised': Eardley to JLM, 7 March 1959 (Beinecke)

244. 'there must be something behind this': VSW to ALM, 9 April 1959 (Berg)

245. 'I introduced [Jim] to the Browne boy': HN to VSW, 9 April 1959 (Lilly)

245. 'I don't see why Jim': VSW to HN, 22 April 1959 (Lilly)

246. 'He says that it is intolerable': HN to VSW, 9 July 1959

246. 'Charm, yes; and very easy to get on with': VSW to ALM, 14 October 1960

246. 'Alvilde never gives it time to wither': HN to VSW, 29 June 1960

246. 'the mere sight of a postcard': JLM to Eardley, 18 September 1959

247. 'take the kettle off the boil': Eardley to JLM, 22 June 1961 (Beinecke)

247. Alvilde scolds HN: HN to VSW, 21 September, 28 September, 4 October, 19 October 1961 (Lilly); HN diary (Balliol), 3 October 1961

247. 'got in her car and drove across country': Frances Partridge, *Life Regained: Diaries, 1970–72* (Weidenfeld, 1998), entry for 27 July 1971

247. 'If you have any influence with Alvilde': JLM to Freda Berkeley, 23 February 1961 (Lady Berkeley)

248. 'distressed by the way Alvilde tells and retells the story': HN to VSW, 9 July 1959, 25 July 1961, 26 July 1961

248. 'takes such matters very grimly': *ibid.*, 20 October 1959

248. JLM to Jamesey, 6 December 1959, in Pope-Hennessy Papers, Getty Research Institute

248. Eddy finds Alvilde trying: HN diary (Balliol), 26 February 1961

248. 'our friends will undoubtedly think badly of A.': Diary, 18 November 1982

249. For history of Alderley Grange, see JLM's chapter on the house in *Some Cotswold Country Houses* (1987), and article in *House & Garden*, June 1968

250. Alvilde objects to JLM visiting Dyrham: JLM to Eardley, 2 December 1961

250. 'the charming exterior': VSW to ALM, 17 June 1961

251. VSW writes to JLM care of JKB: VSW to JLM, 30 September and 20 October 1961 (Beinecke)

251. 'unsavoury stratagems': VSW to ALM, 25 October 1961

251. 'immensely irritated': Diary, 13 February 1953

251. JLM's mother's second marriage: Diary, 31 May, 23 August 1953

251. 'Not unadulterated': Diary, 16 November 1973

251. 'Nothing can ever hit me so hard': JLM to James Pope-Hennessy, 9 June 1962 (Getty)

252–3. difficulties encountered by JLM in writing Shell Guide discussed in his letters to Betjeman, 1963–4 (UBC)

253. 'Let me, dear boy, say at once': John Betjeman to JLM, 6 June 1963 (Beinecke)

253–4. 'Who Cares for England?' reproduced in *Listener*, Vol. LXXI, No. 1825, 19 March 1964

254. 'Within the last two or three years': Diary, 11 April 1964

255. JLM's efforts at Hanbury: *P&P*

255. 'When one thinks of the N.T.': JLM to Eardley, 28 June 1961

256–7. Crisis in the NT, 1960s, described in Jenkins & James, pp. 219 ff.

257. 'The truth is I don't yet know': JLM to Michael Rosse, 27 February 1966 (Birr)

CHAPTER 12: ALDERLEY

258. 'a glorious success': Frances Partridge Diaries, entries for 5 June 1968 and 27 July 1971 (see fourth note to chapter)

258. 'fragrant with roses': Diary, 12 July 1971

261. 'I have seldom met a human being': Diary, 4 October 1971, 3 November 1971

261. Frances Partridge Diaries: *Other People* (1993), entry for 20 November 1965; *Good Company* (1994), entries for 14 January 1967 and 5 June 1968; *Life Regained* (1998), entry for 27 July 1971

261–2. 'she has created . . . a work of art': Diary, 12 July 1971

263. 'Your previous letter': JLM to Eardley, 26 July 1965

263. 'deeply and devoutly': Diary, 5 March 1972

263. 'like my son': Diary (unpublished), 26 July 1971

263. 'John's criticism is always sound': Diary, 15 December 1972

263–4. JLM's correspondence with George Rainbird in Beinecke – filed under 'G'

265. 'although we are bitterly disappointed': George Speaight to JLM, 29 November 1967 (Beinecke)

265–6. St Peter's Chair episode described in *A Mingled Measure* (November 1968)

266. JLM's undated draft letter to Pope Paul VI in Beinecke – filed under 'P'

267. JLM's disenchantment with Roman Catholicism: Diary, 9 February 1977

267. 'Now I regard Holy Communion as commemorative': *ibid.*

267. 'would be shocked if he knew of my lapse': Diary, 29 May 1972

267. 'a splendid old boy': Diary, 22 May 1973

268. 'In that Broadway church': Diary, 5 February 1979

268. 'It is as clear as day that he was . . . homosexual': Diary, 9 December 1972

269. 'Few English houses so dominate their surroundings as Chatsworth': *English Country Houses: Baroque*, p. 70

269–70. 'Before dinner I walked with Debo': Diary, 16 September 1974

270. 'to face the inevitable question, "Is it true?"': Diary, 27 November 1996

270. Huxley quotation (source not given) included in the file on *Another Self* in the 'writings' section of JLM's papers in Beinecke (also containing the reviews quoted from here)

272. 'I got so worked up': Diary, 8 May 1982

273. 'I know of no greater agony': Diary, 13 August 1971

273. 'Blessed be God for being good to me': Diary, 7 April 1972

273. 'suffered from terrible *Angst*': Diary, 8 September 1971

273. 'unpublishable because of the subject': Diary, 22 December 1972

274. 'Lois . . . was sick of training': *Round the Clock*, pp. 29–30

275. 'you have the perfect equipment for a diarist': Rosamond Lehmann to JLM, 16 February 1974 (Chatto & Windus papers, Reading University)

277. 'Last night before going to bed': Diary, 1 January 1974

277. 'telepathic intuitions': Diary, 8 November 1971

277. 'God, there is something maddening': Diary, 11 October 1971

277. 'I think with dread of the awful possibility': Diary, 14 August 1971

277. 'confidences, fun, folly, tears, wisdom': Diary, 21 March 1972

277. 'moody and restless': Diary, 17 October 1971

278. 'must be, no *is*, the centre of attention': Diary, 24 June 1973

278. 'the sweetest fellow': Diary, 22 August 1971

278. 'unwittingly makes mischief': Diary, 6 November 1971

278. 'indulges in grief': Diary, 24 May 1972

278. 'tucking into a huge meal': Diary, 19 January 1974

278. 'charm is limitless': Diary, 16 November 1973

278. 'has little natural charm': Diary, 23 April 1974

278. 'full of vitality and cheer': Diary, 28 June 1972

278. 'dread of death governs all thought': Diary, 22 January 1973

278. 'a very harrowing experience': Diary, 9 July 1973

279. 'He's a fiend': Frances Partridge's diary, 14 January 1967

279. 'The police station is opposite Jamesey's flat': Diary, 25 January 1974

280. 'about the handomest boy I have ever seen': Diary, 11 October 1971

280. 'better looking than words can describe': Diary, 4 January 1972

280. 'The boys most strange': Diary, 26 April 1973

280. 'He is an exceedingly clever boy': Diary, 28 April 1975

280. 'some of the most understanding, cultivated, earnest men': Diary, 8 November 1973

281. 'didn't mind in the least': Diary, 19 May 1972

281. 'betray my best friend': Diary, 14 June 1972

281. 'beauty of landscape is absolutely at a discount': Diary, 25 November 1972

281. 'I know that people say change is always resented': Diary, 19 January 1973
281. 'Our earth is like an apple being eaten by maggots': Diary, 28 February 1972
281. 'The thugs of this world': Diary, 27 August 1972
281. 'I was right about the danger': Diary, 6 October 1974
282. 'What the hell does it matter': Diary, 26 May 1973
282. 'a lot of old fogies': Diary, 7 February 1974
282. 'You may appear to strangers': Diary, 5 June 1973
282. 'The terrible truth is that one cannot trust anyone': Diary, 21 November 1971
282–3. 'undoubtedly our most intimate friend': Diary, 23 March 1973
283. 'While carrying [Fop's] . . . basket . . . I burst into tears': Diary, 20 December 1973
283. '"we" have only three months': Diary, 12 December 1973
283. 'Diana Westmorland . . . was blazing with fury': Diary, 16 December 1973
283. 'Never have affairs been worse': Diary, 6 January 1974
283. 'that anything may happen overnight': Diary, 6 February 1974
283. 'the City . . . expects a complete economic collapse': Diary, 17 February 1974
284. 'We are finished': Diary, 1 March 1974
284. 'this government is determined to finish off the capitalists': Diary, 9 April 1974
284. 'the revolution would undoubtedly come': Diary, 17 June 1974
284. 'The last straw': Diary, 28 May 1974
284. 'positively sick with sadness': Diary, 8 July 1974
284–5. 'I hope unemployment leaps': Diary, 3 August 1974
285. 'I am no longer heartbroken': Diary, 15 August 1974
285. 'seven-eighths of our beloved possessions': Diary, 1 March 1974
285. 'said goodbye to Alderley': Diary, 1 December 1974

CHAPTER 13: BATH AND BADMINTON

286. JLM's early memories of Bath in article of May 1990
287. 'It has upset me dreadfully': Diary, 28 April 1942
287. 'Your readers may be interested': *The Times*, 2 September 1970
288. 'not without embarrassment': Diary, 6 July 1971
288. JLM's *Times* article on Bath, 22 April 1972
288. 'Goodbye to old Bath': quoted in Adam Fergusson, *The Sack of Bath* (Michael Russell, 1973)
289. 'the ticking of some cursed jack': quoted in *William Beckford*, ch. 7

289. 'neither of us wants to go there': Diary, 3 May 1974
290. 'we are delighted with our new little dump': JLM to Norah Smallwood, 13 December 1974 (Chatto & Windus papers)
290. 'I am so steeped in Beckford': Diary, 18 April 1975
291. 'and these diaries too': Alistair Forbes in *TLS*, 10 October 1975
291. 'that D.H. ought to be flattered': Diary, 19 November 1975
292. JLM's diaries banned by NT: Diary, 13 October 1983
292. difficult to 'preserve anonymity': Diary, 16 April 1975
293. 'the grandest seat in Gloucestershire': 'Badminton House' in *Some Cotswold Country Houses* (1987)
293. 'Badminton is a village isolated from the present': Diary, 8 December 1975
294. 'A. is delighted to be in the country again': JLM to Anne Hill, 12 October 1975 (Lilly Library)
295. 'She has a funny, little-girl manner': Diary, 2 January 1976
295. 'The Duke has a limited charm': Diary, 24 January 1976
295. Badminton invitations 'torture': Diary, 23 July 1982
295. 'Leaving the church this morning': Diary, 26 November 1978
295–6. 'Mary Beaufort had hired a "funny man"': Diary, 21 April 1979
296. 'Huge portraits of nineteenth-century Beauforts': Diary, 14 August 1976
296. 'not only had he not written them': Diary, 8 July 1981
296. 'When engaging servants today': Diary, 27 April 1978
296–7. '[I]t was traditional for an annual meet': Diary, 8 July 1989
297. 'a super day': Diary, 3 October 1976
297. 'I took the dogs round the village': Diary, 21 May 1979
297–8. 'Such a Trollopean scene': Diary, 16 December 1979
298. LMs and *Portrait of a Marriage*: Diary, 14 March 1973, 14 October 1973
298. 'indecision, perplexity and wonder': Diary, 24 June 1976
299. 'affectionate, fair, honourable': Diary, 26 June 1976
299. 'talked about their parents dispassionately': Diary, 23 February 1977
299. 'It wouldn't matter much if they were lost': Diary, 17 October 1976
300. 'dealt with fully': Diary, 20 July 1976
300. 'begged me not to analyse': Diary, 10 March 1977
300. 'promised to be discreet': Diary, 9 March 1977
301–2. 'struck by his intense patriotism': Diary, 27 August 1977
302. 'even cigarette ash can be preserved': Diary, 3 March 1978
302. 'a decent character, easy to get on with': Diary, 22 February 1978
302. 'Boothby showed me several letters': Diary, 10 July 1978
302. 'For who are the heavyweights?': Diary, 19 September 1976
303. 'Now that I have divested myself of Harold': Diary, 30 April 1979
303. 'we are all of us dying over seventy': Diary, 9 December 1979
303. 'not including articles, or parts of books': Diary, 6 January 1972

304. JLM 'gets kicks' from seeing friends' obituaries: Diary, 2 June 1975
304. 'He held my hand': Diary, 9 May 1975
304. 'she retains for me the same ineffable magic': Diary, 23 November 1977
304. 'I had misgivings': Diary, 23 October 1978
305. 'the little of life . . . to be left to them': Diary, 17 January 1978
305. 'It is absurd that after twenty years and more': Diary, 7 January 1979
306. 'highly intelligent . . ., albeit neurotic': Diary, 5 April 1977
306. 'charmer of all time': Diary, 27 February 1985
306. 'I can't get out of my head those two boys': Diary, 14 July 1978
306. 'would have preferred less talk about literature': Diary, 10 November 1975
307. 'Oh Colin, Colin': JLM to Eardley, 13 May 1974
307. for JLM and Hugh Massingberd, see 'Saint Jim' in Hugh's memoirs *Daydream Believer: Confessions of a Hero-Worshipper* (Macmillan, 2001)
309. 'Strange how he is not interested in art': Diary, 12 June 1980
309. 'He reminds me . . . of Jamesey': Diary, 13 April 1979
309. 'nephew Nick': Diary, 10 March 1979
310. 'the two young I am most fond of': Diary, 25 August 1987
310. 'hardly recognisable': Diary, 18 June 1980
310. JLM appoints Nick executor and MB literary executor: Diary, 9 September 1979
310. 'supposing Reynolds dies': Diary, 21 June 1979
310. 'How long am I to suffer?': Diary, 15 July 1979
311. 'M.B. has, I suppose, disturbed the hitherto acquired equanimity': JLM to ALM, 10 September 1979 (Nick Robinson)
311. 'A letter this morning from M.': Diary, 10 December 1979
311. 'told me how unhappy A. was being made': Diary, 6 January 1980
313. 'with oh what ease and affection': Diary, 16 December 1980
313. 'very happy indeed about this relationship': Diary, 7 February 1980
313. 'my dependence on M. is such': Diary, 11 June 1980

CHAPTER 14: STRUGGLING ON

314. 'far less entertaining': Diary, 31 December 1981
314. 'Wish I had never published these bloody diaries': Diary, 8 June 1983
314. 'a nice young man indeed': 5 March 1980
315. 'As the English countryside dwindles': Gervase Jackson-Stops (ed.), *Writers at Home* (Trefoil Books, 1985), p. 33
315. 'besieged with requests': Diary, 14 June 1982
316–17. 'How much do I want to tackle this man's life?': Diary, 22 July 1981
317. 'a beastly building': Diary, 22 October 1982

317. 'concentrate on that to the exclusion of all else': Diary, 2 November 1982

317. 'I was almost certainly the first human being': quoted in *The Enigmatic Edwardian*, pp. 136–7

318. 'produced an infant': Diary, 12 June 1980

320. 'what do oldest friends talk about on walks?': Diary, 6 September 1979

320. 'no wish to be taken up by royalty': Diary, 15 August 1987

320. 'an undistinguished youth': Diary, 2 June 1981

320. 'not gracious and a little brash': Diary, 22 May 1983

321. 'the best complexion of a young man': Diary, 26 December 1976

321. 'artificial and profitless': Diary, 10 February 1981

321. 'She said, "Are you an author?"': Diary, 17 March 1982

322. 'With a rush of Pentacostal wind, *She* appeared': Diary, 23 August 1983

323. 'The truth is one cannot dislike the Princess': Diary, 15 August 1987

323. Master's death and funeral: Diary, 5–8 February 1984

323. 'David kept asking how I liked what they had done': Diary, 13 March 1985

324. 'a small coronary attack': Diary, 8 May 1982

324. 'What are my feelings?': Diary, 7 March 1984

324. 'Motoring into Bath yesterday': Diary, 28 April 1984

325. 'enhanced detachment': Diary, 27 July 1985

325. 'as if part of my own life is draining away': Diary, 24 April 1984

325–6. 'Anyway, I have paid my respects': Diary, 23 May 1984

326. 'Regy's vicarious enjoyment of his son's affairs': Diary, 22 November 1985

326. Queen shocked by Esher biography: Diary, 20 June 1986

326. 'Carried my Regy typescript': Diary, 18 December 1985

327. 'I hope I am immune': Diary, 15 July 1985

327. 'like a steamroller': Diary, 10 February 1982

328. 'I was no longer the least interested': Diary, 7 June 1980

328. Exchange with Roger Scruton in *The Times*, 21–24 February 1984

328. 'an utterly charming man': Diary, 20 April 1986

328–9. JLM's tours with David Burnett: Diary, 10–11 March, 18 March, 8 April 1987

329. 'How sad I am': Diary, 27 November 1987

329. JLM's visit to Venice: Diary, 22 April to 1 May 1986

330. 'There was sex': Diary, 25 February 1987

330–1. 'He knew everyone in London': Diary, 13 November 1987

331. 'After all, my life is almost done': Diary, 30 December 1987

331. 'truly, I don't remember ever suffering such agony': Diary, 17 February 1988

332. 'The law is not just an ass': Diary, 7 April 1988

332. 'Just before I left Bath': Diary, 2 February 1988

332. 'Flat Broke' in *Spectator*, 28 January 1989 and *Bath and West Chronicle*, 1 February 1989

CHAPTER 15: GRAND OLD MAN

334. 'At my age': Diary, 18 November 1992

334. 'A thrill to be published at last': Diary, 10 May 1990

334. 'lacked sparkle': Diary, 16 November 1989

334–5. 'I consider Debo': Diary, 18 April 1989

336. 'out for revenge': Diary, 11 January 1985

336. 'almost incestuous': Diary, 8 November 1989

336. 'clever and civilised': Diary, 17 December 1985

336. 'write a book about what he called "my babies"': Diary, 10 September 1990

338. 'not one person of the next generation': *P&P*, Introduction; Diary, 20 October 1991

338. 'somehow the new curtains seem too sumptuous': *P&P*, 'Hanbury'

338. NT refuse to sell *P&P*: Diary, 21 September 1992

338–9. 'most public officials would run for the door': Simon Jenkins, 'The Noblest Nationalisation' in *The Selling of Mary Davies and Other Writings* (John Murray, 1993)

339. 'at moments euphoria has wafted me': Diary, 31 October 1992

339. 'hold desperately on to my wits': Diary, 24 April 1992

339. 'You see, Jim': Diary, 27 October 1989

339–40. 'She was a spoilt, snobbish and vulgar woman': Diary, 9 July 1989

340. 'A grievous loss to literature': Diary, 19 January 1989

340. 'an unaccountable feeling of release': Diary, 16 August 1988

341. 'extremely good-looking and stupid': Diary, 3 April 1991

341. 'Christ-like looks': Diary, 9 April 1993

341. 'an odd feeling as though of disappointment': Diary, 24 March 1990

341–2. 'I have to recognise': Diary, 26 May 1992

342. 'how long shall I have A. for?': Diary, 4 January 1994

342. 'Time has somehow ceased': Diary, 28 March 1994

342. 'I am haunted': Diary, 6 April 1994

343. 'At four, the undertaker called': Diary, 31 March 1994

344. 'eager for any information': Diary, 6 August 1996

345. Hugh Massingberd's landlady: Diary, 11 January 1973; Massingberd, *Daydream Believer*, pp. 165–6

345. 'difficult to like': Diary, 5 August 1993

345. 'places which have coloured my life': Diary, 19 January 1989

347. 'one hundred per cent hetero-platonic': Diary, 15 June 1995

347. regarded homosexuality with 'distaste': Diary, 19 November 1996

347. dismissed it as 'a mistake': Diary, 1 December 1995

347. 'Their mannerisms, their social contacts': Diary, 25 May 1997

347. 'end up like Jamesey': Diary, 3 January 1987

347. 'an honourable and decent man': Diary, 3 April 1995

347. 'he can't both go "back to basics"': Diary, 8 January 1994

347–8. 'bitterly opposed to the bloody Maastricht Treaty': Diary, 27 May 1993

348. 'No doubt they are responsible for ghastly atrocities': Diary, 10 February 1996

348. 'far too many spivs': Diary, 3 May 1997

348. 'What a lot they are': Diary, 10 June 1988

348. 'two hours of sheer banality': Diary, 23 July 1990

348. 'The snobbery, hauteur, stupidity, insolence': Diary, 18 October 1997

349. 'I feel this very sweet man is deadly serious': Diary, 19 January 1992

349. 'an astonishing performance': Diary, 21 November 1995

350. 'A feeling of intense loneliness': Diary, 8 November 1994

Index

Index

JLM = James Lees-Milne; ALM = Alvilde Lees-Milne; NT = National Trust
Works by JLM are given separate entries; works by others are listed under the
author.
Persons are listed under the names by which they are principally known in the text,
with alternatives in brackets.